A PICTORIAL HISTORY OF BOXING

A Pictorial History of

HAMLYN

LONDON · NEW YORK · SYDNEY · TORONTO

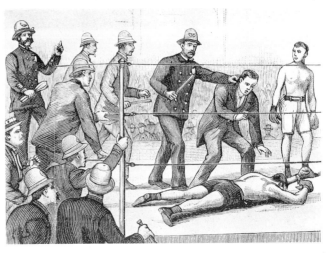

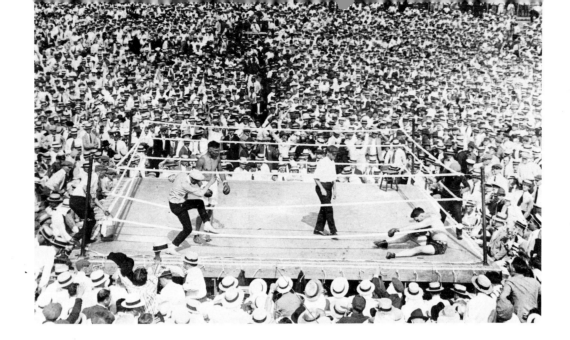

BOXING
by Nat Fleischer and Sam Andre

Revised and brought up to date by Sam Andre and Nat Loubet

MARQUIS OF QUEENSBERRY

CONTENTS

INTRODUCTION

Over the years, hundreds of books have been published about boxers, boxing champions, and boxing in general. The missing link among them, however, has been a complete pictorial history of the sport. It has long been our aim to complete the chain, and we believe we have accomplished it in the present volume.

A *Pictorial History of Boxing* is the product of more than five years of research and planning. It was made possible by pooling our vast personal collections of photographs and illustrations. We were especially fortunate, too, in having at our disposal the rich files of *The Ring* Magazine, without which no history of boxing can be written.

We believe that this book justifies the monumental task involved in preparing it for publication. We regard it lovingly as a valuable contribution to boxing history, with its pictures of all the great champions and thrilling scenes of their famous battles assembled in one volume. Many of the portraits and fight scenes are very rare and, in most instances, are being published for the first time.

We have begun the book with "the father of modern pugilism," James Figg of England, who in 1719 introduced the sport, defeated all opponents, and was recognized as first champion. Although the history of boxing stretches back into the mists of antiquity, it is with Figg that the art and science of modern boxing begins.

Emphasis has been laid on picturing as many of the champions and the top contenders as possible in every division.

Producing this volume has been a pleasure for us, and our greatest hope is that it will give sports fans throughout the world many hours of enjoyment.

NAT FLEISCHER
SAM E. ANDRE

THE HEAVYWEIGHTS

This portrait of James Figg, boxing's first champion, was painted by William Hogarth, famous 18th-century English artist.

PUGILISM'S FIRST HEROES

It was not until the early part of the eighteenth century that boxing became popular as a sport in the British Isles. Though the start of fist fighting in England coincided with the arrival of the Romans, boxing as we know it really got under way with the acknowledgement of James Figg as first British heavyweight king in 1719. Through the pages of ring history, the story of the heavyweights is the story of boxing itself.

When James Figg announced the opening of his Amphitheatre, his name became the first on the long roll of British prize ring champions, and because he was the first to advertise openly the teaching of boxing and exhibitions of skill, he has become known as the Father of Boxing. He was more expert as a cudgeller than as a pugilist. A master with the sword and an expert fencer, he attracted the patronage of the English "bloods," the sports element of the country.

It was Figg who popularized sparring exhibitions, and his initiative was responsible for the opening of many other amphitheatres. In these, wooden rails instead of ropes formed the ring enclosure, which was elevated upon a stage, the referee officiating outside the ring.

Figg died in 1740 and George Taylor, one of his pupils, succeeded to the championship.

Taylor was followed by the father of boxing rules, Jack Broughton, who in 1734 formulated the first code and invented the boxing glove, which at the time was used only in sparring exhibitions.

Figg's card *(left)* was designed by his great friend Hogarth, and was distributed among the patrons at his Amphitheatre and booths at Southwark Fair and elsewhere. This was the first advertisement used to promote the new sport of boxing. Figg resigned his title in 1734 and died in 1740, leaving a wife and several children. George Taylor *(above)* opened a booth when Figg retired, and claimed the title. He defended it against all comers until 1740, when he was soundly beaten by Jack Broughton before a large crowd in Taylor's own booth.

Southwark Fair, London, where Figg's booth was patronized by both aristocrats and the more lowly followers of pugilism. The spectators were entertained here with fencing, cudgelling, backsword, and well-organized and lively boxing exhibitions.

Broughton studied defense and attack and depended on the use of this style. Previously boxing was a toe-to-toe match, but Broughton introduced into the sport stopping and blocking, hitting and retreating. He was six feet tall, weighed 196 pounds and was quite intelligent.

The Duke of Cumberland took a deep interest in him, and obtained for Broughton a position with the Yeomen of the Guard which he held until his death at the age of eighty-five. Broughton's Rules governed boxing

from August 18, 1743, until 1838, when a new code, "The London Prize Ring Rules," was adopted.

From Figg to Muhammad Ali is a long stretch—over 250 years—and in that period many famous heavyweights came to the fore. There were big men, small men, fat and lean ones; men of the rough-and-tumble school and men of science; fighters who were sluggers and those who were cool-headed boxers; men of culture, some of only an ordinary education, and others with none at all. But each was a champion

—a heavyweight who had gained the top rung of the pugilistic ladder.

Eliminating the bare-knuckle and skin-tight gloves era, which covered a century and three-quarters of boxing, and coming down to the period governed by the Marquis of Queensberry Rules that called for glove contests, we find twenty-five heavyweights as kings of the division and one claimant, Marvin Hart. Many thrilling battles were fought in the reign of these Kings of Pugilism, and the majority are vividly portrayed in this volume.

Badly battered and with both eyes closed, Jack Broughton (*right*) protested bitterly when beaten by Jack Slack in 1750. Appealing to his patron, the Duke of Cumberland, who had wagered heavily on him, Broughton cried: "I'm blind, but I'm not beat!"

As champion, Broughton (*left*) won impressively in a gruelling 45-minute battle with George Stevenson, known as "the Coachman." This mezzotint by John Young (after John Henry Mortimer) was one of the first art representations of a boxing match.

Introducing many innovations to the prize ring, Broughton became known as the "Father of British Boxing." in 1743 he devised "mufflers" (gloves) to minimize the risks of facial damage to students at his private school, many of whom were of aristocratic families.

"Broughton's Rules" (*left*), the first ever written for boxing, were adopted on August 16, 1743. The rules barred gouging and hitting a fallen opponent, but wide latitude was left for wrestling and rough-and-tumble fighting. Despite his long, rugged career, Broughton lived to be 85 and was buried with Britain's great in Westminster Abbey. John Smith (*below*), an ugly, misshapen character called "Buckhorse," often appeared in Broughton's exhibitions.

RULES

TO BE OBSERVED IN ALL BATTLES ON THE STAGE

I. THAT a square of a Yard be chalked in the middle of the Stage; and on every fresh set-to after a fall, or being parted from the rails, each Second is to bring his Man to the side of the square, and place him opposite to the other, and till they are fairly set-to at the Lines, it shall not be lawful for one to strike at the other.

II. That, in order to prevent any Disputes, the time a Man lies after a fall, if the Second does not bring his Man to the side of the square, within the space of half a minute, he shall be deemed a beaten Man.

III. That in every main Battle, no person whatever shall be upon the Stage, except the Principals and their Seconds; the same rule to be observed in bye-battles, except that in the latter, Mr. Broughton is allowed to be upon the Stage to keep decorum, and to assist Gentlemen in getting to their places, provided always he does not interfere in the Battle; and whoever pretends to infringe these Rules to be turned immediately out of the house. Every body is to quit the Stage as soon as the Champions are stripped, before the set-to.

IV. That no Champion be deemed beaten, unless he fails coming up to the line in the limited time, or that his own Second declares him beaten. No Second is to be allowed to ask his man's Adversary any questions, or advise him to give out.

V. That in bye-battles, the winning man to have two-thirds of the Money given, which shall be publicly divided upon the Stage, notwithstanding any private agreements to the contrary.

VI. That to prevent Disputes, in every main Battle the Principals shall, on coming on the Stage, choose from among the gentlemen present two Umpires, who shall absolutely decide all Disputes that may arise about the Battle; and if the two Umpires cannot agree, the said Umpires to choose a third, who is to determine it.

VII. That no person is to hit his Adversary when he is down, or seize him by the ham, the breeches, or any part below the waist: a man on his knees to be reckoned down.

As agreed by several Gentlemen at Broughton's Amphitheatre,
Tottenham Court Road, August 16, 1743.

JOHN SMITH, Generally called BUCKHORSE.

PERIOD OF DOUBLE-CROSSES

When Broughton passed out of the picture, boxing suffered because it had lost the man who was recognized as the "Father of the English School of Boxing." His rules formed the groundwork of fair-play and his introduction of gloves, or "mufflers," added to the sport's popularity. His honesty made him beloved by his patrons. They expected emulation of his conduct by those who followed him.

But they were in for a shock. Shortly after Broughton's retirement, crookedness crept into the sport. It made its appearance during the reign of Broughton's successor, Jack Slack, the Norwich Butcher, the first "Knight of the Cleaver" to win an English title. Slack not only "tossed" fights but assisted in the arrangement of other "cross affairs of the knuckles."

Slack's early triumphs were gained more through fearlessness than ability. He introduced the "chopper," which was the equivalent of the modern rabbit punch.

Slack's reign extended from 1750 to 1760, and during that decade British boxing was almost at a standstill. The public lost interest and faith in it because of charges of crookedness made against outstanding fighters.

The Duke of Cumberland became Slack's backer in the fight for the crown with Bill Stevens, "The Nailer"; the Duke of York was the challenger's patron. That contest took place on June 17, 1760, and another surprise was furnished the Corinthians when "The Nailer" won the title. The victor was a notorious character whose double-crosses had brought pugilism to a low level.

After Slack had been shorn of his championship, he became the backer of George Meggs and arranged a battle for the crown with Stevens, whom Slack had bought off. The champion,

Jack Slack, a Norwich butcher and the conqueror of Broughton, was known as the "Knight of the Cleaver." Slack, the grandson of James Figg, held the title for ten years—1750 to 1760.

Bill Stevens, "the Nailer," beat Slack in 1760. Slack's patron was the Duke of Cumberland who again lost a large amount on the outcome. Convinced he was sold out by Slack, the Duke became an arch-enemy of boxing.

George Meggs, "the Collier," came from the pugilistic nursery of Bristol and won from Stevens in 1761. Meggs was trained for the fight by the canny Jack Slack, and Stevens boasted he was paid to lose to the inferior Meggs.

The battle between defending champion Bill Darts *(left)* and Tom Lyons, "the Waterman," in 1769. After dethroning Darts, Lyons gave up the title and retired.

Monsieur Petit, the giant, was the first Frenchman to take up boxing. Standing six feet, six inches, and weighing 220 pounds, he met British title-holder Jack Slack and was defeated in less than 25 minutes.

for a financial consideration, agreed to permit Meggs to win, and for arranging the "cross," Slack received fifty guineas from Meggs.

From 1761 to 1783, a period of twenty-two years, the championship was in an unsettled state. It was knocked about from one head to another.

Meggs, who bought the title from "The Nailer," soon saw it wrested from him by Baker Milsom, and the Baker in turn soon was dethroned by Tom Juchau. Then followed Bill Darts, who won the crown from Juchau. Darts held the title for nearly five years before losing it to "Waterman" Lyons in a desperate struggle.

Lyons thought so little of his exploit, or the fame thereby attained, that at the expiration of two weeks he retired and returned to the peaceful pursuit of ferrying passengers across the Thames. Darts regained the crown, only to lose it in the shortest bout for a heavyweight title in fistic annals to Peter Corcoran of Ireland, the first of his race to win a British championship. The contest lasted less than one minute.

After Tom Lyons retired, Bill Darts reclaimed the title, but didn't hold it long. In a meeting with Peter Corcoran in 1771, Darts *(left)* was knocked out with one punch in less than a minute. Corcoran was the first Irish-born pugilist to win a British championship.

Peter Corcoran of Ireland, who invaded England, fought his way to the championship, and reigned for five years, lost, in a questionable match, to Henry Sellers in 1776.

Corcoran's first important fight took place near Hyde Park on September 4, 1769, with Bill Turner, who previously had defeated Bill Stevens, a former champion of England. Corcoran gave Turner an unmerciful beating.

While in London, Corcoran was introduced to Colonel O'Kelly, a conspicuous character on the turf. He was the owner of Eclipse, the famous race horse, and became Corcoran's sponsor. Colonel O'Kelly arranged a bout for Corcoran for Derby Day, May 18, 1771, against Bill Darts, the English title holder, and the Colonel backed his countryman heavily and collected a handsome sum when Corcoran knocked out Darts in less than one minute of the opening round. The Colonel was accused of bribing Darts to "lay down" in order to make the wagering a "sure thing."

As Corcoran had whipped Bob Smiler, the brickmaker, Tom Dalton, and Joe Davis, and had challenged Lyons, who a few months before had won the title from Darts, Corcoran claimed the championship and was duly recognized.

In 1774 Corcoran fought Sam Peters at Birmingham, the battle taking place near Waltham Abbey. In that contest also there was considerable dissatisfaction, the spectators calling the affair a fake.

Then came the set-to with Harry Sellers, the West of England fighter who hailed from Jack Slack's Bristol School. They clashed at the Crown Inn, Staines, on October 10, 1776, and on this occasion, the flag of the Irishman was lowered, Sellers winning.

The English reported this fight as one sold by Corcoran and the report proved a sad blow to the former champion. Though he prospered out of the proceeds of the fight, he lost the friendship of his admirers and when he died he had to be buried by subscription.

Thus ended the career of the first Irishman to be crowned champion of England. Sellers, who took the crown from Corcoran, held it for four years and was deposed by another Irishman, Duggan Fearns by name. Fearns' victory, like that of Corcoran over Darts, was gained in quick time. The fight lasted only a minute and a half, Sellers falling after the first punch and declining to continue. Fearns was an Irish boatswain.

Following Sellers' dethronement, the championship of England fell into the hands of Tom Johnson, who put in his claim for the title and supported it with dignity and courage. Through him boxing regained public confidence. Johnson, christened Thomas Jackling, ruled from 1783 to 1791.

From the time he assumed the crown until 1789, Johnson waded through his opponents as if they were so many novices. A search was made at Bristol, the hotbed of pugilism, and there an opponent was found in Bill Warr, but he was polished off as easily as were others. Then came a battle with Isaac Perrins at Banbury, Oxfordshire, on November 22, 1789, and this likewise resulted in victory for Johnson.

In 1791, however, the Duke of Hamilton came forth with a challenge for Benjamin Brain (Big Ben), and in this fight Johnson was struck heavily on the nose in the second round. Bothered considerably by this damage and the breaking of the metacarpal bone of the middle finger of his right hand by striking it on a spike, he lost the crown. Thus was the renowned Tom Johnson deprived of the title he had so long held with honor.

With the victory of Big Ben and the defeat of Johnson ends the first period of heavyweight boxing. The second starts with the rise of the great Daniel Mendoza and ends with the reign of John Belcher.

A PARTICULAR and SCIENTIFIC ACCOUNT of the most tremendous BATTLE that ever occurred either in the Broughtonian or Johnsonian Schools, fought at WROTHAM, in Kent, between BIG BEN, alias BENJAMIN BRIAN, and THOMAS JOHNSON, on the 17th of January, 1791.

This portion of Lord Byron's screen depicts the tremendous battle for the championship between Tom Johnson and Big Ben Brain, on January 17, 1791. Johnson *(left)*, unable to avoid Big Ben's blows after breaking his hand on a ring post, lost in 21 minutes.

Tom Johnson *(left)* demolished the giant challenger Isaac Perrins in one hour and 15 minutes, on October 22, 1789. Perrins, six inches taller and 70 pounds heavier, was slowly weakened by body blows and finished with an attack to the head.

FIRST JEWISH CHAMPION

A large portion of the glory of the prize ring has been contributed by men whose forebears centuries ago fought against the Philistines, the Egyptians, the Arabians, the Babylonians, and the Romans. The Jews, like the Irishmen, took to boxing like a duck to water. They accepted the sport as an institution in which they could use the weapons God gave them—their fists—to settle their disputes, and in which they could face an enemy, man to man, in a test of individual skill and courage.

Daniel Mendoza, whose keen, flashing eyes and aquiline features are portrayed in old English prints, was the first Jew to gain a championship. He was much above the intellectual level of his contemporaries.

Prior to Mendoza's advent as a pugilist, brute strength and endurance, rather than scientific finesse, were the qualities most esteemed in the ring. However, after his first battle in which, though the victor, he sustained severe punishment, Dan set his active brains to work to study new means of defense. For three years he devoted himself assiduously to perfecting a system of guarding, sidestepping, and effective use of the straight left, before he again ventured on the test of actual battle.

The development of boxing as a really scientific proposition reached its first polished stage in the able hands of the extraordinary young Israelite. His new tactics were crowned with success. The men of the old-style school attempted in vain to stem the victorious march onward of scientific Daniel. By defeating Bill Warr on Bexley Common, November 12, 1794, Mendoza became champion.

Many boxing critics of his day wrote enthusiastically about the swiftness and grace of the Jewish lad. They praised his generalship and superb science. Others, though these were in the minority, complained that there was something cowardly about a fighter who frequently retreated and relied on superior agility and speed to win rather than standing up in true British bulldog style and hammering away doggedly until he or his opponent dropped.

Thus he revolutionized the Prize Ring. His advent ended the reign of

Daniel Mendoza, a Spanish-English Jew, was boxing's first prominent Jewish boxer and 16th champion of England, reigning from 1791 to 1795. Standing 5' 7" and weighing 160 pounds, Mendoza developed and cultivated ring science. After retiring he became a celebrated boxing instructor and died at the age of 73. Richard Humphries (*below*) known as "the Gentleman Fighter," whipped Mendoza twice, in 1787 and 1788, before the latter became champion. Humphries lost to Mendoza in 1789 and again on September 29, 1790, after which he retired.

Richard Humphries (*left*) and Daniel Mendoza meet in the center of the stage to start their second battle at Odiham, in Hampshire, on January 9, 1788. As in their first contest at Epping, the year before, Humphries again won, this time in 29 minutes.

William Wood, known as "the Coachman," claimed the crown in 1794, following the severe illness and sudden death of the champion, Big Ben Brain, with whom he had been matched.

William Hooper, "the Tinman," a skillfull boxer backed by Lord Barrymore, stopped Wood in 1795 and was recognized as champion. Hooper was one of many star pugilists from Bristol.

Another of the many scenes that decorated Lord Byron's screen shows the former champion, Tom Johnson, interfering with Mendoza (right) during the 1788 battle with Humphries. Rushing to aid Mendoza are his seconds, Jack Jacobs and Harry Isaacs.

Tom Owens is credited with the invention of the dumbbell. A native of Hampshire, he defeated William Hooper, on November 14, 1796, in Harrow, winning in 50 rounds. He claimed the title, but failed to get any recognition. On July 4, 1820, at the age of 52, Owens defeated Dan Mendoza, aged 56, in 12 rounds at Banstead Downs.

the crude slugger. Even the conservative critics who decried Mendoza's prowess were compelled to admit that his rapid thinking and fine strategy had never heretofore been exhibited in ring warfare.

Mendoza had wrought this miracle and convinced the younger generation that while a strong offensive sometimes makes for victory, careful attention to a proper means of defense was no means to be despised. He had introduced this new type of fighting—the scientific style—and it soon became the rage, particularly among the amateurs.

The Celtic race is proverbially a fighting race, yet, strange as it may seem, it was this Jewish boy, Daniel Mendoza, to whom the Irish owe much for popularizing the fistic sport in Ireland, where he established a school in which he taught the art after his defeat of Squire Fitzgerald, the pride of Erin, during a tour of the Emerald Isle. Following Fitzgerald's defeat, Ireland developed many great gladiators and much of their success may be traced directly to Mendoza's tour.

Like Mendoza, another heavyweight pugilist, John Gully, who wore the championship crown in 1807, attracted considerable attention from the literary tribe, due to the fact that he became a Member of Parliament and was received in London society. Gully's whole life reads like a romance.

The son of a merchant, he embarked in business for himself, failed signally and landed in the King's Bench Prison as a debtor, with extremely poor prospects of ever being discharged. The law against debtors, as it then existed, could hold an unfortunate in jail for the rest of his natural life, unless some kind Samaritan paid the money and set him free.

Gully had a friend in Henry Pearce, known to the Fancy as the "Game Chicken." Pearce, born in Bristol, the town in which Gully first saw the light of day, was then champion and he visited his luckless pal in prison. As an amateur boxer, Gully could hold his own with the best, and to please some of his fellow prisoners, John consented to spar a few rounds with the title holder.

The mufflers were produced and, much to everyone's amazement, the youthful prisoner had no trouble in outpointing Pearce, whose fame, be it said, rested more on his strength than cleverness. The story of the remarkable amateur's feat became the talk of London town, with the result that Gully's debts were paid by a prominent sportsman on the condition that he fight Pearce for the title.

To a young athlete pining for his freedom and with a strong liking for the game, this way of escape was ideal. Accordingly, Gully and Pearce met in the ring, but the veteran was too much for Gully.

Gully's showing was so good, despite his defeat, that when ill health forced Pearce to retire, the "Game Chicken" declared that young John was the only man fit to succeed him. This election was approved by the Pugilistic Club, a sort of Boxing Commission of the time which regulated ring affairs. But neither the public nor Gully was entirely satisfied until the

John Gully, the son of a Bristol butcher, was released from debtors' prison, after his debts were paid by sportsman Colonel Harry Mellish, on condition that he fight the champion, Henry Pearce. He lost to Pearce in a fierce 64-round fight, but later became a great champion, wealthy bookmaker, and member of the British Parliament.

right to hold the championship crown had been duly established by a signal victory.

So it was not until Gully had thoroughly whipped Bob Gregson, the Lancashire Giant, that he really was accorded the plaudits of the Fancy as a genuine king. Gregson, not satisfied that Gully was the better man, challenged him again for the title, and in a mill lasting an hour and a quarter Gregson was unable to answer the call of time for the twenty-eighth round and Gully bowed his acknowledgements to a wildly cheering crowd.

Bob Gregson, "the Lancashire Giant," lost two slashing fights to Gully, which determined the successor to Hen Pearce's crown.

The excellent engraving of John Gully (left) and Henry Pearce was part of the lower section of Lord Byron's screen. The shortening of Pearce's given name to "Hen" prompted his followers to dub him "the Game Chicken," a name he lived up to throughout his career. Pearce, a product of the nursery of British boxers in Bristol, was invited to London by Jem Belcher in 1803 to qualify for the title. Belcher, the champion, when he was only 22 had an eye knocked out in an accident during a game of racquets. Believing his career at an end, Belcher gathered the top men in England for an elimination tournament, which Pearce won. The bruising fight (below) between Pearce and Gully, on October 8, 1805, ended after one hour and 17 minutes, when Pearce (right) landed a powerful blow on Gully's throat. Gully's breathing was affected and the fight was stopped.

A remarkable young man in several respects was Gully! Although he entered the prize ring through a prison gate and won the highest honors pugilism could accord him, it is probable that had not Fate forced him into the fistic game, he would never had turned professional. At heart, his ambition was to belong to the gentry. He had little use for the professional ring and its shady followers, who had once picked clean his financial bones. Immediately following his second victory over Gregson, he made a speech to the spectators in which he thanked them for their applause, but stated that he was absolutely through with fighting and would remain a private citizen in the future.

He kept his word. Vainly did sportsmen of wealth and influence try to coax Gully back for "just one more mill." It is said that even Royalty, in the person of the Duke of York, deigned personally to plead with the retired champion to break his pledge.

Gully remained obdurate. He would henceforth have nothing to do with fighting save as an observer. On the turf, the ex-champion accumulated a fortune. He had great success as a stable owner, winning the English Derby twice. He became a rich land proprietor, and, as before mentioned, a Member of Parliament.

Gully died in 1863 at the ripe age of eighty, leaving a large family in comfortable circumstances.

THE TRANSITION PERIOD

Among top pugilists who at various intervals wore the heavyweight crown, "Gentleman" Jackson and Jem Belcher are listed as two of the most popular. Each had a colorful background which had an appeal for fiction writers.

Jackson at the age of nineteen, despite parental objections, decided on a boxing career, and his initial contest was a victory over a renowned pugilist, Fewterell of Birmingham, a giant in stature and scaling 230 pounds. Jackson weighed only 195. The battle took place at Smitham Bottom on June 9, 1788, and was attended by a distinguished group including the Prince of Wales.

A year elapsed before young Jackson again appeared in a bout. He then fought George Ingleston, known as "The Brewer," and at Essex on May 12, 1789, on a floor made slippery by a heavy downpour, Jackson turned his ankle and was forced to quit. The defeat hurt his pride and he retired for six years, during which Mendoza ruled the roost as champion.

It was only after Mendoza's rise to fame and the praise he was receiving as a master of boxing that Jackson, now called "Gentleman" Jackson by the Fancy, decided to return to the ring. He fought Mendoza on April 15, 1795, at Hornchurch in Essex, in a swift and melodramatic combat in which his ring generalship electrified the spectators. Jackson was crowned new champion after eleven minutes of activity.

With that victory began a new era in British boxing. Jackson was the first to show that a hit was not effective unless distance had been properly judged. He also was the first to give

William Futrell (above) had an unbeaten string of victories until he was defeated by "Gentleman" John Jackson, in one hour and seven minutes, at Smitham Bottom, Croydon, on July 9, 1788. Futrell was publisher of the first boxing paper.

John Jackson (right), called "Gentleman" because of his polished demeanor and excellent reputation, was an all-around star in track and field as well as boxing. He possessed a finely-built body, standing 5' 11" and weighing 195 pounds. Jackson was only 18 years old when he slaughtered the huge Futrell before astonished spectators, among them the Prince of Wales, later George IV.

The Jackson-Futrell (sometimes spelled Fewterell) battle scene above shows how the seconds operated during a fight. Note, too, Jackson holding the wrist of Futrell while about to deliver a blow to his head. Two panels from the famous Lord Byron screen *(below)* give a general idea of what the screen consisted of. The panels were completely covered with scenes and clippings of the famous pugilists in the early era of boxing in England. Byron was a boxing enthusiast and attended many of the bouts during 1811 to 1816, when he was in England. His favorite was "Gentleman" Jackson, who had retired in 1795, and he titled him the "Emperor of Pugilism."

Jem Belcher, 20th champion of England, came from fighting stock. He was the grandson of Jack Slack. Belcher introduced the Ascot tie, which he is shown wearing.

Joe Berks, of Shropshire, had a violent temper. He was knocked out three times by Belcher in championship contests.

Jem Belcher, the "Napoleon of the Ring" (below), after losing an eye in 1803, retired in favor of Henry Pearce, who qualified for the crown. Belcher (above, left) returned to fight Pearce on December 6, 1805, and was soundly beaten in 13 rounds.

considerable attention to footwork.

Among his numerous admirers was Lord Byron, who paid him many tributes in his literary works. His was a warm friendship for the gentleman pugilist.

Jackson did more for the uplift of boxing in his era than any of his predecessors. He died on October 7, 1845, at the age of seventy-seven.

Jem Belcher, known as the "Napoleon of the Ring," was the grandson of Jack Slack, fourth boxer to hold the heavyweight crown. Like Jackson, he was a magnificent boxer, lithe and graceful. His brother Tom also was a pugilist. Jem was born April 25, 1781. He was eighteen when he made his boxing debut. His agility and speed in hitting were his best assets.

On December 6, 1805, at Blyth near Doncaster, Belcher, handicapped by an injured eye, lost the title to Henry Pearce, the "Game Chicken." Friends urged him to quit, but twice more he fought, each time against Tom Cribb. In the first bout at Mousley Hurst on April 8, 1807, Belcher was forced to retire at the end of forty-one rounds. He was whipped again in the second contest two years later at Epsom Downs when he broke his right hand. He was the originator of the use of "colors" attached to a post in the ring.

THE NEGRO INVASION

For many years after prize fighting flourished in England, the white man reigned supreme and it was seldom that a principal with black skin ventured to dare fortune in the ring. Here and there in the old records, we read of a Negro donning the mufflers, generally some servant of a spark of nobility who had taught his valet a little of the science which he himself had learned from a pugilistic star.

Bill Richmond, the son of a Georgia-born slave who drifted North as the property of Reverend John Charlton, was the first to cross the Atlantic Ocean and display in British rings the science he had absorbed while working on a plantation. He was born on August 5, 1763, on Staten Island, New York, and was the forerunner of a great array of Negro ringmen whose deeds have gained for them a niche in the Boxing Hall of Fame.

During 1777, while New York was held by British troops, Richmond, by whipping in quick succession three English soldiers who had set upon him in a tavern, attracted the attention of General Earl Percy, who afterwards became the Duke of Northumberland. The British General took Richmond into his household, and under his patronage the Negro, who was only a middleweight, defeated several top heavyweights. His first defeat was at the hands of George Maddox.

With several victories under his belt, Richmond looked for bigger prey and challenged Tom Cribb. Cribb accepted and knocked Richmond out.

That defeat was taken to heart by Richmond. He temporarily retired and didn't appear again in a public ring until he faced Jack Carter at Epsom Downs on April 25, 1809. Though he clashed with one of England's best heavyweights and was knocked down in the second round, Richmond quickly recovered and at the end of twenty-five minutes he battered his man into submission.

In his next contest, the American beat Atkinson of Bandbury in twenty minutes and followed that with a victory over Ike Wood, a waterman, on April 11, 1809, in twenty-three rounds.

On August 9, 1809 Richmond again faced his first conqueror, George Maddox, and the latter, then fifty-four years old, was stopped in the fifty-second round.

For four years Richmond remained idle, then at the age of fifty-two he

This magnificent etching, "Boxeurs," was done by the great French painter, Théodore Géricault. It represents the combat between British champion Tom Cribb (right) and the American, Tom Molineaux. Many great painters immortalized masters of the ring.

made a successful comeback by beating Tom Davis and Tom Shelton.

In 1818 Jack Carter, then aspiring to the championship, threw down the gauntlet to the American invader, who accepted the defi, and on November 12, the former slave, despite his fifty-six years, downed his man and emerged the victor. That fight was Richmond's last.

Richmond died on December 28, 1829, in London at the age of sixty-six. He was the first native-born American to acquire high honors in the ring. It was his success that induced another Negro warrior, also hailing from this side of the Atlantic, the celebrated Tom Molineaux, to invade the London field.

Tom came from a family of fighters. He was born in Virginia on March 23, 1784.

When he landed in England, he resolved to follow in Richmond's footsteps. With Richmond's help, he found a backer who matched him with Burrows, the "Bristol Unknown." The latter was a protégé of Tom Cribb, who won the championship in 1809 and then retired.

Much to Cribb's chagrin, Burrows was hopelessly outclassed and Cribb, determined on avenging this defeat, selected Tom Blake, a veteran of many battles, as the Negro's next opponent. Blake was also defeated. Cribb's choice proved a disappointment and it was this defeat and Molineaux's claim to the heavyweight title that caused Cribb to accept Molineaux's challenge.

This international title bout on December 18, 1810, at Copthall Common, was the first between a Negro and white man in which the crown was involved. Cribb was returned the victor in thirty-three rounds and he retired temporarily.

Unable to coerce Cribb into a return engagement, the American issued a challenge to any man in England, and this was accepted by Joe Rimmer. Molineaux once more claimed the heavyweight championship after defeating Rimmer, and Cribb came to his country's rescue by agreeing to fight Molineaux again.

Bill Richmond (above), called "the Black Terror," weighed between 165 and 170 pounds and stood 5'6". Although born in America, all of his battles were fought in England. Tom Molineaux (left), who was two inches taller than Richmond, weighed 185 pounds. Both enjoyed great success in the British ring, but neither could whip Tom Cribb, the British champion. Richmond was knocked out by Cribb in 1805 and Molineaux, who was known as "the Moor," succumbed to him twice, in 1810 and 1811.

Tom Cribb was one of England's most celebrated champions, whose performances won national prominence for him. Cribb was born in Hanam, Gloucestershire, on July 8, 1781. Big and strong for his age, he went to London when only 13 years old and worked as a stevedore, then as a coal heaver. He was named "the Black Diamond" when he engaged in his first fight, in 1805, against George Maddox. He defeated Maddox in 76 rounds. He won from Jem Belcher in 41 rounds in 1807. When he again defeated Belcher in 31 rounds, in 1809, he was presented with a championship belt and a silver cup (below).

The fight took place at Thistleton Gap, Leicester, with a crowd computed at 25,000 in attendance, and lasted nineteen minutes and eleven seconds with Cribb the victor. Molineaux died on August 4, 1818, at the age of thirty-four.

Tom Cribb, still champion, had fought his last battle, and on May 18, 1822, he named Tom Spring as the successor to his throne.

Cribb, born at Hanham, Gloucestershire, July 8, 1781, engaged in eleven contests, then retired. He opened a public house, "The Union Arms," and was well patronized. He died in his sixty-eighth year.

In the first battle between Cribb and Molineaux, in a chilling rain and heavy wind, Molineaux, badly battered, had to be carried from the ring when the end came in the 33rd round. The bout was hard-fought throughout, with Molineaux suffering many hard knockdowns. In the last round he collapsed, raised his hand, and said to Bill Richmond, his second, "Me can fight no more." He then fell into a stupor, amid the frenzied cheers of Cribb's followers.

The engraving (below) by George Cruikshank illustrates the end of Molineaux in the second great battle, held on December 18, 1811. The contest was staged in a 25-foot ring, before a crowd of 25,000. Early in the fight Cribb's eye was closed tight by one of Molineaux' blows. Cribb had a difficult time, until his second, John Gully, lanced it. From then on, Cribb slowly wore down the American Negro, and with a vicious assault in the 11th round, ended the fight.

The memorable contest between Tom Spring and Jack Langan for the championship, on January 7, 1824, was the first in boxing for which a grandstand was erected. An enormous crowd of 30,000 came from all parts of England to witness the battle, which took place on the Worcester race course. Just before the contest started, one of the quickly-erected stands collapsed, sprawling hundreds of spectators among the wreckage. One person was killed and others were injured. The fight was viciously fought, both men taking severe punishment, but neither giving way. As Spring and Langan sparred for the lead in the ninth round, another section of the stand gave way. Both men fell back, dropped their hands and waited for the confusion to subside. The excitement among the spectators was so intense that they surged forward, giving the ring-keepers a terrible time driving them back. At times the fighters had but five or six feet to fight in. Despite the recurrent invasions of the ring, the fight went into the 77th round. With Langan severely cut and bleeding and barely able to stand, Spring's last blow crashed him to defeat.

The second Spring-Langan contest, on June 8, 1824, ended a round earlier. Langan was brutally beaten, and Spring's hands were so damaged that he never fought again.

Tom Hickman, "the Gasman," who appears in William Hazlitt's literary classic "The Fight," was a terrific whirlwind hitter. A challenger for Spring's crown in 1821, he met Bill Neate on December 10, and was knocked out of time in 18 rounds.

RING'S GREATEST RISE

With the passing of Molineaux and the rise of Cribb to fistic heights, boxing took an upward trend. Cribb took a fancy to a seventeen-year-old boxer whose name was Thomas Winters but who started boxing under the name of Tom Spring. So pleased was Cribb with Spring's first performance against "Hammer" Hollands, a fighter with great hitting power, that he became Tom's coach and teacher and imparted to him much of the ringcraft and generalship which had gained fame for Cribb.

Spring had defeated Jack Stringer in twenty-nine rounds, following which, through Cribb's influence, he was matched with Ned Painter and Cribb's protégé again triumphed. A return bout was arranged in which Spring injured his right eye and had to default in the forty-second round. This was the only time in a long and honorable career that Spring suffered defeat.

The youngster whipped in turn Jack Carter, Ben Burn, Bob Burn, Joshua Hudson, called the "John Bull Fighter," and Tom Oliver, all top pugilists. It was because of those victories that Cribb announced his retirement as champion and named Spring his successor. But Bill Neate of Bristol, whose battle with Tom Hickman, "The Gasman," gained international recognition through William Hazlitt's literary classic, *The Fight,* challenged the procedure.

Spring accepted Neat's challenge and the latter was forced to surrender after thirty-seven minutes of fighting on May 17, 1823, at Hinckley Downs. Following his successful title defense, Spring engaged Jack Langan in two bouts, winning each, and then retired.

The years between 1814 and 1824 saw the greatest rise in British pugilism, with the Spring-Langan contests the outstanding ones. The champion scaled 190 pounds to 176 for his challenger. Spring, with his fighting career ended, became an innkeeper and prospered. He died on August 20, 1851, at the age of fifty-six. Langan became a hotel proprietor in Liverpool. He died on St. Patrick's Day, 1846, at the age of forty-seven.

Bill Neate, "the Bristol Bull," was lacking in skill but could hit like a pile-driver and absorb punishment. In his championship fight with Tom Spring, Neate suffered a broken arm and was forced to quit.

Josh Hudson, known as "the John Bull Fighter," was one of the many tough contenders for the championship crown. He battled Tom Spring at Mousley Hurst in 1820 and was scientifically cut down within six rounds.

Champion Tom Spring (right) was almost six feet tall. He excelled in scientific boxing but was never a hard hitter. He did much towards eliminating the crude slugging methods of the ring. Starting his career in 1814, he retired after his second battle with Jack Langan in 1824.

Tom Cannon, "the Great Gun of Windsor" (above), gained recognition as champion after the retirement of Tom Spring. He was unknown until his first defeat of Josh Hudson, when he was over 30 years old. He met and was easily beaten by Jem Ward at Warwick, July 19, 1825. The intense heat of the sun exhausted Cannon and made him an easy target for Ward to pick up (left) and slam down on the boards. The fight ended in 10 minutes with Cannon hopelessly limp and bleeding profusely.

Spring's successor to the heavyweight crown was Tom Cannon, who was named champion after his defeat of Joshua Hudson in two contests. With Spring and Langan retired, Hudson's victory over Jem Ward, gained him recognition by the Corinthians as leading contender for the throne. Cannon disputed the claim and their two bouts followed to settle the matter. Cannon won the first encounter in the seventeenth round and the return affair in one round less. Thus he was acknowledged Spring's successor.

Jem Ward relieved him of the crown the following year. Cannon entered the ring for the last time with Ned Neale as his opponent and won in thirty minutes. He retired and spent his last days in poverty. He died on July 11, 1858, by his own hand.

Ward was the twenty-sixth champion, an excellent fighter but a man of ill repute. Twice he was accused of

Jem Ward was 5' 10" tall and weighed 175 pounds. He accepted Peter Crawley's challenge, to clinch his title claim.

Peter Crawley, called "Young Rump Steak," was six feet tall and weighed 180 pounds. He held the crown only two days.

Peter Crawley and Jem Ward, after close exchanges of blows, often fell upon each other. Crawley, suffering from a hernia, tried to avoid such falls. In the 11th round, he knocked out the tiring Jem Ward with a solid blow to the mouth.

engaging in fake contests. Despite his skill, his reign brought disgrace to himself and undermined his profession. In each he wagered on himself to lose. He was the first pugilist to receive a championship belt.

He held his honors until Peter Crawley, the "Young Rump Steak," a butcher boy by trade, stopped him on January 2, 1827, in the eleventh round. Peter held the crown only two days, the shortest in ring history. He announced his retirement; Ward reclaimed the title and successfully met a challenge by Jack Carter on May 27, 1828, stopping Carter in the seventeenth round.

Simon Byrne also disputed Ward's claim and he and Jem fought for the right to wear the crown. Their battle at Warwick on July 12, 1831, ended with Byrne the loser after an hour and seventeen minutes of fighting. Ward was now for the second time proclaimed the heavyweight king, the only person to regain his throne in that division either in the bare-knuckle or gloves era. On June 25, 1832, Ward announced his retirement. He died at the age of eighty-one.

James Burke, "the Deaf 'Un," fought the longest championship bout on record, 99 rounds in three hours and 16 minutes, against Simon Byrne. Byrne was punished so badly that he died. Burke was exonerated and claimed the crown.

Simon Byrne, the Irish champion, who died as a result of the beating by Burke on May 30, 1833, was himself the cause of a ring death. On June 2, 1830, at Selcey Forest, Byrne gave a brutal beating to Sandy McKay in 47 rounds. When McKay died from injuries, Byrne was arrested, tried for manslaughter, and acquitted. Among the top men Byrne met in combat was Jem Ward, who won in 33 rounds.

The first globe trotter in ring history followed Ward as wearer of the crown. His name was James "Deaf" Burke. Although born in England, he had the Celtic tag pinned on him because his parents were Irish. He was the twenty-ninth champion of England and his bouts were more numerous than those of any who preceded him. He fought twenty times and lost only twice. He was a strong, well-built boxer with an abundance of stamina and a master in rough-and-tumble battling.

After Jem Ward, who had whipped Byrne for the heavyweight title of England, announced his retirement, Burke laid claim to the crown. His record entitled him to the laurels but Harry Macone challenged the claim and was accommodated and defeated in fifty rounds of tough milling. Thus Burke clinched the title.

Now Simon Byrne of Ireland came forth to contest Burke's right to such honors and in a struggle at St. Albans that lasted ninety-eight rounds for a total of three hours and sixteen minutes, the longest championship fight on record, Burke won. Unfortunately, however, his opponent died from a ring injury and thereafter Burke was hounded both in his own country and in America, where he went in disgust at the treatment he was receiving.

In America his arch enemy, Samuel O'Rourke, who had crossed the Atlantic to make his fortune, slandered Burke and took every opportunity to antagonize him. In this he succeeded and because of their feud, a fight was arranged for New Orleans where O'Rourke, a gambler and gangster, awaited his arrival, prepared with a mob to do Burke bodily harm.

Their rough battle went only three rounds when Burke was attacked by O'Rourke's gangsters, who cut the ropes and engaged Burke's followers in a free-for-all in which even firearms were used. Burke escaped and came to New York, where he had one more bout at Hart's Island with Paddy O'Connell. After winning that fight he returned to England, where he lost his championship to William Thompson, known as "Bendigo."

O'Rourke's end was written in blood. He drifted to a lumber camp in Canada, lost his money in gambling and turned to smuggling. He was found murdered by a fellow lumberjack. Thus came to an end the career of one of the most notorious characters in the early history of American fisticuffs.

William Thompson (above), called "Bold Bendigo," won the crown from Burke on a foul, but retired with a knee injury. Six years later, September 9, 1845, he returned to fight Ben Caunt, a 6'2'' giant, weighing 196 pounds. Bendigo was 5'9'' tall and weighed 164 pounds. The fight was bitter. Caunt often tried to raise Bendigo by the neck (right) and fall over him on the ropes, to break his back. In the 93rd round, Caunt was disqualified for falling without being hit.

Upon his death in 1861, this death mask was made of the very popular Ben Caunt.

"Bendigo" retired after an accident which injured his left kneecap, and Ben Caunt, better known as "Big Ben," claimed the title. Five years later "Bendigo" recovered from his injury sufficiently to re-enter the ring. Twice "Bendigo" and Caunt had fought, each scoring a victory on a foul.

In the third bout they fought seventy-five bitterly contested rounds, when "Bendigo" slipped to a fall and the referee awarded the decision to Caunt on the plea that "Bendigo" had violated the Prize Ring rule which disqualified any boxer who went down without being hit.

"Bendigo's" last fight resulted in a victory for him over Tom Paddock on a foul. Then he retired to become a clergyman. He was the first man in ring history to leave a championship for the pulpit. He died following internal injuries sustained by a fall

William Perry, "the Tipton Slasher," who became champion after the retirement of Bendigo by winning over Tom Paddock.

Harry Broome, a Birmingham pugilist whose triumph on a foul over William Perry enabled him to mount the throne.

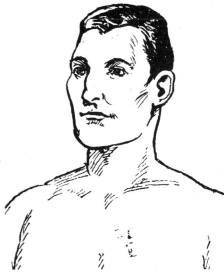

Nick Ward, younger brother of Jem Ward, held the crown from 1835 to 1841. He died in 1850, after a successful career.

Charles Freeman, "the American Giant," who fought Perry in England and won on a foul, died shortly after of tuberculosis.

down a flight of stairs on August 23, 1880.

Ben Caunt, a giant in size, lost the championship to Nick Ward, a younger brother of the veteran ex-champion, Jem Ward, but recaptured the title from his conqueror in a return match. Caunt then adventured abroad, visiting America, where he scored a big financial success with exhibitions throughout the country.

Receiving a challenge from Charles Freeman of Michigan to fight for $10,000 and the world's championship, Caunt returned to New York. He declined the challenge when he learned that Freeman was six feet ten inches tall. Instead, he took Freeman on a tour of Europe.

When they reached England, William Perry, "The Tipton Slasher," decided to tackle the American. Seventy rounds were fought when the referee called a halt on account of the gathering shades of night and ordered the

bout continued the following day. However, Perry, who had suffered severely, succeeded in having the continuation of the battle put off for two weeks.

The referee disqualified Perry in the thirty-seventh round in the second stage of the battle and Freeman was declared the victor.

Shortly after that, Freeman became seriously ill, a victim of tuberculosis, and died on October 18, 1845.

Perry, outside of his defeat by Freeman, decisively defeated the best men of his day in England, and when "Bendigo" retired in 1850 he was matched with Tom Paddock in a battle for the championship that terminated in a victory for the Slasher in the twenty-seventh round on a foul.

On September 29, 1851, Perry dropped the title, losing on a foul to Harry Broome.

Tom Paddock, who had three times contested for the championship, was the man to wrest the title from Broome on May 19, 1856, winning in fifty-one rounds of gruelling fighting. About two years later, on June 16, 1858, the greatest fighting man of his inches in England—Tom Sayers—defeated Paddock for the heavyweight crown in a battle lasting one hour and twenty minutes.

William Perry *(left)* batters the right eye of Harry Broome, whom he has brought to his knees. Perry was disqualified for foul tactics. The battle, which took place in 1851, ended in the 33rd round. Peter Crawley, former champion, refereed the contest. Perry had protested the choice of Crawley, fearing a "raw deal." The fight was rough from the beginning, not only in the ring but outside it, for each man had violently partisan fans.

Tom Sayers, only a middle-weight by modern standards, was one of Great Britain's most prominent fighters. He reached the top rung of the ladder, after a long uphill climb, on June 15, 1858, when he beat Tom Paddock in 21 rounds for the championship. The illustration below shows Sayers delivering the knockout punch that won him the crown. As in all early fights, the spectators crowded around the ring and partisan feeling ran high.

Tom Hyer, America's first heavyweight champion, was born on January 1, 1819. He stood over six feet and weighed 185 pounds.

AMERICA TAKES UP THE SPORT

By a sort of traditional consent, the fight between Jacob Hyer and Tom Beasley in New York in 1816 is established as the first ring battle in America in which the public-at-large was represented and in which the rules that governed boxing in England were accepted by the principals. We accept Jacob Hyer of New York as the first American to fight professionally in public, and his son Tom as the first American heavyweight king.

After Tom Molineaux and Bill Richmond, each of whom had gained prominence as fighters in England though each was an American, there is a long hiatus in U. S. heavyweight history, the first advertised ring affair thereafter being the Hyer-Beasley mill. While pugilism was flowering in England, it was only budding in America, where the majority of those who took part in fights were sailors who had come to the Eastern ports in ships that crossed the Atlantic.

Their contests were usually staged in the back rooms of taverns, in stalls and out-of-the-way places where they could steer away from the police, since fights were prohibited by law.

Thirty-three years after the Hyer-Beasley battle, the first heavyweight championship bout took place in the United States with Tom Hyer, son of Jacob, facing "Yankee" Sullivan for a $5,000 side bet and the championship of America. It was fought at Still Pond Creek, near Baltimore, on

Jacob Hyer (above), father of Tom, is generally accepted as the "Father of the American Ring." He gained fistic fame when he defeated Tom Beasley in 1816. This was his only bout. The affair was the first ring battle in America in which the rules of boxing were observed. He was 6'2" tall and weighed about 182 pounds. Born in New York, he came from Dutch stock.

Yankee Sullivan (right) was born James Ambrose, in Ireland. He won over good men in England and came to America in 1841, becoming a power in politics and the ring. In a fight for the title, he lost to Tom Hyer.

The great fight between Tom Hyer *(right)* and Yankee Sullivan, for $10,000, took place on a cold day with a layer of snow on the ground. In this Currier and Ives print, referee Steve Van Ostrand is on the ropes at the left. The seconds kneel in their corners.

February 7, 1849, with Hyer the victor in sixteen rounds. Hyer decided to remain inactive thereafter due to the failure of Sullivan's backers to put up a side bet of $10,000 for a return bout.

Though William Fuller, a Britisher of mediocre talent, visited America to open a public gymnasium and academy for boxing and declared himself the champion, he had no basis for this since he was a citizen of England and had also been badly whipped by Tom Molineaux at a time when the Negro was well past his prime. Fuller returned to England and was followed in this country by Deaf Burke and O'Rourke, whose presence aroused interest in boxing. But still the game lagged until after Tom Hyer became the first acknowledged champion heavyweight of America.

Boxing and politics went hand-in-hand in those days, with the Native Americans pitted against the Irish every time a ring battle was staged. After Hyer's gruelling contest at Caldwell's Landing, New York, on September 9, 1841, against George McChester, known as "Country McCluskey," Yankee Sullivan and his mobsters picked on Hyer and his supporters and frequent encounters followed. The bout with McCluskey took two hours and fifty-five minutes to decide, with Hyer winning in 101 rounds.

The bitterness between the Hyer and Sullivan ranks resulted in a bout for the title that took place at Rock Point, Maryland, February 7, 1849, and ended in sixteen rounds with Hyer retaining his crown. Hyer retired following his failure to entice William Perry, "The Tipton Slasher," to come to America to fight him for world honors. Tom Hyer died in New York on June 26, 1864.

From the time of the Hyer-Sullivan feud until well into the twentieth century, boxing in America could be dubbed the history of Irish supremacy. Hibernians from abroad, and some of those who lived in America, ruled the roost for many years. Shortly after Hyer whipped Sullivan, another good

heavyweight appeared in the person of John Morrissey, a son of Erin who came to this country at the age of three and with his parents settled in Troy, New York. He was born in Templemore, County Tipperary, February 5, 1831.

Morrissey was a leading politician, became a power in Irish-American affairs, was a top man in the strong political institution, Tammany Hall, and fought for his rights at the drop of a hat. In his later years after retirement, he opened a gambling house in Saratoga, New York, owned race horses, and was the first Congressman and Senator to be elected from among boxers in our country.

After Hyer retired as champion, he went to California, but upon his return, his sparring partner, who had accompanied Tom as a prospector, remained and to earn extra money fought a friend of Morrissey, John Willis. Morrissey, who was present, wagered heavily on his man and had many of his followers on hand to see that "justice" was done to his boy.

Yankee Sullivan, here seen dressed for a Tammany Hall organization parade, was killed in California by the Vigilantes.

John Morrissey packed a remarkable amount of strength in his six-foot frame. He was not too good as a boxer, but his power and ability to take punishment wore his opponents down. His battles with Sullivan and John C. Heenan were ring classics.

George Thompson, Hyer's pal, had all the better of the milling, but sighting danger ahead, he deliberately fouled to lose the fight, thus saving his neck. Morrissey cleaned up on the victory of Willis and on returning to New York, he made an unsuccessful attempt to match Willis with Hyer or with himself. He then accepted a defi from Sullivan to battle for Hyer's crown and on October 12, 1853, he whipped Sullivan at Boston Corners, New York, Sullivan quitting in the thirty-seventh round.

Upset by losing to his bitter Tammany Hall rival, Sullivan quit New York and went to California to try his luck as prospector. He got in difficulties there and was hounded by the Vigilante Committee. Following

his arrest, he was found dead in his cell, apparently a victim of a Vigilante's deed.

The bitter rivalry between Sullivan and Morrissey found a counterpart in that between Morrissey and his fellow townsman, John C. Heenan, known as the "Benicia Boy." Their feud reached its culmination at Long Point, Canada, on October 20, 1858, when Morrissey gained the right to the American heavyweight championship by defeating his rival, who had lost the use of his right hand when it struck a stake in a neutral corner.

Morrissey then retired and operated his luxurious gambling houses both in New York City and Saratoga. He served two terms in the U. S. Congress and was also elected in the New York

Senate but never served because of illness. He died on May 1, 1878, at the age of forty-seven.

With the retirement of Morrissey, Heenan had the field to himself. He was the outstanding heavyweight of his period in America and was generally recognized as title holder because Morrissey had refused to give him a return bout following the mishap he had suffered in their Canadian bout. With no suitable opponent in America, Heenan's friends urged him to issue a challenge to Tom Sayers, British title holder, for the highest honors in fistiana. Adah Isaacs Menken, who later became his wife, was instrumental in forcing the issue, and it was her influence, combined with that of George Wilkes, editor of the *Spirit of the Times* of New York, who challenged Sayers on behalf of Heenan, that resulted in the match being made. It was the first in which an American heavyweight title holder was pitted against a British champion.

Thus, with Heenan's trip overseas, ended the first phase of boxing in the United States.

An artist representing *Leslie's Weekly* drew these scenes of the John C. Heenan-John Morrissey fight for the American championship. Steamboats, filled with 2,000 thugs, thieves, gunmen and so-called sportsmen, sailed from Buffalo at midnight and arrived at Long Point, Canada, at daybreak, October 20, 1858. Sand bars prevented the steamers from landing close to shore, so small boats were used. The ring was pitched next to the lighthouse and a second ring was set up to keep the crowd 20 feet away. In this area 50 ring-keepers were on duty to keep order. Morrissey was in better physical condition than Heenan, who had been ill for a week before the fight, with a festering leg ulcer. They bashed each other for 11 rounds, and only the fifth round ended with a knockdown, by Heenan. The others ended with falls. Heenan collapsed in the 11th round and was carried to his corner. When he failed to come out for round 12, Morrissey was crowned the new champion.

BATTLE OF CHAMPIONS

Of all the names of champion heavyweights who upheld ring prestige, that of Tom Sayers stands out in bold relief. His great contest with John Camel Heenan of America at Farnborough, England, on the morning of April 17, 1860, was the first international ring combat that stirred public interest to fever heat on both sides of the Atlantic. His fighting weight was only 140 pounds, less than the welterweight limit in these days, yet he opposed the leading middleweights with success. Later he fought in the heavyweight division though he seldom scaled beyond 152 pounds.

His only setback was at the hands of Nat Langham on October 18, 1853, in which bout Sayers was blinded and was forced to retire. He tried to obtain a return bout but Langham retired rather than face Tom again. In British ring history, Sayers is rated among the greatest of all time. He was an amazingly clever pugilist. For his pounds and inches he was listed a marvel.

On June 16, 1857, Sayers clashed with William Perry, the celebrated "Tipton Slasher," in a match for the heavyweight crown. It took Sayers an hour and forty-five minutes of battling before he could down his man and win the championship. Perry's seconds tossed in the sponge.

The following year, Sayers added to his laurels by twice defeating Bill Bainge, known as "Benjamin," and whipping Tom Paddock and Bob Brettle, each of whom he knocked out.

The Sayers-Heenan match was a great international event in which both countries, aroused by what might be termed "wild patriotic enthusiasm," heavily supported the native son. Not only was the British press represented at the scene by special writers, but the New York *Spirit of the Times* and Frank Leslie's *Illustrated Weekly*, the leading sports journals, assigned their best reporters and artists to cover the event.

Never before had a prize fight drawn together such a huge and

England's champion, Tom Sayers *(left)*, and America's title-holder, John C. Heenan, met in England, for the world's championship on April 17, 1860. This first international fight, for $1,000 a side and to a finish, was given wide coverage by the British and American press. British police had plans to prevent the fight but were unsuccessful—and probably reluctant.

Heenan's training in England was often interrupted by warnings that the police were on their way to arrest him. Because of this constant threat, he had to move from village to village. His final weeks of training were done in a barn *(above)* in Haram, Wiltshire, where he kept a pit-bull dog, to prevent any tampering with equipment and to scare off strangers. Heenan and his trainer, Jack Macdonald, are seen inspecting the punching bag, filled with 30 pounds of sand, one of the first bags used in training. When the day of the fight approached, Sayers, after nine weeks of training, left Newmarket secretly in a horsebox *(below)* to avoid police on arrival at London Bridge station, where a train was to leave for the scene of battle.

varied gathering. They flocked in thousands to the field near the town of Farnborough in which the ring was pitched.

If the records of the chroniclers of the early American ring history are to be taken at their face value, Heenan was the most terrific hitter of the bare-knuckle days, a fighter with indomitable courage, of great strength and endurance. No fight in the history of the sport ever received more comment, no fight has had so much written about it, than the famous Heenan-Sayers affair.

Heenan was a native son, born in America of Irish parentage. He first saw the light of day in Troy on May 2, 1833. When he left school, his father taught him the trade of machinist and at the age of seventeen he had mastered the profession and gained the rank of first-class mechanic.

Although his father had mapped out the plans for the boy's future, he filed no objection when young Heenan made known the fact that he would like to see life and had decided to

Sayers *(left)*, and Heenan, both in disguise, met for the first time at London Bridge station on the morning of the fight. The police could have prevented the bout, since all London was wild with excitement, and two long trains were filled with spectators waiting to leave for the battle scene. Instead, police were stationed within 15 miles of London, knowing full well the fight would not be held inside that area. Sayers was first to scale officially *(below)* for the bout.

visit the Pacific Coast to try his luck there. On his arrival in San Francisco he found immediate employment in the workshops at Benicia belonging to the Pacific Mail Steamship Company, and it was here that he gained the reputation as a pugilist of note and was called "The Benicia Boy."

When Heenan returned to New York he was hailed by the sporting fraternity. He reached New York City on December 4, 1857, with James Cusick, a friend, and on December 10, he gave an exhibition at the National Hall on Canal Street and was wildly received. Shortly after, he became the most talked of man in ring history.

Joe Coburn consented to put on the gloves with Heenan after the crowd had repeatedly called for a demonstration, and the sports were electrified by Heenan's style, his hitting and countering. Coburn, at that time the most scientific boxer in the world, praised Heenan by declaring he had everything a champion needs.

There are some tales which the fight fan is never tired of hearing and one of these is the great international fight at Farnborough. After bitter battling,

The Heenan-Sayers fight at Farnborough attracted celebrities from all parts of England and France and special correspondents from the *Police Gazette*, *Leslie's Weekly* and other American newspapers. There was a great difference in size when both men stripped for action. Heenan weighed 195 pounds and stood 6'2". Sayers scaled only 152 pounds and was 5'8" tall. Newbold, in his *Great Battle for the Championship*, writes: "The crowd was the most representative ever seen at a fight in our country. Compared to former mills, the present congregation must unhesitatingly be pronounced the most aristocratic ever assembled at a ringside. It included the bearers of names highly distinguished in British society, officers of the Army and Navy, of Parliament, justices of the peace and even brethren of the cloth. The muster of literati included William Thackeray and Charles Dickens."

the ropes were cut in the thirty-seventh round, the crowd surged into the ring and a free-for-all followed. The referee disappeared, but the fighters decided to continue and for five rounds they fought without an official.

The British were certain that Sayers had won the contest while the supporters of Heenan took the opposite side.

In America it was the universal opinion, based on reports that came from abroad, that had the ropes not been cut, Heenan would have carried off the honors. Thus, after two hours and twenty minutes of terrific battling, the first heavyweight championship bout for the world title ended in a draw and a championship belt was given to each man.

The American, a true sportsman, viewed the attacks on Sayers as unjust. He and Tom became friendly and went on an exhibition tour together. Heenan's contention was that Sayers was not to blame for the rowdyism of the mob.

Heenan, on Sayers' retirement, was universally acknowledged as champion of the world, and he decided to return to Europe. Once again the "Benicia Boy" crossed the Atlantic and entered the ring on December 8, 1863, with Tom King for his opponent and Tom Sayers as Heenan's second. This time the gods were unkind to the American, for he was beaten in the twenty-fourth round, after thirty-five minutes of milling. Heenan then retired.

He was thirty-eight when he died at Green River Station, Wyoming Territory, October 28, 1873, and his remains were brought to Albany where he was buried.

When Sayers showed signs of tiring in the 37th round, Heenan rushed him against the ropes, forced his neck across the top strand (above) and pressed down on his throat. The partisan gathering around ringside went wild. They stormed the ring and several thugs cut the ropes. Sayers' seconds interfered and Heenan had his hands full warding them off. The referee had abandoned the scene, but they fought on for five more rounds. Heenen demanded that a new site be found to continue the battle, as stated in the rules, but the fight was called a draw. Heenan, angry at the decision, ran to the train pursued by a mob (right). British and American writers differed as to who was leading when the fight ended.

ENGLAND LOSES PRESTIGE

Boxing was forced into the background in England for a time following the disorder in the Sayers-Heenan battle. The police became more belligerent, the clergy more alert, the attacks on the sport more prevalent. The sport had entered into a rough period. But two men's names stood out prominently: Tom King, who conquered Heenan; and the great Jem Mace, known as the "Swaffham Gypsy," one of the greatest ring men with the gloves that boxing has produced.

On Tom Sayers' retirement, Tom Paddock claimed the British title, and in a bout with Sam Hurst, his challenger, the latter, a 210-pound giant, clinched the championship by stopping Paddock in nine minutes and thirty seconds. But Hurst lacked color and ability and his reign failed to arouse enthusiasm among the British followers of boxing. It remained for Mace to bring new life into the sport.

A cabinet-maker by trade, he was born at Beeston in Norfolk, on April 8, 1831. He was one of four brothers, three of whom were blacksmiths. He was extremely fond of music and in his youth he frequently traveled the country as an itinerant fiddler. Though called a gypsy, he and his family denied he had any Romany blood.

Mace learned his boxing in the booths where he would offer his opponent the choice of gloves or bare-knuckles, but invariably he succeeded in having the former used. He discouraged bare-fist fighting and thus brought public attention to the use of the mitts, a procedure later followed by John L. Sullivan.

He won the British middleweight crown and after defeating Slasher Slack and Bill Thorpe, a clever middleweight, he lost to Bob Brettle, then whipped "Posh" Bill and Bob Travers. In a return bout with Brettle, he was returned the victor. By this time Mace had grown heavier and he resolved to try for heavyweight honors. He was matched with Sam Hurst for the British title and stopped Hurst in eight rounds lasting fifty minutes.

Thus Mace won the British crown on June 18, 1861. On January 28 of the following year he defended his crown successfully against Tom King, who outweighed him by thirty pounds. The bout went forty-three rounds.

In a second encounter on November 26, 1862, King, on the verge of exhaustion, landed a wild swing on Mace's temple, flooring him. Mace collapsed two rounds later and a new champion was crowned.

Tom King at once announced his retirement. But with Heenan clamoring for the world's championship by virtue of his memorable struggle with Sayers, British sportsmen insisted that King should fight the "Benicia Boy." Public opinion was too strong and King came out of retirement and beat Heenan, who was forced to quit.

Jem Mace *(left)*, known as the "Swaffham Gypsy," was the greatest ringman with gloves England ever produced. He was called the father of scientific boxing. Sam Hurst *(below)*, the "Stalybridge Infant," followed Sayers as champion, but lacked support.

The engraving above shows clearly every person who witnessed the battle between Tom King *(left)* and Jem Mace on November 26, 1862, at Medway. In the 19th round King landed a wild blow on Mace's temple. Mace weathered the storm of blows that followed, but in the 21st round he collapsed and King was awarded the championship of England. On December 3, 1863, King knocked out John C. Heenan for the world's title.

Having regained the world's championship for his country, Tom King declared he had fought for the last time. True to his word, he remained in retirement.

Later, he became a familiar figure on the English turf. Dame Fortune followed him, for when he died in his fifty-fourth year, October 3, 1888, his estate was estimated at $300,000, a very respectable fortune in those days.

With King definitely out of the fistic picture, Mace was again universally recognized as world's heavyweight champion. In a battle with Joe Goss on September 1, 1863, Mace won in one hour, forty-five minutes and thirty seconds, and proved that as a scientific artist, he stood head and shoulders over all contemporaries.

While Mace was enjoying his victories overseas, Joe Coburn clinched his claim to the American championship after Heenan's retirement, by defeating Mike McCoole at Charlestown, Maryland, on May 5, 1863.

A year later, Coburn went to England for the purpose of fighting Mace.

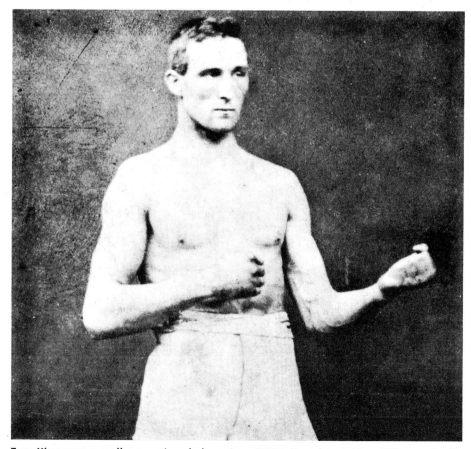

Tom King was a well-proportioned champion, 6'2" tall and weighing 175 pounds. He learned to box in the Royal Navy, where he engaged in many bare-knuckle and glove bouts. After retiring from the ring, he amassed a huge fortune.

After Tom King abdicated the throne, Jem Mace decided he was entitled to wear the crown, and received recognition as champion. Another Englishman, Joe Goss, challenged his right to the title. On September 1, 1863, they met at Thames in a bout that lasted almost two hours. Goss *(left)* was game, but he was outclassed and stopped by Mace in 19 rounds. Goss tried twice more, in 1866, to gain Mace's crown, but was held to a draw and was stopped again, in 21 rounds, on August 6.

Ned O'Baldwin, born in Lismore, Ireland, in 1840, was called the "Irish Giant." He stood 6'5" and fought at 210 pounds. Upon arriving in America, he visited the durable John Morrissey, who was to test his ability. In a 20-minute sparring match with gloves, Morrissey was floored twice. Mike Donovan, the master, always insisted that O'Baldwin was the greatest fighter he ever saw. O'Baldwin was shot and killed in 1875 by his liquor store business partner in New York.

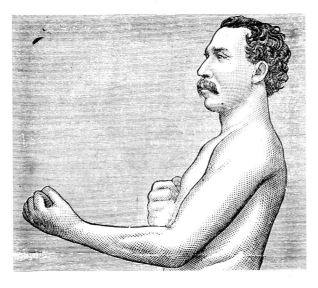

Mace, but the bout had to be cancelled. He then went to America. Tom Allen, Joe Wormwald, Joe Goss and others did the same.

The fistic tide was now rising in the United States, where champions in all classes were developing.

With no opponents in sight at home, Mace departed on a tour of Australia, where he gave boxing exhibitions.

In the meantime, O'Baldwin and Joe Wormwald met in a battle at Lynnfield, Massachusetts, on October 20, 1868. The police interfered, and since Wormwald declined to "fight out matters" later, O'Baldwin was declared the winner. There was no title involved, since Mace still reigned as monarch.

By this time Mace decided that his proper base of operations was in the New World and he joined the exodus of pugilistic talent. On his arrival in America he was matched with Tom Allen. The latter, born in Birmingham, England, had beaten "Posh" Price, Parkinson, Illes, and fought a thirty-four rounds draw with Goss.

Before Allen took up his residence in the United States, Jim Dunn,

Mace accepted the challenge and a match was arranged to be fought in the vicinity of Dublin, Ireland, on October 4, 1864. The affair ended unpleasantly when Coburn refused to accept any referee but his personal friend, James Bowler, and the bout was called off. Coburn returned to America and Mace remained idle until May 24, 1866, when he again clashed with his former foeman, Joe Goss, in an unsatisfactory bout that ended in a draw.

Mace was accused of not trying; with his reputation at stake, he offered Goss another match. On August 6, 1866, Mace gave Joe a terrific beating, stopping him in twenty-one rounds.

At this time, public feeling in England was decidedly opposed to the activities of the brethren of the thudding fists. A reform wave swept the country. The clergy preached against the "ruffians of the ring" and staging fights became a perilous pastime.

Ned O'Baldwin was matched with

Joe Goss, born in England in 1838, started boxing in 1859. He lost to Jem Mace in 19 rounds in 1863, held Mace to a draw in 1866, and was again defeated by Mace in London in 21 rounds that same year.

The Jem Mace (right)-Tom Allen contest at Kennerville, Louisiana, on May 10, 1870, gave Mace a firm hold on the world heavyweight championship. Allen could not cope with Mace's scientific plan of battle and proved an easy victim in ten rounds.

Jimmy Elliott, and John Dwyer had each claimed and held the American championship at intervals.

Coburn had retired temporarily. Mike McCoole won from Allen on a foul, and since McCoole refused to meet Allen again, the latter was recognized as the best man to face Mace for the world's title.

The Mace-Allen battle took place at Kennerville, Louisiana, on May 10, 1870, and Mace won in ten rounds.

Coburn then challenged Mace and they met at Bay St. Louis, Mississippi, on November 30, 1871. It was a hard-fought combat and was declared a draw.

Mace retired immediately after the Coburn engagement. His name was held in great esteem by his country-men. He did more to foster the pure science of boxing than any other man of his era.

Great as Mace was when fighting under London Rules, it was as a glove artist that he appeared at his best. Following his retirement, his friends in New York presented him with a huge, handsome silver belt which now rests in "The Ring" Museum in Madison Square Garden in New York City.

Mace passed away on November 30, 1910, in Liverpool, England, at the age of seventy-nine.

Joe Coburn fought Mace twice in 1871. Neither struck a blow in the first bout and the second was a 12-round draw.

Jem Mace, photographed in Liverpool, England, in 1909, was 79 years old and active until his death on Nov. 30, 1910.

51

THE END OF AN ERA

In the long history of boxing there have been many romantic figures, but few who gained such prominence as Ben Hogan, born in Wurtemburg, Germany, in 1844, the first German to lay claim to the American bare knuckle heavyweight crown, though he was never recognized as a champion. His fame rests on his battle with Tom Allen in 1872 for the championship, a contest that ended unsatisfactorily when Hogan refused to continue after he had been fouled in the third round.

He was one of the most picturesque characters in American ring history: a Union and Confederate spy during the Civil War, a gambling house operator, oil magnate, theatrical producer, and the inventor of the floating palace gambling house, in addition to being a professional pugilist. He was baptized Benediel Hagen, but following his arrival in New York he changed his name to Hogan.

The story of Hogan is vibrant with human interest. It is the tale of a man who sought adventure and got a bellyful before he settled down to the life of an evangelist. He married a Salvation Army worker, opened a flophouse in Chicago and there preached the Gospel to those who sought shelter.

Following the retirement of Heenan after his defeat by Tom King, there was speculation among Americans as to who would be Tom's successor. Opinion favored Jimmy Elliott, a powerful man with a pugnacious temperament, and Joe Coburn. They were the two best bare knuckles artists in America.

After a few side-bet contests, Elliott challenged Coburn to fight him for the championship and when the latter refused, following the procedure of those days, Elliott's friends claimed the crown. On May 10, 1867, he and Bill Davis clashed in a ring pitched at Point Pelee Island, Lake Erie, Canada, to decide the championship issue. Elliott won by a knockout and was proclaimed the new title holder.

The following year, on November 12, 1868, Elliott fought Charley Gallagher at Peach Island, near Detroit. Gallagher's backer withdrew his man at the end of the twenty-third round after several appeals to the referee for action on Elliott's foul work, and the latter retained his title.

On May 9, 1879, he and John Dwyer of Brooklyn fought at Long Point,

Jimmy Elliott (left), a mean, tough ring veteran, was sent to prison for assault and robbery. Released with a pardon, he was matched to fight Johnny Dwyer of Brooklyn, (below) for the American championship, May 8, 1879, at Long Point, Canada. Badly punished for nine rounds, Elliott wet his hands with turpentine and blinded Dwyer. Fresh water restored Dwyer's sight and from then on he beat Elliott unmercifully, finally knocking him out in the twelfth round. Dwyer never fought again.

Mike McCool *(left)* and Joe Coburn, both claiming the title, met for the championship and one thousand dollars a side on May 25, 1863. After 67 rounds of vicious fighting near Cumberland, Maryland, McCool's seconds were forced to throw in the sponge.

Mike McCool, born in Ireland, was a riverman in Cincinnáti who developed a powerful body ad packed a terrific punch.

Joe Coburn, Irish-born and one of the cleverest men of his time, was fast, strong and could hit hard with both hands.

Canada, in a bout listed for the American championship. In a gruelling affair, Elliott was stopped in the twelfth round, following an injury to his ribs.

He was an able boatman, an adventurer, a handy man with fists and gun, and an able wrestler. In a tavern brawl he was shot and killed by Jere Dunn, a notorious character who had been the Chief of Police of Elmira.

Mike McCoole, known as the "Deck Hand Champion of America," born in Ireland, March 12, 1837, was another of the many sons of Erin who ruled the roost as U. S. title holders. He was the first heavyweight developed outside New York City to gain the top rung of the ladder. From Tom Hyer, who reigned in the Forties, to John L. Sullivan, the East held a monopoly of heavyweight stars, but McCoole changed that. He went to the Midwest at an early age because of difficulties with the police, and as a bargeman the six feet, two inches tall pugilist carried his battering ram wallops into the ring in impromptu battles quite often.

McCoole and Joe Coburn fought for the championship on May 5, 1863, in Maryland, Coburn winning. A return bout with Coburn was arranged

for Cold Springs Station, Indiana, May 27, 1868, but Coburn was taken into custody by the police and McCoole, having put on his fighting togs and entered the ring, claimed the crown and was acclaimed champion. He then fought Tom Allen of Birmingham, England, for the championship at Foster Island near St. Louis, June 15, 1869. He was badly punished, but the referee awarded the decision to Mike. In their return engagement near St. Louis in 1873, Allen won decisively

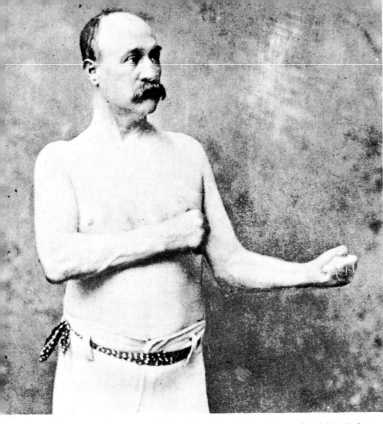

Tom Allen, an Englishman, born in 1840, did much of his fighting in American rings. Upon retiring in 1876, after his loss to Joe Goss, he settled in St. Louis and opened a saloon.

Joe Goss, born in England in 1838, had eleven fights in the Empire. In his only bouts in America, he won over Tom Allen in 1876 and was knocked out by Paddy Ryan in 87 rounds in 1880.

Paddy Ryan, a handsome gentleman, retired in 1886 and settled at Green Island, near Troy, N. Y., where he died in 1901.

in twenty-nine rounds and McCoole retired.

He died in the Charity Hospital of New Orleans on October 17, 1886. He was the last of the slugging bare knuckle pugilists, if we except John L. Sullivan, who later returned to boxing with gloves.

After Tom Allen had stopped Mike McCoole in their return engagement on September 23, 1873, and McCoole retired from pugilism, Allen claimed the heavyweight crown but found himself challenged by Joe Goss, rated next to Jem Mace. Goss defeated Allen on a foul and he became the undisputed king of the division. Now a new American menace had made his appearance in this country, a young giant from upper New York whose physical prowess was such as to make him the talk of the fistic circles.

His name was Paddy Ryan.

Like Morrissey, Paddy Ryan was a Tipperary man, and like Morrissey and John C. Heenan, Ryan brought fistic fame to Troy, which he made his home when he first came to America.

The Trojan Giant, as he was dubbed, was born in the town of Thurles, County Tipperary, Ireland, March 15, 1853. He was five feet, eleven inches tall and weighed far more than the majority of his predecessors among the champions, his normal weight being 200 pounds.

He had only two battles under the London Rules: in the first he captured the title from forty-two-year-old Joe Goss; and in the second, he lost the crown to John L. Sullivan, when Ryan refused to continue after he had been badly whipped in nine rounds. In his youth he had lost a bout to Joe McAuliffe with skin tight gloves.

Ryan's battle with Goss took place on May 30, 1880, at Colliers Station, West Virginia. In this bout, Ryan did what no other fighter in American ring history has ever accomplished—he won the championship in his first professional battle!

In the eighty-sixth round a severe right-hand cross counter felled Goss and his seconds claimed a foul, but this was disallowed. They carried Joe

Paddy Ryan's reign as champion was brief. Winning the title in his first bout (*below*), he lost it in his second, when John L. Sullivan knocked him out in the ninth round in 1882 (*above*). The match was held in a ring pitched in front of the Barnes Hotel in Mississippi City, Mississippi, and lasted only ten minutes and 30 seconds. The stakes were five thousand dollars and the title.

Crude, but extremely powerful, Paddy Ryan needed 87 rounds to dispose of lighter but more experienced Joe Goss in their championship meeting at Collier's Station, West Virginia, in 1880. The fight lasted one hour, 24 minutes. When Goss could not get up to toe the mark, his seconds conceded victory to Ryan. Collier's Station, situated on the Pennsylvania-West Virginia border, was the scene of many notable bare-knuckle bouts during the days when London Prize-Ring Rules governed boxing.

to his corner and when time arrived for the start of the eighty-seventh session, his seconds called a halt. Thus we have the remarkable feat of a heavyweight champion being crowned whose only fistic contests prior to the titular mill were encounters in ordinary bar-room fights!

Within two years after Ryan had defeated Goss, dark clouds began to gather on the Trojan's horizon. The clouds took the shape of John L. Sullivan, whose friends issued a challenge for the American title. Ryan accepted the Sullivan defi and at Mississippi City, Mississippi, on February 7, 1882, just thirty-three years to a day after Tom Hyer and Yankee Sullivan had engaged in the first recognized heavyweight championship of America, Ryan was stopped in the ninth round.

Later, on November 13, 1886, Sullivan knocked out the Trojan again, this time in the third round. Never before in the history of pugilism did a fighter win the title in his first contest and lose it in his next. With the crowning of John L. Sullivan as champion, a new era in boxing began.

FIGHTING has changed. On March 10, 1888, this writer saw John L. Sullivan and Charles Mitchell fight in a muddy, slippery twenty-four-foot ring on Baron Rothschild's training grounds near Chantilly in France. It was not like arrangements for tomorrow's fight.

Thirty or forty men stood around the ring. One was Billy Porter, the bank burglar, who afterward died in the German salt mines. He had a revolver in each overcoat pocket, and notified those in Mitchell's corner that Sullivan was to have fair play. Sullivan got it.

The men fought with bare fists soaked in walnut juice, and had long spikes on their shoes. Sullivan requested Mitchell to "be a gentleman, you ———— ———— if you can," when Mitchell drove a spike into Sullivan's instep.

The fight was under London prize ring rules, each round ending when either man went down with one knee on the ground. No gate receipts, no purse, only a side bet.

When the fight ended in a draw, both men were locked up by French gendarmes at Senlis, bombarded by Germans. This writer saw them there. The French jailer had taken away their silk handkerchiefs "to prevent their hanging themselves." Both wept. Both are dead. What would they think of a modern fight with $3,500,000 gate receipts?

John L. Sullivan, photographed on left at the height of his career, was five feet, 10½ inches tall and weighed 190 pounds. He faced 35 opponents, won 16 by knockouts, was held to a draw three times, and was knocked out once, when he lost the crown to Jim Corbett. The late Arthur Brisbane, brilliant columnist for the Hearst newspapers and close friend of Sullivan, made the above comments in his column on the eve of the Dempsey-Tunney fight in Philadelphia in 1927.

JOHN L.'S ENTRANCE AND EXIT

Like the red planet Mars, shining emblem of war, the bright star of John L. Sullivan suddenly flared into flame on a fistic horizon hitherto dimly outlined in mists of mediocrity. For three years prior to his New York debut there had been considerable talk in metropolitan circles about this heavy-hitting Boston youth who scored victories over such men as Cockey Woods, Dan Dwyer, Mike Donovan and George Rooke within the precincts of the cultured Hub and had beaten Professor John Donaldson in Cincinnati, Ohio.

But it was not until New York saw him in action that the wise men of Gotham realized his standing as a combatant extraordinary. The speed and ferocity of his attack not only amazed the spectators, but led many of them to conclude that the likes of this savage young conqueror had never before been seen in a ring.

In or out of the ring, "John L." was quick to wrath and a bad hombre to cross at any time. Yet he won the whole-hearted devotion of fistic followers as no other pugilist before or after him succeeded in doing.

Not even those later day idols, Jack Dempsey and Joe Louis, exercised such a lasting spell of fascination on the public mind as did the picturesque, indomitable biffer from Boston. When the ring followers called him "The Champion of Champions" it was no idle phrase. They really meant it. In their eyes Sullivan had attained the status of a god, all-powerful, super-human, the world's greatest fighter with bare fists or the padded mitts.

John Lawrence Sullivan was born on October 15, 1858, in Concord Street, Roxbury, Massachusetts, in the Highlands of Boston. He came of hardy Irish stock, his father, Michael, hailing from Tralee, County Kerry, and his mother from Athlone, County Roscommon. His paternal grandfather was a noted Celtic wrestler and champion performer with a shillelagh. His dad was agile and pugnacious, of diminutive stature, but big of heart, as savage as a wild cat if aroused and kingpin with the fists among the hod carriers with whom he worked.

A victory over Cockey Woods, a husky Boston scrapper, launched Sullivan on the pugilistic ocean. That triumph brought him an exhibition tour and the following year a bout with Dan Dwyer in Revere Hall, Boston, where he easily won. As Dan was the recognized champion of Massachusetts, the fact that Sullivan slapped him around light-heartedly was a big feather in the youngster's cap. He followed this by decisively whipping Tommy Chandler, a well known and formidable heavyweight.

Fight fans now began to talk about the young New England sensation, and his big chance that opened the way to a dazzling future came when Professor Mike Donovan, then world middleweight champion, visited Bos-

In the engraving on the left, the artist portrayed the "Fighting John L." You can see alertness in his eyes, powerful arms, chest and shoulders, and almost feel the fierce mood and challenging attitude.

The fight that established Sullivan (*right*) as a potential champion was the one in which he scored over John Flood in 1881. It was Sullivan's first appearance in the New York area, and the fight was held on a barge anchored in the river off Hastings, near Yonkers. The Bostonian lived up to his exciting advance notices by winning decisively in eight rounds (16 minutes).

John Flood, known by the inspiring title of "Bull's Head Terror," wasn't so inspiring against John L. He was knocked down in every round until he finally quit.

ton to give an exhibition in the latter part of 1879. The professor, who later held the post of boxing instructor at the New York Athletic Club, was deservedly rated as one of the most scientific boxers of the day. Yet the young Boston "Strong Boy" battered him and all but knocked him out.

"You're the goods, young fellow, and I'm betting you'll go far in this game!" said Donovan after the set-to.

Besides William Muldoon, the latter's friend Billy Madden had seen Sullivan fight. The two were staging a variety show in Boston and they agreed to put "John L." on in an exhibition bout. Joe Goss, once claimant of the heavyweight title, was to appear in a benefit arranged for him at the Hub and Madden induced him to take on Sullivan for four rounds.

Goss was clever and tricky, but despite all his cleverness, he was clearly outclassed.

Following the Goss affair, Sullivan earned new prestige by giving George

Rooke a terrific beating. Rooke was knocked down seven times.

By now Sullivan's fame had spread to America's sporting centers and he was much in demand. Macon McCormick, America's ace sports reporter, then editor of the *Cincinnati Enquirer*, was an ardent fight-patron and made up his mind that this new knockout artist must show his wares in the Midwest, and he arranged to have Sullivan box John Donaldson. In the third round, Donaldson decided that he had had enough and quit. But the crowd grew hostile and Donaldson consented to resume sparring, but a moment later, he threw up his hands and quit again.

Two months after the Cincinnati affair, they again faced each other in a contest, without gloves, held in a back room of the Atlantic Garden in the same city, and in the tenth round Sullivan cornered his elusive opponent and knocked him out.

Sullivan's first important fight around

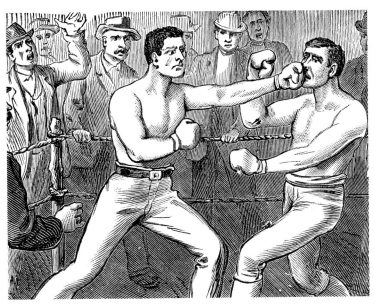

Fighting with the gloves was preferred by John L. Sullivan to battling with the bare knuckles. One of his earliest glove contests was with Professor John Donaldson *(right)* at Cincinnati in 1880. John L. won by a kayo.

(Above) The artist's conception of the bare-knuckle fight between Paddy Ryan *(left)* and John L. Sullivan, in 1882, included the huge camera perched high above ringside, a novelty in those days. Pictured in the foreground are many notables of the day, among them, Richard K. Fox *(extreme right)*, Ryan's backer. Ryan *(below)* was badly outclassed and knocked out by Sullivan in nine rounds after absorbing a great amount of punishment. With this victory, Sullivan became American champion.

New York State took place on a barge anchored in the Hudson River off Yonkers. John Flood, known as the "Bull's Head Terror," was his opponent. Five hundred sports paid ten dollars each to see the battle. Sullivan and Flood fought with skin-tight gloves, under London Prize rules, for a stake of $1,000, of which $750 went to the winner and $250 to the loser.

The fight lasted sixteen minutes, with Flood down in every round. The latter's seconds threw in the sponge in the eighth, acknowledging defeat.

The Philadelphia fans saw him knock out Fred Crossley in less than a round, followed by John L. whipping two well known sluggers for the edification of Chicago ring patrons: Captain James Dalton, a tugboat skipper, in four rounds; and Jack Burns in two minutes of the first frame.

When Sullivan and Madden returned to the East, negotiations were well under way for John's title shot at Ryan's crown. These were concluded on October 5, 1881, when articles were signed for a fight to a finish with bare knuckles, to take place the following February, for $2,500 a side.

This battle for the heavyweight championship was held at Mississippi City on February 2, 1882, the "Boston Strong Boy" stopping his man in nine rounds.

For the first time in American journalistic history, the newspapers hired famous novelists, dramatists, and even members of the clergy to write their impressions of a prize fight, so deep an interest was there in this title bout. Among those so employed were Henry Ward Beecher and the Reverend Thomas De Witt Talmage. Nat Goodwin represented the dramatic brotherhood in that capacity, and Oscar Wilde, then on a lecture tour of the United States, accepted an assignment to write a story for a British publication.

The Sullivan-Ryan battle, as already told, was exciting and yet a rather one-sided affair. Sullivan, the more powerful of the two, had much the better of Ryan in the wrestling mixups permitted by London rules, and he threw Paddy frequently.

When time was called for the ninth round, Ryan could scarcely move. He staggered out gallantly and Sullivan wasted no time. He tore in like a human battering-ram and it was all over. A new champion had been crowned.

Thereafter, for ten long years, the

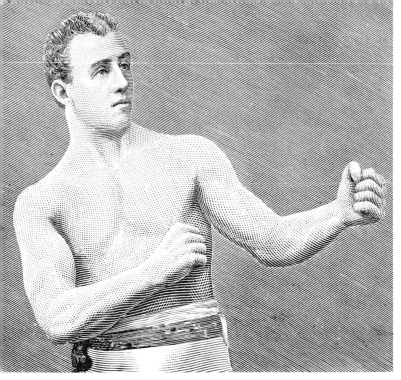

Charlie Mitchell, England's best pugilist, was a skillful boxer with a sharp punch. He came to America and spread the word that he was here for one purpose: "To knock out Mr. Sullivan."

Jake Kilrain (right) of Quincy, Massachusetts, was groomed and backed by Richard K. Fox, editor of the *Police Gazette*, to dethrone John L. Before meeting Sullivan, Kilrain had some tough battles.

Below is the scene in Mechanics Hall, Boston, where an overflow crowd saw Charlie Mitchell and Jake Kilrain engage in a 4-round draw on May 26, 1884. The contest followed the appearance of the Britisher in several New York bouts and served as a test for the rising young star, Kilrain. Mitchell was beaten by Sullivan in 1883, but Kilrain did not get his chance until 1889.

Charlie Mitchell finally got his chance to meet John L. Sullivan, May 14, 1883, at Madison Square Garden, but lasted only three rounds. After giving Sullivan a battle the first round, Mitchell was knocked out of the ring in the second *(left)* and floored in the third round, when Police Captain Williams *(right)* ordered the fight stopped to save Mitchell from any further punishment.

"Boston Strong Boy" met all comers in the heavyweight division except Negroes.

In 1883, Sullivan faced Charley Mitchell of England in a glove bout staged in New York City and stopped him in the third. The police intervened.

Herbert A. Slade, the Maori, was Sullivan's next opponent. Slade made his American debut before a New York gathering and early in the third round the man from the Antipodes was hurled across the ring by the impact of a clubbing right to his jaw and was unable to continue.

These successive victories over foreign invaders naturally added fresh lustre to Sullivan's laurels. But what finally established him on the pinnacle of public fame was a tour he made of the United States, during which he offered the sum of $1,000 to any man who could stand up to him for four rounds, with the gloves.

First Sullivan beat Slade on August 6, 1883, and the following month he began his trip, meeting all comers. Across the continent he went, never evading a challenger.

From January, 1884, to December, 1886, Sullivan reigned the undisputed monarch of all he surveyed in the fistic world, adding fourteen victories to his credit and fighting a four round draw with Duncan McDonald at Denver. In a battle with Patsy Cardiff at Minneapolis on January 18, 1887, Sullivan broke his left arm; nevertheless he succeeded in securing a draw in 6 rounds.

The most notable contests in his career, other than the Ryan mill, were his thirty-nine rounds draw with Mitchell at Chantilly, France, his seventy-five rounds kayo of Jake Kilrain, the last bare knuckle championship contest, and his defeat by Corbett.

The site selected for Sullivan's fight with Mitchell was Baron Rothschild's picturesque estate at Chantilly, France. Most of the spectators were British, and owing to the secrecy maintained in order to avoid interference and arrest by the authorities, the crowd was strictly limited in number. Only a handful of sports saw the contest and among these were Sullivan's *chère amie*, Ann Livingston, dressed as a boy, a role which that talented young lady had frequently filled on the American stage.

The ring was set up in the rear of a stable, on ground utilized as training quarters for the Baron's racing steeds. For thirty-six hours a heavy rain had been falling. It had stopped when the fighters were squared off, but it left the ground so soggy that the battlers were ankle-deep in mud. Intermittent showers after the combat got under way persisted, a fact which did not add to the gladiators' comfort.

The fight did not come up to expectations, but it was so important that the result was eagerly looked for in boxing circles all over the world. There was a wide difference of opin-

The first round of the international "passage at arms," in which John L. Sullivan and Charlie Mitchell faced each other on the estate of Baron Rothschild near Chantilly, France, on March 10, 1888. The contest was staged during a heavy rain, which made the footing precarious. After 39 rounds the seconds decided to call a halt, and the bout ended in a draw.

Sullivan, his head bandaged, sits in a jail cell, where he was temporarily held after the contest. Both boxers suffered injuries, but Mitchell's were more serious. He is seen here (right) awaiting an examination by a doctor.

When Richard K. Fox challenged Sullivan, on behalf of Jake Kilrain, to a title fight and Sullivan turned it down, Fox announced through the *Police Gazette* that he claimed the crown for Jake and he presented Kilrain with a belt. Whereupon, the citizens of Boston, angered at this action, collected $10,000, bought a gold belt (above), with 397 diamonds, and presented it to Sullivan.

ion regarding the showing of the men. The Sullivan cohorts insisted the champion had by far the better of the milling and based this assertion on the fact that the Englishman had often fouled by going down without being hit.

Mitchell's adherents declared that he had proved his superiority and that the decision to call off hostilities at the end of the thirty-ninth round and make the affair a draw was fortunate for Sullivan.

Back in America, Sullivan was hounded by Richard K. Fox, owner of the *Police Gazette,* who sought a match between "John L." and Jake Kilrain, to whom Fox had awarded the *Police Gazette* championship belt because Sullivan had refused to accept Kilrain's challenge. But now things were different. Riled by his poor display in France, Sullivan signed for a Kilrain bout.

He and Kilrain clashed under the London Prize Ring rules, bare knuckles, for a side bet of $10,000, at Richburg, Mississippi.

The twenty-four-foot ring was pitched on the turf. Kilrain was first to climb through the ropes and then John entered, accompanied by William Muldoon and Mike Cleary. A blazing sun beat down on the strange scene.

John Fitzpatrick, who later was elected Mayor of New Orleans, was the referee. Bat Masterson, once sheriff of Dodge City and in later years

Jake Kilrain's battle with England's champion, Jem Smith, at Isle des Souverains, France, on December 19, 1887, hastened the match with Sullivan. Kilrain dropped Smith in the 17th round (below), but both carried on for 106 gruelling rounds before the contest was stopped because of darkness and called a draw. As a result of this fight, Sullivan claimed the world title after beating Kilrain in 1889.

the boxing expert of the *Morning Telegraph* of New York, was the timekeeper for Jake while Tom Costello held the watch for John.

The fight lasted two hours and sixteen minutes, Kilrain's seconds throwing in the sponge in the seventy-fifth round. From the outset Sullivan forced matters, but was met halfway by Kilrain in the early stages of the battle when Jake fought with great gallantry and spirit.

The Sullivan-Kilrain encounter was the last heavyweight championship fight held under London Prize Ring rules. Henceforth, the gloves were to

The Sullivan-Kilrain fight, last of the bare-knuckle era, was well represented by artists from the various sporting papers then in vogue. The artist from the *Police Gazette* depicted the fight in close-up form *(above)*, showing Sullivan, on the left, poised to counter any move made by Kilrain. The scene shows Sullivan's corner in the background. The second man from the left is Dan Murphy, an important corner-man, whose duty is to guard against tampering with the water. Sullivan's other seconds were Mike Cleary, next to the ring post, holding a round fan, and William Muldoon, next to Cleary.

In this rare photograph *(below)*, showing Sullivan and Kilrain clinched in the center of the ring in the seventh round, the camera recorded the actual details of the over-all scene. The day was reported as blistering hot, but note the men wearing coats.

The artist from the *Police News*, rival to the *Police Gazette*, injected much more detail in his version of the fight. In the center of the ring are Sullivan (*right*) and Kilrain. To the left are Kilrain's corner-men, Charlie Mitchell, Mike Donovan and bottle-holder Johnny Murphy. The timekeeper, holding a watch in the center, is Tom Costello. Around the ringside holding Winchesters, are Captain Tom Jamieson and his twenty Mississippi Rangers. Sullivan objected to their appearance, but was assured they were necessary "to keep the peace." Standing in the second ring, in the foreground, is referee John Fitzpatrick. The three illustrations below were the artist's version of crucial moments during the fight: Both go down (*left*) in the first round; Sullivan scores the first knockdown in round seven (*center*); and Kilrain, very weak, is carried by his seconds in the 65th round.

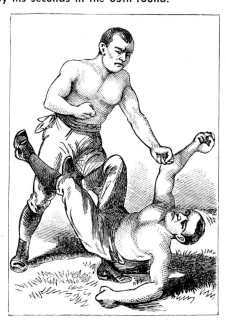

John L.'s popularity on the stage, in plays or personal appearances, was tremendous. Wherever he appeared the theatre was sure to be sold out. Sullivan's theatre earnings, ending in 1915, were over $900,000.

decide the arguments of title-claim-ants. The fighter, discarding Nature's weapons, was translated into the boxer. The bare knuckle man had had his day.

During 1890 John L. Sullivan appeared on the stage as the hero of a melodrama entitled *Honest Hearts and Willing Hands*. On June 4, 1891, he boxed a four round exhibition bout at San Francisco with Jim Corbett, prior to sailing for a tour of Australia. On March 10, 1892, he signed articles to fight Jim Corbett with five ounce gloves before the Olympic Club of New Orleans for a $25,000 purse and $20,000 stake, the bout to take place on September 7th.

More than three years had elapsed since Sullivan beat Kilrain. During that period "John L." had not donned a glove except for exhibition purposes. Idleness, the enervating life of the stage, long nights of carousal with boon companions, had taken toll of his vitality, shortened his breath and in-creased his stomach's circumference.

Sullivan underestimated Corbett, believing firmly that, in or out of condition, he could defeat the Californian easily. He had reached that stage in a fighter's career where training is a thing of horror.

At his best, "The Boston Strong Boy" heartily disliked the task of conditioning himself. At his worst, with no William Muldoon, who trained him for the Kilrain fight, to drive him, he went through daily exercises in de-

While Sullivan was busy with his exhibition tours, a new heavyweight threat appeared in the person of Frank Slavin of Australia. Claiming the British Empire title, Slavin was eager to meet the American champion. To force the issue, the Australian's first match in the United States was with John L.'s old rival, Jake Kilrain. The bout, held in Hoboken, New Jersey, in 1891, resulted in a decisive victory for the Australian, who needed only nine rounds to dispose of Kilrain. The referee *(bearded)* was Jere Dunn, who shot and killed Champion Jim Elliott in 1883.

With the swashbuckling Sullivan as champion and the United States being invaded by challenging Britishers, interest in American boxing was increasing. Negro ringsters were becoming more numerous. The best of the lot was George Godfrey, of Chelsea, Massachusetts, who advertised himself as the "American colored champion." Godfrey's ambitions were dealt a crushing blow, however, when "Old Chocolate" faced Joe Choynski, young San Franciscan, at Coney Island in 1892 and was kayoed *(below)* in the 15th.

One of the most elaborate programs in boxing history was the three-day "Carnival of Champions" staged at the Pelican Athletic Club in New Orleans, Louisiana, on September 5, 6 and 7, 1892. The principals were heavyweights John L. Sullivan (1) and James J. Corbett (2), lightweights Jack McAuliffe (3) and Billy Myer (4), and featherweights George Dixon (5) and Jack Skelly (6). McAuliffe and Dixon were successful in defending their titles, but the "cycle of three" was shattered when Sullivan lost his laurels.

to Sullivan's face. The opening was there and Corbett saw it, made mental note of it and afterward repeated the operation, though the second time he failed to withhold his fist and swung the blow flush to Sullivan's face, to the undoing of the Boston man.

The articles of agreement for the first championship battle under Queensberry rules were entered into without any of the quarrelling and bickering that have marked the agreements of more recent years. Each man was anxious for the contest; neither desired an

He had his battle completely planned in his mind and it is a fact that he won the fight just as he had planned, forcing Sullivan to the final count one round earlier than he had expected.

Trained on the Cars.

In the baggage car attached to the train which took Corbett to New Orleans a gymnasium had been fitted up. There Corbett continued his training as he sped through the country, and just as the train entered New Orleans he authorized a friend who was with

had been making another effort to discourage opponent.

There was a hush through the building as the clanged, a little after nine o'clock, and broug two men together. Sullivan rushed, and age proached Corbett he swung his left, which C ducked under and hopped away just in time to a vigorous right intended for the jaw. Sulliva carried almost off his balance, but he steadied self by catching the rope with his left hand.

Again he plunged toward Corbett, swinging and left, while the crowd was inclined to jeer C for his evasive tactics. Rush after rush was by the champion. Again and again he swung b mendous right, followed by his no less tremendou It seemed that Sullivan expected the jeers o

Aging, dissipated Sullivan *(left)* proved an easy victim for young, clever Jim Corbett, who cut him to shreds in 21 rounds. This newspaper illustration tells the complete story, with Sullivan making a futile attempt to rise after being counted out.

sultory fashion. The result? Corbett knocked the "Boston Strong Boy" out in the twenty-first round.

The title passed from America's most popular gladiator to the lithe, handsome youth, the "California Dandy" whose fistic prowess flowered to full bloom on the sun-kissed slopes of California. Coincident with the crashing of the premier pugilistic idol from his pedestal, the bout definitely set the seal of public approval on the use of gloves in heavyweight championship contests as opposed to the

bare knuckles and rough mauling tactics of the London Prize Ring.

The Queensberry era of boxing came triumphantly into its own with the successful staging of the Battle of New Orleans.

There isn't much to the story of that battle. Corbett, young, active, and brainy, stepped jauntily around the massive hulk of what had once been a great fighting man and evaded Sullivan's sweeping leads, hooked, countered on the retreat and cut and jarred "John L." incessantly. Sullivan rushed

in vain. His formidable right hand, which had won for him so often, was useless in this crisis and he was an easy victim for his young challenger.

It was a fight in which speed, youth, and scientific generalship were pitted against bulky muscular power slowed down by age and fast living, a gifted exponent of a new style of boxing against old traditional slugging methods and archaic milling tactics which were doomed to defeat. One hour and twenty minutes after the start, the cool, smiling youth from California

William Muldoon, noted wrestler, physical conditioner, trainer, and friend of Sullivan, later became a New York boxing commissioner.

Richard K. Fox, editor and publisher of the *Police Gazette*, was an enthusiastic sportsman but a bitter enemy of Sullivan. Fox, who popularized the custom of presenting championship belts, supported many of John L.'s foes.

John L. Sullivan as he appeared in later years, when he became a teetotaler and toured the United States giving lectures to the public on the "Evils of John Barleycorn."

was crowned the new world champion in the first battle staged for that title under the Marquis of Queensberry rules with gloves.

It was the herald of a new day in boxing. The game was destined henceforth to rise to recognized respectability as a means of entertainment for all classes of both sexes, and ultimately to attain the commercial rating which culminated in the establishment of the 20-million dollar gate!

The shock of the Sullivan idol crashing from its pedestal rocked the sporting kingdom to its uttermost confines. Men of "John L.'s" generation didn't regard his defeat as a mere misfortune—it was a catastrophe. The Battle of New Orleans was to Sullivan admirers what Waterloo was to the French!

The legend of invincibility woven around Sullivan persisted even after his signal defeat.

After his retirement, Sullivan went on the stage and later became a prohibition lecturer. He died at Abingdon, Massachusetts, on February 2, 1918.

SCIENCE REPLACES FORCE

James J. Corbett lifted boxing out of the barroom slough, the evil influences of its habitués, and started it towards its moral revolution. Prior to his rise to pugilistic heights, his predecessors for the most part were men who scorned the conventionalities of decent social life. Corbett changed that. He won the support of a better class of patrons for the sport.

At the zenith of his career there wasn't a man in the ring who could be compared favorably with him in cleverness and quick thinking. He was not of the slugging type as was Sullivan, but he was by no means a weak hitter, as Bob Fitzsimmons, who wrested the title from him, testified when interviewed on Gentleman Jim's punching powers.

Corbett was born in San Francisco, California, September 1, 1866, of Irish parents. He was one of twelve children.

After leaving school, Corbett entered a mercantile establishment where he became a clerk with a reputation for quick figuring. He quit that job for one as a teller in a bank and retained the latter position until he turned to professional boxing for a living.

His real boxing education began when he became a member of the famous Olympic Club, where Professor Watson tutored him.

After he started his professional career, his greatest rival was Joe Choynski, a clever, fast, hard hitting battler. On May 30, 1889, they engaged in their first mill at Fairfax, California, with two-ounce gloves, but the police interfered and the bout was halted in the fourth round. Hostilities were resumed on June 5 to settle the matter of supremacy, this time on a

James J. Corbett, ex-bank clerk who became champion of the world, was six feet, one inch tall and weighed about 185 pounds. His manager Bill Brady (insert) also handled all theatre bookings for "Gentleman Jim," who had a natural acting aptitude.

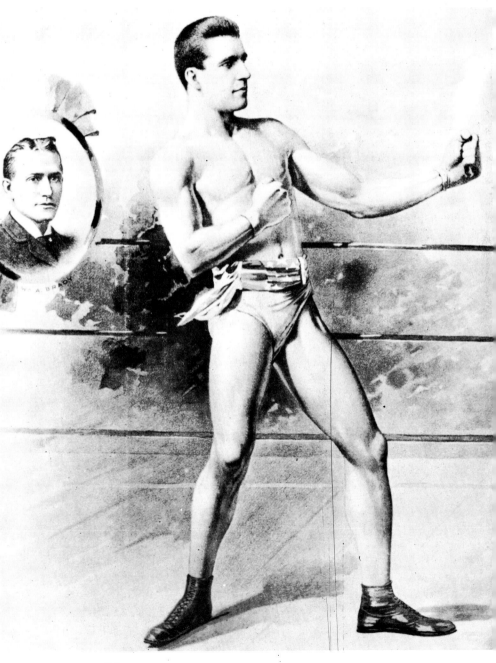

Peter Jackson, born in the West Indies in 1861, began his boxing career in Australia in 1882. A fine physical specimen, he was six feet, one inch tall, weighing 200 pounds.

Eager to meet Sullivan, Jim Corbett *(right)* took on the great Peter Jackson in 1891 and held him to a bruising 61-round draw. Corbett's followers saw it as a victory for Jim, since he conceded thirty pounds and less experience to Jackson.

barge anchored near Benicia. After twenty-seven furious rounds in which Choynski bled profusely from the mouth and nose, Joe quit. A third bout was arranged and this one went only four rounds, with Corbett the winner.

Corbett's defeat of Jake Kilrain in New Orleans on February 18, 1890, brought the young Californian into national prominence.

On May 21 of the following year, Gentleman Jim astonished the boxing world by holding the great Peter Jackson to a sixty-one rounds draw before the California Athletic Club. This bout stamped him as ready for a crack at Sullivan's crown, a bout already discussed.

Following the defeat of the "Boston Strong Boy," Corbett made his very successful stage debut. He appeared in a melodrama, *Gentleman Jack,* and thereafter did considerable theatrical work, his vocation after his retirement. After winning the heavyweight title, Corbett retired for more than a

CORBETT AND COURTNEY FOUGHT BEFORE THE KINETOSCOPE.

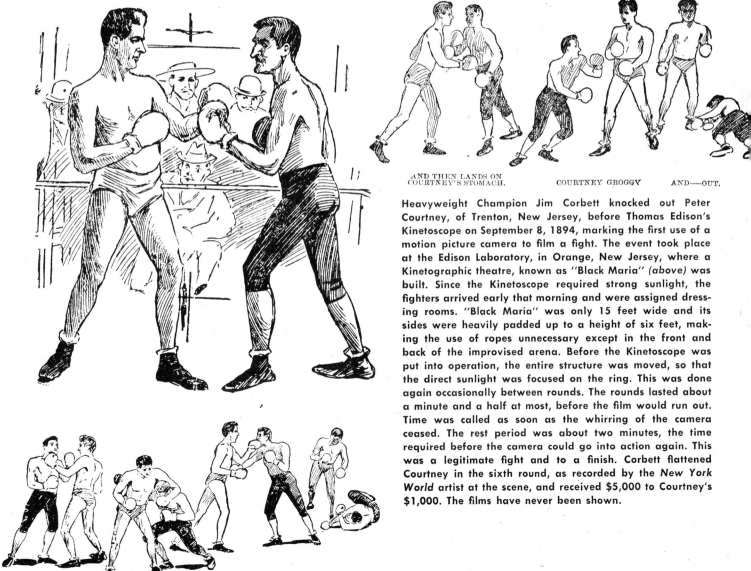

AND THEN LANDS ON
COURTNEY'S STOMACH.   COURTNEY GROGGY   AND—OUT.

Heavyweight Champion Jim Corbett knocked out Peter Courtney, of Trenton, New Jersey, before Thomas Edison's Kinetoscope on September 8, 1894, marking the first use of a motion picture camera to film a fight. The event took place at the Edison Laboratory, in Orange, New Jersey, where a Kinetographic theatre, known as "Black Maria" *(above)* was built. Since the Kinetoscope required strong sunlight, the fighters arrived early that morning and were assigned dressing rooms. "Black Maria" was only 15 feet wide and its sides were heavily padded up to a height of six feet, making the use of ropes unnecessary except in the front and back of the improvised arena. Before the Kinetoscope was put into operation, the entire structure was moved, so that the direct sunlight was focused on the ring. This was done again occasionally between rounds. The rounds lasted about a minute and a half at most, before the film would run out. Time was called as soon as the whirring of the camera ceased. The rest period was about two minutes, the time required before the camera could go into action again. This was a legitimate fight and to a finish. Corbett flattened Courtney in the sixth round, as recorded by the *New York World* artist at the scene, and received $5,000 to Courtney's $1,000. The films have never been shown.

In his first title defense Corbett knocked out British veteran Charlie Mitchell *(left)* at Jacksonville, Florida, in 1894. (The artist who drew this sketch couldn't have seen the bout, which was fought with gloves, not bare knuckles.)

At the Olympic Club in New Orleans, on March 2, 1892, Bob Fitzsimmons and Peter Maher, both potential champions, fought a slashing 12-round bout, with Fitzsimmons the winner by a knockout. Note the second ring, built to prevent any mob interference.

year from ring affairs, but persistent abuse from the Britisher, Charley Mitchell, finally got Corbett back into harness. He handed Mitchell a shellacking in their bout at Jacksonville, Florida, on January 25, 1894, stopping him in the third round.

With that bout, the champion decided to quit and announced that he had turned over his crown to Peter Maher, the Irish heavyweight. It was a good gesture on his part, but futile, since the public didn't take it seriously. Nor did Bob Fitzsimmons, who was eager for a shot at the title. Fitzsimmons took on Maher and knocked him out in one round, thus forcing the hand of Corbett.

At Carson City, on March 17, 1897, in the first open-air arena built especially for boxing, Corbett was knocked out by Fitzsimmons in the fourteenth round. In that fatal round, "Freckled Bob" shot several lefts to the face, then feinted with a right for the jaw.

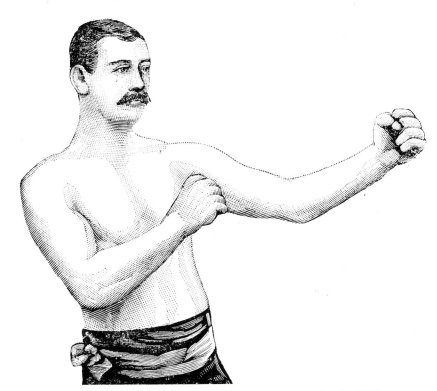

Peter Maher, born in Galway, Ireland, in 1869, came to America in 1891 with a good record. He was six feet tall, weighed about 190 pounds, and carried a powerful wallop in his right arm. He fought all of the best men in America from 1891 to 1907.

A champion five years, Corbett seemed destined to extend his reign when he dropped the spindly-legged Cornishman, Bob Fitzsimmons, in the sixth round at Carson City, Nevada, in 1897. Bleeding and battered, Fitz's chances appeared to be hopeless.

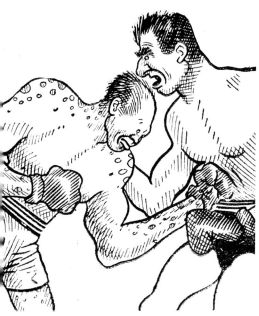

The crafty, hard-hitting Englishman survived the early drubbing and just kept waiting for the opening he knew was sure to come. Early in the fourteenth round, Fitz sidestepped one of Corbett's blows and, seeing an opening, came in with a left hand to the stomach and, without changing the position of his feet, shot the same hand to the jaw. The "solar plexus" blow (above) was born, and Fitzsimmons (right) watches Corbett take the count.

As Corbett raised his arm to protect himself, Fitzsimmons executed his famous shift, bringing his right foot forward. Then, like a bolt from the sky, he shot a right to the heart and a left that landed with paralyzing force into the pit of Corbett's stomach for the knockout. A new champion had been crowned and with that knockout was born the "Solar Plexus" blow.

On May 11, 1900, Corbett put up his greatest battle when he almost succeeded in regaining the crown from James J. Jeffries at the Seaside A.C. of Coney Island, New York. For twenty-two rounds Corbett had far the better of the fighting with his spectacular footwork and two-handed attack, but in the next frame Jeffries cut loose with the winning wallops. A right to the jaw then put Corbett on the canvas, his head resting on the lower rope. In this position he was counted out by Referee Charley White. It was one of the finest exhibitions of science versus brute strength that the ring had known.

The following August, Corbett and Kid McCoy fought in Madison Square Garden of New York in an unsatisfactory bout that ended in the fifth round and created considerable talk. An investigation was held and the unsavory taste left by the bout resulted in the repeal of the Horton Law, under which boxing was permitted in New York, and put a temporary end to public bouts. Corbett had won on a questionable knockout.

For three years Corbett eschewed the temptations of the roped square. Then on August 14, 1903, he again attempted a comeback, this time against Jeffries in San Francisco, and the "Grizzly Bear" of the West put Corbett away in the tenth round. With that bout Corbett quit. Henceforth his entire attention was devoted to the stage.

Corbett appeared in *The Naval Cadet* and *Byron Cashel's Profession*.

He died from cancer in his Bayside, Long Island, New York, home on February 18, 1933, in his sixty-seventh year.

His name shines as the Master Scientist of the Squared Circle.

JOHN KELLY. REFEREE

Towards the close of his ring career, Corbett's splendid record was tainted by a suspicious bout with Tom Sharkey at the Lenox Athletic Club in New York, on November 22, 1898. While Corbett and Sharkey were exchanging punches in the ninth round, Connie McVey, one of Corbett's seconds, crawled through the ropes (above). This action prompted referee "Honest John" Kelly to call all bets off and award the fight to Sharkey on a foul. There were cries of "fake," and newspapers rapped the event in the same tone. An investigation was started but soon forgotten. (Right) Corbett as he looked when appearing in a Broadway play.

77

LANKY BOB FITZSIMMONS

Robert Fitzsimmons was not as fortunate as his predecessor, who ruled his kingdom for five years. "Freckled Bob's" reign lasted only two and a quarter years. He was shorn of his crown by a comparative novice, James J. Jeffries, a twenty-four-year-old California boilermaker to whom Fitzsimmons spotted thirteen years.

Fitzsimmons was born on June 4, 1862, at Elston, Cornwall, England. When he was nine years old his family moved to Lyttleton, New Zealand, where Fitz went to school and distinguished himself in athletic lines, specializing in sprinting and football.

Below the waist Ruby Robert looked like a featherweight. One could scarcely believe that in bruising fights his sketchy legs could successfully bear the weight of his muscular upper frame.

His first ring battle was with a huge blacksmith named Tom Baines, better known as the "Timaru Terror." The youngster tamed the "Terror" by knocking him out in less than a round, after which Fitzsimmons was selected to represent Timaru in a boxing tourney promoted by Jem Mace, world's champion then touring the Antipodes. Bob weighed only 140 pounds, but

he was large of frame and loose-jointed, with sinewy arms and fine back muscles, and in that tournament the young blacksmith knocked out four men in a row.

A year later, Mace again made his appearance with a show of fistic stars. Mace at that time was grooming Slade, the Maori heavyweight who he fancied had the making of a champion, and he arranged for his charge to box Fitzsimmons, who pounded the Maori so fast and viciously that Mace stopped the battle in the second round. Fitzsimmons now proceeded to take up fighting professionally.

He made a fine beginning, knocking out Arthur Cooper in three rounds, Jack Murphy in four, and Jim Crawford in three.

There was little money to be made in Timaru and Fitzsimmons decided to go to New South Wales. On December 17, 1889, he whipped Dick Ellis in three rounds before a Sydney club and was matched with Jem Hall for February 10 of the following year, a bout in which Fitzsimmons was counted out in the fourth round.

In his first fight in America, Fitzsimmons met Billy McCarthy at the California Athletic Club for a $1,250 purse and stopped him in the ninth round.

On June 28, 1890, Fitzsimmons met Arthur Upham and stopped him in five rounds before the Audubon Club of New Orleans. "Freckled Bob's" fame as a new star was now sufficiently established to warrant a match with middleweight champion Jack Dempsey, the celebrated "Nonpareil." He stopped Dempsey at the Olympic Club in New Orleans, January 14, 1891, and won the world's middleweight crown. The end came in the thirteenth round of a vicious battle in which Dempsey was dropped several times.

Dempsey answered the call of time in the thirteenth, but was dazed after the severe punishment he had received in the previous sessions. Fitzsimmons sent the "Nonpareil" down with a right-hander to the mouth and then followed with a vicious dig to the

Bob Fitzsimmons had the legs of a lightweight, but above the waist he was a heavyweight, with powerful shoulder muscles developed during his days as a blacksmith.

Wyatt Earp, famed marshal of the Old West, gave a flagrantly unfair decision when he refereed the Fitzsimmons-Sharkey bout.

To avoid the ever-vigilant Rangers (prize fighting was illegal in Texas), the bout between Peter Maher *(left)* and Bob Fitzsimmons was moved from Langtry to Mexican territory across the Rio Grande. Fitz flattened Maher in one round.

right side which hurled Dempsey panting to the ropes. Fitz landed on Dempsey's jaw and put him down again. Weak and exhausted, he tried to regain his feet but could not, and his seconds threw up the sponge.

During the next two years, Fitz-simmons, who had almost fought himself out of opponents in the middle-weight division, stopped Peter Maher, Irish heavyweight champion, in twelve rounds. He also scored a signal revenge on his old rival and former conqueror, Jem Hall, by knocking the latter out in four rounds before the Crescent City Club of New Orleans.

A bout between Joe Choynski and Fitzsimmons at catchweights on June 17, 1894, was stopped by the Boston police in the fifth round, after Choynski, repeatedly floored, was about to be counted out. The following September, Fitz fought his last battle as a middleweight, knocking out his fellow countryman Dan Creedon in two rounds.

On February 21, 1896, Peter Maher, chosen as successor to the heavyweight title by Jim Corbett when the latter retired, was knocked out again by Fitzsimmons near Langtry, Texas.

In December of the same year, Tom Sharkey was declared winner on a foul over Ruby Robert in eight rounds at San Francisco. This was a flagrant example of ring robbery, the verdict being rendered by Wyatt Earp, a Western marshal, after Sharkey had been knocked out by a blow which landed fairly above the belt.

Fitzsimmons won the world's heavy-weight championship from Corbett, as already stated, in fourteen rounds on March 17, 1897, at Carson City, Nevada. Fitzsimmons' weight was officially given as 167 pounds, Corbett's 183.

I AM THE WHOLE THING *Fitz dopey*

EVERY FIGHTER MUST LICK EVERY OTHER FIGHTER BEFORE I FIGHT *Y ORDER OF Robt Fitzeverything*

CORBETT'S OFFER

LEO THE NEW LION

McCOY'S Challenge   MAHER'S DEFI   *Give me a chance Gus Ruhlin*

TRYING TO HOIST FITZSIMMONS INTO THE RING.

CORBETT, McCOY, MAHER, RUHLIN AND SHARKEY ALL WANT A CRACK AT "THE CHAMPION WHO WON'T FIGHT." LANKY BOB THINKS HE WILL GO ON SHOWING AND FAKING FOREVER AND FOREVER, BUT THERE'LL COME A TIME SOME DAY.

Bob Fitzsimmons did no fighting for two years after winning the title from Corbett. Instead, he toured the country with a theatrical group and cashed in handsomely. For this he was widely criticized in print, as shown in the cartoon above.

For more than two years after winning the heavyweight championship, Fitzsimmons toured the country with a theatrical show. Then he put his title on the line in a bout with young James J. Jeffries at Coney Island. The unexpected result of the battle, a knockout of Fitzsimmons in the eleventh round, was a stunning surprise.

Knockouts of Jim Daly, Ed Dunkhorst, Gus Ruhlin and his oldtime enemy, Tom Sharkey, qualified him for a second chance with Jeffries.

They clashed on July 25, 1902, at San Francisco and for nearly eight rounds Fitzsimmons hammered the giant mercilessly with both hands, breaking his nose, cutting both cheeks to the bone and opening gashes over each eye, until it seemed as though the downpour of blood and consequent blindness must compel the big fellow to surrender.

But Jeffries, a mountain of a man, all solid bone and sinew, a miracle of endurance, kept pressing doggedly

HOW
Fitzsimmons
WILL Knock Out
THE

Drama in His New Play

In Many Respects the Most Unusual Play Ever Written.

✿ ✿ ✿ ✿

HIS WIFE STARS WITH HIM.

forward and suddenly sank a terrific right to the stomach, followed with a crashing left hook to the jaw, and Fitz was counted out.

Fitzsimmons had seen his best days but obstinately refused to retire. In 1903, he defeated George Gardner in

twenty rounds at Mechanics Pavilion, San Francisco, winning the title of light heavyweight champion, a newly constituted class only recently recognized by sporting authorities. This was the third crown he had gained, the first fighter in ring history to gain such laurels.

On December 20, 1905, with the light heavyweight title at stake, Philadelphia Jack O'Brien, one of the fastest and most scientific fighters of his day, stopped Fitzsimmons in thirteen rounds at Mechanics Pavilion, San Francisco.

Two years later, Jack Johnson knocked out the sturdy old veteran in two rounds. Revisiting Australia, Bob engaged in a contest with Bill Lang, then champion of his country, and was defeated in twelve rounds at Sydney. His final ring appearance was at Williamsport, Pennsylvania, where Dan Sweeney and Fitzsimmons (now fifty-two) fought a no-decision six rounds bout.

Fitzsimmons retired and went into vaudeville. He died from influenza in Chicago on October 22, 1917, at the age of fifty-six.

JEFFRIES, THE IRON MAN

It was a great occasion in ring affairs when James J. Jeffries defeated Fitzsimmons to win the heavyweight title.

Jeffries was taken in hand by three wise ringmen, Billy Delaney, Bill Brady, and Tommy Ryan, and they developed him into one of the greatest pugilists of modern times. Born in Carroll, Ohio, April 15, 1875, he came from stock that traced its ancestry back to Normandy. His family moved to California in 1881, and Jeffries lived in that state until his death on March 3, 1953 at Burbank, California.

Jim was six feet, two inches tall and weighed 220 pounds stripped when he was only sixteen years old. He was a gruff, taciturn man whose ox-like strength gained for him the heavyweight crown. He lacked style, dash, boxing skill, and other assets of an excellent fighter when he made his climb, but by the time he reached the heights, he gained international acclaim.

In action he looked like a big bear, with his massive hairy chest, and he fought with the ferocity of one. Such giants as Gus Ruhlin, Bob Fitzsimmons, Jim Corbett, Tom Sharkey among others, tried to subdue him, but without success.

Jeffries was an iron worker, and while in that employ he learned how to box. He won a couple of contests and then Harry Corbett, a California sportsman, introduced him to Billy Delaney, who was looking for a sparring partner for Jim Corbett, then in training for his fight with Fitzsimmons.

He wanted one who was big and husky, one who could take Corbett's punches without wilting. Jeff accepted the post, and in camp he absorbed the knowledge that enabled him to climb to the top. Billy Delaney saw a find in him, took him in hand, and trained him. A couple of years later Jeffries surprised the world by trouncing Fitzsimmons to gain the world heavyweight championship.

He was called the Iron Man of the Roped Square. He could batter an opponent into submission with his TNT wallops but could easily be hit and often took severe punishment until he perfected his crouch as a means of defense. In his first battle with Corbett, and his twenty-five round bout with Tom Sharkey in which he broke two of Tom's ribs, Jeffries received as much as he gave, but his endurance surpassed his rivals' and he won.

The same happened in his fights with Bob Fitzsimmons. When Jeffries faced Ruby Robert for the first time, he scaled thirty-eight pounds more than his freckled opponent, who came in at only 167. Fitzsimmons was an old man as boxing ages go, thirty-seven years, when he faced Jeff, thirteen years his junior. Here is how their bout ended:

Jim Jeffries, who stood 6' 2" and scaled a solid 220 pounds of beef and brawn, was one of the most formidable fighting machines the prize ring ever produced.

Rated among the all-time classics was the meeting of champion Jim Jeffries *(right)* and challenger Tom Sharkey, on November 3, 1899, at Coney Island. This was the first fight in which motion pictures were made under artificial lights. Despite the heat of day and 400 arc lamps, the fight went 25 slashing rounds, with Jeffries the winner of a sensational battle. A rare photo *(below)* of ex-sailor Tom Sharkey, shows his cauliflower left ear and the famous star and ship tattoo on his chest.

Jeffries advanced carefully. Then his long left crashed to the jaw of the champion. A feint at the body was followed by a powerful left again to Fitzsimmons' jaw. His knees buckled, and his brain was benumbed.

Jeffries launched his right with 205 pounds behind the toss and it landed with a thud against "Freckled Bob's" jaw. He fell. Jeffries stood and looked down on his defeated opponent while Referee George Siler counted the doleful decimal.

Fitzsimmons lay on his back. His eyes were closed. His blood-stained shoulders quivered. The great arms that had wrenched the crown from Corbett, doubled up the powerful Tom Sharkey, and hammered Gus Ruhlin into submission, lay inert at his side. Over him swept the cheers that he had so often heard before, but this time they were not for him. They were for a new fistic hero from the Golden West.

Five months after winning the crown, Jeffries tackled Sharkey in a twenty-five rounds bout in Coney Island, New York, that developed into one of the most brutal seen during the early days of the gloves era. The former gob, who had previously lost a decision to Jeffries in twenty rounds,

Jeffries *(left)* and Sharkey were showing the effects of the brawl and were "resting" in a clinch when referee George Siler pulled them apart as the bout ended.

Marvin Hart of Kentucky claimed the title when he knocked out Jack Root, on July 3, 1905, in Reno, Nevada. Jeffries, who chose both to fight for the title, refereed.

was a much improved battler this time. Though he failed to win, he made a desperate effort to do so.

Before the gong sounded for the last round, it was obvious that only a knockout could win for Sailor Tom, but he still was full of fight despite two broken ribs and severe lacerations brought on by Jeff's cutting, stinging blows. Jeffries charged from his corner and overwhelmed his opponent with a fusillade of lefts and rights that forced Tom to retreat. At the bell ending the fight, Sharkey was in a sorry state. Referee Siler held up the hand of Jeffries, the victor. Sharkey had to be removed to a hospital.

An exhibition tour followed and several minor contests were staged by Jeffries. In one, he faced a burly miner, inexperienced but powerful Jack Munro, who surprisingly dropped Jeffries with a blow to the jaw. Jack Curley, a promoter, took advantage of the situation and through ballyhoo aroused sufficient interest to rematch the pair. This time, Munro was knocked out in the second round. During World War One he joined the Princess Pat Regiment of Canada and was one of the outstanding heroes in the famous outfit.

It was after that bout on August 24, 1904, that Jeffries, unable to obtain suitable opponents, retired and selected Marvin Hart and Jack Root to fight for the vacated throne, with Jeffries to act as referee. When Hart knocked out Root in the twelfth round, he was proclaimed new champion.

But dissension arose. There were other excellent heavies in the field who protested Jeffries' act. One of these was Tommy Burns (Noah Brusso of Canada, born June 17, 1881). He challenged and cleaned up the field, taking on all comers in various parts of the world. Through his triumphs he received universal recognition as champion.

Jack Johnson, the Galveston Giant, was one of several top ringmen who contested the right of Burns to the crown. He followed Tommy all over the world to force him to accept a challenge to settle the matter of supremacy. Burns was finally cornered

Tommy Burns (left) was an overblown middleweight when he wrested the title from Marvin Hart. Burns won easily in 20 rounds at Los Angeles, on February 23, 1906. After following Burns to England and Australia, Jack Johnson proved too big and powerful for Tommy, when they met at Sydney in 1908. Shorter and 20 pounds lighter, the courageous Burns was far outclassed. With Burns helpless in the 14th round, the police stepped in and ordered the bout stopped.

in Australia, where Snowy Baker guaranteed Tommy $30,000 to fight the Negro at Rushcutter's Bay, Sydney, on Boxing Day, December 26, 1908.

That huge sum, the largest offered to any fighter up to that time, was the golden egg from which were hatched the millions Dempsey, Tunney, Joe Louis and others later drew. Tommy received a shellacking from his tormentor, who in an avenging spirit took pleasure in cutting up his opponent. The police stopped the bout in the fourteenth round.

When he beat Burns, Johnson had a record of sixty-seven ring battles. He was a cautious, tantalizing performer. He stood six feet, one-quarter inch and at his best scaled 210 pounds. He possessed great ring science, was a master of the now lost art of feinting, and carrying punishing power with his stiff jabs, he could make things most uncomfortable for an op-

Despite great disadvantages in height, weight and reach, middleweight champ Stanley Ketchel met Johnson at Colma, California, on October 16, 1909. Ketchel had the satisfaction of flooring Johnson in the 12th, but was knocked out in the same round.

Joe Jeannette and Sam McVey, two great fighters who fought Johnson often, met in Paris in 1909. After a total of 38 knockdowns—Jeannette 27 and McVey 11—McVey quit in the 49th round. McVey is shown below, down for the 10th time.

ponent. He was a fighter with a perfect stance.

Following his triumph in Australia, he fought Victor McLaglen, the movie actor, Philadelphia Jack O'Brien, and Al Kaufman, and won from each handily. Then came his historic battle with Stanley Ketchel, middleweight champion, in which, though an agreement was reached whereby there would be no knockout, Ketchel, seeing an opening, lashed a powerful blow to Johnson's jaw in the twelfth round and dropped the big heavyweight king. So angered was Johnson that, quickly rising, he squared off, let go his left, and it was curtains for Ketchel. He was knocked flat on his back and was counted out.

The quest of a "White Hope" was now on. In every country, enterprising managers were scouting for a Caucasian to whip Johnson, whose escapades and marriages to white women

In trouble with the Federal authorities, Jack Johnson avoided arrest by skipping the United States in 1912. With him, in Paris, is Lucille Cameron, first of several white wives.

Sam Langford, (above) in action against Ian Hague in London, in 1909, gave Johnson such a rough time in their fight in 1906 that Johnson avoided any second meeting with Langford.

A momentous occasion in boxing history was the signing of Jack Johnson and Jim Jeffries (second from right), who came out of retirement after six years. The signing, in Hoboken, New Jersey, was attended by a gathering of newspapermen and sportsmen.

had turned public sentiment against him. Charged with violation of the Mann Act, for which he later served a year in Leavenworth Prison, Johnson left America for Europe and later South America, while promoters were kept busy digging up talent to obtain an outstanding Caucasian as an opponent for Galveston Jack.

Before going overseas, however, Johnson had one more important contest in the States. Jeffries, urged by his friends, particularly Jack London, the author, who had been present in Sydney and following the Burns slaughter had written to Jeffries pleading for him to come out of retirement and bring back the title to his race, signed for a fight with Johnson. Tex Rickard, who was both promoter and referee, staged it at Reno, Nevada, July 4, 1910.

Jeffries, a shell of his former self, proved easy for the Galveston Giant,

The once-mighty Jeffries, now only a hollow shell, reached the end of the trail when, battered, bleeding, and exhausted, he was stopped by Johnson in the 15th round *(above)*. Awaiting the opening bell *(below, left)* is a grinning, confident Johnson. In the audience *(below, right)* were former rivals James J. Corbett *(left)* and John L. Sullivan. Corbett was one of Jeffries' chief advisors and Sullivan was reporting his observations in a special series of articles for a Boston newspaper.

who handed the Boilermaker a severe beating, almost as terrible as he had given to Burns. In the middle of the fifteenth round, Sam Berger, Jeff's chief second, tossed in the sponge in token of defeat and Rickard, acknowledging the gesture, held up the hand of Johnson.

That victory redoubled the action of the promoters seeking someone who might take the crown from the Negro. The "White Hope" race was now on in earnest.

With Johnson's triumph ended another era in the heavyweight division —an era that boasted of the greatest array of talent since Tom Hyer's installation as America's first champion.

It seemed now that a White Race cult had suddenly come into existence that took the stand that only a Caucasian heavyweight could hold the championship—a ridiculous situation.

When on January 1, 1914, Gunboat Smith knocked out Arthur Pelkey in fifteen rounds in San Francisco, the New Yorker laid claim to the "White Heavyweight Title." The "White Hope" craze suddenly went into crescendo. Among the leading boxers were Luther McCarty, a giant cowboy, Carl Morris, Tom Cowler, Fred Fulton, Arthur Pelkey, Gunboat Smith,

Luther McCarty *(above, right)* was the No. 1 "white hope" when he posed before fatal bout with Arthur Pelkey on May 24, 1913.

The tragic ending of McCarty, who collapsed from a light punch in the first round at Calgary and was counted out. Carried from the ring and laid on straw on the arena floor, Luther died without regaining consciousness. (Manager Billy McCarney can be seen in background, with hands on head.) The untimely passing of the youthful McCarty (he was only 21) was attributed to an earlier accident in which the husky Nebraskan suffered severe neck injuries after being thrown by a stumbling horse. Ed Smith refereed fatal bout.

Frank Moran, Al Palzer and Jess Willard. They were the more prominent from among whom it was expected the man to beat Johnson would be found. And he was.

The "White Hopes" thrived between 1910 and 1915, and they were a mighty impressive lot, far better than the majority of the contenders in recent years. For a time it seemed that Frank Moran might be the successful candidate, and then the eyes of the boxing world became centered on a better all-around heavyweight, Luther McCarty. Unfortunately, in a bout for the championship of the Caucasian race, staged by Tommy Burns at Calgary, Canada, McCarty died a few minutes after his contest with Arthur Pelkey got under way, not from a blow he had received, but, as the autopsy showed, from a broken collarbone, an ailment not disclosed prior to the affair.

With him out of the way, all eyes became focused on another giant, Jess Willard of Pottowatomie, Kansas, who through a number of knockouts over pretty good heavyweights and a na-

tional ballyhoo campaign by Billy McCarney, who was handling his affairs, gained national recognition.

He started his career in 1911, and by the time he was ready for the leap into the field of challengers he had taken into camp, among others, Sailor White, Soldier Kearns, Billy Young, who died following a knockout in the eleventh round, and Boer Rodel, with

whom he previously had gone ten rounds in addition to fighting ten rounds no-decision contests with such stars as Pelkey, McCarty, and Carl Morris.

It was after his knockout of Rodel in Atlanta, Georgia, that Willard's preliminary work had been completed and he was ready for the shot at the crown.

JOHNSON, RING MARVEL

The reign of Jack Johnson lasted from 1908 until April 5, 1915, when he was deposed by Jess Willard at the Oriente Race Track of Cuba, in the outskirts of Havana. Johnson, rated by most experts as the best all-around heavyweight since the Corbett-Sullivan bout, was born on March 31, 1878, at Galveston, and was known as the Galveston Giant. He developed the art of feinting to a high degree, had a rapier-like left and superb defense.

When he fell into disfavor with the U. S. Government, due to his escapades, he exiled himself following his bout with Jim Flynn in 1912 in Las Vegas, which was stopped by the police in the ninth round, with Jack the winner. He went to Europe, where he lived a gay life, squandered his fortune and engaged in three title-defense bouts. He stopped Andre Sproul in two rounds, fought an unsatisfactory draw of ten rounds with Jim Johnson, and beat Frank Moran in twenty rounds. Then he went to Buenos Aires and disposed of Jack Murray in three rounds.

The champion, homesick, in poor physical condition at the age of thirty-seven, and in financial distress, was now ready to accept a bout with the outstanding Caucasian of the "White Hope" era. The Negro had the men who could stage the bout in Jack Curley and Harry Frazee, a theatrical producer. Big Jess Willard, the Pottowatomie Giant, was the choice of the promoters, and under a broiling sun Johnson was knocked out in the twenty-sixth round. The bout was the longest under modern rules.

"The Battle of the Camera Shot" is what the Willard-Johnson affair might be termed, since the photo of the knockout has received more prominence in sports than any ever snapped in the roped square. It is the picture showing the Negro resting on the canvas, flat on his back, shading his eyes from the terrific sun's rays, while Referee Jack Welsh is counting him out.

Had the arrangement been made for a twenty rounds bout instead of

At the age of 37, after years of careless living, Jack Johnson lost the title to Jess Willard in 26 rounds at Havana, Cuba. Johnson claimed that he threw the fight, offering this photo as proof that he used his gloves to "shield his eyes from the sun."

Regarded by many authorities as the best all-around mechanic in heavyweight history, ex-stevedore Jack Johnson stood slightly over six feet in height and at his peak *(right)* he scaled 195 pounds. He combined power with clever boxing skill, two-handed punching power and shrewd generalship. *(Above)* Johnson as he appeared around 1930.

forty-five, the last such in boxing, Willard would not have captured the title. Johnson had a good lead at the time the affair was terminated.

In the first twenty rounds, the Galveston Giant hit Big Jess with stinging blows frequently, but couldn't down him. He repeated to a great extent the tactics he had used to annoy Jeffries.

Jess was no boxer. He was an ungainly fighter who previously had lost a twenty rounds decision to Gunboat Smith and in 1914 was whipped by Bearcat McMahon in twelve. His size, more so than his fighting qualities, plus shrewd management, got him the shot at the title.

However, Jess worked hard to offset Johnson's superiority by employing a wearing-down system. He kept plodding and figured that with the extreme heat that lowered the vitality of the contestants, and with his weight

Jess Willard (left), the giant Kansan, stood six feet, six inches, and weighed 250 pounds. He had not proved himself the best of the "white hopes"—he lost several decisions to lighter rivals—but because of his tremendous size, strength, and durability, he was considered to have the best chance to beat Johnson in a 45-round bout and "restore the prestige of the white race." Johnson (above, right) did all the leading in the early rounds. In the final round (below) Johnson's knees begin to sag after Willard landed a right-hand blow to the jaw.

and height, he would tire the champion. That's just what happened as the affair progressed.

In the ninth round Willard had a deep cut on his right cheek and was bleeding from the mouth. From the tenth round through the twentieth, Johnson made every effort to end the fight by a knockout and his performance in those rounds clearly indicated the falsity of the charge that he had faked his knockout.

In the twenty-first round it became apparent that Johnson had worn himself out. He couldn't go much further.

He had shot his bolt, tossed away his Sunday punch without being able to stop his rival.

He was slow in answering the bell for the twenty-sixth round, before which, realizing his condition, he motioned to his wife at the ringside to leave the arena as he didn't want her to see him knocked out. Jess met Jim two-thirds across the ring and let go a powerful blow to the face. Johnson's head snapped back. The Kansas Giant smashed home a right to the stomach.

That proved Jack's undoing. Another left to the same place, and as

Johnson lowered his guard, a right to the jaw put him down. He was counted out by Referee Welch while Johnson was shading his eyes.

The detractors of Johnson point to the photo as proof that he "laid down" for Big Jess, and his "confession," purchased by *The Ring Magazine* tends to bear this out, though *The Ring* editor, who reported the fight and bought the "confession," is confident the affair was on the level and that Jack sold the "confession" because he was urgently in need of funds.

Johnson was far in the lead when he

Nearly a year after winning the title, Willard made his first appearance in the ring as champion. In the spring of 1916 he outpointed hard-hitting but slow-moving Frank Moran of Pittsburgh in a ten-round no-decision bout in Madison Square Garden.

finally caved in from the heat, physical exhaustion, and the spurt of his rival in the fatal round.

Johnson was killed in an automobile accident at Raleigh, North Carolina, on June 10, 1946.

It is quite a paradox that Willard, one of the poorest of the heavyweight champions, should have taken the crown from one of the greatest. Big Jess was a slow-moving pugilist who disliked training as much as he disliked the sport itself. He went into boxing to obtain what he could out of it financially and the lackadaisical manner in which he tuned up for his contests, his disinterest in camp life, proved costly.

He quickly left Havana for the States after winning the crown, got into entanglements with his group of managers and trainers, joined a circus group, and the following year, March 25, 1916, he fought Frank Moran in the old Madison Square Garden in a no-decision ten-rounder in which he could not lose the crown unless he was knocked out.

When he placed the title on the

Willard didn't fight again until 1919, when he faced Jack Dempsey in Toledo, Ohio. At his training camp Big Jess (far right) is pictured with (left to right) sparring partner Jack Hemple, ex-champion Jim Jeffries, sports writer Bob Edgren, another ex-ring great, Kid McCoy, and sports enthusiast Army Major Cushman Rice.

block again on July 4, 1919 in Toledo, he collected his largest purse, $100,000 and took a terrific battering from Jack Dempsey, losing the title by quitting at the end of the third round. Willard's heart was never really in the fighting game, but he displayed an abundance of courage and fortitude while taking his shellacking from the Manassa Mauler.

With his downfall, Dempsey, the most popular boxer since Sullivan's rise to fistic fame, was crowned king of the heavyweights.

DEMPSEY AND THE FABULOUS TWENTIES

In every sport there emerges one person who stands out so prominently that he is referred to as "The Idol." Such a man was Jack Dempsey in boxing. While in there tossing punches, he was the most spectacular heavyweight since John L. Sullivan. He participated in the first million-dollar gate — $1,789,238 — when he fought Georges Carpentier and before he hung up his gloves, the receipts of four other contests in which he fought

Jack Dempsey (*above*) as he looked during his rugged early days in the ring, when fights were tough, purses small and discouragement frequent. Dempsey (*left*) at the peak of his career and bursting with power. Middle-aged Dempsey (*right*), the successful business man. Still a rover, with his varied and scattered activities keeping him constantly on the move, "Manassa Jack" remains a popular figure with the sports-loving public. To them, he is always "The Champ."

The most spectacular fighter-manager combination in ring history was dynamic Dempsey *(left)* and flamboyant Jack Kearns. Their partnership began with a casual meeting in a San Francisco bar in 1917. Dempsey, then 22, was a small-time slugger who, except for one brief and not too impressive visit to New York, had done his battling on the "tank-town" circuits of Colorado, Utah and Nevada. He had just drifted to California, looking for fights and a manager. Destiny steered him to Kearns, an experienced pilot, colorful showman, and ballyhoo artist. The tie-up was an immediate success. Within a year Dempsey became the outstanding contender for the championship. Promoter Tex Rickard entered the scene and the "Golden Triangle" of Rickard-Dempsey-Kearns introduced the million-dollar gate in boxing. Rickard promoted most of Dempsey's important bouts—the one in which Jack won the title from Jess Willard and his subsequent clashes with Bill Brennan, Georges Carpentier, Luis Angel Firpo, Jack Sharkey, and the two with Gene Tunney. Five of the bouts drew $1,000,000 or more in receipts, the second Tunney match setting an all-time record of $2,658,660.

exceeded those figures. His last fight with Gene Tunney grossed $2,658,660, for a grand total in five bouts of $8,453,319.

Every time Jack defended his crown an epic battle ensued. His sensational mixup with Luis Angel Firpo, the Wild Bull of the Pampas, was one of the most thrilling in pugilistic annals, and his joust with Tunney in Chicago, the "Battle of the Long Count," is the most controversial.

He scored the quickest knockout in a heavyweight bout of national importance when he flattened big Carl Morris in New Orleans in fourteen seconds on December 16, 1918, bettering by four seconds the time in which he disposed of Fred Fulton, the Sepulpa Plasterer, in Harrison, New Jersey, on July 27 of the same year. Both were non-championship affairs, since the Manassa Mauler had not yet won the title.

It was the start of his career as world champion that got the Golden Era of Boxing under way, with him as the ace pugilist; Jack Kearns, his manager, as the king of the ballyhoo artists who beat the publicity drum; and Tex Rickard, as the promoter.

It was in the fall of 1917 that Dempsey, born in Manassa, Colorado, June 24, 1895, six feet, one inch tall and scaling 180 pounds, met Kearns, the man who through extraordinary ballyhoo steered Dempsey into the million dollar class of fighters and a world crown. It was the turning point in young Dempsey's career and a lucky stroke for the kid from Colorado.

Up to the time that Jack Dempsey had stopped Willard, he had scored forty-two knockouts, but it wasn't until after he had put big Fred Fulton down for the count that he received sufficient recognition to be considered a proper challenger for the champion. The quick Fulton victory gained for him the bout with Jess Willard.

William Harrison Dempsey was a tough young hobo. He had fists of iron and a granite jaw.

The Manassa Mauler, who rode the rods on his way to fame and fortune, landed in New York broke and pleaded for a chance to display his

Dempsey held a deep affection for his family and kept in constant touch with them. Here he and Kearns are seen visiting Dempsey's brother, Bernard *(far left)* and Bernard's wife and three children.   Unidentified man in center was hired farm hand.

George Lewis ("Tex") Rickard, erstwhile cowboy, town marshal, prospector, honky-tonk proprietor and gambler, who got into boxing by accident but went on to become the greatest promoter the rugged prize fighting business had yet known.

Most spectacular of Dempsey's triumphs on his march to the championship was the quick demolition job on Fred Fulton in 1918.

fighting qualities. He had many managers but only Kearns gets credit for Dempsey's fabulous career. Kearns' publicity campaign, following Dempsey's triumph over Fulton, succeeded in getting Rickard to stage the Dempsey-Willard match.

It was on July 4, 1919, that Dempsey reached the goal of his ambition —the world championship—when he battered big Jess Willard into submission in three rounds. Willard regarded Dempsey as easy prey, did little training, and paid for it with a merciless beating, one of the worst ever suffered by a heavyweight king. Not in the memory of the oldest fan could anyone recall when a title holder received

such murderous punishment as did Jess. Yet he responded after each knockdown by rising from the rosin canvas to absorb more punishment.

Willard, scaling 245 pounds to 187½ for his opponent, was dropped for counts seven times in the opening round and was reeling, dazed, in a stupor, when the gong came to his rescue as he was sitting on the canvas, mouth wide open, eyes glazed, blood streaming from the nostrils and gushing down his parched throat. He was staring wearily and aimlessly into space as his seconds dragged him to his corner. The broiling sun added to his discomfiture.

The referee, Ollie Pecord, hadn't heard the bell ending the round and held up Dempsey's hand in victory, but after Jack had left the ring and Pecord was apprised of his error by Warren Barbour, the official timer, he quickly recalled Dempsey and the bout continued.

Willard made a game attempt for a comeback in the second round but fared little better than in the opening frame.

Now the claret was flowing freely from mouth and nose, both cheeks were puffed, two front teeth had found their way to the canvas. His right eye was closed and the right side of his head was swelling rapidly. He looked as if he were struck by a blackjack. Yet he fought on.

In the third round he walked out of his corner a pitiful object. He faced another severe attack, but handed back a number of solid punches. Soon his left eye was tightly closed, his face looked as if it had passed through a threshing machine. The bell sounded and the fight was over for

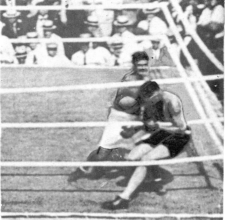

Conceding five inches in height, the same in reach and 58 pounds in weight, an irresistible Dempsey swarmed all over Willard and battered the aging giant to the canvas seven times in the thrilling first round of their championship battle on the sun-drenched holiday afternoon of July 4, 1919, in Toledo, Ohio. Willard was game, however. Surviving the cruel beating in these opening three minutes, Jess fought courageously for the next two rounds, and Dempsey was unable to drop him again. But Jess absorbed such a frightful lacing he was utterly exhausted when he stumbled back to his corner at the end of the third round. During the minute's rest he announced he was unable to continue. How badly the big Kansan was hurt is evidenced in photograph at right. After having his gloves removed, Jess needed the help of his handlers to lift himself to his feet and leave the ring. He had been champion four years and three months, and was 37 when he lost to the 24-year-old Dempsey.

In the excitement, nobody heard the bell ending the first round, with Willard down for seventh time, and Dempsey, thinking the fight was over, scrambled out of the ring. Notified the bout was still on, Manager Jack Kearns (arrow points to him) yelled for Dempsey to return.

The colorful combination of French idol Georges Carpentier and his manager, François Descamps. Although Carpentier actually was only a light heavyweight, the American public believed that his sharpshooting right gave him a chance against Dempsey.

In his first start as champion Dempsey met Billy Miske at Benton Harbor, Michigan, in 1920. Miske gave Dempsey two hard battles before Jack won the title, but he was now a sick man, recovering from serious illness, and Dempsey knocked him out in the third round.

In his second appearance as champion Dempsey encountered unexpected opposition when he faced Bill Brennan in Madison Square Garden in 1920. Brennan actually outpointed Dempsey for 10 rounds, but Manassa Jack rallied to knock durable Bill out in the 12th.

Big Jess. He called the referee to his corner, where he had been virtually dragged by Walter Monahan, his second, and announced his retirement.

The King had abdicated; a new King was crowned.

Prior to the Dempsey-Carpentier fight on July 2, 1921, Dempsey had stopped Billy Miske in a title defense in three rounds at Benton Harbor, Michigan, on September 6, 1920, and Bill Brennan in Madison Square Garden on December 14, 1920, in twelve rounds.

The Golden Era got under way when the champion faced the Orchid Kid from France, a popular boxer who had previously annexed the world light heavyweight championship.

The bout, called "The Battle of the Century," took place at Boyle's Thirty Acres in Jersey City, New Jersey, and ended with the dramatic knockout of

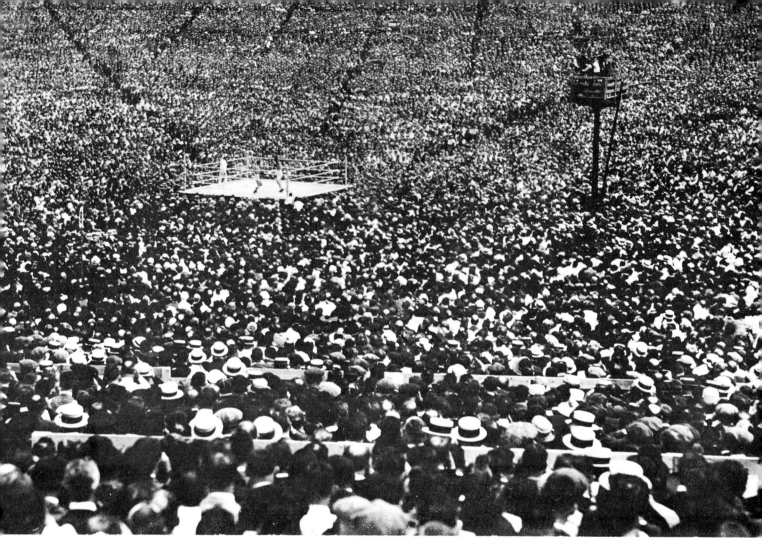

A view of the tremendous crowd that turned out for boxing's first million-dollar extravaganza, which pitted Dempsey against Carpentier on July 2, 1921, in a vast wooden bowl built especially on Boyle's Thirty Acres in Jersey City. The bout attracted an overflow attendance of more than 80,000 and gross receipts of $1,789,238. (Below) Referee Harry Ertle instructing the fighters before the start of bout.

Carpentier in the first million dollar gate in ring history.

Tex Rickard's enterprise at Toledo, on the shores of Maumee Bay, was a piker's gamble compared to what he faced when he undertook to stage the Dempsey-Carpentier mill. But he was amply rewarded with a record attendance and receipts. The colorfulness of the contestants brought out more persons, including the cream of the social set, than ever before in boxing. The success of the venture proved the crowning point in the career of Tex Rickard.

The Frenchman took the offensive at the clang of the gong in the second round after Jack had easily won the opening one, and for one complete round had the greatest boxer of recent years rocking and backing under the fury of the onslaught. A swooping overhand punch was responsible.

The end of a gallant challenger came in the fourth round when heavier, stronger Dempsey knocked Carpentier out, but not until after the "Orchid Kid" had supplied a real thrill for the onlookers by staggering the champion in the second round.

Following his victory over Carpentier, Dempsey didn't fight again for two years. Among his "outside" interests was a horse racing stable, and on a visit to New Orleans he posed with 16-year-old Ivan Parke, a riding sensation at the time.

Then came the turn of the battle. With 80,000 cheering the Orchid Kid as he came out for the third round, Jack leaped forth with an attack and shot in several hard right hand blows to the face and a solid right smash to the stomach that changed the tide. The Frenchman covered up, was cornered and bombarded with body blows. He looked like a weakling in the hands of his now vicious opponent. The bell was sweet music to his ears.

It took but little time in the fourth and final round to end the fray. The champion's deadly left hook found its mark to an unguarded body and the Frenchman slipped limply to the canvas. He took a count of nine. Through all this, scarcely a sound was heard as the huge gathering gasped in astonishment at what was happening.

Dempsey swung against the jaw of the challenger and again he went down, his body stretched across the floor. He didn't move until eight was counted and then attempted to get to his feet but couldn't make it. The fight was over and Dempsey became a national hero.

Dempsey returned to the ring in July, 1923, to meet aging but clever Tom Gibbons in Shelby, Montana. Dempsey had trouble with the light, speedy Gibbons, but strength eventually prevailed, and the champion retained his title on a 15-round decision.

Younger, heavier brother of "Phantom Mike," Tom Gibbons (seen here with son) was 34 when he was given the chance to wrest the heavyweight title from Dempsey.

New York State Athletic Commission chairman William Muldoon supervised the weighing-in of the crude but powerful South American, Luis Angel Firpo, for his championship meeting with Dempsey at the Polo Grounds on September 14, 1923.

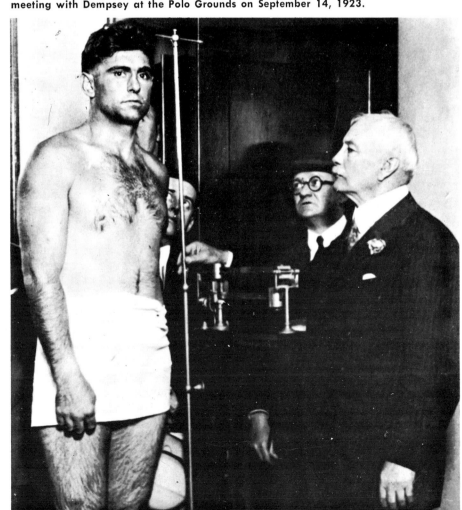

Following two years of idleness, Dempsey tackled Tom Gibbons at Shelby, Montana, on July 4, 1923, and the best he could do was to win a decision in fifteen rounds before only 7,202 paid spectators, the lowest in Dempsey's championship career. The city went bankrupt through its guarantee of $300,000 to the Manassa Mauler, a sum that was far beyond what had been taken in at the gate.

The fight was a financial flop and four Shelby banks went broke.

The Shelby fiasco was followed by Dempsey's greatest battle—that in which he knocked out Luis Angel Firpo of Argentina in the second round at the Polo Grounds in New York on September 14, 1923.

The champion floored the Wild Bull of the Pampas seven times in the opening round and twice in the second before putting him away. A short right uppercut to the jaw ended the thriller.

But in those three minutes and fifty-seven seconds of fighting, there was crowded more action than ordinarily

The big thrill of the Dempsey-Firpo bout occurred in the first round, when the "Wild Bull of the Pampas," knocked down seven times, became infuriated, rushed Jack across the ring and battered the champion through the ropes. (Below) Dempsey, assisted by occupants of the working press section, clambered back into the ring in time to avoid being counted out by Referee Johnny Gallagher.

Dempsey's tumble out of the ring only delayed the inevitable. The champion resumed his savage assault in the second round and within 57 seconds Firpo was down twice, the second time for the full count. After his unfortunate experience in Shelby, Dempsey had returned to the promotional banners of Tex Rickard, and the Firpo bout drew a turnout of 82,000 and gross receipts of $1,188,603.

On a tour of Europe in 1925, Dempsey and his wife, motion picture star Estelle Taylor, were given an enthusiastic reception in Berlin. Introduced by American and British troops after World War I, boxing was becoming popular in Germany, and the visit of the colorful world heavyweight champion helped to establish the sport on a major scale there.

is witnessed in fifteen rounds of a championship match. In those minutes of thrilling, whirlwind, terrific battling. Dempsey was knocked through the ropes, out of the ring, and hadn't friendly hands pushed him back, he would have lost his title.

In that space of less than two rounds, Firpo gave a marvelous exhibition of gameness. Battered and bloody, groggy from the severe punishment, he showed a fighting

heart by coming back following those crushing drives and almost relieving Jack of his crown.

It was the most dramatic fight in the history of modern pugilism. It was a gripping, nerve-shaking contest between lion-hearted, heavy-hitting ringmen.

Firpo had the world within his grasp, the richest title in pugilism almost in hand, yet failed to triumph because he lacked one great essential

in boxing—a fighting brain. Twice he floored Dempsey in the first round but couldn't take advantage of the opportunity by following up his attack properly. The wild-eyed, excited, infuriated giant, who saw his opponent swaying groggily before him, was unequal in the emergency. Dempsey, fully recovered in the second round, made quick work of his task with speed, agility, and fighting fury.

When Dempsey decided to return

A public clamor for a match between Dempsey and Negro challenger Harry Wills resulted in several futile efforts to bring the pair together. Floyd Fitzsimmons (*above*) signed bout for Benton Harbor, Michigan, and (*below*) Rickard even had date set and tickets printed for Jersey City promotion.

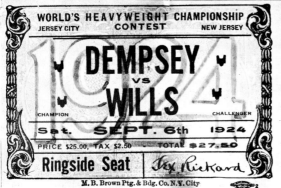

Gene Tunney moved into a contender's role in 1925 by knocking out the veteran Tom Gibbons in 12th round in New York. His decisive victory over the man who had gone the 15-round route with Dempsey spurred Tunney to challenge for the championship.

to the ring in 1925, he was pressed by the New York State Athletic Commission to accept Harry Wills, a Negro of national prominence, as his challenger, but he refused. This was done after a previous agreement for such a match had fallen through. His decision resulted in Jack's being barred in the Empire State. Tex Rickard was appealed to by the Boxing Board and he decided against staging a mixed bout, declaring that he had received a hint from Governor Al Smith that such a contest was not desired in New York, but James A. Farley, Chairman of the New York Commission, emphatically denied the report.

When Rickard arranged to have Gene Tunney face Dempsey and selected the Yankee Stadium for the bout, the Commission put its foot down and refused to sanction it. The Boxing Board drove the fight out of New York, and the Sesquicentennial Stadium of Philadelphia was awarded the promotion for September 23, 1926. In that bout Jack lost his title.

It was another million-dollar bout and drew an attendance of 120,757, the largest in boxing history. The gate was $1,895,733.

The fight took place in a driving rainstorm that made the canvas slippery and drenched spectators and participants alike. Tunney, far better physically, was master of the situation in all except two rounds, in one of which, the fourth, he was on the verge of a knockout.

In several rounds Tunney made the champion look foolish as Jack missed and floundered about the ring. He was far off his usual tearing-in, fast-punching style. He seemed to have lost his punch, his vicious attack and all that in his heyday made him the "Man Killer."

The champion was awkward, slow, and couldn't follow through as he did in the famous battles with Willard, Carpentier, and Firpo. Some blamed it on the weather conditions; others on his difficulties with his manager with whom he broke following his marriage to Estelle Taylor, the movie actress.

Gene, on the other hand, exhibited cleverness and sharp hitting. He fought his greatest battle. He often beat Jack to the punch and several times rocked his head. He opened a gash over Jack's eye in the fifth round. In the sixth, Dempsey succeeded in checking his rival's attack, but Tunney came back with power in the last portion of that round and the next to

Rusty from three years of ring inactivity and beset by domestic and professional worries, Dempsey (*left, above; right, below*) was beaten decisively by younger, well-conditioned Tunney in 10 rainy rounds in Philadelphia on September 23, 1926.

toss punch after punch to the head and body without a return from the champ.

And that's how it went from then to the tenth and final session with Tunney always leading, striking effectively, and Jack missing. For the first time in his career, the Manassa Mauler found himself entirely on the receiving end.

His left eye was closed, his face puffed, and he was wobbly when the gong ended the affair. Tunney, the New York boy who had won the light heavyweight crown in the American Expeditionary Force in France, was now the world heavyweight champion.

Both Rickard and Dempsey were eager to obtain a return engagement, but Tex had to get Manassa Jack back into the top challenger's post before he could sell Dempsey to the public again.

The heavyweight chosen to give

A product of the sidewalks of New York, 28-year-old Gene Tunney (*above*) awaits the official decision that would crown him the new heavyweight champion of the world. The one regret in Tunney's triumph was that, because of political pressure, he was deprived of the chance of winning boxing's highest honors in his home town. (*Below*) Tunney, who had served with the United States Marines in World War I, and had won the American Expeditionary Forces light heavyweight title in France, stages a lively reunion with his former buddies. The Leathernecks, proud of Gene's accomplishment in defeating the mighty Dempsey, promptly commmissioned him an "honorary colonel."

Gene Tunney, shown as he looked at the height of his career, boxed from 1915 to 1928 and lost only one battle—to Harry Greb, whom he later defeated. In 77 bouts, he scored 40 kayoes, won 15, drew once, won on a foul, had one no-contest and 18 no-decisions.

One month after Tunney dethroned Dempsey, Jack Sharkey exploded the Harry Wills "bubble" by thrashing the Negro and winning on a foul in the 13th round in Brooklyn.

With Tunney signed to meet the winner, Dempsey and Sharkey clashed in New York on July 21, 1927. This shot shows Sharkey (*left*) grimacing from a low punch, just before Dempsey shifted to his chin and knocked him out in the seventh round.

Dempsey a tryout was Joseph Paul Zukauskas, otherwise known as "Jack Sharkey," who figured as the outstanding fighter among the big fellows plodding toward the championship goal. Sharkey had a good record, his most noteworthy performance being a victory over Harry Wills, the Negro gladiator who for years had vainly challenged Dempsey. It was this removal of what had come to be known as "The Black Menace" from the roster of title-contenders which boosted Sharkey's stock and gained for him the match with the ex-champion.

The bout took place at Yankee Stadium, New York, on July 21, 1927, Dempsey winning by a knockout in the seventh round before 75,000 fans who paid $1,083,530, the fourth million-dollar gate. In the contest's early stages, Sharkey elected to fight at long range. A fast boxer, he outpointed Dempsey, whose speed did not equal that of his antagonist.

But Sharkey, abandoning his cautious attitude, unwisely went in to mix matters, a style of milling which exactly suited the iron-fisted Dempsey. The latter pounded Sharkey's body savagely and in the seventh round landed a stomach punch at close quarters which seemed to some of the spectators to be a trifle low. Sharkey imprudently turned his head to protest to the referee and in the same instant, Dempsey smashed a hook to the jaw which sent the ex-gob down and out. He claimed a foul, but Referee Jack O'Sullivan disallowed it.

Opinions were about evenly divided among the spectators as to whether Sharkey had actually been fouled. With that victory, Rickard announced the Dempsey-Tunney rematch.

They met at Soldier's Field, Chicago, September 22, 1927 in a title match that has gone down in ring history as "The Battle of The Long Count," the fifth in the series of million-dollar-gate contests in which Dempsey took part, with 104,943 persons paying the all time record sum of $2,658,660.

It had been agreed before the fight that the neutral corner rule be observed and that in the event of a knockdown, the man scoring it should go to the farthest neutral corner. When Dempsey dropped Gene in the seventh round, he refused to obey that rule and Referee Dave Barry stopped the count until Jack did. Thus, Dempsey was penalized and Tunney received additional time to regain his senses.

As in Philadelphia, Dempsey was defeated. This time he came pretty close to winning by a knockout in the seventh round, but his failure to obey the rules and go to a neutral corner cost him the victory. Though Tunney has often declared he could have gotten to his feet at any time within the allotted ten seconds, the photo of the knockdown with Gene resting against the ropes, glassy-eyed, indicated otherwise.

Second Tunney-Dempsey bout, September 22, 1927, drew a crowd of 104,943 and all-time record receipts of $2,658,660 to Soldiers Field, Chicago. Tunney won again, but had a close escape from defeat in the "long count" episode in the seventh round.

How long Tunney actually was down was never determined, but estimates ranged from 12 to 16 seconds. Dempsey's hesitancy in going to a neutral corner when Tunney sank to the canvas was responsible for Referee Dave Barry's delay in starting the count. That one flash was the nearest Dempsey came to regaining the title. Tunney, arising at the official count of nine (*above*), recovered from the knockdown and resumed his systematic battering of the former champion. Dempsey was tiring rapidly in the eighth round and sagged to one knee (*below*) from a volley of Tunney punches. Dempsey was near exhaustion at the final bell in the 10th round.

Yet in the next round, Tunney, his brain cleared, danced around the ring, tossed jabs and then dropped Dempsey with a right to the jaw. He quickly got to his feet but was outpointed by a wide margin in that and the succeeding two rounds, with Gene getting a well deserved decision.

The long count knockdown has become one of the most talked about, controversial points in boxing. Some of the ringsiders said Gene received a fourteen count, as did the official timekeeper, while others, mostly newspapermen, said it was seventeen. The writer's stop watch caught it at fourteen. Here is what happened:

Gene opened the round with a right to Dempsey's head then delivered several effective jabs. Dempsey rushed him and smote two rights to the head that landed Gene against the ropes. The last punch was hard enough to drop him to the canvas, where he lay in an awkward position in Dempsey's corner with body half twisted and eyes glassy.

In interviews he declared that he knew what was going on, however. He watched Dave Barry closely and when Dempsey went to a neutral corner and Barry's count was started, Gene slowly worked his way upward. Dempsey rushed in, but Gene, his equilibrium regained, moved about the ring, making Jack miss, and the round ended with both hugging each other.

Thus ended the fighting career of one of the great ringmen of all time. Though Dempsey tried a comeback and gained a fortune in exhibitions after the second defeat, his real fighting terminated with the "Long Count" battle.

James Joseph Tunney, born May 25, 1898, the first New York-born ringman to win the crown under glove rules, had a proud record before winning the heavyweight title. Prior to joining the Marines and gaining the A.E.F. light heavyweight title in Europe, he had a few contests, but it was after his return from World War One that he took to the sport in earnest and set the championship as his goal.

He defeated Battling Levinsky for the American light heavyweight

In his last title defense, on July 23, 1928, Tunney gave a masterful exhibition in whittling Tom Heeney of New Zealand into defeat in 11 rounds at New York's Yankee Stadium. Heeney had won an elimination tourney to determine Tunney's opponent, but he proved no match for the champion. A few days later Gene announced his retirement.

crown, January 13, 1922. At that time he had won twenty-nine contests and didn't experience a single setback. He lost the title to Harry Greb in May of that year, regained it from Greb on February 23, 1923, and never again did he suffer a defeat.

In 1925 he threw down the gauntlet to the heavyweight class, scored knockouts over Tommy Gibbons and Bartley Madden, and defeated Johnny Risko in twelve rounds.

From a slender, though sinewy athlete, he had developed into a splendid specimen of muscular manhood, with massive shoulders, deep chest, and stalwart frame. His weight and punching power increased without sacrificing the agility and speedy footwork for which he was celebrated. Not the least surprising thing about the Philadelphia meeting with Dempsey when the heavyweight title passed to Tunney, was the unsuspected strength of the victor which enabled

him to tie up and control in the clinches a pugilist who had hitherto been deemed invincible in a test of roughing it at close quarters!

Nearly a year passed before Tunney again defended his title. This time Tom Heeney, known as the "Australian Hard Rock," was selected to oppose him. Out of a lot of rather mediocre heavies in an elimination tournament conducted by Tex Rickard at Madison Square Garden, Heeney and Sharkey had forged to the front. A meeting between the two pugilists resulted in a draw, but as Sharkey had already been knocked out by Dempsey, the Australian was awarded the match for the championship.

Tunney and Heeney met on July 26, 1928, at the Polo Grounds in New York City. The fight was halted by Referee Eddie Forbes eight seconds before the conclusion of the eleventh round, when Heeney, game to the core, but literally cut to pieces by the

Man of many interests, Jack Dempsey, operating the Dempsey-Vanderbilt Hotel in Miami Beach in 1938, often took his daughters for a run on the sands. (Right) Dempsey's duties with the Coast Guard in World War II included athletic instruction.

(Left) Three months after retiring from the ring, Gene Tunney, followed by fiancée Polly Lauder, disembarked at Naples, Italy, en route to their marriage in Rome.

As a Navy Commander (below) in World War II, Tunney kept distinguished company. On a visit to the Mitchell Field Air Force base on Long Island in 1942, Tunney appeared (second from left) with Brigadier General Jimmy Doolittle; Colonel Douglas Johnston, commanding officer of the post, and Lieutenant Colonel John S. Allard, former vice-president of Curtiss-Wright.

champion's unerring punches, was blind and utterly helpless. From first to last Heeney never had a chance. The man who stood off the best of the heavyweight contenders was little better than a novice in the hands of the most scientific pugilist since the day of James J. Corbett.

Financially the bout was a dismal failure. It was the first non-profitable championship battle staged by Rickard. It resulted in a loss of $152,000. Gene was guaranteed $500,000.

The glamor and color of Dempsey's name was missing. Despite the most frantic efforts of the press agents, the public remained coldly indifferent as to what would happen to Tom Heeney. There was nothing spectacular about the man from the Antipodes. He was a persevering, dogged, plodding fighter and the fans guessed correctly in advance as to what his fate would be.

Speculation as to Tunney's next opponent ceased suddenly when the champion announced his retirement. There were no "if's" about Gene's statement. It was short, definite, to the point. He was through forever with the ring.

Tunney married an heiress, Miss Polly Lauder, and became a very successful businessman.

THE CROWN GOES OVERSEAS

After Tunney's retirement, Jack Sharkey, Young Stribling, Johnny Risko, and Germany's Max Schmeling were the leading contenders for Gene's vacated throne. An elimination was ordered by the National Boxing Association and the New York Commission.

Tex Rickard set about to get such a tourney under way. He went to Miami, Florida, with the intention of matching Sharkey and Stribling, but while

there, Rickard died following an appendix operation. Jack Dempsey, who had been associated with the promoter in several ventures, accepted a call from the Madison Square Garden Corporation, and in association with that organization promoted the fight on February 27, 1929, with Sharkey gaining the decision.

In the meantime, Schmeling, who had knocked out Joe Monte in the Garden in eight rounds and followed

that with a knockout of Risko in the same arena in nine rounds, was clamoring for a shot at the winner. This was temporarily denied him, and while waiting, he won a thrilling fifteen-rounds contest from Paulino Uzcudun, the Basque, while Sharkey put Tommy Loughran out in three rounds.

The heat was now on for a Schmeling-Sharkey fight, but the Garden officials decided to have the German,

William Lawrence (Young) Stribling, the pride of Dixie, became one of the leading contenders for the vacant title when Tunney retired from the ring wars. Stribling began boxing as a bantamweight and fought in every division up to heavyweight. He was only 28, but a veteran of nearly 300 bouts, when his life ended tragically in a motorcycle crash in 1933.

A newcomer flashed across the heavyweight scene in 1928 when a young German, Max Schmeling, scored a one-round knockout over the Italian Michele Bonaglia in Berlin.

Recovering from knockout by Dempsey, clever Jack Sharkey (*below*) went on to establish himself as one of the best of the American bidders for Tunney's vacated laurels.

As a preliminary to the championship bout with Schmeling, Jack Sharkey was awarded a knockout victory over Phil Scott of England, on February 28, 1930, in Miami. Scott, a boxer with fair skill, but fragile, refused to continue after three knockdowns in the third round, claiming that all of the blows were foul. Referee Lou Magnolia stopped the proceedings and declared Sharkey the winner.

The meeting between Jack Sharkey and Max Schmeling, to decide the successor to the heavyweight crown, ended in complete confusion. Schmeling, sitting on the canvas claiming foul, insisted Sharkey's left to the stomach landed below the belt.

a young, well built, scientific boxer who possessed a powerful right, wait it out while the Boston gob and Phil Scott of England engaged in an international elimination at Miami Beach in which the Britisher was halted in the third round. The stage was now set for the final in the elimination series, Schmeling representing Europe and Sharkey, America; this despite a British howl that Scott had been fouled and that Sharkey should have been disqualified.

In the Miami bout, Sharkey, outboxed in the opening round, dropped Phil in the second with a punch and a push, and in the third, put the Englishman on the canvas with a left hook to the stomach. Phil cried foul.

Twice again he was floored by similar blows and when he refused to get to his feet, declaring all punches were below the belt, Referee Lou Magnolia halted proceedings, insisted on Scott deciding whether he wanted to continue or quit. Phil chose the former, but when he went down from another punch in the mid-section, he remained squirming on the canvas and Magnolia gave the decision to Sharkey.

On June 11, 1930, Sharkey and

In the sequence above, the camera recorded the controversial blow. Referee Jim Crowley (*below, left*) not in position to see the blow, took the word of one of the judges who saw the foul and awarded the title to Schmeling. While Schmeling is carried to his corner, his manager, Joe Jacobs, protests to Crowley that the blow was foul.

Schmeling clashed in the Yankee Stadium before a gathering of 79,222 fans. The gross gate of $749,935 was the first during the Golden Era that failed to reach the million dollar mark.

Sharkey's stock had been given a scant boost because of the besmirched victory he had achieved. The fans were in no mood to wax enthusiastic over the ex-gob's triumph over "Phainting Phil" and gave Schmeling more than a fighting chance to win the crown. And that's what he did.

Max was proclaimed world champion following a blow to the stomach that had left him reposing on the canvas, writhing in pain. It was a powerful drive which he and Joe Jacobs, his mentor, insisted was low and in that they had the heavy support of Arthur Brisbane, editor of the Hearst publications, who demanded that Referee Jim Crowley disqualify Sharkey or Brisbane would have the Walker Law repealed. Neither Harold Barnes, a judge, nor the referee had seen the low punch, but Charles F. Mathison, the other judge, agreed with Schmeling, and for the first time a challenger gained the world heavyweight title while resting on his haunches.

Max Schmeling, in his first defense of the title, knocked out Young Stribling (above) in the 15th round. Referee George Blake stopped the bout with one minute to go. Schmeling (below, left), just over six feet tall and weighing 195 pounds, was a very good boxer and a methodical ringman. He carried dynamite in his right hand, and his record, from 1924 to 1948, is studded with knockouts.

Jack Sharkey, an ex-gob from Boston, was a good boxer, but his temperamental nature led to many erratic performances. In 55 bouts, from 1924 to 1936, he lost 13, and scored 15 knockouts.

Prior to the incident, Schmeling had been outpointed. It was the first time under modern rules that a Teuton had won the crown.

The New York Commission was hotly in favor of a return match, but Schmeling and his manager turned thumbs down. As a result, New York vacated his throne until such time as Sharkey was given an opportunity to fight for the championship again. In the meantime, Young Stribling, who had a huge knockout record and had stopped Otto Van Porat in one round and Phil Scott in two in London, was accepted by Schmeling as a suitable opponent. The German put his title on the line in the Cleveland Stadium on July 3, 1931, Herr Max winning by a knockout in the fifteenth round with only fifteen more seconds to go. Stribling had been outclassed and Referee George Blake halted the affair.

Only in the five opening rounds did Stribling look like he would carry off the honors. From then on it was all Schmeling's bout. He carried the battling to the challenger all the way and it was simply a romp after the sixth round.

Two years and nine days after their first engagement, Max and Sharkey clashed again, this time in the Garden's Long Island Bowl, and the title changed hands on what many thought was an unfair decision. Schmeling, as in the first bout, raised a cry, but to no avail. There was little over which to enthuse in that contest, most of the fighting being done after the affair.

Most of the effective work was accomplished by Schmeling, who carried the fight to Sharkey, maneuvered his opponent cleverly, and landed the best punches of the few that really meant something.

Max's next fight of importance was his best—other than his first contest with Joe Louis. The mill took place on September 26, 1932, with Mickey Walker, former welter and middleweight king, as his opponent. Mickey was knocked out in the eighth round of a thrilling affair, a hair-raiser, one of the best seen in New York in years. Sixty thousand persons saw the Ger-

On the night of June 21, 1932, Sharkey (*right, above*) and Schmeling met in a return championship bout, in which Sharkey won the decision and title, in 15 rounds. The fight was not exciting, both men depending on left hand jabs throughout. Most of the sportswriters decided in Schmeling's favor. However, the championship was back in America, at least for a whiile. The third man in the ring is former heavyweight Gunboat Smith, a good referee.

Schmeling's next fight, after losing the title to Sharkey, was a sensational battle with Mickey Walker, slated for 10 rounds. In the eighth round, Schmeling had Walker badly cut and bleeding. After flooring him with a powerful right, Schmeling pleaded (*right*) to referee Denning to stop the fight, which he did.

man vanquish his rival in Schmeling's greatest fight since coming to America.

The last round was one of three minutes of action. Floored in the opening frame, Mickey shaded Max in the second and at the end of the seventh was leading four rounds to three. Then came the turn. Max battered

Walker's body and face until Mickey was helpless. A powerful right dropped him. He was bleeding from mouth, nose, and cuts over his face, and one eye was closed. Referee Denning stopped the bout.

The following June, in another thriller, Max Baer halted Schmeling

Several times in his first fight with Schmeling, Louis, befuddled, struck his opponent low and after the bell. Here Referee Arthur Donovan warns the Brown Bomber. 39,878 persons saw the bout and the paid attendance was $547,531. Both fighters received the same amount, $125,535, which was 30 per cent of the net. Louis, a hot favorite, cost his backers heavily when he was knocked out.

in the tenth round in the Yankee Stadium and that was followed by a loss in twelve to Steve Hamas, former four-letter man at Penn State University. Max then went home, drew with Paulino in Barcelona in twelve rounds, stopped Walter Neusel in eight, Steve Hamas in a return bout in nine, and Paulino again in twelve, and now came back to America for another campaign.

Joe Louis was now coming along as a threat to the heavyweights and Mike Jacobs was priming him for a title shot. Believing that Max was ready to be taken into camp by Joe, he arranged to have them meet in the Yankee Stadium on June 19, 1936. To the surprise of all, Schmeling gave his greatest performance in knocking out the Brown Bomber in the twelfth round, a triumph that put Max back into the championship picture as the outstanding challenger.

The left side of Louis' face was so swollen that it appeared he had a double cheek. He was staggered often and received severe punishment. His left eye was completely closed and his lips were bleeding.

Max scored his first knockdown in the fourth round and henceforth, a more determined Schmeling never faced an opponent. When the fight ended, Louis was resting in a praying position supported by the ropes.

The dramatic finish of the first Louis-Schmeling fight. Louis (*left*) stands groggy and helpless; a powerful right lands on his jaw; and he drops to a praying position. It was a stunning blow to the reputation of the Brown Bomber, who had been touted as invincible. (*Below*) Trainer Max Machon (*left*) and second escort Schmeling to his corner in glee. Manager Joe Jacobs is at right.

Now Schmeling pleaded for another chance at the championship, but complications arose that paved the way for Louis to obtain the lucrative bout.

After Schmeling had lost the title to Sharkey, the latter, in an unsatisfactory affair that created considerable discussion, dropped the championship to "Satchel Feet" Primo Carnera of Italy. The Italian, a crude heavyweight who lacked both science and hitting power, stopped the Boston Gob on June 29, 1933, in the Garden Bowl in the sixth round.

Following that victory he went back home and in Rome he outpointed Paulino Uzcudun in fifteen rounds, then trimmed Tommy Loughran in Miami in a bout of fifteen rounds in which he had a weight advantage of eighty-six pounds. But on June 14, 1934, he was shorn of his crown by Max Baer of Livermore, California. The bout was staged in the Garden Bowl.

The "Comedy Battle" it has been dubbed, because there were many knockdowns and tumbles. Baer dropped the Italian Goliath eleven times before the bout was halted.

Baer, known as the "Merry Madcap" for his eccentricities, was a playboy, like Harry Greb, who paid little attention to training, and his tenure as world title holder lasted only one year. He had an excellent record, but success doomed him and he fell prey in his first and only championship defense to the cleverness of James J. Braddock, who came off the relief rolls to gain a place in the Fistic Hall of Fame.

Baer continued to ply his trade for several years, during which he faced the cream of the division, among them Joe Louis, who stopped him; Tommy Farr, who beat him in London, Eng-

Primo Carnera (above), the Italian giant who was dubbed "Satchel Feet," was one of the poorest of all heavyweight title holders. He was a crude fighter with little skill. (Left) A knockdown in the Carnera-Sharkey fight, in which Sharkey lost his title by a knockout in the sixth round at Madison Square Garden's Bowl.

Clever, hard-hitting Ernie Schaaf, a young heavyweight title contender, was knocked out by Primo Carnera at Madison Square Garden, on February 10, 1933. Schaaf went down from a light blow in the 13th round and was rushed *(above)* to a hospital, where he lingered a few days, then died as the result of a brain injury. It was believed that Schaaf entered the ring concealing an injury sustained in an earlier bout with Max Baer. Ernie, 25 when tragedy struck, was born in Elizabeth, New Jersey.

Max Baer *(right)* over six feet tall and weighing 195 pounds, had the finest physical equipment a ringman could want. He had massive shoulders, long and supple muscular arms, slim waist, strong legs, and a deadly right hand. Unfortunately, he never took boxing seriously, always clowning and depending upon his right hand to end matters. In his fight with Carnera for the title Max swang the huge champion in the clinches and knocked him down 11 times, joining him on the canvas once *(below)*. Greatness might have been his, had he learned to box and set up a defense.

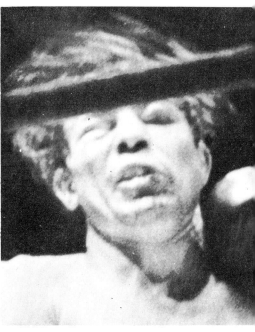

land; Lou Nova, by whom he was knocked out twice, and Two-Ton Galento, who was halted in eight. Each was a sensational affair, thanks to the showmanship of Max. He retired in 1942 when he enlisted in the U. S. Army.

Braddock, the "Cinderella Man," born in New York on December 6, 1905, fought as a light heavyweight for a number of years with ordinary success. His triumph over Baer was one of the biggest upsets in the history of the division. He fought Tommy Loughran for the light heavyweight title on July 18, 1929, and lost in fifteen rounds. Thereafter he dropped decisions to such top men as Leo Lomski, Maxie Rosenbloom, Yale Okun, Babe Hunt, Ernie Schaaf, Al Gainer, Tony Shucco, and Lou Scozza, who knocked him out.

But with talent scarce at the time the Garden was seeking an opponent for Baer, Braddock came out of retirement to stop Corn Griffin in three

Jimmy Braddock did the unexpected when he knocked out Tuffy Griffiths on November 30, 1928. He hit the downgrade afterwards, until he made his new start in a comeback.

Braddock, the "Cinderella Man," as he looked when he recorded the upset of the year, June 13, 1935, when he gained the decision over Max Baer at the Garden Bowl in a bout that went the limit of 15 rounds. Jimmy, in contrast to the man whom he dethroned, was a serious fighter that day as can be seen in the lower photograph, in which he is ready to crash his right into Baer's jaw. Throughout the fight Baer clowned, to the astonishment of a large crowd.

rounds on the Baer-Carnera card and then whipped Art Lasky in fifteen rounds. Those victories, especially the last named, since Art was being groomed for the title shot, put Braddock in line for the bout that gained him the world championship. The "Cinderella Man" he was called thereafter.

Now came an historic turn in boxing. The Garden Corporation had a contract with Schmeling to fight Braddock for the championship, but Mike Jacobs, who owned the Twentieth Century Club, a Garden rival, had the biggest attraction in America in Joe Louis, the young Detroit Bomber who, after an unsullied record studded with knockouts, had been stopped by Schmeling. It was Jacobs' intention to keep Louis in the headlines by matching him with Braddock. So good was the inducement that Braddock turned against the Garden and accepted Jacobs' offer. The agreement called for the champion to receive his percentage of the gate in

Jim Braddock, the guy who kept trying, who couldn't be discouraged, even against all odds, has his hands raised *(above, left)* in token of victory over Max Baer and is declared the new heavyweight champion of the world. In the press room of the Twentieth Century Boxing Club *(left)* in the old Hippodrome, Braddock is in discussion with *(left to right)* Walter Stewart, now sports editor of the *Memphis Commercial Appeal*, Lester Scott, trainer Doc Casey, Tommy Farr and a sports writer from Europe. *(Above)* Braddock, battered by Joe Louis, went out like a champ, in eight rounds, on June 22, 1937, in Chicago.

addition to ten percent of Jacobs' share of all Louis' championship fights should he gain the crown.

Despite protests by Schmeling and his country, he was shunted to the sidelines and the Braddock-Louis bout took place in Chicago on June 22, 1937, with Louis a winner by a knockout. Braddock dropped the Bomber in the opening round but Louis stopped him in the eighth and carried off the world championship.

Jimmy engaged in only one more bout after that, whipping Tommy Farr in ten rounds. He then retired and became a captain in the U. S. Army during World War Two.

In the Chicago contest, Braddock was on his feet until his brain was numbed by a right hand wallop, his eyes were dimmed and his body paralyzed from the vicious attack of the Brown Bomber. Jimmy went down a fighting champion.

Braddock won 51 of 85 career bouts, 26 by KO. Born December 6, 1905, Jimmy died of a heart attack on November 24, 1974, at North Bergen, N.J.

Battered and bruised, lips badly cut, a severed artery bringing forth the claret in spurts, face cut into crimson ribbons, one eye closed and the other puffed, but game to the very last, Braddock lay unconscious on the rosin-covered canvas, a champion shorn of his crown. He fell like a poled ox, while the spectators, intense with excitement, looked on in awe.

For Louis it was the kind of finish that adds to ring romance. The blasting right that landed with a thud against Braddock's chin in the fatal round, turned the trick for the newly crowned king. The end came in 1.10 of the eighth round.

ERA OF THE BROWN BOMBER

Joe Louis was one of the greatest and most colorful boxers in modern fisticuffs. Only Dempsey since the gloves era got under way and Sullivan in the bare knuckle and skin-tight gloves periods compared to him in popularity and ability. This Alabama-born boxer who first saw the light of day on May 13, 1914, and whose father, "Mun" Barrow, was a cotton picker, was a pugilistic symphony with a tempo geared to bring him across the ring with all the grace of a gazelle and the cold fury of an enraged mountain lion. He combined excellent harmony of movement with crushing power stored in each hand.

His career was one that won't be

Mike Jacobs and Joe Louis leave Yankee Stadium after Joe's knockout of Schmeling. Jacobs promoted all of Joe's major fights after 1935. Louis' gross earnings in all fields, including his final bout with Rocky Marciano, amounted to $4,626,721.

forgotten in a hurry. The Brown Bomber did everything expected of a champion. He pulverized, paralyzed, or poked his way beyond a larger number of challengers than any heavyweight king who wore the Royal Robe before him.

He lacked the technique of the masterful Johnson, the powerful offense of Jeffries from a crouching position, the sinking body clouts of Freckled Bob Fitzsimmons, the beautiful ring science of Jim Corbett and the speed of Dempsey in carrying the fight to an opponent. But he combined a good portion of each of the assets of these great ringmen in addition to a mighty punch to roll up the largest string of successes ever attained by a heavyweight champion. Long before he retired, the Bomber's place among ring immortals had become a topic of world-wide discussion.

Louis brought back to boxing life and color that was sadly needed, and when he had no more worlds to conquer he retired.

In his rise to fame he faced the good and mediocre, and in his entire career he lost only three contests: his knockout by Schmeling before he became a title holder, and his loss to Ezzard Charles and knockout by Rocky Marciano after he made his comeback attempt.

Louis started his professional career following his defeat by Max Marek in the finals of the national amateur championships. Henceforth he was to make a steady rise until he gained the top rung of the ladder.

Prior to the knockout he had suffered at the hands of Schmeling, he had won twenty-seven consecutive bouts, all except four by knockouts. Among his victims were many of the better class heavyweights, including Stanley Poreda, Charley Massera, Patsy Perroni, Natie Brown, Roy Lazer, Roscoe Toles, and Hans Birkie.

Then those who had launched his professional career—John Roxborough and Julian Black—aided by Mike Jacobs, who promoted all of his major fights after March 28, 1935, when Joe had won the decision over Brown in

Joe Louis knocked out three former heavyweight champions before winning the title from Braddock. He knocked out game but ineffectual Jack Sharkey in three rounds on August 17, 1936.

Louis knocked out Max Baer in four rounds on September 24, 1935. Max made only token attempts at fighting back and, absorbed a great number of Louis' punches before succumbing.

Detroit, figured that the Bomber was ready for the top men of his division. In successive bouts, Joe knocked out Primo Carnera, in six rounds; King Levinsky in one; Max Baer in four; Paulino Uzcudun in four; and Charley Retzlaff in one. Then came the only setback he suffered during his pre-championship and championship day, the knockout by Schmeling.

So thorough and masterly a job did the Uhlan perform, that the thousands who had come in expectation of seeing the Brown Bomber put another opponent to sleep because of his supposed invincibility sat dumfounded watching the so-called Executioner executed. Not since the day when the great John L. Sullivan was dethroned by James J. Corbett had such a jolt been meted out to the fight public. The "Superman of Boxing" was a pathetic figure as he sat in his corner, first aid administered to him by his trainer Jack Blackburn and his man-

agers after the fatal ten had been counted over him. Face puffed, mouse under his eye, thumbs sprained, he looked nothing like the man who had been mowing down opponent after opponent.

When the fight was over, Joe's mind was set on only one thing—revenge. He quickly decided on plans to prepare himself for a return bout and Mike Jacobs arranged for his comeback with the aim of building him up for a title bout.

Jack Sharkey was his first victim. He went out in three rounds. The murderous fists of the Brown Bomber worked beautifully that night. Next came Al Ettore of Philadelphia. He lasted through part of the fifth session. Jorge Brescia went out in three, Eddie Simms in one, and Steve Ketchell in two.

The start was most satisfactory. Joe's handlers and Jacobs were delighted with his comeback. Uncle

Primo Carnera, completely outclassed, took an unmerciful beating, lasting six rounds with Joe Louis, on June 25, 1935.

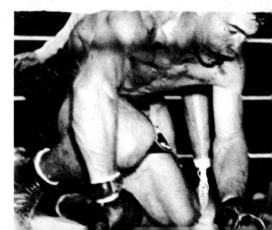

Prior to winning the title, Louis won a 10-round decision over Bob Pastor (*right*), shown waiting for the verdict. Tammy Farr (*above, left*), a tough Welshman, lost a fifteen round decision to Louis, in Louis' first defense of his crown. Farr put up a game, tough fight, making his American debut before 32,000 fans in New York.

Trainer Jack Blackburn laces Louis' gloves, while the champ sits calmly in his corner before his second meeting with Schmeling.

Smiling Max Schmeling sits in the opposite corner, looking confident, as he waits to be introduced to a crowd of 70,000.

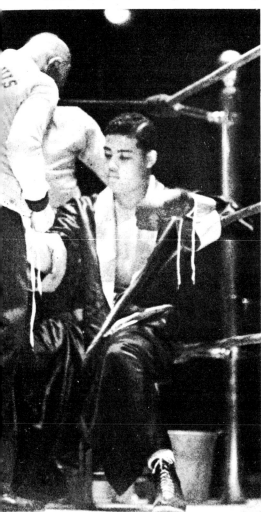

Mike then matched Joe with Bob Pastor of New York, who temporarily halted the steady stream of kayoes by lasting ten rounds of what the scribes termed a running match. Bob back-pedalled throughout the ten frames.

Another knockout of Natie Brown followed, and in the next session, Louis defeated Braddock to win the world crown. The goal of his ambition had been reached but what he wanted most, next to that, was to avenge his knockout by Schmeling. He sought a quick return bout and this he received after he had outpointed Tommy Farr of Wales in an international championship bout.

Tommy gave an excellent performance against the Bomber, and those among his countrymen who saw the affair both at the ringside and in the movies were strongly of the opinion that Farr had won. But the majority of the scribes and the judges thought otherwise and correctly so, for Louis, despite the aggressiveness of Tommy, tossed leather at a steady gait in the majority of the rounds. His effectiveness was far superior to that of the

A scared Schmeling faced Louis in their second bout. In this fight the Brown Bomber went all out from the start to avenge the knock-out he had suffered previously. As Louis kept tossing rights, Max twisted his body and took the punches on his side. After the fight he declared he had been fouled.

Welshman. It was a stirring bout and an excellent final tuneup for Louis.

His triumph over Schmeling followed. He scored the second quickest knockout in the history of the heavyweight championship bouts, 2:04 of the opening round, and in accom-plishing this wonderful feat he handed Schmeling a terrible beating. Joe collected $349,288.40, an average of $2,832 per second, the record up to that time in any championship fight.

The fists of the Bomber crushed his former conqueror in a manner that left no doubt about his superiority. Though Schmeling complained bitterly about being struck foul kidney punches, every blow was a fair one. Any that struck Max in the kidneys were caused by the twisting of Schmeling's body as he held on to the

A right that landed with a thud caused Schmeling to reel, topple on his side, roll over and land on all fours, from which position Referee Donovan counted him out. Though Max Machen, who seconded Max, tossed in the towel, under New York rules this was not permitted and Referee Donovan hurled it out of the ring. It landed on the upper strand where it remained until the count on Schmeling had been completed.

upper strand and tried desperately to avoid the vicious attack of his opponent. The first two punches, powerful left hooks, started Schmeling on his downfall. Once Louis got the range, he kept up a steady bombardment until Max had been halted.

The first knockdown followed a right to the chin. The German fell on his shoulder and rolled over twice before coming to a rest with his feet in the air. Louis did most of his attack with his right. Nine such blows landed with accuracy in the first minute. Max was down twice more. The second time, after a count of two, he got to his feet, a powerful right crashed against his jaw and Max went down on all fours. He tried to straighten himself to rise, but while in the process, his chief second, Max Machon tossed in the towel. Since this is not permitted under New York rules, Arthur Donovan, the referee, hurled it back, took a good look at Schmeling, and as Timekeeper Eddie Joseph had reached eight, Donovan halted the bout.

The King had proved his right to the throne.

With that great victory, a series of contests was arranged for Louis before his enlistment in the Army, in which he tackled all comers in what became known as the "Bum of the Month" battles. Louis disposed of John Henry Lewis, Jack Roper, Tony Galento, and Bob Pastor in 1939, all by knockouts. Galento floored him but suffered a severe shellacking.

Louis started the next year with a discouraging affair with Arturo Godoy of Chile, who lasted the fifteen rounds as a result of unorthodox tactics, but later Joe got even with him by stopping him in a return engagement after first halting Johnny Paycheck. A kayo over Al McCoy ended that year's campaign.

His biggest successes were registered in 1941 when Red Burman, Gus Dorazio, Abe Simon, Tony Musto, Buddy Baer, Billy Conn, and Lou Nova were taken into camp. The Simon bout in Detroit, as well as that with Pastor two years previous, was scheduled for twenty rounds but

Four months after Joe Louis won a 15-round decision over Arturo Godoy of Chile, they met again and Louis won in eight rounds, when the bout was stopped. Godoy, angered at the referee, refused to go to his corner insisting he be allowed to continue. Louis got protection from trainer Jack Blackburn (left) and manager Julian Black.

Lou Nova is helped to his corner by manager Ray Carlin, Dr. William Walker and his second, Ray Arcel, after being knocked out by Joe Louis. Nova, who practiced Yoga for this fight, was an easy six-round victim for the champion.

133

"Did you ever see a ghost walking? I did." That's what one reporter wrote following the two-round knockout of an outclassed Johnny Paychek by Joe Louis.

Abe Simon (*left*) went thirteen rounds with Joe Louis before being stopped in 1941. Abe convinced his manager, Jimmy Johnston (*right*), that he would win the title in a re-match. Simons, a huge, 255-pound heavyweight, met the Brown Bomber—who was outweighed by 48 pounds—again, on March 27, 1942 and was knocked out in six rounds. Louis donated his purse to Army and Navy relief. Abe was a very successful actor on stage and television. He died of a heart attack on February 7, 1970, at New Paltz, N.Y., at the age of 56.

Buddy Baer knocked the Brown Bomber through the ropes in the first round of their bout on May 23, 1941. When Buddy refused to come out for the seventh round, the fight was awarded to Louis. Baer claimed he was hit after the bell sounded ending the sixth round and Louis should have been disqualified. They met again on January 9, 1942, and Louis knocked Buddy out in one round and donated his purse to the Naval Relief Fund.

neither went the distance. Simon was knocked out in the thirteenth round and Pastor in the eleventh.

The bout with Baer resulted in Buddy's disqualification when he refused to come out for the seventh round, claiming a foul. He had put Joe through the ropes in the opening round of that mill. Buddy asserted that Joe had struck him after the bell had sounded ending the sixth round.

Joe's victory over Baer marked the champion's sixth outing in as many months. It had been a busy and wearying campaign of continuous training and fighting, but Louis wasn't prepared as yet to call it quits. He wanted to keep going.

Tony Galento, a wild-swinging, rough and tumble ringman, possessed no talent other than hitting power. Though he took a severe shellacking from Louis in Yankee Stadium (*top*), where he was stopped in four rounds, Galento had the satisfaction of putting the Bomber on the canvas (*above*) with a round-house blow. Joe, surprised at finding himself on the deck, got to his feet and lambasted his rival, until referee Arthur Donovan stopped the fight. Galento's manager, Joe Jacobs and chief second Whitey Bimstein (*right*), after hauling the game, but badly beaten, challenger to his corner, worked feverishly to get Tony in condition so that he could leave the ring.

Billy Conn, a brilliant light heavyweight champion, had been clamoring for a crack at Louis. Billy, a flashy boxer, had been enjoying consistent success against the bigger fellows, and a thirteen round kayo of Bob Pastor had convinced him of his ability to cope with Louis.

Louis wanted a June fight, and since Conn shaped up as the only possible opponent in sight, the match was arranged for the Polo Grounds.

The battle was to prove one of the most tumultuous of Louis' career, for Conn, outweighed more than twenty-five pounds and at further disadvan-

tages in height and reach, came within the proverbial eyelash of dethroning Louis.

In this contest, the bludgeon was too much for the rapier. For the greater part of thirteen rounds, the beautiful jabbing, clever maneuvering of Conn gave him the advantage.

If Billy Conn had been more cautious when he faced Joe Louis in a title fight in 1941, he might have won the heavyweight crown. He was ahead on points going into the 13th round, then decided to slug it out with Louis, and was knocked out.

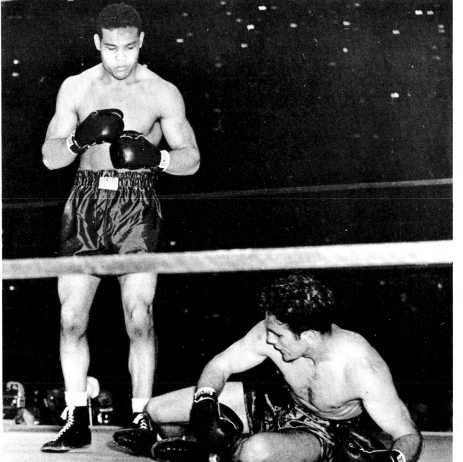

Then Billy, cocky, confident he was Louis' master, gambled a fortune on a knockout. He elected to trade punches with his heavy hitting rival and with only two seconds more to go before the bell would end the thirteenth frame, he was counted out by Referee Eddie Joseph.

A finishing right from the Bomber's TNT fist rang down the curtain on the dazzling show. The game Pittsburgher was within grasp of the crown yet tossed it away by attempting to outslug Joe at a time when the champion was a bewildered title holder and not too steady. From the eleventh through to the finish, Conn had suddenly turned aggressor and handed the champion a sound thrashing, much to the amazement of 54,487 fans who rocked the stands with their enthusiasm.

Overconfidence caused Billy's downfall. They were slugging it out, Billy with a grin on his face and Joe with a look of bewilderment, when Louis landed a powerful left hook to the jaw. He followed that with even a harder right and Conn was in a state of collapse. He had little left after that but courage as Louis battered his body with lefts and rights until the finishing right hand wallop came with only seconds more to go.

Billy Conn came nearest to defeating Louis. When he was halted by Joe, he was ahead on the cards of two of the officials. Judge Marty Monroe had the tally seven to four for Conn with one round even, Referee Eddie Joseph, seven to five for Billy. Judge Healy tabbed it six to six.

After enlisting in the U. S. Army, Louis went overseas on many exhibition tours. Before doing so he fought a return contest with Buddy Baer for the Naval Relief Fund and stopped Buddy in one round. He then tackled Simon in an Army Relief Fund bout and halted him in six.

When Louis and Conn were discharged from the Army, Mike Jacobs decided to match them in a repeater, figuring the public was ready, now that World War Two had ended, for a big time promotion in boxing. He was correct. With a ringside top of $100 for the first three rows, that bout, staged on June 18, 1946, at the Yankee Stadium, drew a paid attendance of 45,266 with a gross gate of $1,925,564, but the affair wasn't worth more than a $10 tops show.

From the standpoint of the fans, it was a flop, with little in it to arouse enthusiasm. It was one of the dullest in Joe's career, owing entirely to the tactics of Conn, who, fighting an entirely different battle from his first encounter with the Bomber, elected to back step. He took no chances.

Of the twenty-three minutes involved, more than three-quarters was packed with dullness and inaction. Conn offered the patrons nothing but flying feet and was knocked out in 2.19 of the eighth round. Louis couldn't catch up with Conn to make the bout interesting and Billy wouldn't mix it. It was inconceivable that these were the same two who had thrilled a vast gathering only five years before!

Up to seven rounds little had been

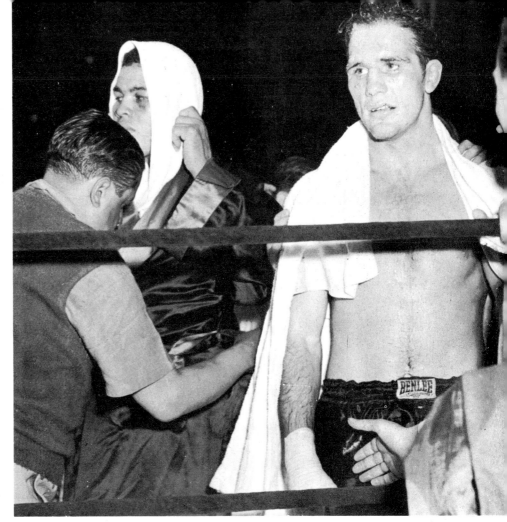

The disappointed Billy Conn *(right)* stands bewildered in his corner after being kayoed by Joe Louis, who nearly lost his title. After winning over Henry Cooper, J. T. Turner and Tony Zale in January and February of 1942, Conn entered the Army.

Joe Louis *(center)* and two buddies, in a U.S.O. canteen. Joe defended his title against Lou Nova in September of 1941, then joined Uncle Sam's Army. While in service, he twice defended his title and donated his purses to the Army and Navy Relief Funds.

Out of the Army after four years, Louis renewed his argument with Conn at Yankee Stadium on June 19, 1946. Conn also had put in four years of Army service, but hadn't retained as much of his former skill as had Louis. Joe had an easy time of it in the return bout; Conn offered feeble resistance and was knocked out in the eighth round of a slow, disappointing affair. The match attracted an attendance of 45,266 and the second highest gate of all time for boxing, $1,925,564.

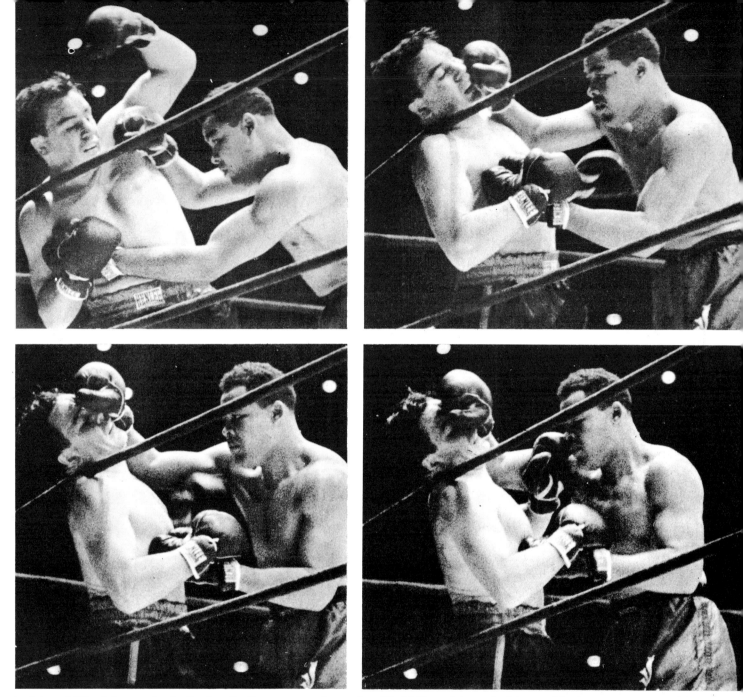

Louis' next title defense, also in Yankee Stadium, was on September 18, 1946, and it resulted in a quick victory over Tami Mauriello. At the opening bell Mauriello rushed out of his corner and nailed Louis with a right that staggered him and sent him reeling back into the ropes. An annoyed Louis smeared Tami's face, then cut loose with an attack that finished Tami in two minutes and nine seconds.

accomplished by either. Here and there a weak-hearted jab was tossed. Conn threw nothing that even looked like a punch. Louis tried, but his delivery was ineffective because of the roaming tactics employed by his opponent.

When Conn landed on the canvas he assumed exactly the same posture as did Jack Johnson in Havana—he shaded his eyes from the hot lights, as Johnson did from the sun, while being counted out.

The one round knockout of Tami Mauriello followed, a bout in which Tami came close to dropping the champion in the first half minute. But Louis, after being hurled almost across the ring with the blow, rushed into his opponent with a vicious attack and it soon was all over.

Then came a series of exhibitions before the Bomber accepted another title defense, this time against aged Joe Walcott of Camden, New Jersey. That historic battle in the Madison Square Garden Arena on December 5, 1947, almost saw the termination of Louis' long successes.

Louis retained his crown because

Despite easy victories over Conn and Mauriello it became evident on December 5, 1947, when Louis met Jersey Joe Walcott in Madison Square Garden, that advancing years and his long Army hitch had taken much of his former ring stuff away from the champion. Expected to be another easy victim, Walcott gave a surprising performance which included two knockdowns over Louis. A bruised, bleeding champion (*below*) received the decision in 15 rounds, but it aroused a storm of protest among many who felt Walcott had won.

he received a split decision verdict, unpopular with the fans and scribes. Walcott lost his chance to take the crown through his back-pedalling. Never in the history of the division has a boxer won a championship running away without attempting a defensive counter-fire. Though Joe won the decision, he was nearer to dethronement than he ever had been through his ten years reign as world champion.

He was knocked down twice. The first occurred in the opening round for a count of two and the next in the fourth for a count of seven. The Brown Bomber was battered hard and bleeding. At times he looked foolish as he tried to catch up with his elusive target. His reflexes were bad and his defense poor. All that was revealed plainly to 18,194 persons who paid $216,477 to see the battle, which was considered so one-sided when it was arranged that the odds were 1 to 10.

Referee Ruby Goldstein saw the challenger the victor, crediting Walcott with seven rounds to six with two even. Marty Monroe, one of the judges, gave the decision to Louis, nine to six, and Judge Frank Forbes called Louis the winner, eight to six and one even.

140

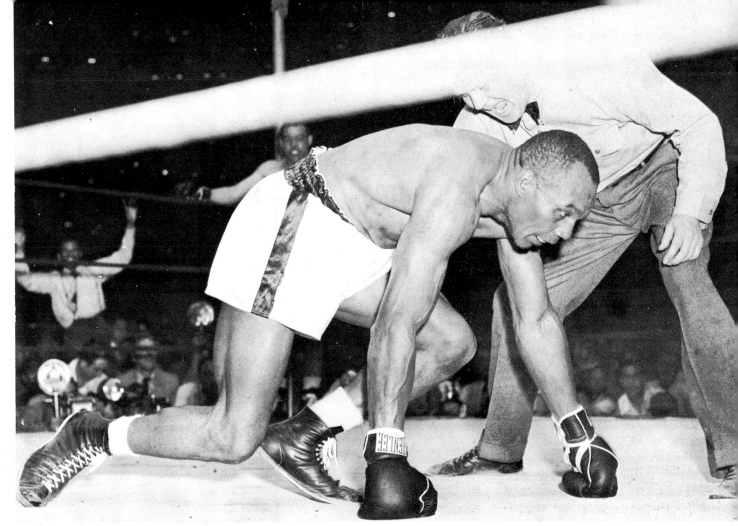

Walcott's finish in the second bout. The unpopular verdict in the first meeting resulted in a Louis-Walcott rematch on June 25, 1948, at Yankee Stadium. Dropping Louis again, Jersey Joe was ahead on points when the champion rallied in the 11th round for a knockout victory.

Left jabs and several hooks baffled Louis in the opening round and a solid, short right to the jaw dropped him. The fourth was not a minute old when Walcott crashed his right to the jaw, again toppling Louis in his tracks.

Not until the ninth round did Louis catch up with his foe. Like a maniac he went after Jersey Joe. Though the blows carried jarring force, Jersey Joe withstood them. From then on Walcott missed many roundhouse rights and kept racing madly away from Louis, only occasionally halting momentarily to toss effective jabs to the head. It was the sprinting tactics of Jersey Joe which cost him the fight.

In a return bout six months later, June 25, 1948, at the Yankee Stadium, 42,657 persons saw Louis decisively whip his tormentor by knocking Wal-cott out in the eleventh round. It was Joe's twenty-fifth and last title defense. Louis came back a long way to overcome a crafty antagonist who had baffled him for ten rounds, then crumbled to the canvas when the Bomber caught up with him.

Two minutes of the eleventh round had slipped away in a contest that had been quite tame and had drawn the boos of the crowd. Louis kept pressing, Walcott kept slipping aside, but the champion was in no mood to go through a repetition of their first encounter. Walcott was leading during the first two minutes of the round when his antagonist suddenly attacked with fury. Lefts and rights landed on Walcott's head, but he made the error of coming off the ropes to swap blows with the Bomber. Jersey Joe thought he had the fight cinched and there's where he erred.

Louis nailed him with a right after three beautiful straight lefts to head and face had numbed Walcott's brain. His legs were now rubbery. A right to the body and he dropped his guard. As he began to sag, a fast and furious barrage followed.

Louis went after the kill, backed his man against the ropes, pounded away with both fists and while Louis set himself for the knockout punch, Nature beat him to it. Walcott collapsed, rolled over on his back, struggled to his knees, and began to crawl as the eight and nine counts were recorded by Referee Frank Fullam. Jersey Joe was still down when the fatal ten was reached.

With that victory, Joe Louis made

James D. Norris *(left)* took over the boxing empire of the ailing Mike Jacobs in 1949, formed the International Boxing Club, and ushered in boxing's TV era, backed by John Reed Kilpatrick *(right)* chairman of the board of Madison Square Garden.

Former light heavyweight champion Gus Lesnevich *(left)* congratulates Charles after Ezzard knocked him out in the 7th round of their Yankee Stadium bout in 1947.

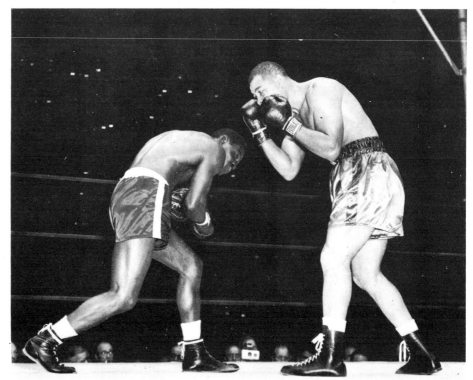

Louis *(right)* attempted a comeback on September 27, 1950, facing Charles in Yankee Stadium, but was badly beaten in his effort to regain the laurels. Charles was too young and too speedy for the faded veteran.

up his mind to quit. He went on another long exhibition tour and on March 1, 1949, he announced his retirement.

Louis requested that Ezzard Charles of Cincinnati, and Walcott, who hailed from Camden, New Jersey, fight for the right to succeed him, since they were the outstanding heavyweight contenders. In a contest in Chicago on June 22, 1949, Charles was returned the winner over his Jersey opponent in fifteen rounds.

The National Boxing Association accepted this as a world title match, but neither the European Federations nor the New York Commission acknowledged Charles as the new champion. To prove his right to the crown, he stopped Gus Lesnevich, former light heavyweight king, and Pat Valentino of California, each in eight rounds. Then he added New York to his supporters by stopping Freddie Beshore in Buffalo in fourteen rounds.

Unlike Jack Dempsey, with whom Louis has frequently been compared, the Brown Bomber had a vulnerable chin. He couldn't take it as the Manassa Mauler could. That was evidenced by the number of times Louis was dropped to the canvas.

In addition to being floored twice by Jersey Joe Walcott, he was put down by Buddy Baer, Tony Galento, and Jimmy Braddock in championship contests, and by Max Schmeling twice before, and by Rocky Marciano after returning as champion.

He grossed $4,626,721.69 during his fighting career, yet following his retirement he owed more than a million dollars in taxes to the U. S. Government due to the loss of his fortune in poor investments and high living.

Louis was not the last of the champs in a million dollar gate promotion.

Louis' friends were now clamoring for him to return to the ring and attempt to regain the throne he had abdicated. He challenged Charles. The champ accepted and further clinched his claim to world laurels. He gained universal recognition as Joe's successor when he easily outpointed the Brown Bomber in fifteen rounds at Yankee Stadium.

142

The boxing writers estimated at least a million dollars in flesh was introduced to the fight fans, when former champion Ezzard Charles *(left)* and champion Jersey Joe Walcott, flanked Joe Louis, greatest of all champions since Dempsey. They were introduced to 61,370 fans, from the Polo Grounds ring on September 12, 1951, in ceremonies just before the start of the Ray Robinson–Randy Turpin title fight.

One of the big boxing surprises in the summer of 1951 was the knockout of Ezzard Charles by Jersey Joe Walcott, in Pittsburgh. This was their third in a series of title bouts and Charles, a 1 to 6 favorite, lost his crown in the seventh round.

Knockouts of Nick Barrone in eleven rounds, Lee Oma in ten, a victory over Walcott in fifteen rounds in Detroit and one over Joey Maxim at the same distance, brought Charles into another engagement with Walcott. In that contest, staged in Pittsburgh, a new champion was crowned.

Jersey Joe surprisingly knocked out the defending title holder in the seventh round. In a return bout, Walcott, whose age at the time was officially listed at thirty-eight years, but who was reported to be close to forty-two, gained a points verdict in fifteen rounds, June 5, 1952, and three months later, September 23, the title changed hands to Rocky Marciano, the Brockton Blockbuster, who crashed a knockout blow to the chin of the champion.

Father Time caught up with Joe Walcott just as it seemed he would be acclaimed the "winner and still champion." One short, powerful right hand punch and age were sufficient to bring about his downfall. The manner in which Marciano ended the tough, brawling, furious battle in forty-three seconds of the thirteenth round was a reminder of the days

An elated Rocky Marciano lets out a whoop after seeing Referee Charles Daggert complete the count that gave the Brockton Blockbuster the championship. Daggert, with count completed, stoops to help the defeated title holder to his corner. But Jersey Joe was so helpless that his seconds and the medical advisor rushed to his aid. The kayo wallop was one of the hardest punches ever landed by Marciano.

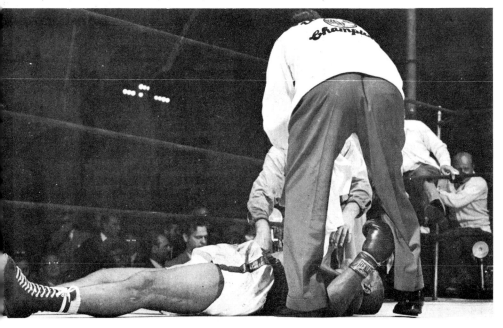

when another New Englander, John L. Sullivan, ruled the roost by virtue of his mighty fists.

At the time of the knockout, according to the official tallies of the judges, there was only one way in which Rocky could win—via the knockout route. And he did it with one solid crash.

The ending was as unexpected as was the knockout of Ezzard Charles by the man whom Marciano had dethroned. The clout struck its mark with such suddenness and swiftness that many in the vast Municipal Stadium of Philadelphia didn't see it. But what they did see was old Jersey Joe sprawled against the ropes in a grotesque position, an inert mass.

Charley Goldman (*above*), a crack bantamweight in the early days, is the alert teacher and trainer who developed Rocky's technique. He changed Marciano's awkward stance and taught him proper balance, to get the most out of his punching power. Rocky's greatest disadvantage, was his 67-inch reach, shortest of all heavyweight champions. He often had to leap at his opponents to score (*right*).

Under the impact of the punch that made him helpless, Jersey Joe's body began to sink as he was resting against the ropes, then he slid down on his left side. Walcott's left hand grabbed instinctively at the middle strand as he went down on one knee. He slumped slowly forward and he landed on his head. His face was on the canvas as Referee Charley Daggert counted him out.

The new champion, a product of the Army and amateur ranks, born on September 1, 1923, takes his place like Louis and Dempsey, among the world's top clouters, a fighter with iron fists. He was the only heavyweight who went through a career without a loss. Starting as a profes-

When Joe Louis tried a comeback in 1951, he felt confident that he could put Rocky Marciano away as he had done so often with other opponents. Rocky surprised him by landing a haymaker in the eighth round. This bout set Marciano up for a title shot.

sional in 1947, he scored forty-nine victories, forty-two by knockouts, and retired undefeated.

It was not until he fought Roland LaStarza in 1950 and gained a disputed decision that he became a headliner. He continued his rise by shunting to the sidelines mediocre talent until the mid-summer of 1951, when his knockouts of Rex Layne in six rounds and Freddie Beshore in four brought him into the championship spotlight. He continued his rise by handing Louis a terrific beating, stopping the erstwhile Bomber in the eighth round, after which Lee Savold, Gino Buonvino, Bernie Reynolds, and Harry Matthews were put out of the picture. With those triumphs he was now ready for a shot at the world crown, which he won when he defeated Walcott.

Marciano defended his title six times. In his initial defense, a return

End of the trail for the Brown Bomber. After being knocked through the ropes, Louis made an attempt to fight back his rushing opponent, but Marciano, with the stakes high, didn't let Louis get away from him. He pounced on the former champ and soon had him helpless. Referee Ruby Goldstein stopped the fight. Note Joe's look as he is attended by Dr. Nardiello.

Harry Matthews came out of the West with an idea that he could check Marciano's rise toward a title shot. But Rocky knocked him out in the second round and his next bout was with Walcott for the championship. Matthews is resting comfortably in his corner.

Marciano found Walcott a much easier victim when they met again in Chicago on May 15, 1953. With Rocky's first offensive outburst, Jersey Joe was knocked to the canvas and counted out in two minutes, 25 seconds.

(*Below*) Outboxed for six rounds, Marciano's heavy guns eventually began to reach the target and clever Roland LaStarza (*right*) was battered into defeat in 11 rounds at the Polo Grounds, New York, on September 24, 1953.

First clash (*above*) of Marciano and Charles at Yankee Stadium on June 17, 1954, was one of history's most gruelling battles for the heavyweight championship. It was a savage give-and-take brawl with Marciano's youth and stamina deciding the issue. With blood streaming out of a gash above his left eye, Rocky staged a roaring finish to edge out a close decision. (*Below*) Charles was a disappointment in a return match in the same ring three months later. He seemed too scared to fight. Although he ripped Marciano's nose early in the bout, he devoted his time mainly to skittering around the ring, trying to avoid Marciano's punches. He was finally knocked out in the eighth round

bout, he knocked out Walcott in the opening round of a disappointing fight in Chicago. Four months later in New York he disposed of Roland LaStarza in the eleventh round.

The following year he fought two thrillers with Ezzard Charles. In the first, on June 16, 1954, at the Yankee Stadium, Rocky retained the throne, gaining the decision in fifteen rounds; and in the second, on September 17, in the same arena, Ezzard was knocked out in the eighth round. Each bout was replete with action and drama. The knockout was a stunner The power behind Rocky's punches was in evidence.

Then came the international championship mill in San Francisco where he easily stopped Don Cockell, British

After causing a sensation by knocking Marciano down early in bout, light heavyweight champion Archie Moore found Rocky's youth, strength and stamina too much for him, and he collapsed in his own corner in ninth round of a furious battle in Yankee Stadium on September 21, 1955. (*Below*) Marciano heads for opposite corner as the referee, Harry Kessler, begins the final count over Moore.

The first international heavyweight title fight since Louis defeated Farr found Don Cockell, British Empire champion, an easy mark for Rocky Marciano, who stopped him in the ninth round at San Francisco (1955). The Britisher walked into a buzz saw and was battered into helplessness. A Cockell handler is seen entering the ring to save Don, but the referee halted the one-sided bout.

Empire champion, in the ninth round and followed that with his farewell fight, a contest in New York in which he stopped Archie Moore, holder of the light heavyweight crown, in the same number of rounds. With that knockout ended the brilliant career of the Brockton Blockbuster. Only one other heavyweight king retired undefeated and made it stick, Gene Tunney.

His six title defenses netted Marciano purses totaling $1,462,961. With his pre-championship income and his side income following his rise to the top, his earnings were well beyond the $2,000,000 mark.

John L. Sullivan popularized boxing in the United States; James J. Corbett set the model for scientific boxing; Jack Dempsey set the record for the million dollar gate; Gene Tunney was the first to retire undefeated and remain so; Joe Louis established an all-time record for title defenses; and Rocky Marciano is hailed as the only heavyweight king who not only won every bout in which he engaged as a professional but hung up his gloves with that clean slate and stuck to his decision.

Marciano's retirement brought about a world elimination in which Archie Moore received a bye and Floyd Patterson and Tommy (Hurricane) Jackson entered the final elimination, with Floyd winning a twelve rounder on a split decision. He then tackled Moore in the Chi-

Under manager Al Weill's (*above*) piloting, Rocky rose to the top of the heavyweight division and divided a fortune with Weill. From 1947, when he began as an unknown preliminary boy, until he retired in 1955 as champion, Marciano's ring purses grossed $1,462,291. Undefeated in his career of 49 bouts, Rocky scored 43 knockouts, while six opponents went the route. Marciano, shown with wife Barbara and daughter Mary Ann, died in an airplane crash in Newton, Iowa, August 31, 1969, the day before his 46th birthday.

Floyd Patterson, who on August 30, 1956, became the youngest world heavyweight champion, successor to the throne left vacant by Marciano, had his ups and downs as an amateur. In the Eastern Golden Gloves tourney he won a decision over Mike Zecca of the U. S. Marines in the eliminations. The next night he lay flat on his back (above) after being put to sleep in the quarter-finals by Charley Williams of Buffalo. In the picture below Patterson annexes the world title by halting Archie Moore in the fifth round.

Floyd Patterson holding bouquet awarded him when he beat Vita of Roumania to win the Olympic middleweight championship.

cago Stadium on November 30, 1956, and in a surprising upset put Moore, the favorite, away in the fifth round to become Marciano's successor.

Born in Waco, North Carolina, on January 4, 1935, the former Olympic middleweight king who won his crown at the Helsinki Games in 1952, became the youngest professional ever to gain the top rung of the ladder. He is a fast moving, clever heavyweight with a snappy punch, though his blows lack the steam of those Louis, Marciano, and Dempsey could deliver.

He made his professional start after returning from his successful trip to Helsinki. His most important bouts prior to winning from Moore were those with Joey Maxim, in which the latter won an unpopular decision—

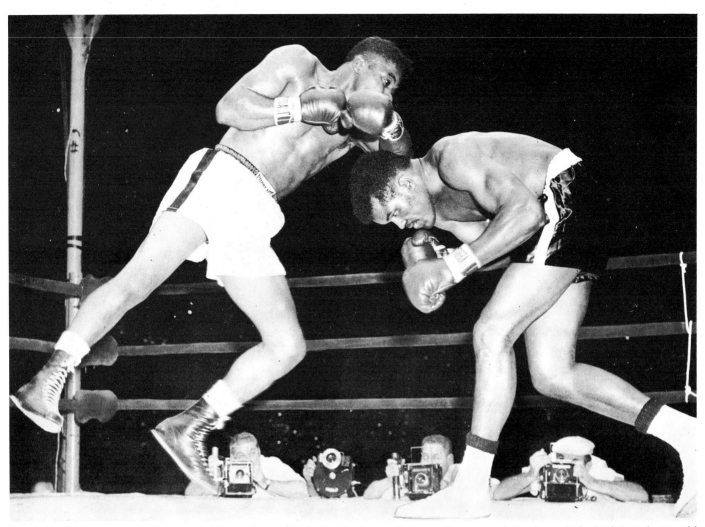

In his first title defense, Patterson *(above, left)* knocked out Hurricane Jackson. The eccentric Jackson lacked ability, but could absorb an enormous amount of punishment. Referee Ruby Goldstein stopped the bout when Jackson, dazed and helpless, was floored in the 10th round *(below)*. The New York boxing commission suspended Jackson's license to protect his future well-being.

the lone loss suffered by Patterson; his knockouts of Jimmy Slade and Willie Troy; and his twelve rounds victory over Jackson.

In the fight with Moore, the panther-like son of a Brooklyn sanitation truck driver disposed of his opponent in 2.27 of the fifth round before a roaring gathering in the Chicago Stadium.

Patterson was piling up a lead on the official score cards against a wildly-missing Moore when he crashed home a terrific left hook to the jaw. The blow had a delayed action effect on the old warrior. He started to step forward then he spun and fell on his face. Moore barely beat the count of Referee Frank Sikora.

As Archie wobbled, Patterson finished him off with another powerful left, sinking him to his haunches. Moore started to pull himself up, and just as he was getting to his feet, Sikora had completed the count.

The attendance was 14,000, with gross receipts of only $228,145—far from the figures Joe Louis' bouts registered.

On July 29, 1957, at the New York Polo Grounds, Patterson engaged in his first championship defense. He defeated Tommy (Hurricane) Jackson.

In that contest, Patterson accomplished what had been expected. The 14,458 persons who paid $156,936 to see the affair witnessed a bout in which the defending title holder was never in danger. Referee Ruby Goldstein halted it in one minute and fifty-two seconds of the tenth round after a smashing left and right to the jaw had placed Jackson at the mercy of his opponent. Many protested the referee's action, but he was justified. Jackson was dropped in the first round as the bell sounded; went down for a count of two in the second, though the knockdown timer continued to toll off six; and was floored again in the ninth for a count of four.

It was the first independently promoted heavyweight championship bout in many years, with Emil Lence, a New York dress manufacturer, in-

Peter Rademacher, Olympic heavyweight king, the first amateur to challenge for the world professional crown, dropped Floyd Patterson in the second round at Seattle but thereafter took a shellacking. Patterson retained the title by a kayo in the sixth round.

stead of the International Boxing Club, in charge. Jackson received $61,929.81 for the lacing he took, and the champion, after agreeing to cut $50,000 off his guarantee to save Lence from losing heavily on the promotion, got $123,859.62.

Jackson started off well, but as the fight progressed, he couldn't defend himself. He absorbed terrific body clouts and many to the jaw. Though floored three times, he continued to display raw courage in his attempt to go the route.

Three days following that fight, Patterson went into training again, this time to face the world amateur champion, Peter Rademacher, Olympic title holder in the latter's debut as a professional, an unheard of procedure. Boxing commissions throughout the world appealed to both Gov-

ernor Rosselini of Washington and his commission to prevent the staging of the bout, but the appeal was vetoed. The fight took place on August 22, 1957 at Seattle and the amateur title holder was knocked out. Tommy Loughran, the referee, counted off the doleful decimal. The time was two minutes and fifty-seven seconds of the sixth round. Rademacher had been sent to the canvas seven times.

The Olympic champion surprised by not only remaining in action so long following the pre-fight predictions that he would be lucky to last two rounds, but winning the opening round and decking Patterson for a count of four in the second frame. Thereafter, however, he was never in the running.

Rademacher was down for nine in the third round, four times for nine

Pete Rademacher *(above, left)* won the 1956 Olympic heavyweight title on December 4, when he clobbered Russian L. Moukhine so fiercely in the first round that the referee stopped the bout. Rademacher was the first amateur champ to fight for the professional heavyweight title in his first bout. In the fifth round of his bout with Floyd Patterson, Pete *(above, right)* heard referee Tommy Loughran toll the count of nine for the fourth time, as Patterson stood in a neutral corner.

Roy Harris, dead game but badly outclassed in his title bout with champion Floyd Patterson, gasped for air as he took the count of nine on one knee *(below)* in the 12th round. Harris returned to his corner with his face a bloody mess from cuts and his legs on the verge of buckling from Floyd's body blows. The fight ended when Roy's seconds would not let him come out for the 13th round.

in the fifth and once prior to the final count in the sixth round. Four times Referee Loughran faltered at the count of nine when he could have counted Peter out.

The history-making fight, the first time an amateur fought a professional heavyweight champion for the crown, brought out a gathering of 16,961 persons for a record Northwest gate of $243,030 and a net of $209,556. Youth Unlimited which backed Rademacher, lost close to $120,000 on the promotion. Peter received nothing for his services while Patterson, guaranteed by his backer $250,000, received that amount.

Floyd Patterson made his second title defense in Los Angeles on August 18, 1958, against Roy Harris of Cut and Shoot, Texas. After being decked in the second round, he battered the Texan into submission. Referee Mushy Callahan halted the bout when Harris' trainer, Bill Gore, told him that Roy could not come out for the twelfth. Attendance was 21,680 and the gate amounted to $234,183. Another 196,762 fans paid $763,437 to see the bout on closed-circuit TV. Harris, though game, was outclassed.

On the rainy evening of June 26, 1959, 18,215 fans at Yankee Stadium in New York watched 196-pound, 4-to-1 underdog Ingemar Johansson of Gothenburg, Sweden, win a knockout victory over 182-pound Floyd Patterson. Referee Ruby Goldstein halted the bout in 2:03 of the third round.

After two rounds of minor action, Johansson let loose a stunning right, his much vaunted "hammer of Thor,"

which sent Patterson reeling and flat on his back.

Six more times Patterson went down. When he staggered up after the seventh knockdown, Goldstein stopped the fight. By scoring seven knockdowns in one round, Johansson had equaled a heavyweight-title-fight record set by Jack Dempsey against Luis Firpo in 1923.

In terms of the live gate, the fight was a financial failure for promoter William Rosensohn, but it grossed more than $1 million in closed-circuit telecasts. This was the dawning of an age when money was to be made, not from the live audience, but from TV.

Johansson, born September 22, 1932, was lively, handsome, and gregarious, with a lust for life that he shared with his lovely fiancée, Birgit Lundgren.

A many-sided man, Johansson showed ability not only as a sportsman, but also as a singer, actor, and businessman who made a sizable fortune outside the ring.

Having won the International Golden Gloves in 1951, and eighty of his eighty-nine amateur matches, he went on to participate in the 1952 Olympic finals in Helsinki, but was disqualified for "not trying" in his fight with Ed Sanders of the United States.

From the time he turned professional until his ascension to the heavyweight throne, Johansson scored

Floyd Patterson, an easy target, rubs his nose as Johannson's left is on its way to Patterson's head. Floyd, on all fours, suffered seven knockdowns before the end.

Ingemar Johannson stands over badly battered Floyd Patterson who is trying to regain feet as referee Ruby Goldstein rushes in. Johannson's victory was a stunning upset.

Floyd Patterson became the first man in ring history to regain the heavyweight title when he knocked out Ingemar Johansson in the fifth round of their return match. Arthur Mercante counts the Swede out. Floyd, humiliated in their first bout, was never better.

Referee Bill Regan signals that it's all over for Ingemar in the rubber match with Floyd at Miami Beach in 1961. Not too much was heard from Johansson after this knockout.

twenty-two straight victories, fourteen by kayos. Included in the string was the defeat of Franco Cavicchi, of Italy, in 1956, for the European heavyweight title.

When he fought Patterson the second time, at New York's Polo Grounds, on June 22, 1960, Johansson faced a man who was looking, not for revenge, but rather for personal redemption from the humiliation he had suffered in losing his title. A bigger, stronger, and restyled Patterson knocked out Johansson in 1:51 of the fifth round.

From the beginning, Patterson, weighing 190 pounds, was the aggressor, keeping the 194-pound defending champion off balance with left jabs and two-handed flurries. By the fourth round Johansson was standing off balance, with his feet wide apart, but he kept boxing himself out of serious trouble.

Forty-nine seconds into the fifth round Patterson landed a blazing left hook to the jaw that sent Johansson down for a count of nine. On his feet again, Johansson tried to keep going, but a barrage of lefts and rights and a final left hook caught Johansson's chin and knocked him cold.

A crowd of 31,892 who paid $824,-814 and a closed-circuit-TV audience of 500,000 who paid $2 million were witnesses while Patterson, by reclaiming the heavyweight crown, accomplished what other heavyweight champions had attempted and failed to do. *The Ring Boxing Encyclopedia* lists unsuccessful attempts by James J. Corbett, Bob Fitzsimmons, James J. Jeffries, Jack Dempsey, Max Schmeling, Joe Louis, Ezzard Charles, Jersey Joe Walcott, Ingemar Johansson, Sonny Liston.

A third Patterson-Johansson bout took place in Miami Beach on March 13, 1961. Patterson and Johansson were the heaviest in their careers at $194\frac{3}{4}$ and $206\frac{1}{2}$ respectively.

Patterson retained his title by knocking out Johansson in 2:25 of the sixth round with a sharp left, then an overhand chopping right that struck Johansson high on the side of his head. Johansson started to get to his feet, then pitched forward. He got up a split second after referee Bill Regan reached the count of ten. Films confirmed the referee's decision.

The fight was clumsily sporadic. What the crowd of 13,984 spectators saw was the bloody pounding of two fighters out to annihilate each other.

The scorecards of referee Bill Regan and judges Carl Gardner and Gus Jacobson all showed Patterson ahead in four of the five rounds before the knockout.

Johansson's boxing career wasn't quite over. He won back the European heavyweight title on June 17, 1962, by knocking out Dick Richardson. Then he retired in mid-1963 to devote his full time to business.

Patterson's last successful defense of his crown was against the strong, game, but woefully inexperienced Tom McNeeley, December 4, 1961, at Toronto. A crowd of 7,813 watched McNeeley hit the canvas ten times. A left to the jaw ended the fiasco in round four.

After two years of waiting in the number-one contender's spot, Charles (Sonny) Liston got his chance against Patterson September 25, 1962, in Chicago. At 212, he outweighed Patterson by 25 pounds and outreached him thirteen inches.

Sonny was in control from the beginning, pounding both hands to Patterson's body and jabbing accurately. The end came when the second of two powerful lefts decked Patterson in 2:06 of the first round. The 18,894 fans were stunned at the speed with which the bout ended. Liston had the honor of landing the third-fastest knockout in heavyweight history. The fastest was 1:28 credited to Tommy Burns in his match with Bill Squires, while Joe Louis scored the second-fastest when he dispatched Max Schmeling in 2:04 in their return bout.

Liston was born May 8, 1932, on a marginal farm in Arkansas, to a field hand. He was probably the most disliked heavyweight the United States had spawned since Jack Johnson won the title in 1919 and had the newspapers calling for a "white hope."

Reputedly one of twenty-five children, Liston ran away to St. Louis, where at the age of thirteen he joined a bad crowd that, in his words was "just always lookin' for trouble." After serving time in prison, he became associated with unsavory underworld characters. His 6-foot-1½-inch height, 220-pound weight, 17½-inch neck, 14-inch fists, an often sullen expression, and his checkered past all contributed to his being cast in the role of bad guy.

When Liston was eighteen, the Missouri penitentiary athletic director, Father Alous Stevens, encouraged Liston to take up boxing. Five years later, in 1953, he won the Golden Gloves. He turned pro shortly afterward.

On the way up, Liston fought thirty-four fights, knocking out twenty-three opponents and losing only to Marty Marshall in an eight-round decision in 1954.

Patterson was given a rematch on July 22, 1963, at Convention Hall in Las Vegas, with the odds 5 to 1 against him. Again Liston outweighed his opponent 215½ to 194½, and again Patterson could do little to retaliate for the torrent of powerful blows Liston delivered. Counted out in 2:10 of the first round by referee Harry Krause, Patterson had landed only one substantial punch, a hard right to the jaw following his own first knockdown. Patterson was decked once more before the knockout, preceded by a flurry of rights and lefts to his head. Liston's left hook and crushing right to the ribs set Patterson up for a right and left that crumpled the ex-champ.

Charles (Sonny) Liston waited a long time for his shot at the title but it was well worth it as he dispatched Patterson in the first round at Chicago in 1962 (above), then repeated the act in Las Vegas the following June (below). The "Ugly Bear" as he was referred to by Cassius Clay, was thought to be practically invincible by most experts.

ALI, MASTER SHOWMAN

When loquacious Cassius Clay signed for a match with Liston, only three of the forty-six "experts" polled failed to pick Liston to be an easy winner over the "Louisville Lip," or "Mighty Mouth, as Clay was dubbed. His bravado made people overlook the fact that the Louisville, Kentucky, youth had fought his way up, starting boxing at the age of twelve. When he won the light-heavyweight championship at the 1960 Olympics in Rome, eighteen-year-old Clay had won 108 amateur bouts, including 6 Kentucky Golden Gloves titles and the 1969 International Golden Gloves heavyweight crown, while losing only 8 fights.

After Clay returned to Louisville, a syndicate of businessmen managed his pro career, and Angelo Dundee managed his training. Clay's gibes, poems, predictions, and antics mounted along with his pro victories, which numbered twenty by the time he entered the ring against Liston.

Clay had a genius for getting attention, and mass media made instant copy of his clowning and physical appeal. Color and excitement, which had been missing in boxing since the time of Jack Dempsey, returned.

Surprisingly, the Clay-Liston bout, on February 25, 1964, in Miami, was a financial fiasco for promoter Bill MacDonald, with a turnout of only 8,297. Even more surprisingly, Clay won the fight when Liston failed to answer the bell for the seventh round.

Clay charged out in the first round and failed to land any telling blows, although he demonstrated his speed in delivering quick jabs to Liston's head while dancing and moving away from Liston's vaunted left hook. Early in the third round, Clay opened a nasty gash under Liston's left eye, but the champion retaliated well enough in that round and the following one to keep the score fairly even.

The fifth round brought a dramatic turn as Clay stopped punching and kept moving away from Liston, claiming he couldn't see because of some foreign substance on Liston's gloves.

Clay balked at coming out for the sixth round because of blurred vision, but with the prodding of his second, Angelo Dundee, Clay answered the bell, recovered his vision, and fought a furious round that tired Liston badly.

As the seventh round was about to get underway, referee Barney Felix announced that Liston refused to continue, owing to eye cuts and an injury to his left shoulder. When the fight was stopped, the officials, Felix, and judges Bill Lovitt, and Gus Jacobsen, had scored the bout a draw.

Cassius Marcellus Clay, son of a sign painter, was born January 17, 1942, in Louisville, Kentucky. He decided early in life that he wanted to be both rich and heavyweight champion of the world.

At the age of twenty-one, Clay had obtained half of his dream, the heavyweight crown, as well as a new religion, Islamism, and a new name, Muhammad Ali. Shortly after his bout with Liston, Ali entered into the first round of what was to be a long-drawn-out battle with the United States armed forces after flunking two intelligence tests for the draft and being classified 1Y.

No title fight in any class ever stirred up so many questions, charges, suspicions, or angry reverberations as did Ali's 1:42 knockout of Liston in Lewiston, Maine, on May 25, 1965.

Ali leaped out of his corner and

While Liston is being checked at the weigh-in for their bout in Miami Beach in 1964, Clay (rear) heckled the proceedings and continuously shouted at the champion.

Cassius Clay, later to become Muhammad Ali, becomes the new champion as referee Barney Felix declares the bout ended with Liston sitting on his stool claiming an injury.

Clay seemingly taunts Liston as the latter sprawls on the canvas in the first round of a return match at Lewiston, Maine. In a most confusing ending, Liston was finally declared to have been stopped at 1:42, though referee Jersey Joe Walcott did not halt it until 2:12 upon hearing shouts from *Ring* editor Nat Fleischer that Liston was out.

immediately connected with a right and a left to Liston's head. Suddenly he landed a corkscrew right to the left side of the head, and Liston sagged to his knees, then rolled over onto his back. Liston struggled to get up but again fell on his back. Ali danced over to the fallen man, calling him names and telling him to get up and fight, ignoring the exhortations of referee Jersey Joe Walcott to go to a neutral corner.

The rules say that there can be no legal count over a fallen boxer, so long as the standing fighter refuses to go to a neutral corner; nevertheless, knockdown timekeeper Frank McDonough started counting when Liston hit the canvas. He eventually got as far as twenty-two before Liston lurched to his feet. Both fighters began to throw punches, and then referee Jersey Joe Walcott heard Nat Fleischer shout, "Joe, the fight is over!" Although Ali had not gone to a neutral corner, Walcott accepted the timekeeper's count, separated the men, and declared Ali the winner.

Aside from the controversial issue of whether the knockdown timekeeper

calling a fight, experts argued whether the knockdown blow had really been hard enough to knock down the massive Liston. When films of the fight were examined, with watches synchronized to TV film frames, the velocity of Ali's punch remained unresolved. All that was proved was that Liston had hit the mat in 1:42 and that the referee had stopped the bout at 2:12.

Although Liston continued to fight, he was never again considered a major contender. Five years later, on January 5, 1971, his wife found him

Another view of the knockdown of Liston in the controversial Lewiston match; Clay is already signalling a knockout victory.

Former champ Patterson takes a mandatory eight-count in the 6th round against Clay, who administered a frightful beating.

dead in his Las Vegas home. The circumstances surrounding his death remained mysterious, even sinister— a balloon of heroin was discovered in his kitchen at the time he was found.

On November 22, 1965, Patterson stepped into the ring with Ali in Las Vegas, hoping to win back the heavyweight title for a third time. Instead, the ex-champion received a merciless beating from a younger, taller, heavier, and sharper opponent. Ali, at 210 pounds, bewildered the 194-pound contender with left jabs and jolting rights to the body. The one-sided affair was halted at 2:18 of the twelfth round by referee Harry Krause.

Although 1966 was a successful year for Ali pugilistically, it opened by taking an emotional toll. Since becoming a Muslim he had become increasingly involved in his adopted religion. In January he divorced his wife, the former Sonji Roi, a model, because, he said, "she would not abide by the Muslim standards" by giving up her flashy dressing and makeup.

Then, in February, a reporter showed up at Ali's home to tell him that his local draft board had reclassified him 1A and that he could expect to be called up shortly. With what turned out to be unfortunate timing, the media picked up Ali's "I got no quarrel with them Vietcong," and a brushfire of "patriotic" reaction raced across the country, causing the cancellation of a proposed fight with Ernie Terrell.

Public sentiment drove Ali out of the country to seek matches on foreign soil for almost a year while he waited for a decision on his appeal for draft deferment as a conscientious objector and then as a Muslim minister.

Prior to his bout with Henry Cooper in London, Ali fought unpolished but lion-hearted George Chuvalo in Toronto on March 29, 1966. Chuvalo managed to stand up for the full fifteen rounds but the game Canadian took a terrible beating.

England welcomed Ali with open

George Chuvalo, the hard rock from Canada, went 15 rounds with Clay in 1966. He was never knocked down in his career.

162

arms since he offered Britain the possibility of regaining the heavyweight title lost back in 1898 by Bob Fitzsimmons. Accordingly, a sellout crowd paid $450,000 to watch 188-pound Cooper try to flatten 201¼-pound Ali with his powerful left hook. In June 1963, the Englishman had come close when he knocked Ali off his feet at the end of the fourth round, the bell just barely rescuing Ali. However, Cooper was stopped in round five when facial cuts made it too dangerous for him to continue.

On May 21, 1966, Cooper got a second chance, but his hope was quenched suddenly in the sixth round when Ali landed two swift punches to the head, opening up a deep, jagged wound over Cooper's left eye and sending cascades of blood down his face. Referee George Smith halted the fight.

Three months later, badly outclassed Brian London, at 200½ pounds, landed only two punches of minimal potency before Ali hit him with a right to the jaw in the third round, sending London down on his face. At the count of seven he raised himself partially, looked at referee Harry Gibbs, and went down again to be counted out as 11,000 fans booed their countryman.

Ali defended his title for the fourth time in five months when he met the 194½-pound champion of Europe, Karl Mildenberger, on September 10, 1966, in Frankfurt, Germany, before an audience of 45,000.

Ali toyed with the German until late in the fourth round, when the champion became angered after Mildenberger landed two jolting lefts to the liver and launched a two-fisted attack that drove Ali across the ring. Ali recovered and delivered a left-right combination that opened a gash over Mildenberger's right eye.

From the sixth round on, Ali battered Mildenberger, then stepped back occasionally to survey his handiwork.

Englishman Henry Cooper, who had put Clay on the deck in their first meeting in 1963, became a bloody mess during their second bout in 1966, stopped in the 5th round.

Another Englishman, lantern-jawed Brian London, soon became Clay's next victim, going out in three rounds. In an earlier title bout against Patterson, London was also stopped.

In what turned out to be one of the tougher fights of his career, Clay, by now known as Muhammad Ali, finally halted German southpaw Karl Mildenberger in the 12th round.

Tired and bloody, Mildenberger managed to come out for the twelfth round. After Ali backed the German into the ropes and belted him with a flurry of lefts and rights, referee Teddy Waltham stopped the bout.

"The Big Cat," Cleveland Williams, received a similar beating from Ali on November 14 that year, in Houston, Texas. Ali decked the 210½-pound challenger three times in the second round and once in the third before referee Harry Kessler stopped the fight.

Three months later, Ernie Terrell, weighing 212½, suffered the slow punishment and humiliation Ali had promised him for refusing to acknowledge the champion's adopted Muslim name. The fight went the full fifteen rounds, but Ali's superiority was obvious, and referee Kessler and judges Jimmy Webb and Ernie Taylor unanimously awarded thirteen rounds to the champion.

New York's Madison Square Garden drew a gate of $244,471 on March 22, 1967, as 13,780 fans watched thirty-four-year-old Zora Foley succumb to an extremely fast Ali in the seventh round.

Ali gave the first three rounds to his opponent as he danced around the ring. At the opening of the fourth round, chief second Angelo Dundee told Ali to "get going," at which point Ali showed what a breathtaking fighter he really was. Every punch he delivered was sharp and on target.

At the start of the seventh round, Ali maneuvered Foley into position. A short downward right, similar to the "phantom" punch that had decked Liston at Lewiston, downed Foley, and the fight was over.

While Ali was busy piling up victories, the U.S. government was reviewing and turning down Ali's request for a ministerial deferment.

On April 28, 1967, Ali was ordered to report to the Houston induction

In what was to be his final bout as champion before being stripped of his title by various boxing bodies, Clay administered the quietus to Zora Folley, counted out in 7th.

Many thought Cleveland Williams, the Big Cat, would give Clay a tough battle, but Cassius took care of him in three rounds, knocking down the challenger four times.

6'-6" Ernie Terrell, his left eye bandaged due to what he claimed was thumb-gouging by Clay, went 15 rounds with the champ in a one-sided bout, Clay winning 13 rounds.

center. He reported but refused induction. On May 9, a federal grand jury indicted him on the charge of failing to submit to the draft. Within a few hours both the New York Boxing Commission and the World Boxing Association stripped Ali of his title and banned him from fighting anywhere in the United States.

Ali was tried on June 19 and 20 in the United States District Court for the Southern District of Texas, in Houston, presided over by Judge Joe Ingraham. With the judge's emphatic statement that the court was to consider only whether Ali had refused induction, not the fairness of the 1A classification or Ali's status as a Muslim, there was little surprise at the guilty verdict. What caused surprise was the maximum penalty of a five-year sentence and a $10,000 fine. Ali was released on bail, and his lawyer, Hayden C. Covington, of New York, filed an appeal. Meanwhile, Covington had also initiated a civil case questioning the legitimacy of the Louisville, Kentucky, and Houston draft boards because there were no blacks on either board.

Shortly thereafter, the Fifth Circuit Court of Appeals in New Orleans upheld the district court's verdict of guilty, and a further appeal was filed with the U.S. Supreme Court. On August 3 Judge Ingraham refused Ali's request for permission to travel to foreign countries to honor fight contracts. Ali was ordered to turn in his passport.

One bright light appeared for Ali. On August 17, he married seventeen-year-old Muslim Belinda Boyd.

While the case was pending in Supreme Court, the federal government disclosed that five telephone conversations involving Ali had been tapped by the F.B.I. The Supreme Court ordered the district court to reconsider the case, and on July 24, 1969, Judge Ingraham ruled that all five conversations were irrelevant to

Ali, his title taken away, was soon found guilty of refusing to be inducted. In photo above, Ali leaving court with attorney Hayden Covington (*center*) and Lt. Col. Edwin McKee, commanding officer at U.S. Army induction center. *Below*, Ali, holding pack of records, is interviewed at Houston Army center.

Obtaining a license in Georgia to return to ring action, Clay (*left*) stopped Jerry Quarry in three in Atlanta.

the conviction.

A year elapsed before the Fifth District Court of Appeals upheld the lower court's decision. During that time Ali had held a press conference —on February 3, 1970—to say emphatically that he would not enter the ring as a professional. He called Nat Loubet, editor of *Ring*, to inform him that he had quit boxing. At this time *The Ring* magazine acknowledged the vacancy the New York and World boxing associations had declared two years earlier.

Two years after Ali's match with Foley, he managed to get a license in Georgia to fight an eight-round exhibition against three minor heavyweights in September, and then to fight Jerry Quarry, whom he kayoed in three, on October 25 at Atlanta, Georgia.

A breakthrough occurred when Federal Court Judge Walter E. Mansfield nullified the New York Commission's refusal to give Ali a license, calling it "arbitrary and unreasonable action." Despite his insistence that he

Returning to a New York ring for the first time since stopping Folley, Ali scored a KO in the 15th round over Argentina's Oscar (Ringo) Bonavena, who was a tough hombre.

George Chuvalo's face was pounded into a bloody pulp by the up-and-coming Joe Frazier, 1964 Olympic gold medal winner, in July 1967, as Joe marched onward.

was through with professional boxing and no longer the title holder, on December 7, 1970, Ali met and kayoed Oscar Bonavena of Argentina in the fifteenth round in New York.

Finally, on June 28, 1971, the Supreme Court handed down its long-awaited ruling. The decision was eight to nothing in Ali's favor, with Justice Thurgood Marshall abstaining. Ali was back in the boxing game.

Nothing caused so great a muddle around the heavyweight title as had Ali's draft case. The W.B.A. had taken the title from him, and now it had to find a replacement. Three months later it sanctioned the organization of an eight-man elimination tourney headed by Mike Malitz's Sports Action, Inc., a New York-based firm, to determine who would take over Ali's "vacated" title.

The intent of the tourney was somewhat thwarted when officials of New York's Madison Square Garden arranged a bout between George Chuvalo, of Canada, and Joe Frazier, of Philadelphia, for July 19, 1967. Frazier knocked out Chuvalo in the fourth round, then refused to join the elimination group. The group consisted of Frazier, Thad Spencer, Ernie Terrell, Oscar Bonavena, Karl Mildenberger, Jimmy Ellis, Floyd Patterson, and Jerry Quarry.

In retaliation, the W.B.A. dropped Frazier from number one to number nine in its ratings, to enable Leotis Martin to get into the number-eight spot as Frazier's substitute.

The New York Boxing Commission further complicated matters by declaring that the winner of the W.B.A. tourney would not be recognized unless that champion defeated Frazier.

The round-robin began on August 5, 1967, with Spencer pitted against Terrell, and Ellis against Martin, in Houston, Texas. Spencer, from Portland, Oregon, won a twelve-round decision over Terrell, of Atlantic City, New Jersey. On the same day and in the same arena, Ellis, from Louisville, kayoed the Philadelphian, Martin, in the ninth.

In Frankfurt, Germany, Bonavena beat Mildenberger in twelve rounds on September 16, 1967.

The final match in the first round was fought between Patterson and Quarry on October 28 in Quarry's home state, California. Quarry won a split decision in which referee Vern Bybee voted a draw while judges Lee Grossman and Joey Lomas gave the fight to Quarry.

Now Mexico and Britain entered the picture. Mexico's governing body for boxing tried but failed to get Manuel Ramos placed in the W.B.A. listings. Ramos had stopped Terrell on October 14. Likewise, the British couldn't get Eduardo Corletti, victor over Johnny Prescott on October 17, into the tourney.

In the final round, on December 2, 1967, Ellis and Bonavena met in Louisville, Kentucky, where Ellis decked Bonavena twice and went on to win a unanimous decision in twelve rounds.

In Oakland, California, Quarry stopped 6-foot, 4-inch Spencer in the second semifinal, three seconds before the bell ended the twelve-round fight on February 3, 1968.

The final bout of the tournament took place on April 27, 1968, in Oak-

In a W.B.A.-staged tournament for the vacant crown held in 1967, Thad Spencer (*above, left*) easily defeated Ernie Terrell (*on floor*) at Houston. A bit later on, Floyd Patterson (*on canvas, above right*) dropped a split decision to Jerry Quarry in 12 rounds.

Quarry (*below, left*) gained the tournament final by halting Spencer in the 12th round at Oakland in early 1968. (*Below, right*), Jimmy Ellis, who was to go on to the final, disposes of Leotis Martin via a nine-round stoppage at Houston's Astrodome.

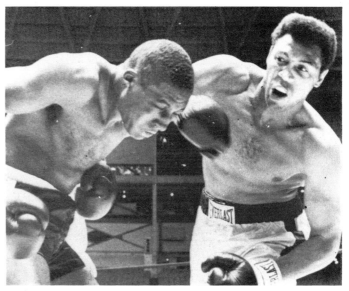

Quarry and Ellis met in the final of the W.B.A. tourney at Oakland. Jimmy (*above*, *right*) was given a split nod and lifted by handlers (*below*) after being awarded the partial title.

Joe Frazier's face is contorted after absorbing a blow from Oscar Bonavena during their first meeting in 1966. This was the first of Frazier's big wins on the road to the title.

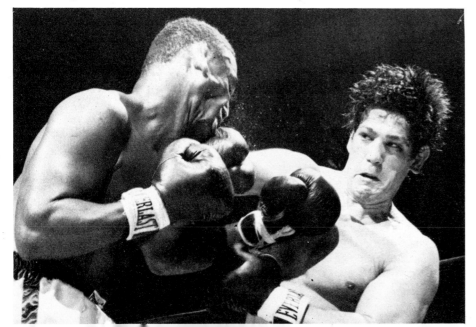

land, where the 197-pound Ellis won over the 195-pound Quarry in a fifteen-round split decision. The referee, Elmer Costa, and judge Fred Apostoli, the former middleweight champ, awarded the fight to Ellis, while judge Rudy Ortega scored the match a draw. The 11,356 fans brought a gate of $186,700.

Ellis was the W.B.A. champion, but the New York Boxing Commission announced that it would recognize the winner of the Joe Frazier–Buster Mathis bout as the new champion. Five state commissions, as well as those of Mexico and South America, followed New York's decision. Thus, when Frazier stopped Mathis in the eleventh round, New York, Maine, Pennsylvania, Texas, Massachusetts, and Illinois recognized Frazier as the champion while the others recognized Ellis.

The opposing powers were reconciled when Frazier stopped Ellis in the fifth round on February 16, 1970, at New York. The title, stripped from Ali, had finally been filled.

Joe Frazier, born in Laurel Bay, South Carolina, on January 12, 1944, was the youngest of thirteen children. He started his fistic career at age nine, when he rigged up a homemade punching bag of moss and leaves.

Twelve years later, after having married at sixteen, he moved to Philadelphia, where he won the Golden Gloves in 1962, 1963, and 1964 and won America's only gold medal in boxing at the Tokyo Olympics.

With a group of businessmen from Philadelphia, Cloverlay, Inc., as his sponsor, Frazier launched his professional career on August 16, 1965, with a one-round knockout over Woody Goss. He piled up ten straight kayos before meeting Oscar Bonavena on September 21, 1966.

Bonavena floored Frazier twice in the second round, but Frazier rallied to win a ten-round decision. After four more victories, three of which were kayos, Frazier was pitted against George Chuvalo on July 19, 1967. In the fourth round, the tough Canadian was knocked out for the first time in his fifteen-year career.

When Frazier fought Buster Mathis on March 4, 1968, he was determined to clear any hint of tarnish from his Olympic medal. (Before Frazier went to Tokyo, he had won thirty-eight of forty fights. His two losses had been to Mathis in the Olympic trials. When Mathis had broken a knuckle, Frazier had substituted.)

"Smokin' Joe" flattened Mathis with a left hook in 2:33 of the eleventh round.

Frazier became undisputed world champion on February 16, 1970, when the gong rang for the opening of the fifth round and the W.B.A.'s champion, Jimmy Ellis, couldn't come out.

After the first round, in which Ellis held a margin, Frazier dominated the match with a steady and relentless style of strong, heavy pressure. As the end of the fourth round approached, Frazier bombarded Ellis's body and head until the Kentuckian sank to the mat for a count of nine,

Frazier won recognition as champion in six states after halting hulking Buster Mathis on the opening card at the newly-built Madison Square Garden in March of 1968.

Frazier eyes Ellis after flooring him in the fourth round of their contest to determine an undisputed titleholder in February, 1970. Ellis was unable to answer fifth-round bell.

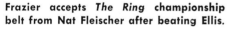

Frazier accepts *The Ring* championship belt from Nat Fleischer after beating Ellis.

In the most electrifying moment of their so-called "Fight of the Century" in 1971, Frazier sends Ali to the canvas in 15th round.

during which the bell rang. Raising himself at nine, Ellis managed to get to his corner. When the fifth-round gong sounded, manager Angelo Dundee motioned to referee Tony Perez that Ellis could not continue.

The first of three encounters with Ali took place on March 8, 1971, at Madison Square Garden before 20,445 fans plus 1.3 million watching closed-circuit theater TV. Ali, who described his own fighting style as "Float like a butterfly, sting like a bee," was slowed down by Frazier's constant pounding.

Ali's strategy was to let Frazier become arm weary while flicking tiring jabs at his opponent, but despite a 6½-inch disadvantage in reach, Frazier managed to get in under Ali's jab to land countless left hooks to the Muslim's body.

Frazier suffered a swollen jaw and lumps around both eyes, while Ali merely sported a hematoma on the

It happend in Chicago, but not as a result of the famous fire. Fans wrecked the Coliseum when closed-circuit showing of Ali-Frazier was cancelled due to projector failure.

170

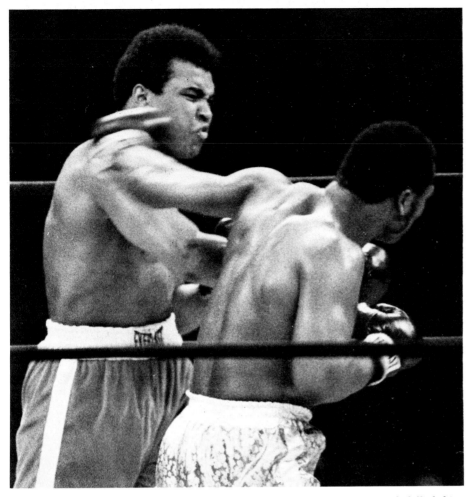

Good shot of famed Frazier left hook as it landed on Ali's jaw and felled him.

The ubiquitous Ali upstages television sports personality Howard Cosell, who has interviewed Muhammad on numerous occasions, sometimes with rather bizarre but entertaining results.

right side of his jaw. Frazier won unanimously, with referee Arthur Mercante giving him eight rounds, six to Ali, with one even. Judge Artie Aidala awarded nine to Frazier and six to Ali, and judge Bill Recht awarded eleven to Frazier and four to Ali.

The only knockdown occurred in the fifteenth round, when Ali was dropped for the third time in his career but bounced back after the mandatory eight count.

Before facing George Foreman, Frazier fought Terry Daniels in New Orleans on January 15, 1972, then Ron Stander, in Omaha, on May 25, 1972. The odds against his two opponents were 15 to 1 and 20 to 1 respectively. Daniels lasted four rounds; Stander, five.

On January 22, 1973, at Kingston, Jamaica, Frazier, a 3-1 favorite, was

Manager Yank Durham raises Frazier's arm in victory after decision over Ali was announced. It was unquestionably the high point of Joe's professional fistic career.

floored six times by Foreman before referee Arthur Mercante stopped the action at 1:35 of the second round before 36,000 fans.

Frazier pressed the attack, but was met by a challenger who moved not a step backward. A right to the jaw by Foreman achieved the first knockdown midway into the first round. Frazier got up, exchanged a few punches, and was down again from a series of rights to the head.

Again Frazier rose quickly, but obviously dazed, and was decked a third time as the bell ended the round. As set down by the rules, counting did not end with the bell, but was continued until Frazier struggled up at the count of three.

Frazier opened round two with a rushing attack and a left hook to the head, but it was a short rally. Foreman, who weighed 217 to Frazier's 214, sent the champion to the mat for the fourth time with a left-right to the jaw. Up at the count of two, Frazier was dropped by two left hooks. Again Frazier struggled up but then went down for the last time from a series of punches.

Frazier gamely got to his feet, but referee Arthur Mercante looked at his glazed eyes and reeling figure and signaled that there was a new champion.

Foreman had come a long way since his first bout January 26, 1967, in the Parks Diamond Belt Tournament, which was fought during the period in which he was being trained by the Job Corps.

"Doc" Broadus, Parks Job Corps Center vocational-guidance director, noticed Foreman's size and speed playing football and persuaded him to try his hand at boxing.

Born in Marshall, Texas, January 22, 1948, to a railroad construction worker, Foreman, fifth of seven children, spent most of his early youth in trouble. In his words, "You name it, I'd done it." He credits the Job Corps,

In a shocking development Frazier, the 1964 Olympic hero, was floored six times by the 1968 Olympic champion, George Foreman, in two rounds, being virtually demolished.

Referee Arthur Mercante signals the end of the bout as manager Dick Sadler and handlers rush to congratulate Foreman, the new titleholder. Pilot Yank Durham assists Frazier.

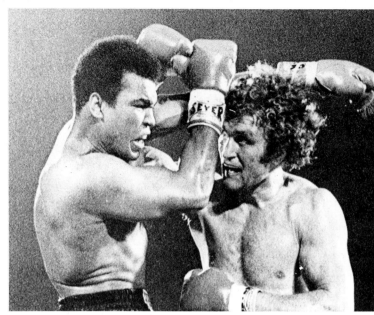

Muhammad Ali suffered a broken jaw during a 12-round loss to Ken Norton in March, 1973. He avenged it in a return 12-rounder.

Before taking on Norton, Ali fought Joe Bugner, an Englishman born in Hungary. Muhammad outpointed the European in 12.

which he joined in 1965, with his complete turnabout in attitude and direction.

In 1967, he terminated his training in the Job Corps after winning the National A.A.U. heavyweight title in Toledo, Ohio. This assured him a spot on the ten-man Olympic team to compete in Mexico.

While Foreman was deciding whom to take on as his first challenger, former champions Ali and Frazier

worked toward what they hoped would be comebacks.

Ali had fought thirteen times since losing to Frazier. These included six kayos, one a broken-jaw loss to Ken Norton, whom he beat in a rematch, and six wins, including a decision over the European heavyweight champion Joe Bugner in a twelve-round bout on February 14, 1973, in Las Vegas, Nevada.

Frazier also beat Bugner in twelve

rounds on July 2, 1973, in London.

On January 28, 1974, "Smokin' Joe," at 209 pounds, and Ali, at 212, faced each other in Madison Square Garden before a crowd of 20,746, who paid a live gate of $1,053,688, and a theater-TV audience that paid $25,-000,000. The closed-circuit TV audience reached 1,100,000 with a gross gate of $10,000,000. The gross revenue for the fight, including foreign film rights, etc., came to $25,000,000.

Joe Frazier (*left*) and Muhammad Ali connect with punches at the same time. The impetus of winning a close decision over Frazier led to Ali's bout with Foreman.

If Foreman didn't have a reputation as a man-killer previously, he got it after knocking out Ken Norton at Caracas.

George Foreman *(above, left)* displays the cut eye, heard about around the world, suffered by him during training for his bout with Muhammad Ali. Foreman and pilot Dick Sadler *(above, right)* acknowledge applause at Kinshasa's soccer stadium.

As in their previous bout, Frazier bore in while Ali sidestepped and countered. Frazier scored decisively and often to the body. Ali hit only to Joe's head, but more often and with more power than previously.

The most controversial moment of the fight occurred in the second round when referee Tony Perez stopped the fight for twenty seconds, thinking he had heard the bell ring. It was a crucial time. Frazier had Ali in a corner, but Ali spun and jabbed out of trouble and hit Frazier solidly on his puffing cheekbone. After taking a long left hook to the chin, Ali came back to confuse and hurt Frazier with lefts and chopping rights to the head. It was at this point that the referee stepped in, stalling the only opportunity Ali had to finish his man.

The seventh was Frazier's big round. The first of several good left hooks connected thirty seconds into the round, stunning Ali.

Ali was off his toes, flatfooted, as Frazier again carried the action in the eighth. Although Ali was tired, he rallied to outpunch Frazier for the last nine minutes and was awarded a unanimous decision for the twelve rounds by referee Tony Perez and judges Tony Castellano and Jack Gordon.

Foreman's first title defense was in Tokyo on September 1, 1973, against the Puerto Rican heavyweight champion, "King" José Roman. The fight was over in two minutes of the first round. The powerful champion, at 219½ pounds, smashed the inept Roman to the canvas three times with devastating right-hand blows.

Foreman's second title defense on March 26, 1974 in Caracas, Venezuela ended in two minutes of the second round when he jolted Ken Norton to the canvas. His 212¾-pound challenger barely beat the count but his trainer, Bill Slayton, jumped into the ring and referee Johnny Rondeau halted the fight which drew 9,000 fans into the Poleidro arena.

Muhammad Ali, on October 29, 1974,* became the second man in boxing history to win the world heavyweight title twice. He accomplished this with a knockout over George Foreman in 2:58 of the eighth round when a left hook, a right to the jaw, and another left hook deposited the champion on the canvas, where he was counted out by referee Zack Clayton.

The only other heavyweight to achieve this feat was Floyd Patterson, who rewon his championship in 1960 by knocking out Ingemar Johannson, who had taken the prize from him the previous year.

Approximately 62,000 fans witnessed Ali's upset victory over Foreman in the 20th of May Stadium in Kinshasa, Zaïre. Foreman, going into the fight as a 3-to-1 favorite, fought according to plan, the only way he knows how to fight, a crowding, pushing, two-fisted flailing attack. From the opening bell up to the ending in the eighth round George had Ali against the ropes while he banged

* October 30, 1974, in Kinshasa, due to International Date Line.

away at Ali's rib cage in an attempt to blast his challenger out of contention.

Foreman looked formidable in the early rounds as he appeared to be overpowering Ali with jolting body blows. George's attempt to land to Ali's head was less successful as Ali used the ropes to advantage, sliding and moving just enough to avoid being seriously damaged.

In the third round, Ali began to use his left and several combinations to Foreman's head, spearing the oncoming champion. By the fifth round it became obvious to those at ringside that Ali was fighting a different type of fight than had been expected. He did not dance around the ring and exhibit the butterfly approach of speed and stinging. Rather, he fought Foreman from a flatfooted stance and used his speed to counterpunch and cover up, avoiding the all-out blitz so characteristic of the champion's mode of attack.

Despite Foreman's statement to the writer in his dressing room after the fight was over that he was never tired during the fight and had never felt as secure as he did during the bout, it was obvious to all at ringside that Foreman was kayoed as much from exhaustion as from Ali's blows.

Foreman's punching power lessened from the fifth round on, and the tide of battle moved from Foreman's high tide, receding to an ebb as his strength failed and Ali began to land the better punches.

The surprise was that it was Foreman who lost his power and stamina while Ali, who many felt would be worn down by the pressing tactics of the champion, was the fresher as the last three rounds of the contest were fought.

After the fight in both dressing rooms the new and old champion played the parts expected of them:

Ali: "I told you all I would do it, but did you listen? He was scared, he was humiliated. I told you I was the

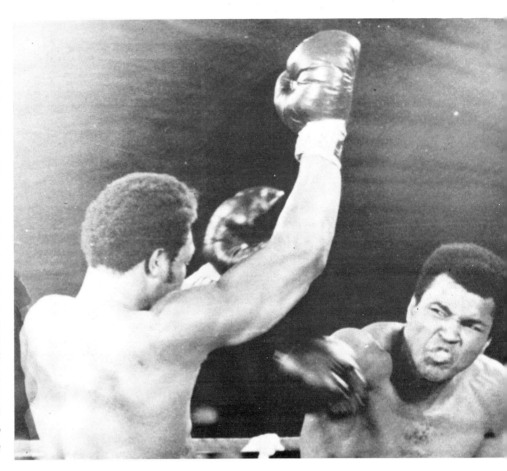

Ali lands a right to Foreman's jaw (*above*) during the early going. Foreman, who got off to a fast start, withered as the bout progressed. Ali, whose pattern evolved into one of fighting off the ropes, connected with a left and right (*below*) to end it in 8th.

greatest heavyweight of all time.

"I didn't dance. I wanted him to tire, to lose power. I decided to use the ropes. He punched like a sissy.

"I kept telling him during the fight to show me something, to come on and punch. Come on, you're the champion! Show me something.

"What you saw wasn't me, it was Allah. It wasn't me, you know I can't punch. Me knock out George? Not me, that was Allah."

If the fight in Kinshasa was one of the most exciting heavyweight title fights of all time, it was not the last peak in Ali's magnificent career. After successful defenses against Chuck Wepner, who was stopped in the fifteenth round at Cleveland on March 24, 1975, Ron Lyle, who was stopped in the eleventh at Las Vegas on May 16, 1975, and Britain's Joe Bugner, who went the distance but lost a clear decision on July 1, 1975, Ali met Joe Frazier for the third time on October 1, 1975. The fight was in the Philippine Coliseum, Manila, and began a few minutes before 11 AM. It was promoted by Don King, before 28,000 people, with 700,000,000 in 68 countries hooked in by satellite television. Ali was guaranteed four and a half million dollars and Frazier two and a half million dollars and Frazier two

million. Ali's pre-fight publicity slogan ran: "It'll be a thrilla, a chilla and a killa when I get the gorilla in Manila".

Ali, who was convinced Frazier was finished as a fighter, had promised to stand his ground and hit Frazier, and in the first four rounds he did this at will. Frazier's legs buckled in the first, and in the third he looked on the point of going as Ali continually jerked his head back and knocked the sweat from his face in showers. But Frazier kept boring in and won the fifth, catching Ali with lefts as Ali fought on the ropes. The sixth was even better for Frazier, and it was Ali's turn to face the black void as two tremendous left hooks ripped into his face. Ali survived the round, but from there to the tenth he fought in short bursts as Frazier continued his relentless assault, burrowing in to score with savage punches. At the end of the tenth, the fight was even, with Ali and his corner showing the more strain. It seemed that Frazier had absorbed Ali's ferocity and had finally dredged the last reserves of strength from the champion's frame.

The eleventh saw the beginning of the third phase of the fight, as Ali fought back to catch Frazier with long shots with both hands. Frazier's

face slowly began to change shape as bumps puffed up around his eyes and blood dripped from his mouth. As Ali drew on his last reserves of strength, and Frazier's power drained from him, Ali in the next three rounds hit Frazier with everything he had left. Frazier could offer no resistance as he stumbled around, his courage alone keeping him upright. At the end of the fourteenth referee Carlos Padilla helped Frazier back to his corner, and despite his protests manager Eddie Futch would not let the near-blind Frazier out for the fifteenth. He had given all he had, as had Ali, who at the end sank to the canvas to rest and escape the clamour. It was a great fight and afterwards Ali, generous in victory to Frazier, talked of the mental and physical strain, hinted at retirement, and admitted that during the fight he had felt like fainting, and that at the end of the tenth he was almost at the point of quitting. For once not showing his elation at victory, he summed it up by saying that a fight like that was next

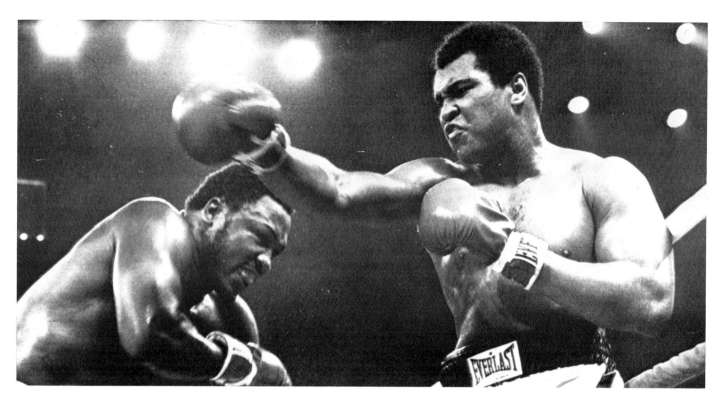

The seventh round of the third Ali-Frazier fight in Manila, and Ali glances a right off Joe Frazier's head *(above)*. Ali, starting strongly, puts his full force from the shoulder in a right to Frazier's face *(right)*.

to death—the closest thing to dying he knew of.

Ali rested for only four months before resuming the defence of his title. He beat four challengers in 1976; on February 20, Jean-Pierre Coopman, the Belgian heavyweight champion, by a knock-out in the fifth round at San Juan; U.S. contender Jimmy Young on points over fifteen rounds at Landover on April 30; Richard Dunn, the British, European and Commonwealth champion, who was stopped in five rounds at Munich, and the man who broke his jaw three years earlier, fellow-countryman Ken Norton, who was outpointed over fifteen rounds on September 28 at Madison Square Garden, New York. Two challengers were satisfactorily dealt with in 1977. On May 16 at Landover, Alfred Evangelista, the European champion, who was beaten on points, and on September 29, Earnie Shavers from Ohio, who was also outpointed in New York.

In his first defence in 1978, however, at Las Vegas on February 15, Ali was surprisingly outpointed by twenty-four-year-old Leon Spinks, from St. Louis, Missouri, who had won

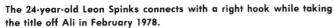
The 24-year-old Leon Spinks connects with a right hook while taking the title off Ali in February 1978.

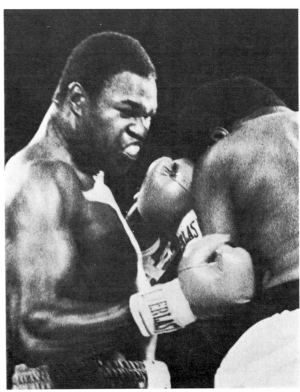
Larry Holmes (left) emphatically beat the ageing Ali to retain his W.B.C. title in October 1980.

the Olympic Games light-heavyweight gold medal in 1976, had turned pro the following year and was unbeaten in his seven paid bouts. His points victory over Ali was on a split decision, Referee Art Lurie, voting for the champion and the two judges for the challenger. The World Boxing Council, however, declared the title as vacant because Spinks refused to meet Ken Norton and the latter was announced champion on March 18, 1978, but on June 10 Norton lost this claim when outpointed by Larry Holmes, from Philadelphia, who was thereupon recognised as world titleholder by the W.B.C., but not by the majority of boxing followers. This claim was made even more absurd when on September 15 at New Orleans, Ali regained the title from Spinks by a unanimous points verdict.

Thus Ali became the first man in Boxing history to win the Heavyweight Championship three times and he had taken part in no less than twenty-four world title bouts. Afterwards he indicated that having

achieved this objective he would retire from the ring thus leaving Holmes as the outstanding contender. On November 10, 1978, he strengthened his claim to titular recognition by knocking out Alfredo Evangelista (Italy) in seven rounds at Las Vegas. Ali received five million dollars in his return fight with Spinks and he will go into the records as having earned in eighteen years of ring warfare, millions of dollars more than any other boxer.

Holmes then disposed of three challengers in 1979, stopping Osvaldo Ocasio (Puerto Rica) in seven rounds; Mike Weaver (Los Angeles) in twelve and Ernie Shavers (Ohio) in eleven, all three contests taking place at Las Vegas, and all were in defence of his W.B.C. title. In 1980 Holmes continued his slaughter of championship contenders by knocking out the European heavyweight champion, Lorenzo Zanon (Italy) in six rounds at Los Angeles on February 3; halting Leroy Jones (Denver) in eight rounds at Los Angeles on March 31. At Bloomington,

Minn. on July 7, he stopped Scott Le Doux (Minneapolis) in seven rounds.

On October 2, however, he made himself the undisputed world champion when he forced Muhammad Ali to retire at the end of the tenth round at Caesars Palace, Las Vegas, after a pathetic display by the former triple titleholder, who had not fought for two years and had undergone a drastic weight reduction that left him a mere shadow of his former greatness.

Meanwhile the W.B.A. confused the heavyweight championship situation by declaring the title vacant and recognising John Tate of Knoxville, Tennessee, as world champion when he outpointed Gerrie Coetzee of South Africa, over 15 rounds at Pretoria on October 20, 1979. Tate did not reign long, being knocked out in the 15th round by Mike Weaver, who already styled himself Heavyweight Champion of America. They met at Knoxville on March 31 and on October 25, 1980 Weaver made his first defence of his W.B.A. title by knocking out Coetzee in the 13th round of a hard fight in South Africa.

THE LIGHT HEAVYWEIGHTS

THE LITTLE BIG MEN

Each division in boxing except the light heavyweight got its start in England. This division, known in Europe as the cruiserweight, was instituted in America in 1903. It was fathered by Lou Houseman, a Chicago newspaperman, promoter, and manager at the time of Jack Root, who after scoring many victories as a middleweight had outgrown the division.

Houseman conceived the idea that there should be a grade established to include boxers between the middleweight and heavyweight sections, since there was a large weight difference in many contests. After receiving the green light from America's leading middleweights and the press, Houseman arranged to have Root fight Kid McCoy. The bout took place in Detroit on April 22, 1903, with Root the winner and champion of the new division.

George Gardner contested the right of Root to the honors and succeeded in proving his point by knocking Jack out on July 4, 1903, in twelve rounds in Buffalo, New York. The British accepted the new class and thereafter it became one of the most popular in Great Britain.

The division has never been too popular in our country, however, because the men who scaled between 160 and 175, the official top weight for a championship match, learned that only occasionally has the group been a good money-making class. Most of the top men have aimed for the heavyweight crown. After reaching the top or getting close to it, they invariably leaped into the heavyweight ranks, where the financial returns were best.

Some of the world's greatest ringmen have fought in the division,

among them such stars as Kid McCoy, Harry Greb, Tom Gibbons, Jack Delaney, Young Stribling, Paul Berlenbach, Billy Conn, Gene Tunney, Jack Dillon, Battling Levinsky, Georges Carpentier, Philadelphia Jack O'Brien, Jimmy Slattery, Tommy Loughran, and Bob Fitzsimmons. Fitzsimmons won the crown after losing the heavyweight title. He gained it when he beat Gardner via the decision route at the end of twenty rounds in San Francisco on November 25, 1903, and he in turn lost it to Jack O'Brien, who knocked him out in the thirteenth round in the same city on December 20, 1905. Thus the title during its first year changed hands three times—unusual in boxing.

Like most of the light heavyweights of later years, Philadelphia Jack O'Brien preferred to confine his ring battles to the higher division and

Kid McCoy (*left*) boxed Jim Corbett before movie cameras in an early attempt to weave a plot around a boxing match. McCoy was past his prime when matched with Jack Root for the first light heavyweight championship in 1903, in which he lost in 10 rounds.

Bob Fitzsimmons (*right*) at the age of 41 gave Gardner a 20-round boxing lesson in San Francisco, thus adding a third crown to his spectacular career. A veteran of 13 years, Fitzsimmons lacked the punching power he once possessed, but his boxing skill and ring-craft befuddled the younger Gardner. The new championship, in its first year, 1903, changed hands three times.

Philadelphia Jack O'Brien, knocked Fitzsimmons out after 13 hard-fought rounds, to become the fourth light heavyweight champion. O'Brien fought 185 battles in his career (1896-1912).

Jack Root easily whipped McCoy to become the first light heavy-weight king. In a 54-fight career (1897-1906) Root scored 24 knockouts and was stopped three times, his only losses.

George Gardner dethroned Root via a knockout in 12 rounds at Fort Erie, Canada. Gardner, born in Lisdoonvarna, County Clare, Ireland, started boxing in 1897 and retired in 1908.

Battling Levinsky whipped Dillon at Boston in 12 rounds and fought many no-decision bouts while defending his title, which could only be won by a knockout. From 1910 to 1929 Levinsky met the the best men around.

Jack Dillon, the "Giant Killer" (left), claimed the title in 1908 when O'Brien failed to accept his challenge. Dillon held the title for eight years, until beaten by Battling Levinsky in 1916. In 14 years of boxing (1908-1923) Dillon engaged in over 240 contests, fighting anyone, anywhere.

made no attempt to defend his championship up to the time of his retirement in 1912. Then Jack Dillon, known as the Giant Killer, born February 2, 1891, in Frankfort, Indiana, claimed it, but like O'Brien he immediately started facing heavyweights until Battling Levinsky, a clever performer, challenged him. Levinsky, born June 10, 1891, in Philadelphia, signed with Dillon for twelve rounds in Boston. In this contest the Battler, avoiding the heavy blows of his opponent through the employment of ring science, emerged the victor on points and the newly crowned king.

It is noteworthy that while many boxers won more than one championship and a number regained the crown after having lost it, no light heavyweight king other than Bob Fitzsimmons ever held more than one title and no light heavyweight ever rewon the championship, though Mike McTigue reclaimed it.

Levinsky laid claim to the world title and was generally recognized in our country, but Georges Carpentier, Champion of Europe, had his share

Georges Carpentier (left) of France, European light heavyweight champ, kayoed Levinsky in Jersey City, New Jersey, and was acknowledged world champion. With him is famed boxing promoter Jack Curley (center) and his manager Francois Descamps.

"Gorgeous Georges" Carpentier (*left*) had a fabulous ring career from 1907 to 1927. Starting as a featherweight, he fought in every division to a shot at the heavyweight title. An excellent boxer with a stunning punch, he fought mostly in Europe. In the photo above Carpentier floors the American Gunboat Smith during their London bout in 1914. Smith lost on a foul in the sixth round.

Willie Lewis, who did most of his fighting in Europe between 1908 and 1914, appears to be knocked cold by Carpentier in 1912 bout in Paris. But Lewis got up to lose 20-round decision.

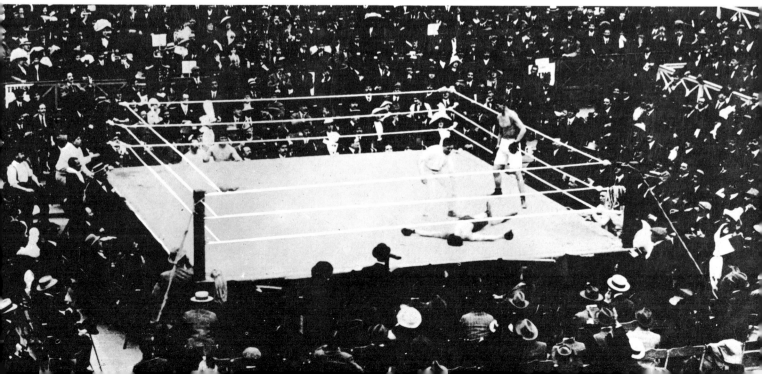

(Above) Gene Tunney and Bob Martin (right) were AEF champs in 1919. Tunney defeated 20 opponents in an elimination series to win the light heavyweight title. He then beat champ Martin in a special four-round bout. After his discharge Gene won 22 bouts, 15 by kayo, and won the American light heavyweight title from Battling Levinsky in 1922. (Above, left) The only loss on Tunney's record came at the hands of the great Harry Greb (left), who beat Gene for the title that same year. The referee is Kid McPartland. (Below) Tunney regained the title from Greb in 1923 in 15 rounds.

of supporters. To settle the dispute, Carpentier and Levinsky fought for world supremacy in Jersey City, on October 12, 1920, with Carpentier clinching the laurels. It was that victory that gained for him the heavyweight championship contest with Jack Dempsey the following year.

Levinsky retained the U. S. title despite his defeat by the Orchid Kid, and on January 13, 1922, he lost it to Gene Tunney in the old Madison Square Garden in twelve rounds.

With his defeat by Dempsey in the higher division, Carpentier returned to France and there defended his world light heavyweight crown against Battling Siki, the Singular Senegalese, who surprised everyone by halting Georges in the sixth round.

Gene Tunney, his mind set on the heavyweight title possessed by Dempsey, once more put his U. S. light heavyweight title on the line against Harry Greb—he had previously lost it to Harry and had then rewon it after defeating him in fifteen rounds. Gene now decided to work towards a heavyweight title bout.

Mike McTigue battered Battling Siki around for 20 rounds (*above*) to win the title on St. Patrick's day, 1923, in Dublin. It was a day of celebration for the Irish, who were enjoying the battle in the indoor arena while Irish rebels were using gunfire against the British outside the stadium. Siki, greeted by "Bold Mike" upon arrival in New York in 1924 (*below*) engaged in 23 bouts before his death.

With Gene's retirement, Mike McTigue, one of the top Americans in the division, went to Dublin, where on St. Patrick's Day, 1923, in the midst of the Sinn Fein insurrection, he whipped Battling Siki in twenty rounds and came back to America with the world crown.

Of those who up to this stage held top honors, Greb and Siki were the most colorful. The Greb-Tunney battles in the light heavyweight class were sensational ring encounters. They faced each other five times, with Greb winning only once. Twice he was defeated in American championship matches with Tunney and twice they engaged in no decision bouts.

Greb was a most unusual fighter. He wasn't a hard hitter but a tantalizing one. Seldom more than a middleweight, he fought the best of the heavyweights with considerable success. He punched with accuracy and rapidity, tossing punches from all angles.

He was blind in one eye, yet fought without others knowing it for the better part of his great career.

In Siki, the sport had a unique, queer character, a fun-making, fight-loving figure whose escapades eventually cost him his life by murder. His real name was Louis Phal, a boy of the jungle who lived his life as a simple lad, with a savage's brain, an uncontrollable temper, and a steady thirst for drink.

When McTigue returned to America he was offered a fight with Young Stribling, the pride of Georgia. He accepted, handed the Georgian a shellacking but received no better than a draw from Referee Harry Ertle, who was threatened by the Southern supporters of Stribling and, fearing violence, figured such a decision would pacify the mob. Despite the verdict, he, McTigue, and the latter's manager Joe Jacobs, had to make a hasty exit from the state when the fans rushed the ring to get at the fighter and official. Stribling faced Mike again in Newark a year later. Though it was a twelve rounder no-decision affair, Mike was on the loser's end.

Mike McTigue was aptly named "Bold Mike." He met Young Stribling, the pride of the South, at Columbus, Georgia, in 1923 (below) and received a draw verdict after a hectic session. He gave Stribling a return bout in Newark, New Jersey, on March 3, 1924. Signing for the match (right) are: (seated) "Pa" Stribling, Young Stribling, Babe Culman, the matchmaker, McTigue, and Paddy Mullins, Mike's manager; (standing) H. G. Gewinner and Harry Blaufuss, promoters, "Ma" Stribling, and J. F. Black, also a promoter. The contest went the scheduled 12 rounds, with no decision.

William ("Young") Stribling had 10 fights as a heavyweight in 1930. He won seven by knockouts, three via decision. One of the knockouts was over Phil Scott (above) in two rounds in London. Stribling was a fine boxer and puncher, and had a yearning for speed. (Left) In his plane, Stribling holds his child with an assist from his wife. Ma and Pa Stribling, looking on, travelled everywhere with Bill. Pa was his manager and Ma, also a familiar figure in boxing, assisted and encouraged her son from his corner.

Paul Berlenbach, who possessed a deadly clout, succeeded McTigue as title holder when he gained a 15-round decision in 1925, in Yankee Stadium. Paul was the 1920 Olympic wrestling champion.

After losing the crown to Jack Delaney, Berlenbach faced Mike McTigue in a return contest in Madison Square Garden, January 28, 1927. The battle was a slam-bang affair until the fourth round, when McTigue staggered and floored Paul for the full count.

In later years, Stribling, who fought both as a light heavyweight and heavy against the cream of both divisions, was killed in a motorcycle accident. His leading battles were against Jack Sharkey, Jimmy Slattery, Paul Berlenbach in a title match which he lost in fifteen rounds in New York on June 10, 1926, and his fight for the heavyweight crown with Max Schmeling in Cleveland in which he was stopped with only fifteen seconds to go in the fifteenth and final round. He, like Siki and Greb, was a colorful figure.

McTigue held on to his throne for two years. On May 30, 1925, he faced a terrific puncher in Paul Berlenbach, an amateur wrestler turned boxer, and Mike was outpointed in New York in fifteen rounds to lose his laurels. He was a clever boxer, one of the smart men of the ring of his era, but couldn't overcome the hitting power of his opponent.

Two years later, after Paul had lost the title, these two former champions engaged in another encounter, a thriller, in which McTigue, now an old man as fighter's ages go, suddenly became a tiger in an effort to avenge the loss of his championship and battered Berlenbach into submission in four rounds, one of the ring's major surprises.

McTigue engaged in a number of additional contests, finally retiring at the age of thirty-eight. In his latter years he fought such stars as Leo Lomski, Tony Maurullo, Armand Emanuel, Tuffy Griffiths, George Hoffman, Bob Godwin and Patsy Perroni, each of whom whipped him. Griffiths stopped him in a round. When he retired, the 1929 crash and depression that followed cost Mike his mind and

Jack Delaney was dropped (*above*) for a short count in his losing battle in 1926 with Berlenbach. But a year later he stopped Paul in six rounds. After entering the heavyweight picture, Delaney was knocked out in one round by Jack Sharkey (*below*) on April 30, 1928, in a controversial bout that was discussed long after the result. Photo shows referee Jack Purdy ordering Sharkey to a neutral corner.

On July 16, 1926, Berlenbach retained his title in a great 15-round fight with Jack Delaney (*right*), a masterful boxer and powerful hitter.

fortune. Confined to a mental institution, he died August 12, 1966.

Berlenbach, unlike many others who have held world championships, didn't place his crown in moth balls for an unlimited time. He defended his title twice during the year in which he won it.

In the first bout he knocked out Jimmy Slattery, a very clever boxer from Buffalo, in eleven rounds, then he and Jack Delaney fought a masterpiece in which Oom Paul retained his laurels via the decision route in fifteen rounds in Madison Square Garden.

The following year, after outpointing Stribling in fifteen rounds in New York, he again tackled Delaney for the Italian Hospital Fund at Ebbets Field, Brooklyn, and in another thriller in which 49,186 persons paid the record sum of $461,789. Delaney gained the crown.

Delaney, a boxer of extraordinary cleverness, with a rapier-like jab, decided there was more to be made in the heavyweight division than his own, and retired to fight in the top class. He fought Berlenbach again in Chicago and stopped him in the sixth round and lost to Jimmy Maloney and Johnny Risko prior to dropping a fifteen round bout to Tom Heeney of New Zealand. Then he was knocked

out by Jack Sharkey in the first round of a much-discussed, controversial affair, and a year later he retired to enter business.

Delaney was born in St. Francis, Canada, March 18, 1900, lived most of his life in Connecticut, and died at Katonah, New York, November 27, 1948.

After Delaney's retirement as light heavyweight boss, McTigue reclaimed the title and on October 7, 1927, Tommy Loughran, another clever boxer who hailed from Philadelphia, relieved him of it by outpointing him in New York in fifteen rounds. Tommy had lots of class.

Jack Delaney's fourth fight as a heavyweight, August 11, 1927, ended in confusion. While Jack is being attended to in his corner, Paolino Uzcudun, the Basque, stands bewildered and angry after being disqualified in the seventh round for hitting low. Pete Reilly, Jack's manager, stoops along ringside, displaying dented cup in an effort to convince skeptical boxing writers, of the foul.

On March 1, 1934, Tommy Loughran, four years a heavyweight, tried unsuccessfully to wrest the heavyweight crown from Primo Carnera. Carnera scaled 270 pounds to Loughran's 186, an 84-pound handicap that created a record for a championship bout.

He put his title on the line against Jimmy Slattery, Leo Lomski, Pete Latzo (twice), Mickey Walker, and Jimmy Braddock, winning each and displaying in those contests the ring cleverness that brought world prominence to Jim Corbett.

After defeating Braddock in fifteen rounds, Loughran retired undefeated to enter the higher division.

He was knocked out by Jack Sharkey in the third round in his first heavyweight attempt but was quite successful thereafter and succeeded in getting a crack at the heavyweight title held by Primo Carnera. In that he gave away considerable weight, eighty-six pounds, yet managed to go the distance, losing the verdict at the end of fifteen rounds in Miami.

In his contest with Leo Lomski, he fought for a time in a stupor due to punishment; in his first contest with Ray Impellettiere, the bout was halted because of a bad cut over his eye, but Commissioner William Brown ordered the bout resumed. Yet Lough-

Tommy Loughran (*right*) was one of the most skillful boxers in ring history. He was a light hitter, but his agile footwork and clever boxing style, frustrated the knockout plans of all but two—Jack Sharkey and Steve Hamas—of the many heavy-hitting opponents he met. Loughran's boxing career, 172 contests, started in 1919 and ended in 1937. After winning the light heavyweight crown from McTigue, in 1927, he defended the title six times before relinquishing it to join the heavyweights. In his first heavyweight bout, Tommy was knocked out by Jack Sharkey (*above, right*) on September 26, 1929, in three rounds. He met all the top men from then on.

In Loughran's second defense of his title, he was floored in the first round by Leo Lomski, a dangerous hitter. Tommy took the count of nine and managed to hold off the onrushing Lomski until the last minute of the round, when a looping right floored him again for another nine count before the bell rang, ending the round. From the second to the 15th round the fight was all Loughran's.

Jimmy Slattery (left) defeated Lou Scozza in 15 rounds on February 10, 1930, in the eliminations final staged by the New York Commission. Slattery's victory made him the new champ.

Maxie Rosenbloom (left) clinched his title claim on June 25, 1930, when he beat Slattery in 15 rounds in Buffalo. In a return match in 1931, Slattery was again defeated in 15 rounds.

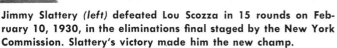

Bob Olin, standing over Rosenbloom who slipped during title bout on November 16, 1934, gained the crown in 15 rounds before a slim crowd in Madison Square Garden. Rosenbloom, a real veteran of the ring, engaged in 285 bouts from 1925 to 1939.

ran managed to win both bouts. He gave up his title in August, 1929, and in a tourney to choose his successor, Maxie Rosenbloom succeeded in clinching the honors by decisively outpointing Jimmy Slattery, who on February 10, 1930, in Buffalo, had outpointed Lou Scozza in fifteen rounds in the final of an elimination staged by the New York Commission. Rosenbloom received world recognition when he beat Slattery in Buffalo on June 25, 1930.

Slapsie-Maxie, as Rosenbloom was called, was a clever boxer but an exceedingly weak hitter. The New Yorker, born September 6, 1904, was a most active battler. He lost only a few of the several hundred bouts he fought. He defended his crown often, his best championship battles being a fifteen rounder with Mickey Walker in New York and one with Lou Scozza in Buffalo.

"Slapsie Maxie" Rosenbloom has enjoyed great success in movies, nightclubs, and TV.

John Henry Lewis, after beating Olin in 15 rounds, gave up the title for a crack at the heavyweight crown and was kayoed by Joe Louis in one round on January 5, 1929.

Melio Bettina (right) of Beacon, New York, scored a nine-round knockout over Tiger Jack Fox in Madison Square Garden and mounted the vacated light heavyweight throne.

Maxie lost his title to Bob Olin in Madison Square Garden in a dull fifteen round affair and thereafter continued campaigning throughout the country. When he retired in 1939, he became an actor and entertainer in night clubs and appeared in many movies and television shows.

It was on November 16, 1934, that Olin gained the crown. He was an ordinary boxer who lacked color. On October 31, 1935 he dropped the championship to John Henry Lewis, a Negro who gained the decision in fifteen rounds in St. Louis.

John Henry, like many of his predecessors, was a clever boxer, but he could also punch. He defended his title twice—against Emilio Martinez, whom he stopped in the fourth round in Minneapolis, and Al Gainer, whom he whipped in New Haven in fifteen. Each was a mediocre affair that lacked interest.

Three months after the last fight, he gave up his title at the request of the New York Commission to enter the heavyweight class and fight Joe Louis. The bout lasted less than one round, with John Henry knocked out. He retired shortly after that dismal contest.

Melio Bettina and Tiger Jack Fox were the survivors in an elimination to decide his successor, and on February 3, 1939, Bettina stopped Fox in the Garden in the ninth round.

Billy Conn, a clever Pittsburgher, came along to depose the southpaw Bettina in Madison Square Garden by outpointing him in fifteen rounds to win world support. Billy, born October 8, 1917, was one of the ring's classiest light heavyweight performers. In that respect he followed the trend of the division.

Billy outpointed Gus Lesnevich of Cliffside Park, New Jersey twice in title contests, once in New York and again in Detroit, then vacated the throne to seek a match with Joe Louis for the heavyweight title. He was stopped by the Bomber in the thirteenth round on June 18, 1941; again on June 19, 1945, in eight.

With Conn's retirement another elimination was started, New York naming its men and the National Boxing Association selecting a field of its own. After each had obtained its top performer, Anton Christoforidis of Messina, Greece, and Melio Bettina faced each other in Cleveland, with the Greek winning. Then he met Lesnevich in Madison Square Garden to decide U. S. supremacy and Gus won.

Since the war was on and European boxers were inactive, it was generally agreed that Lesnevich was the world's best in his division, but to clinch the top honors he accepted a challenge from the leading contender, Tami Mauriello of New York, whom he defeated twice to clinch his place in the sun.

Gus entered the Coast Guard during the war, was inactive until 1946, then on his discharge began to campaign in the States. He knocked out Joe Kahut in Seattle, in one round; was stopped by Lee Oma in four; then went to England to fight the British Empire champion, Freddie Mills, whom he stopped in the tenth round.

Back in the States he kayoed Billy Fox in ten, and again in one in title bouts; defeated Tami Mauriello, then stopped Tami in seven and Melio Bettina in one, in non-title affairs. He then returned to England to give Mills another chance. In this bout the Britisher took the crown from Gus.

HE WON'T GET AWAY
FROM ME WHEN HE'S HURT

DRAWN BY
Billy Conn

Billy Conn, shown on opposite page, was the most handsome of all ringmen. He was an excellent boxer with a fair punch and beat many of the national favorites. Billy outpointed Melio Bettina for the crown on July 13, 1939, and after three title defenses, gave it up to go after Joe Louis. Billy had Louis beaten for 13 rounds in the first fight, got careless and was kayoed. Training for the second Louis fight Conn (above) drew a prediction (right) that came true in reverse.

Gus Lesnevich (above, right) gained National Boxing Association recognition as champion by defeating Anton Christoforidis on May 22, 1941, then clinched the American title by beating Tami Mauriello (below, left) on August 26, in 15 rounds.

By knocking out Freddie Mills in 10 rounds on May 14, 1946, Lesnevich was declared undisputed world champion. The fight, held in London, was vicious, with Gus handicapped by a closed left eye.

Freddie Mills, declared victor over Lesnevich by referee Ted Waltham on July 26, 1948, gained the world title for England.

Joey Maxim, a veteran campaigner from Cleveland, Ohio, won the title on January 24, 1950, by battering Freddie Mills into submission in the 10th round of a 15-round match. Maxim outclassed Mills throughout the fight, which took place at Earl's Court in London. Maxim, still available, started in 1941.

Archie Moore (left), another veteran, outpointed Maxim in St. Louis on December 17, 1952, in 15 rounds and is yet to be beaten for the light heavyweight crown. Moore has engaged in over 195 fights since the start of his career in 1936.

by winning the decision at the end of fifteen rounds.

Gus entered the heavyweight class after losing to Joey Maxim in a contest for the vacant American light heavyweight title. He faced Ezzard Charles for the N.B.A. heavyweight championship following Joe Louis's retirement and was stopped in the seventh round. That ended his career.

After Maxim had annexed the U. S. championship, his manager, Jack Kearns, took him to England to challenge Mills, who accepted. That match, staged in London on January 24, 1950, brought the world title back to America, Joey stopping the Britisher in the tenth round of a thrilling engagement.

Maxim, born March 28, 1922, in Cleveland, Ohio, on returning to America engaged in many contests.

He tackled Ezzard Charles in a heavy-weight championship mill in Chicago and lost in fifteen rounds, then successfully defended his crown against Bob Murphy in New York and stopped Ray Robinson in fourteen rounds after being well behind on points. Ray, the middleweight king, trying to annex another crown, collapsed from the excessive heat in the Yankee Stadium.

In his next defense on December 17, 1952 in St. Louis, Maxim lost his title to the veteran Archie Moore.

After Moore gained the crown, he and Maxim met twice in championship battles. The first, in Ogden, Utah, on June 24, 1953, resulted in Moore's winning a close decision to retain his laurels. In the second, at Miami, on January 27, 1954, Archie won by a wide margin in fifteen rounds.

Light heavyweight champion Joey Maxim (above, left) retained his crown on June 25, 1952, by outlasting middle-weight champion Ray Robinson, who collapsed suddenly from exhaustion. Despite the excessive heat at Yankee Stadium that night, Robinson was well ahead on points until he began to wilt in the 13th round, falling face down at Maxim's feet before the round ended. When Robinson was unable to answer the bell for the 14th round, referee Ray Miller signified the fight was over and declared the jubilant Maxim (right) winner by a knockout.

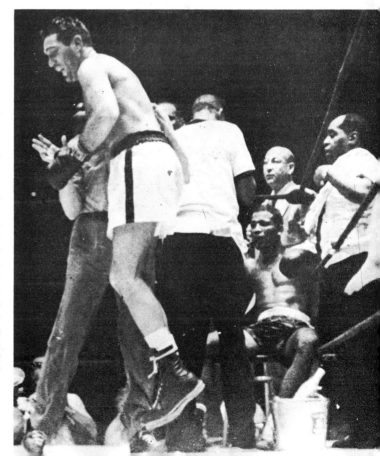

Moore knocked out Harold Johnson in New York on August 11, 1954, in the fourteenth round in defense of his crown; then he stopped Bobo Olson, the middleweight king, in the third round on June 22, 1955, in another title bout.

On September 21, 1955, Moore decided to try for the heavyweight championship and was knocked out by Rocky Marciano in the ninth round. Archie then went to England and on June 5, 1956, halted Yolande Pompey in London in the tenth round of a title mill.

When Rocky Marciano retired undefeated, Moore and Floyd Patterson fought for the vacant heavyweight throne and Floyd stopped Archie in the fifth round on November 30, 1956, to become Rocky's successor.

On July 8, 1957, both the New York Commission and the National Boxing Association declared the light heavyweight throne vacant due to Moore's failure to defend it and ordered Tony Anthony of New York and Harold Johnson to decide supremacy, they being the top contenders. But a day later they rescinded the order and Moore and Anthony were matched for the crown, Los Angeles being chosen as the battleground on September 20.

Though Moore virtually slaughtered Anthony, he actually *talked* him out of the title. All through the early rounds he kept saying to the youngster, "You're looking great. Keep up what you're doing. You're the next champion!"

In the sixth and seventh rounds Anthony took a terrible battering, and the referee stopped the fight in the latter round.

In one of the most sensational fights seen in years, Archie Moore knocked out Yvon Durelle of Baie Ste. Anne, New Brunswick, Canada, in the 11th round (below), to retain his crown. The battle, held in the Forum in Montreal, on December 10, 1958, was packed with thrills. Floored four times, three times in the first round (above), Moore staggered back to knock Durelle down four times, twice in the final round. Ancient Archie now holds the record for career knockouts, with 127.

A schism arose in the light-heavyweight ranks when, on October 25, 1960, the National Boxing Association lifted Archie Moore's title for inactivity and then named thirty-three-year-old Harold Johnson, of Philadelphia, as their champion after he kayoed Jess Bowdry, of St. Louis, forty-five seconds into the ninth round on February 7, 1961. "Old Man" Moore, recognized as world champion by every other boxing board, had beaten Johnson in four out of five encounters between 1949 and 1954, and he still holds the record for longest-held title in his division.

In February 1962, the New York Commission withdrew its recognition of Moore, and when Johnson, a clever pugilist with a classic style, was awarded a unanimous decision over Doug Jones on May 12, 1962, in Philadelphia, he received international recognition.

The champion's superior punching power brought him another victory when he defeated Gustav Scholz, of Germany, in fifteen rounds on June 23, 1967, in Berlin.

A rare event occurred in the Johnson family. On June 22, 1936, Johnson's father, Phil, was kayoed by Jersey Joe Walcott in three rounds

Johnson received international recognition as king of the division after defeating Doug Jones on May 12, 1962.

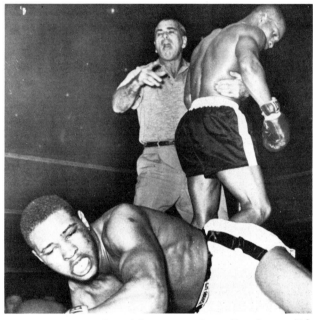

After scoring a technical kayo over Jesse Bowdry on February 7, 1961, Harold Johnson won N.B.A. recognition.

One of Johnson's best triumphs was the 15-round verdict he pounded out over Germany's Gustav Scholz in 1967.

Harold Johnson (left) spars with his father, Phil. Oddly, both were kayoed by Jersey Joe Walcott 14 years apart.

in Philadelphia. Fourteen years later, Feburary 8, 1950, Harold also was kayoed by Walcott in three rounds at Philadelphia.

Willie Pastrano, at 173½ pounds, unexpectedly found himself first Johnson's challenger, then his conqueror, when he outboxed the 174-pound Johnson in fifteen rounds in a split decision on June 1, 1963, in Las Vegas.

With blood flowing from a cut over Gregorio Peralta's eye, Pastrano retained the title with a six-round knockout on April 10, 1964, in New Orleans, after having lost a ten-round decision to the Argentinian in 1963.

The referee and most writers had

the champion leading when he knocked out Terry Downes in 1:17 of the eleventh round, in Manchester, England, on November 30, 1964, to retain his title.

Always a fast-moving, wily, and defensive boxer but never known for his punching power, Pastrano met his match in Puerto Rico's idol José "Chegui" Torres, a recent graduate from the middleweight ranks. On March 30, 1965, Torres decked Pastrano for the first time in Pastrano's career, then kayoed him when the defender was too weary to answer the bell for the tenth round.

An extroverted yet gentle man and a lover of the arts, Torres learned his

peek-a-boo stance from his manager, Cus D'Amato. The stance served him well when he was a member of the 1956 Olympic team and then won the Golden Gloves in 1968, and he continued to use it in his next two title bouts against Wayne Thornton, of California, and Chic Calderwood, the British Empire title holder. Torres beat Thornton in fifteen rounds on May 21, 1966, and kayoed Calderwood in the second round on October 15, 1966.

Richard Ihetu, former middleweight champ and better known as Dick Tiger, ascended the light-heavyweight throne on December 6, 1966, in New York, when officials decided that he had been more aggressive and faster on recoveries over the fiteen rounds than the surprisingly lethargic Torres. Torres's loss was even more surprising considering his seven-year, nine-pound, and two-inch advantages over the thirty-seven-year-old, 167-pound, five-foot-eight-inch Tiger.

Willie Pastrano (*right*) became the new 175-pound champion by scoring an upset 15-round decision over Johnson at Las Vegas on June 1, 1963, outboxing his heavier foe.

It was on November 30, 1964, that Pastrano traveled to Manchester, England, where he halted Terry Downs in the 11th.

Pastrano, retained his title by knocking out Gregorio Peralta (*below, left*) of Argentina in sixth round on April 10, 1964.

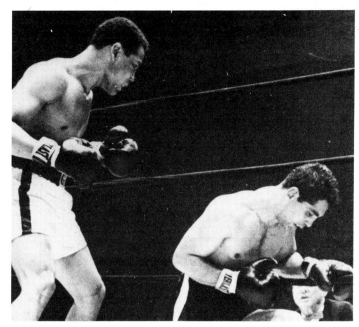

On March 30, 1965, Pastrano was unseated as champion by José ''Chegui'' Torres, who became the new titleholder when Willie was unable to come out for the tenth round at New York's Madison Square Garden. (*Right*) Pastrano on the floor in the sixth round.

Dick Tiger, who had taken the crown from Torres in December, 1966, successfully defended it against Jose on May 17, 1967.

Torres, shown here connecting with a long right to Tiger's head in their first match, looked lethargic for most of the 15 rounds.

Tiger, who grew up in the Ibo tribe of eastern Nigeria, and was trained to box by British army officers, was one of boxing's best-liked heroes. Sincere, modest, affable, and gentlemanly, Tiger was also a man of conscience. When civil war broke out in his native Nigeria, he became a lieutenant in the morale corps of the Biafran army.

Already old for a boxer when he won the title, Tiger was past his peak when he entered the ring against 173¼-pound Bob Foster on May 24, 1968. The 168-pound champ started off well, landing a good left hook early in the first round, but the second and third rounds were Foster's as he eluded Tiger's shots while peppering his opponent with left jabs. A left hook toppled Tiger onto his back and the champ was counted out by referee Mark Conn. This was the only time in Tiger's fifteen-year career that he was knocked out.

Tiger continued to fight until 1971, when he retired. Shortly afterward, on December 14, the Nigerian died of cancer in his homeland.

Foster went on to defend his title fourteen times, the record number for his class. From 1969 to 1973 he kayoed Frank DePaula, Andy Kendall, Roger Rouse, Mark Tessman, and Hal Carroll. He beat Ray Anderson, then kayoed Tommy Hicks, Brian Kelly, Vincent Rondon, Mike Quarry, and Chris Finnegan and ended the string with two decisions over Pierre Fourie of Johannesburg, South Africa.

Stepping up to the heavyweight class, he was knocked out by Joe Frazier in two rounds on November 18, 1970. On November 21, 1972, Ali kayoed him in eight rounds.

On June 17, 1974, Foster met a tartar in Jorge Ahumada, of Argentina. In the University of New Mexico Arena in Albuquerque 13,000 fans watched their "hometown son" fight a fifteen-round draw with Ahumada.

At 174 pounds, Foster was one-half

Bob Foster jumps for joy after winning the light heavyweight title by knocking out Tiger in the fourth round on May 24, 1968. It was the only knockout ever suffered by Tiger.

Foster eyes an unconscious Mike Quarry, who Bob has just stopped in the fourth round of their title bout at Las Vegas on June 28, 1972. Foster defended a record 14 times.

pound heavier than his rival, but his thirty-two-year-old body almost spelled his doom. Nat Loubet, editor of *Ring*, scored the fight thirteen rounds for Ahumada to two for Foster. The draw decision was considered dubious, to say the least, by most of the fans and experts alike.

Foster was the favorite at 8 to 5, and although he had height and reach on his challenger, he never "got off." As the contest progressed, Ahumada gained confidence and finished strongly.

It was the fourteenth title defense for Foster and the least convincing of his career.

On September 17, 1974, Foster, who was 34, announced his retirement. The World Boxing Council then recognized the fight at Wembley on October 1, 1974, between Jorge Ahumada and John Conteh of Great Britain as being for the vacant title. Conteh, 23, from Liverpool, proved too strong and skillful for the Argentine and won a decision to become the first Briton to hold the title since Freddie Mills in 1950.

Meanwhile the W.B.A. recognized the battle between Ahumada's countryman Victor Galindez and Len Hutchins of the U.S.A. Galindez stopped Hutchins in the twelfth to become W.B.A. champion. In 1975 Galindez defended three times, gaining decisions against Pierre Fourie, of South Africa, in Johannesburg, against Jorge Ahumada, and against Fourie again in a Johannesburg return on September 13, 1975.

Conteh defended his W.B.C. title against Lonnie Bennett, of the U.S.A., at Wembley on March 11, 1975, and stopped his challenger, who was led back to his corner with blood pouring from a cut eye after one minute and ten seconds of the fifth round.

Conteh made one defence of his W.B.C. crown in 1976, outpointing Alvaro "Vaqui" Lopez in Copenhagen on October 9, but was stripped of his laurels in May 1977 through his failure to defend it and on May 21 Miguel Angel Cuello, from the Argentine, won the vacant championship by knocking out Jesse Burnett in nine rounds at Monte Carlo. On January

A right from John Conteh smacks home on the side of Jorge Ahumada's face *(above)* in their battle for the light-heavyweight crown on October 1, 1975 at Wembley. After being stripped of his title, Conteh was unsuccessful in a bid to win it back from new champion Mate Parlov of Yugoslavia *(below)*.

7, 1978, Cuello surprisingly lost his title to Mate Parlov, of Yugoslavia, by a knockout in nine rounds at Milan, who kept his crown by outpointing John Conteh at Belgrade on June 17, but it was not a popular verdict as the Englishman appeared to have done enough to get the decision. Parlov did not keep his title for long, being forced to retire to Marvin Johnson, from Indianapolis, in ten rounds at Marsala on December 2, 1978.

Meanwhile, Victor Galindez maintained his hold on the W.B.A. version of the championship. In 1976 he made three successful defences against Harald Skog who retired in three rounds at Oslo on March 28; Richie Kates, who was knocked out in the final round at Johannesburg on May 22, and Kosie Smith, who was outpointed over fifteen rounds at Johannesburg on October 5. In 1976 he

made three more successful defences, outpointing Richie Kates in Rome on June 18, outpointing Alvaro "Yaqui" Lopez in the same city on September 17 and outpointing Eddie Gregory over fifteen rounds at Turin on November 19. In 1978 Galindez defeated Lopez again, this time at Camaiore on May 6, but on September 15 he lost his title to Mike Rossman, from New Jersey, at New Orleans the bout being stopped in round thirteen. On December 5 Rossman made a successful first defence of his W.B.A. crown by stopping Aldo Traversaro in six rounds at Philadelphia.

He remained W.B.A. champion until April 14, 1979 when in a return match with Galindez he was stopped in ten rounds.

Eight days later, Marvin Johnson lost his W.B.A. title to Matt Franklin from

Matthew Saad Muhammad (right) on the point of knocking out Lotte Mwale (Zambia) at San Diego in November 1980.

(Great Britain), who was endeavouring to regain the title he had lost to Mate Parlov in 1978. The champion sustained a badly gashed eyebrow and his seconds used an illegal substance to heal the wound. Conteh gave him a hard fight throughout, but was adjudged a narrow points loser at the end of 15 exciting rounds. A return bout was ordered and they met at Atlantic City on March 29, 1980, but this time Conteh boxed badly and was put down five times before the bout was stopped in round four.

Matthew Saad Muhammad made three more successful defences in 1980. On May 11 he stopped Louis Pergaud, from the Cameroons, in five rounds at Halifax, N.S. On July 13 he beat Alvaro Lopez (Stockton, Cal.) in 14 rounds at Great Gorge, N.J., and on November 28 he ruined the hopes of Lotte Mwale from Zambia, by knocking him out in three rounds at San Diego.

Back to the W.B.A. championships. On November 30, 1979, Marvin Johnson changed sides and won the W.B.A. title by stopping Galindez in eleven rounds at New Orleans, but on March 31, 1980, he was himself stopped in eleven rounds by Eddie Gregory (New York) who got into the fashion by changing his name to Eddie Mustapha Muhammad. Under this guise he beat off challengers: Jerry Martin (Philadelphia) stopped in ten rounds at Mcaffe, N.J., and Dutchman Rudi Koopman, the European champion, stopped at the end of the third round at Los Angeles, to enter 1981 still as champion.

Philadelphia, who knocked him out in eight rounds at Indianapolis. The new champion promptly changed his name to Matthew Saad Muhammad and his first defence, on August 18, 1979 at Atlantic City, was against John Conteh

CRUISERWEIGHT CHAMPIONS

(Weight Limit, 190 Pounds)

MARVIN CAMEL (U.S.A.) WAS THE FIRST WINNER OF THE NEWLY CREATED CHAMPIONSHIP WHEN HE OUTPOINTED MATE PARLOV (YUGOSLAVIA) OVER 15 ROUNDS AT LAS VEGAS ON MARCH 31, 1980.

HE LOST THE TITLE ON NOVEMBER 26 WHEN BEATEN BY CARLOFF "SUGAR" DELEON (PUERTO RICO) ON POINTS AT NEW ORLEANS.

THE MIDDLEWEIGHTS

When British boxing was at the zenith of its glory, the Fives Court (*above*) was crowded with the cream of the aristocracy, applauding the skill of such men as Jackson, Mendoza, Cribb, Molineaux and others. All are shown in the foreground. Boxers used mufflers (gloves) during these exhibitions. Randall and Martin are seen sparring in the ring in a benefit performance. The first historic battle between Randall and Martin (*below*) took place on Crawley Downs, May 14, 1819. Martin was knocked out after 45 minutes of severe fighting. In those days, seconds were allowed in the ring. From left to right are: Tom Jones and Tom Oliver, seconds for Randall; Randall and Martin; Ben Burns and Harry Harmer, seconds for Martin. All of the seconds were celebrated boxers.

MIDDLEWEIGHT'S CLASSIEST

When one discusses great fighters, the stars of both the middleweights and welterweights come in for their share of praise. The middleweight class in particular has been the most colorful and most intriguing. It stands out as the toughest over the years. It is a class in which every asset of greatness must be displayed by those who seek to gain the top rung.

Its stars have been many and their performances occupy a special niche in the Fistic Hall of Fame. Its battles have been thrillers, in number far superior to those of any other class. Boxing ability, speed, stamina, heavy hitting—these have all been on display in the majority of the championship fights in this division.

The list of outstanding boxers in the class comprises names of men whose ring battles are historic. Often listed as tops are Stanley Ketchel, most frequently named as the king of the class for all time; Bob Fitzsimmons, who won the title from Nonpareil Jack Dempsey in a stirring encounter, the first of his three title triumphs; and Sugar Ray Robinson, a ring marvel, whose defeat of Carmen Basilio enabled him to establish a world record. Robinson is the first to win the championship in the middleweight sector five times, regaining it four.

Kid McCoy, the wily corkscrew artist, a cagey, clever battler; Tony Zale, a powerful hitter; Rocky Graziano, a colorful, two-fisted fighter whose championship contests with Zale—the

Jack Martin, born in 1796, was a baker by trade and was dubbed "Master of the Rolls." He had fast hands and won his first fight when he was only 17 years old. Martin, 5'9" tall and weighing 150 pounds, always met heavier men.

Nat Langham (right), born in Leicestershire in 1820, was middleweight king from 1843 to 1857. He weighed only 157 pounds, but he was so good that ring patrons favored him as a candidate for the heavyweight crown. Harry Orme, a 200-pound giant, was the only man to defeat him, but it took 117 rounds and three hours. Langham beat the celebrated Tom Sayers (his only loss) in 61 rounds in 1853.

Jack Randall, the original "Nonpareil," also called the "Prime Irish Lad," was born in London in 1794. Randall was the most accomplished middleweight ever developed in England. During his career (1815-1821) he won all of his 15 bouts by knockouts.

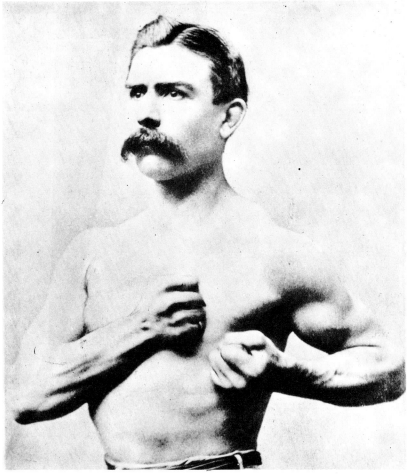

Mike Donovan *(left)* and George Rooke *(above)* were twice matched for a middleweight title bout, but police prevented both meetings. When Donovan decided to join the heavyweights, Rooke declared himself middleweight champion. In later years, Donovan was boxing instructor at the New York Athletic Club.

first of which he lost and the second of which was a sensational victory for him—made ring history; Jake LaMotta, who lost the crown to Ray Robinson; Randy Turpin, who relieved Robinson of the title, then lost a thriller to him before a record-breaking paying gate of $767,626 and attendance of 61,370 at the Polo Grounds on September 12, 1951; Marcel Cerdan, French ace who was killed in an airplane accident; Vince Dundee and Billy Soose—these are only a few of the stalwarts who kept the class in the spotlight.

It is a division that set many records in marks for attendance, receipts, and exciting contests: bouts in which Billy Papke and Ketchel engaged; the clever artistry of Mike Gibbons and Jeff Smith; the short but marvelous career of Les Darcy, Australian champion; the ring science of Tommy Ryan

and the all-around ability of Jimmy Clabby, Eddie McGoorty, George Chip, Harry Greb, Jack Dillon, and Frank Klaus. They all left their mark for future stars to shoot at.

The trio whose names are mentioned most frequently, however, when ring greatness comes up for discussion, are Ketchel, Robinson, and Darcy, whose untimely death deprived the game of one of its luminaries.

Long before middleweights as such were listed as a separate class in the United States, the British had such a division. In our country the middleweights—and even the welterweights—were too busy engaging pugilists who scaled from 160 up to 200 pounds. Fighting heavier men was a steady diet for middleweights.

The first American to obtain recognition as middleweight champion was

Tom Chandler, who defeated Dooney Harris in San Francisco by a knockout in the twenty third round on April 13, 1867. Chandler held on to the crown until 1872 with little fighting, and when challenged by George Rooke he refused to defend the crown and retired. On July 17, 1872, Rooke, was acclaimed title holder.

On March 10, 1881, Rooke tackled Prof. Mike Donovan in the Terrace Garden of New York in a championship match, and so badly was Rooke beaten that the police stopped the affair in the second round, Donovan gaining the crown.

Donovan didn't remain at the head long. He retired the following year to box exhibitions with heavyweights. This left the middleweight throne vacant for two years. Then George Fulljames of Toronto, Canadian title holder, announced that he was pre-

George Fulljames of Canada claimed the title in 1882. In 1884, Nonpareil Jack Dempsey knocked him out for the crown.

George La Blanche, a Canadian known as "the Marine," used the illegal "pivot blow" when he knocked out Dempsey in 1889.

Jack Dempsey, "the Nonpareil," had knocked out La Blanche in 1886, and they met again on August 27, 1889. This time, La Blanche was trained by Jimmy Carroll, a good British lightweight, who taught him the "pivot blow." In the 32nd round, La Blanche started the blow as a left hook, which missed its mark. He quickly pivoted on his heel and brought his elbow back with terrific force on Dempsey's jaw. Had the elbow missed, the fist would have been just as effective. Dempsey fell on his face unconscious. Up to the time La Blanche used the blow, Dempsey had him bleeding and staggering and set for a knockout. The referee awarded the fight to La Blanche, but the sporting world protested the blow as being illegal, since it was not executed with the fist, and Dempsey was still recognized as the champion.

RING Nº1
FIGHTING IN THE RISING TIDE WATER

RING Nº2
THE FINISH

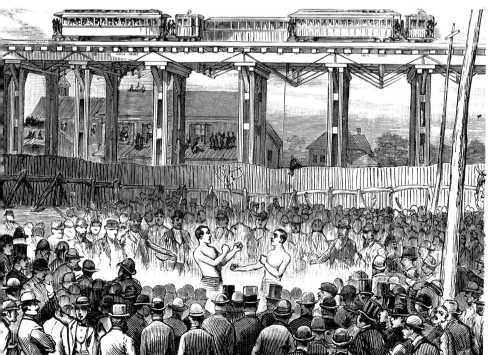

Jack Dempsey and Johnny Reagan, after two postponements due to police vigilance and fog, finally met for their title fight, at Huntington, Long Island, on December 18, 1887. After eight rounds, the rising tide from the nearby Sound flooded the ring and the fight was halted. Reagan refused to fight on sand, so the 25 spectators, led by Dempsey and Reagan, boarded their tug and found a turf spot, 25 miles away. Resuming (above), Reagan was badly outclassed, but gamely went 45 rounds before he was forced to quit.

Dempsey was ambitious to reach the top. In his third fight (left) he met Harry Force, an experienced battler, for $100 a side, at Coney Island, New York. At that time the resort was a dumping ground for derelicts and criminals escaping police. The ring was a circle formed by the fans, who witnessed a rousing battle, until the 11th round, when police raided the scene. The referee set a new date—September 17—for the fight, but Force failed to appear.

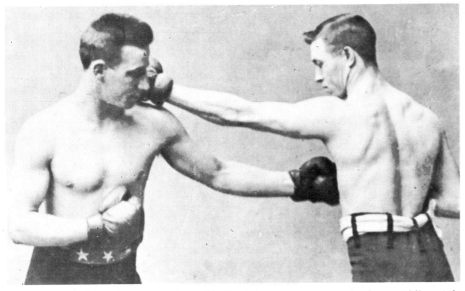

Tommy Ryan (left), shown sparring with Jim Dineen, was recognized as middleweight champ when Bob Fitzsimmons abandoned the class to aim for the heavyweight crown. Ryan had defeated all challengers for the middleweight title.

POISONED GLOVES USED IN

Deadly Oil of Mustard Was Smeared Bonner's Fighting Mits, Nearly Blinding His Opponent.

Tommy West (above) gave Ryan a rough time before being kayoed in the 14th round in 1898. In 1899 West won on a foul over Jack Bonner in the eighth round, when he was blinded (left) by the oil of mustard which had been smeared on Bonner's gloves. In 1900 West forced Joe Walcott to quit in 11 rounds, but the following year he was again knocked out by Ryan at Louisville, Kentucky. This 17-rounder was the bloodiest battle ever seen in the South.

: to a clinch.
to the body
the right on
started to

:o a straight
p early. He
trying with
gave him a
wing to the
tried at the
West's left
He bled a
urriedly got
ey dove into
nt an awful

ind, Bonner
left for the
at the head.
1 the left a
ood. Toward
ried with a
West clinch-
he body, but
 time.

ing.

inual efforts
gan to tell.
n. Then he
d West was
it from gong
wed a bit.
isposition to
lloping.

grind, Bon-
and landing.
calling for
few straight
and one real
close, had a

uneventful.
th the left,
1 the right-
got to Bon-

BLINDED BY A BLOW FROM A POISONED GLOVE:

there was something on the gloves. He staggered back, half blinded, and caught one of the arms, which had blocked Bonner's blow, as if burned. The referee said: "I smell it." and turning to Bonner sent him to the corner.

The police flooded Bonner's corner and took charge of the seconds, while the crowd stood up. West, in the meantime was in agony from the burns he had received, and White was nearly blinded. Bonner finally admitted he had oil of mustard in his corner for his legs. The fight was given to West.

Every circumstance of the fight between West and Bonner points to a job. The betting, which, on the past performance of the men, should have been no better than 6 to 5, was 2 to 1, with Bonner a favorite.

Some were offering 100 to 40, and it is said one man offered to bet 50 to 15 he could name the winner. The betting was all out of keeping with honesty, and those who had thought of betting on West got frightened and refused to bet at all.

Stanley Ketchel, 5' 9" and 154 pounds of fury, was christened Stanislaus Kiecal on September 14, 1887, in Grand Rapids, Michigan. He left farm life at 15 and "rode the rods," wandering through the West where he fought his way out of hobo jungles into the ring. From 1903, when he started, to 1910, when he was murdered, Ketchel fought 63 battles. He scored 46 knockouts, 14 in rapid succession in 1905.

Bob Fitzsimmons knocked out Dempsey for the title and defended it only once.

pared to meet any middleweight in the world, to decide the ownership of the vacant throne. Nonpareil Jack Dempsey, accepted the defi.

The men met at Great Kills, Staten Island, on July 30, 1884. They fought with heavy driving gloves and Fulljames was battered into submission in the twenty-second round. From then on Dempsey successfully defended his crown until he was knocked out by Robert Fitzsimmons on January 14, 1891, in a vicious encounter at New Orleans, in which Dempsey was halted in the thirteenth round.

Previously—in 1886—Dempsey stopped the great George LaBlanche, "The Marine," in the thirteenth round; but in 1889 LaBlanche, with the aid of the pivot punch, knocked out Dempsey in the thirty-second round. Since LaBlanche was overweight, Dempsey retained his crown.

Prior to that, in 1888, public opinion had forced Donovan out of retirement

Exciting battles lay ahead, when Stanley Ketchel, named "the Michigan Assassin," claimed the middleweight crown. On June 4, 1908, he whipped Billy Papke in 10 rounds. They met again on September 7, at Los Angeles, and in a surprise finish, Papke (right), known as the "Illinois Thunderbolt," knocked Ketchel out in 12 rounds. Ignoring the preliminary handshake, Papke floored Ketchel with a terrific right. Down four times in the first round, one eye shut tight, and fighting in a daze, Ketchel took a horrible beating for 12 rounds.

Willus Britt (below, right), who handled Stanley Ketchel's ring affairs, also managed lightweight Jimmy Britt, his brother.

Jack (Twin) Sullivan was knocked out after going 20 rounds with Ketchel. His twin brother, Mike, lasted one round.

to fight Dempsey for the world championship. "The Nonpareil" agreed. They fought on November 15, in Brooklyn, and the contest ended in a six-round draw, with Dempsey retaining his throne.

What Robinson is to the present day school of middleweights, Ketchel was to the old. Stanley, born of Polish parents, September 14, 1887, in Grand Rapids, Michigan, engaged in many scintillating contests, the best of which were those with Joe Thomas and Billy Papke.

He knocked out Mike Twin Sullivan on February 22, 1908 in one round to win the crown and three months later, stopped his brother Jack Twin, in twenty. Then, in successive months, he defeated Billy Papke in ten rounds in a championship match; stopped Hugh Kelly in three; knocked out Joe Thomas in two; and lost his title in the twelfth round of his battle

Two months after being slaughtered by Billy Papke, Ketchel regained his crown, before a packed arena in San Francisco. Ketchel sailed into Papke from the first bell and never let up until he caught him with a clean shot on the jaw in the 11th round.

When Ketchel met Jack Johnson on October 16, 1909, he weighed 160 pounds to Johnson's 209. In rounds 8, 9, 10 and 11, Ketchel pressed the attack. Ketchel's first blow in round 12 put Johnson down *(left)*. But Johnson got up and kayoed him.

with Billy Papke in Los Angeles, September 7, 1908. Two months later, November 26, he rewon his throne, halting Papke in the eleventh round in San Francisco.

The following year Ketchel and Jack O'Brien engaged in a hair-raising affair in New York in which the final gong found Philadelphia Jack's head resting in the sawdust pail. It was a vicious encounter, a no-decision bout, with O'Brien saved from a knockout by the bell. He then stopped O'Brien in Philadelphia in three rounds. Then came his fourth affair with Billy Papke in Colma, California, the most thrill-

Ketchel's next fight after regaining his crown from Papke was with the clever warrior, Philadelphia Jack O'Brien. They met on March 26, 1909, at the Pioneer Athletic Club in New York, which was once a horse market. O'Brien's defensive skill and ring craft warded off many of the boring-in attacks by Ketchel. Most of Jack's blows landed, but they were not good enough to slow Ketchel down. Going into the 10th round, O'Brien seemed to be ahead, though the bout was a no-decision affair. With only eight seconds to go in the 10th and final round, Ketchel unleashed a furious attack *(right)* and landed a deadly right on O'Brien's jaw. Jack toppled over backwards, completely out, with his head resting in the resin box *(below)* in his own corner. The referee tolled off the count, but only reached eight when the final bell rang.

ing of all his engagements. It was fought in a raging storm, and Stanley, now dubbed the "Michigan Assassin," won on points after twenty rounds and held on to his throne.

Three months later he tried to wrest the heavyweight title from Jack Johnson, and though he put the giant Negro down in a surprise maneuver, he was knocked out with the next punch by Johnson after Jack quickly regained his feet in the twelfth round.

On October 15, 1910, Ketchel was killed by a jealous farmhand, Walter A. Dipley.

Pete Dickerson, Stanley Ketchel; Emmet Dalton, the notorious bandit and Joe Harmon, a heavyweight, posed for this rare and unretouched photo, at Joplin, Missouri, in 1909. Ketchel and Harmon were guests of Dickerson at the State Democratic Convention held there. This was Ketchel's last photo.

A jealous ranch hand shot and killed Ketchel, in a brawl over the latter's girl friend. Ketchel fell dead in front of the shack *(left)* on his ranch in Conway, Missouri.

Kid McCoy could have won the middleweight crown without much trouble, but he put on weight to go after the heavyweight title.

Les Darcy, middleweight champion of Australia, was 5' 6'' tall and scaled 158 pounds. He had skill and stamina.

Les Darcy was never seen in an American ring. Judged from his wonderful performances in Australia against the cream of the American talent, had he not died from a combination of a broken heart and pneumonia in Memphis, Tennessee, after he was hounded by U. S. sports writers as a "slacker," there is no telling how far he would have gone in his chosen profession. He might have been greater than Ketchel.

He came to New York on an oil tanker, after leaving his native land without permission. He was signed to fight Jack Dillon in the old Madison Square Garden, but Governor Whit-

man of New York, following concerted attacks, not only refused permission for Darcy to perform in the Empire State, but induced other Governors to do likewise in their domains. He issued a statement declaring that Les had run away from his native land to avoid induction into the Army for World War One service, and wherever Darcy went this stigma followed him.

He enlisted in the National Guard Air Corps in Tennessee but died from what most people thought was a broken heart. Thus, while termed a slacker in our country, this nineteen year old fistic phenom from Australia

passed away as a member of our armed forces.

In Australia, he knocked out Eddie McGoorty twice, George Chip, beat Jimmy Clabby, George K.O. Brown, and Fritz Holland; lost to Jeff Smith in five rounds and beat him on a foul in two. He had an excellent record.

Kid McCoy was another who stood out in the class. He was a clever, sharpshooting boxer with a bunch of tricks up his sleeves. He and Tommy Ryan set the pace for their division in the early days. McCoy killed himself, as did Papke.

With the death of Ketchel, there was a wild scramble for the vacated

217

Billy Papke, shown weaving under Jim Sullivan's left (above), scored a knockout over Sullivan in London on June 8, 1911, in nine rounds, and reclaimed the crown when Cyclone Thompson could no longer make the weight.

Cyclone Johnny Thompson, of Sycamore, Illinois, won handily over Papke in 20 rounds and clinched his claim for the crown. Thompson's ring career started in 1892, when he was 16 years old.

Frank Mantell, who came from Pawtucket, Rhode Island, bolstered his title claim when he beat Papke in 1912. Mantell, a 12-year veteran, retired in 1917, after being knocked out by Harry Greb in one round and Mike Gibbons in three rounds.

throne. Billy Papke claimed the title. Previous to the death of Ketchel, he fought no decisions with Willie Lewis and Frank Klaus and kayoed Lewis in three rounds in Paris, stopped Joe Thomas in sixteen rounds in San Francisco and won from Jack Twin Sullivan in Boston. He was in Australia at the time of Ketchel's demise and as the former champion and number one contender declared himself champion.

On February 11, 1911, he was out-pointed in twenty rounds in Sydney by Cyclone Johnny Thompson. But Thompson couldn't hold on to his newly won laurels because he became overweight and Papke reclaimed the championship.

Frank Mantell disputed the claim and on February 22, 1912, at Sacramento, California, he whipped Papke in twenty rounds and received considerable support as world champion.

Others who were in the field and

Jeff Smith, who had been fighting only two years, was beginning to meet the best men when he put in a claim for the title. Born in New York on April 23, 1891, Jeff boxed all over the United States and Europe for 17 years.

In 1913 Jeff Smith had five bouts in Paris. He drew with Frank Mantell in 20 rounds and later lost a 20-round decision to Georges Carpentier (right).

Mike Gibbons, a boxing marvel, fought 132 bouts in a career from 1908 to 1922.

Jimmy Clabby, another tough ring veteran, battled the best from 1906 to 1923.

Eddie McGoorty won the Wisconsin State Amateur title when only 15. A pro for 11 years, he was kayoed in Australia by Les Darcy in 15 rounds on July 31, 1915.

contested the right of Papke and Mantell to hold the crown were Eddie McGoorty, Jimmy Clabby, Les Darcy, Jack Dillon, Jeff Smith, Mike Gibbons, and Frank Klaus.

For two years the title was in dispute, but after Papke had lost on a foul to Klaus in fifteen rounds on March 5, 1913, in Paris, Klaus received general recognition as world champion. He was knocked out by George Chip at Pittsburgh, on De-

George Chip (above), born in Scranton, Pennsylvania, in 1888, gained the middleweight crown in 1913 by knocking out Frank Klaus in Pittsburgh. Chip's career started in 1909.

Al McCoy (left), after six years of boxing, scored a big upset with a one-round knockout over Chip in 1914. Since the title could be won only by a knockout, McCoy held it three years, before Mike O'Dowd turned the trick on November 14, 1917.

Frank Klaus, after nine years of campaigning, won the crown from Billy Papke in March 1913, lost it to George Chip in October, then retired. Klaus, born in Pittsburgh in 1887, died there in 1948.

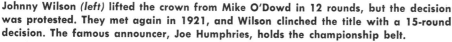

Johnny Wilson (left) lifted the crown from Mike O'Dowd in 12 rounds, but the decision was protested. They met again in 1921, and Wilson clinched the title with a 15-round decision. The famous announcer, Joe Humphries, holds the championship belt.

cember 23, 1913, in five rounds and Chip ascended the throne.

George didn't last long. In a surprise that astounded the boxing world on April 6, 1914, Al McCoy, a southpaw, knocked Chip out in Brooklyn in the opening round. He held the title for three years, losing it to Mike O'Dowd in the sixth round in Brooklyn, on November 14, 1917.

Although Mike protested the decision at the end of twelve rounds

Harry Greb (right) loved "night-life" and cared little for training. In the ring, he was a dynamo, throwing punches from all angles. Because of the fast pace he set in his bouts, he was called "the Human Windmill." His unorthodox style frustrated nearly all of his opponents. In a span of 14 years, he fought over 500 battles, lost 7 and was knocked out once, by Joe Chip, in 1913, his first year in boxing. Greb (below, left) won the crown in 1923 by drubbing Johnny Wilson in 15 rounds. He fought many of his last battles with one eye sightless, and died October 22, 1926, following an eye operation.

Challenger Tiger Flowers (below, right) got a crack at the title and won it from Greb in 15 rounds on February 26, 1926. In a return title bout on August 19, Flowers again won a 15-round decision.

of his contest with Johnny Wilson in Boston on May 6, 1920, Wilson succeeded O'Dowd as crown wearer. Slightly over a year later, July 21, Wilson gained a decision over Bryan Downey in Cleveland on a foul, and despite the refusal of the Cleveland Commission to recognize Wilson as winner, he retained the throne but lost it to Harry Greb on August 31, 1923, in fifteen rounds at the Polo Grounds of New York.

221

Jim Farley *(right)*, the New York State Boxing Commissioner in 1926, weighs in Harry Greb and Tiger Flowers for their last meeting. Boxing Secretary Bert Stand is next to Farley.

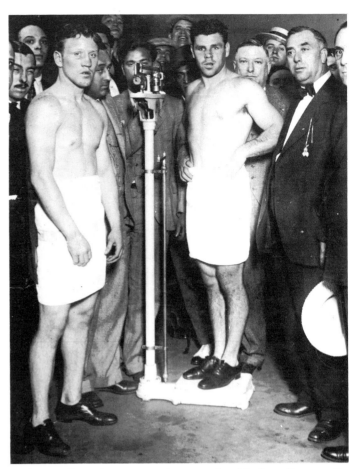

Mickey Walker, shown on scales, won the title from Flowers. He defended it successfully in 10 rounds against challenger Ace Hudkins *(left)* on October 29, 1929, at Chicago.

On February 24, 1925, in Los Angeles, Mickey Walker knocked Bert Colima out cold in his own corner. Dutch Meyers, Colima's manager, is seen about to administer smelling salts to his boy, while Walker protests the action. The referee disqualified Colima, in spite of the fact that he was kayoed.

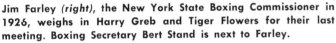

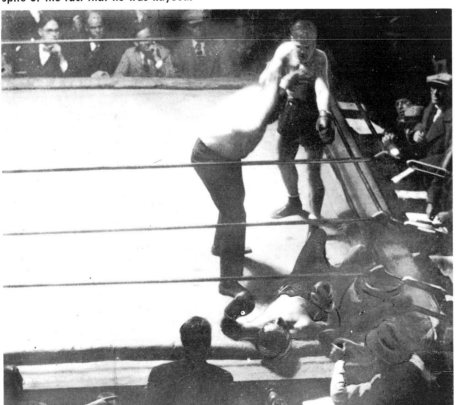

Greb held the crown for nearly three years, when he was deposed on February 26, 1926, by Tiger Flowers, another southpaw, in fifteen rounds at New York City. Flowers was the first Negro to hold the crown.

Mickey Walker, of New Jersey, who held both the welter and middle-weight crowns, succeeded Flowers as banner bearer in the latter division. He rated close to the top. A terrific hitter with an abundance of courage, he fought in every division from welterweight through heavyweight. Though far outweighed, he always gave a thrilling performance.

Walker won the middleweight crown from Tiger Flowers in Chicago, December 3, 1926, in a ten round bout after having dropped the decision to Harry Greb in fifteen rounds in a scintillating, hair-raising mill in New York on July 2, 1925, an affair in which

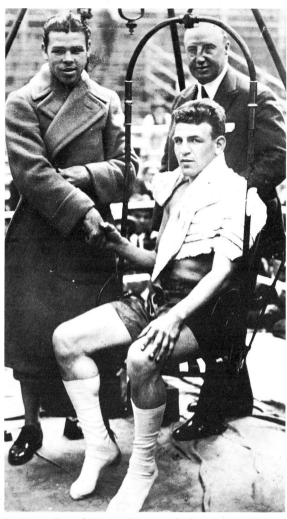

Having relieved Tiger Flowers of the crown, Mickey Walker defended his title against Tommy Milligan, in London. Milligan *(on scales)* and Walker weighed in for the fight, and eight hours later Walker knocked out the European champion in the 10th round *(right)*.

he attempted to annex the middleweight championship while still holding the welter title.

As a middleweight he knocked out Tommy Milligan in London in the tenth round, June 30, 1927; won from Ace Hudkins in ten in Chicago, June 21, 1928; and beat Hudkins in Los Angeles in ten in a second bout for the title. He relinquished his crown on June 19, 1931, to compete against heavyweights.

He drew with Jack Sharkey in fifteen rounds of an interesting contest; knocked out Jimmy Maloney in two; won from King Levinsky and Paulino Uzcudun in ten rounds each; lost to Johnny Risko; knocked out Salvatore

Walker, the undisputed middleweight champion, is bade farewell by British promoter C. B. Cochran and Eugene Corri *(right)*, the sportsman who refereed the fight.

The day after the exceedingly popular "Toy Bulldog" fought a 15-round draw with heavyweight Jack Sharkey, he was on the golf links with tavern owner, Billy LaHiffe *(left)*; Jack Kearns, his manager; his young son; and Senator "Wild Bill" Lyons *(right)*. Since his retirement in 1935, Walker has earned great prominence as a painter *(below)* in the primitive art field.

Ruggirello; was stopped by Max Schmeling in eight vicious rounds of fighting in a campaign that kept him pretty busy during 1932. The following year, unsuccessful in his quest for heavyweight honors, he fought Maxie Rosenbloom for the latter's light heavyweight title and lost a close bout in fifteen rounds.

Mickey wound up his great ring career in 1935, winning six of eight bouts that year, four by knockouts. In his final contest, with Eric Seelig as his opponent, he was stopped in the seventh round and hung up his gloves.

He was a fabulous character, colorful, a powerful puncher; and while for a good portion of his career he was only an overstuffed welterweight, he made the grade in the three top divisions. After retiring, he turned to painting and had several successful exhibitions. He also owned a colorful and popular bar on 49th St. opposite Madison Square Garden. He is currently hospitalized in New Jersey.

The retirement of Mickey Walker brought to the class confusion even more complicated than that following Ketchel's death. Differences of opinion between the National Boxing Association and the New York Commission resulted in two claimants for a num-

Marcel Thil, after winning the middleweight championship of Europe in 1939, was married *(lower right)* to his manager's daughter, Georgette Taitard. With the middleweight class in complete confusion in America, Gorilla Jones, the NBA champ met Thil on June 11, 1932, in Paris and lost on a foul in the 11th round *(right)*.

Lou Brouillard of St. Eugene, Canada, won the New York middleweight title over Ben Jeby in 1933 and lost it the same year to Vince Dundee. Three years later, Lou went to Paris to meet Thil in a title bout and lost on a foul in four rounds. In 1937 they met in Paris for the second time and Brouillard *(below, left)* was again disqualified for fouling in the sixth round.

ber of years before the ascendancy of Tony Zale.

Gorilla Jones came out on top in a National Boxing Association elimination and Ben Jeby was the New York Commission's choice. Marcel Thil, French champion, beat Jones on a foul in Paris, but New York refused to concur. Thil clinched his claim by defeating both the British and German title holders, Len Harvey and Eric Seelig.

The confusion continued with Lou Brouillard knocking out Ben Jeby, Vince Dundee outpointing Brouillard,

Ben Jeby, who lost the middleweight title to Brouillard in 1933 and retired in 1936, is shown giving advice in 1938 to a promising young lightweight named Jackie Savino.

Teddy Yarosz (below, left) of Pittsburgh won the American middleweight title when he decisioned Vince Dundee in 15 rounds on September 11, 1934, in the smoky city. Yarosz boxed from 1929 to 1942. Dundee, who was born in Italy, fought from 1925 to 1937. He died in 1949.

Babe Risko, born in Syracuse, New York, in 1911, won the crown from Teddy Yarosz on September 19, 1935, and lost it to Freddie Steele in 1936. He died in 1957.

Fred Apostoli (below, left) stopped Marcel Thil in the 10th round on September 23, 1937, and should have been declared champion. The New York Boxing Commission did not recognize Thil as champion and insisted the bout be fought as a non-title affair.

Dundee losing to Teddy Yarosz, the last named dropping a verdict to Babe Risko. All of these battles were really for the American crown only.

On February 15, 1937, Brouillard had lost to Thil on a foul in Paris, and when Thil came to America to fight Fred Apostoli on Mike Jacobs' Tournament of Champions program, the New York Commission insisted that the bout be listed as a non-title affair though both men were under the class limit. When Thil was defeated, Apostoli failed to gain the support of the New York Board as world champion, recognition he definitely should have received.

The confusion continued after Apostoli stopped Freddy Steele, who had

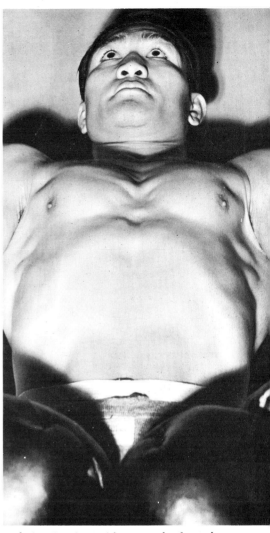

Freddie Steele from Tacoma, Washington, annexed the American middleweight crown from Babe Risko on July 11, 1936, in Seattle. Freddie battered Risko into the ropes (above) and floored him in the first round, then went on to an easy victory in 15 rounds. Steele defended the title in five bouts, then lost it to Al Hostak.

Ceferino Garcia, a title contender from the Philippine Islands, knocked out the New York Commission champion, Fred Apostoli, in seven rounds on October 2, 1939.

Solly Krieger, born in New York City, outpointed Al Hostak in 15 rounds on November 1, 1938, for the NBA title.

Al Hostak regained the middleweight crown in Seattle, when he knocked out Krieger in four rounds on June 27, 1939.

lifted the title from Risko in an overweight match; and when Steele refused to face Apostoli in a bout for the crown, the New York Commission ruled the latter world champion.

In the meantime Steele was knocked out in a round by Al Hostak in Seattle; Solly Krieger of New York gained a decision over Hostak in fifteen rounds, then was knocked out in four by Hostak, both for the N.B.A. crown. When Apostoli was halted by Ceferino Garcia in seven rounds in Madison Square Garden, the situation became still more confused.

Then Tony Zale knocked out Hostak; Garcia was defeated by Ken Overlin; and Overlin lost to Billy Soose. The N.B.A. declared Zale its

The first circular ring in the United States (a round ring was used in England in 1912) was built in a San Francisco shipyard and demonstrated before workmen on May 26, 1944. Former middleweight champ Fred Apostoli, who went into the Navy in 1942, is shown on the left, in an exhibition bout with Vic Grupico of San Francisco. Frank Carter was referee. The ring was made of aluminum tubing covered with heavy velvet cloth.

Tony Zale ended the NBA championship confusion, by knocking out Al Hostak, in 10 rounds on July 19, 1940, at Seattle. In a return title bout in Chicago on May 28, 1941, Zale again knocked out Hostak, this time in two rounds. Tony was a popular ringman and anxiously attempted to get a shot at the New York title-holder.

Ken Overlin shellacked Ceferino Garcia on May 23, 1940. On May 9, 1941, he met Billy Soose and lost the New York title in 15 rounds. Overlin, a ring-cutie *(left, above)*, tried some tricks with Soose, but Billy waltzed away with the verdict.

Billy Soose, unable to make weight, vacated the New York middleweight title for the heavier class. Born in Farrell, Pennsylvania, in 1917, Billy attained ring prominence after attending Penn State College.

The middleweight muddle was finally cleared up in 1941, when Tony Zale was matched to meet Georgie Abrams, an outstanding contender. Zale, shown about to land a right to Abrams' head, won a 15-round decision and the world middleweight crown.

world title holder and the New York Board placed Soose on top.

Before a match could be arranged, Soose outgrew the class, and Georgie Abrams, who had thrice defeated Soose, was named to face Zale. When Tony won a fifteen round decision in Madison Square Garden on November 28, 1941, a universal title holder ruled the middleweight class for the first time in a decade.

Following four years service in World War Two, Zale won a victory over Rocky Graziano on September 27, 1946, that set aside all doubt as to his right to the throne. Rocky knocked out Zale in a return bout in Chicago a year later, and in a third encounter Zale regained the crown by halting Graziano in Newark in three rounds.

Rocky Graziano, the most colorful prize fighter to step into a ring since Stanley Ketchell, was born on the lower East Side of New York on June 7, 1922. Rocco Barbella (his real name) was 5' 7" tall and threw a right hand that was loaded with pure dynamite. He started fighting in 1942. When his career ended in 1952, he had fought 83 battles, winning 52 by knockout, 14 by decision and one by a foul. He drew in six bouts, lost seven decisions and was knocked out three times. Two stages in Rocky's amazing life are shown above. In his early zoot-suit period, Rocky, in the foreground, is leaving Stillman's Gym after a workout in 1943, munching on a Danish bun. The final stage was set in 1953, when Rocky, invited to appear on Martha Raye's television show, delighted audiences for weeks with his humorous speech and antics, as in the scene above with Miss Ray and Cesar Romero.

Thus the middleweight class returned to a normal status after years in which no world champion was recognized.

Graziano, a product of New York's slum districts, made the grade despite his ups-and-downs in a most controversial career. He turned to television and the movies after retirement and made a success of his new venture. The movie *Somebody Up There Likes Me*, the story of his rise to fistic fame, a Horatio Alger tale, earned him more than a quarter of a million dollars.

The Graziano-Zale fights in New York and Chicago went down in boxing history as epic ring battles. They were thrillers.

In the New York affair at the Yankee Stadium, Zale, on the verge of defeat, ready to collapse, suddenly dropped Rocky for the count. The gate for that bout was 39,827 with the gross receipts $342,497, but when

Rocky unleashed a sudden burst of power in the 10th round (above) and Charley Fusari was finished. For nine rounds, Fusari held the lead and had Rocky whipped, but he was unable to stop Rocky's do-or-die spirit in the last round. Graziano had lost the title to Zale the year before and was making a comeback on September 14, 1949, against Fusari, who was a fast-coming prospect from Irvington, New Jersey.

Marty Servo, the welterweight champ, lasted two rounds when he faced Graziano in an overweight match on March 29, 1946. A sudden switch in the odds, making Servo a 10-1 favorite, created rumors of a fix that almost canceled out the fight. Rocky insisted upon going through with the bout, and in less than six minutes, he smashed Servo to the canvas (right) with a broken nose and a face beaten to a pulp.

Rocky Graziano was at the height of his career on September 27, 1946. He had flattened 32 opponents and was ready to do the same to the champ, Tony Zale. Instead, Rocky was knocked out for the first time. He hit Tony with some solid bombs early in the fight and he missed some too, as the sequence above shows. Others had crumbled under Rocky's blockbusters, but Tony fought back with body punches, and Rocky was feeling the effects. By the end of the fifth round they were both getting tired and were both hurt. In the sixth round Zale whipped a solid blow to Rocky's stomach. Rocky went down, got up, and was floored again with a left. He struggled to rise *(left)* but referee Ruby Goldstein counted him out before he was half off the canvas. Once on his feet, Rocky wanted to continue, but the referee and trainer Whitey Bimstein prevented it *(below)*, while Zale, tired but still middleweight champion, was led to his corner.

"Boxer's License No. 514 issued by the New York State Athletic Commission to Tommy Graziano, ring name Rocky Graziano, is hereby revoked." So droned chairman Colonel Eddie Eagan after a hearing charging Rocky with failure to report an attempted bribe to throw a fight with Reuben Shank. Rocky, seated at the table with his lawyer *(right)* with manager Irving Cohen standing between them, appears stunned with disbelief. The bout with Shank, scheduled for December 27, 1948, had been called off when Rocky injured his back while training. Early in January, Graziano was grilled almost 15 hours in the District Attorney's office. They wanted him to name the person who offered the bribe. Rocky insisted that he considered all bribe attempts a joke and never took them seriously.

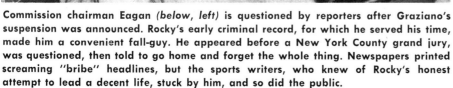

Commission chairman Eagan *(below, left)* is questioned by reporters after Graziano's suspension was announced. Rocky's early criminal record, for which he served his time, made him a convenient fall-guy. He appeared before a New York County grand jury, was questioned, then told to go home and forget the whole thing. Newspapers printed screaming "bribe" headlines, but the sports writers, who knew of Rocky's honest attempt to lead a decent life, stuck by him, and so did the public.

Tony Zale, the man of steel, started his pro career in 1934. When he retired in 1948 after 88 battles, he had won 70 bouts with 46 kayoes, lost 12, drew twice and was stopped four times.

233

In an oven-like atmosphere at the Chicago Stadium in 1947, Zale and Graziano ripped each other apart until the sixth round, when Rocky let loose a barrage of lefts and rights and Tony went down against the ropes, forcing the referee to stop the slaughter. Rocky Graziano, with his left eye slashed open and the right one almost closed, was the new champion. As Rocky explains in his book: "This was no boxing match. It was a war, and if there wasn't a referee, one of the two of us would have wound up dead."

Less than a year later, Tony Zale made Graziano an ex-champion with a long left hook on the jaw. Rocky was counted out flat on his back in the third round.

Zale and Graziano resumed their warfare at the Chicago Stadium, the receipts from 18,547 paid admissions reached a new high for an indoor fight, $422,918.

The spectators in the Windy City were treated to one of the greatest middleweight championship fights on record. In a temperature that seemed to have reached the boiling point, Rocky won the crown July 16, 1947. It was a terrific encounter, and every minute was packed with drama.

Their third bout in Newark on June 10, 1948, lacked the fire of the previous pair as Tony won the title back hands-down.

The middleweight crown went overseas on September 21, 1948, when Marcel Cerdan, of France *(above, right)* defeated Tony Zale so badly that Tony was unable to answer the bell for the 12th round. After this fight, Zale decided to retire from the ring.

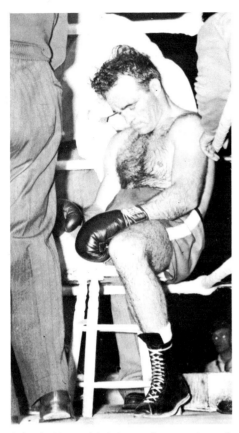

Jake LaMotta *(right)* stands over Marcel Cerdan in their title bout, after Marcel went down from a half push. Cerdan *(above)* could not come out for the 10th round and Jake was declared champion. A return bout was delayed when LaMotta was injured, and Cerdan returned to his home in Casablanca. Returning to the States for the championship match, he was killed when his plane crashed on October 27, 1949. Cerdan had an excellent record. In 111 fights from 1934 to 1949, he won 64 by knockouts and 43 by decision. He lost four—one decision, two fouls and one kayo. LaMotta defended the title twice, then lost it to Ray Robinson.

Three months after Zale had knocked out Rocky, a Frenchman, Marcel Cerdan, dethroned Tony in the Roosevelt Stadium of Jersey City, the champion being unable to come out for the twelfth round. Marcel, after dropping the championship to Jake LaMotta, the "Bronx Bull," in Briggs Stadium of Detroit, June 16, 1949, was killed in an airplane accident in the Azores, while on his way back to the United States to train for a return bout with Jake. He had been halted by LaMotta in their title contest in the tenth round.

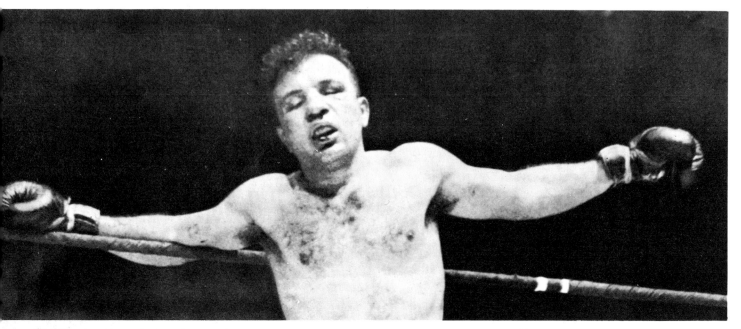

Jake LaMotta leans on the ropes, a courageous but beaten champion, after his bout with Sugar Ray Robinson was halted by the referee in the 13th round. This was Jake's sixth meeting with Robinson. He beat Sugar Ray once and lost four, all by decision. From 1941 to 1952, the "Bronx Bull" had 106 bouts, with 30 knockouts and 53 decisions. He lost 15 and was stopped four times.

Randy Turpin, the British and European middleweight champion, gave the boxing world a big surprise when he outpointed Ray Robinson in 15 rounds and annexed the world title. Turpin is seen lunging with a left past Sugar Ray's head in the action photo on the left, but it was the last round and Randy was all but wearing the crown.

Ray Robinson won the middleweight title for the first time when he halted LaMotta in the thirteenth round in Chicago, February 14, 1951. He then went on a long tour of Europe, neglected to keep physically fit, and in a surprise defeat lost the championship to Randy Turpin in London by a decision in fifteen rounds. That bout took place July 10, 1951. The return contest was staged at the Polo Grounds in New York, September 12, 1951, and a record gate for a non-heavyweight fight was set with a gross of $767,626.17. Ray rewon the crown,

Sugar Ray was in trouble in the 10th round of his return title match with Turpin. His left eye was sliced open and bleeding profusely. If he could go one more round, the bout might possibly be stopped. In desperation, he went all out with a barrage of blows, until Turpin lay flat on his back. Randy got up and, with his back to the ropes (below), swayed helplessly as punches crashed against his jaw. Referee Ruby Goldstein halted the bout and Ray was champ again.

Ray Robinson came out of retirement in 1955 and for the third time recaptured the middleweight crown, when he stopped Bobo Olson in two rounds *(above)*. Five months later, he stopped him again in four rounds. After Ray quit on December 18, 1952, for a career as a night club entertainer, Olson and Randy Turpin met on October 21, 1953 for the vacant throne, which Olson won.

stopping the Britisher in the tenth round at a time when it appeared that Robinson, with a bad cut and on the verge of having the bout halted, landed a barrage that ended the affair in his favor via the knockout route.

As middleweight champion, he tried to wrest the world light heavyweight title from Joey Maxim at the Yankee Stadium, June 25, 1952, but after rolling up a good lead, exhaustion in the terrific heat caused him to collapse in the fourteenth round. He announced his retirement six months later to become an actor in his own stage show.

The various commissions decided on an elimination to obtain his successor. In Europe, Randy Turpin, the British Empire champion, and Charley Humez, French and European title holder, were matched for a bout in London on June 9, 1953, and Turpin won the decision.

In America, Carl "Bobo" Olson of Hawaii and Paddy Young of New York, the leading contenders, were billed for an American championship bout in Madison Square Garden June 19, 1953, and Olson won. Then Olson and Turpin were matched to decide who would succeed Robinson as world champion and Olson outpointed Randy to win the crown.

When Robinson's venture into the theatrical field ended in a failure, Sugar Ray decided on a comeback. He knocked out Olson in the second round in the Chicago Stadium, De-

Gene Fullmer, a worthy challenger from Utah, knocked Robinson out of the ring in the seventh round *(above)* in 1957, and went on to win a unanimous 15-round decision and the middleweight title. Since 1951, Gene had engaged in 40 bouts. He won 37, 20 by knockouts, and lost three. On May 1, 1957, in a return bout, Ray stopped Fullmer in five rounds *(right)* and won the crown for the fourth time.

cember 9, 1955, to seat himself back on the throne which he had abdicated.

Gene Fullmer, a young Mormon from West Jordan, Utah, challenged and relieved Ray of the crown at Madison Square Garden on January 2, 1957, gaining the decision at the end of fifteen rounds. But three months later, Sugar Ray gained the plaudits of the world's boxing fans when in the Chicago Stadium on May 1, he knocked out Fullmer in a return contest in the fifth round to become the first in the history of the middleweight division to win the crown four times.

239

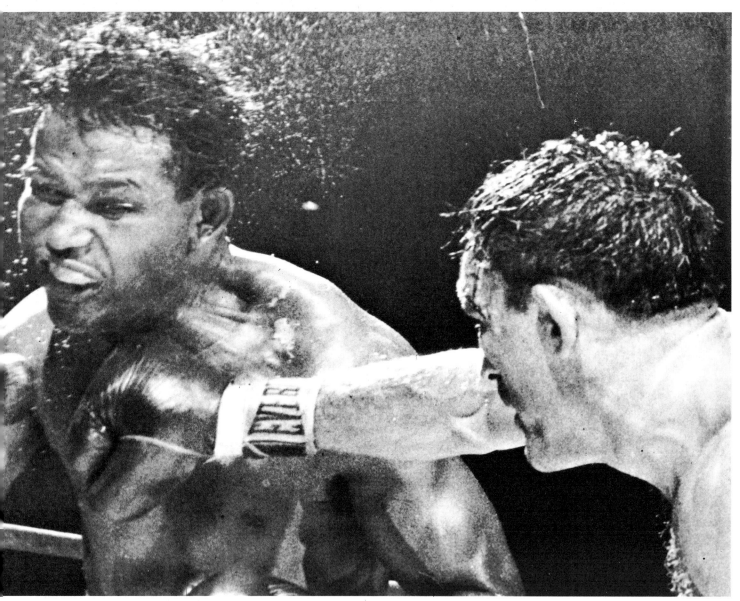

Carmen Basilio, the welterweight champion, connects with a smashing right to Robinson's jaw in the 10th round of their middle-weight championship bout. In the 13th round *(below)* Carmen acted as a leaning post for the tired Sugar Ray.

Carmen Basilio, blood-spattered but determined, won the world middle-weight championship from 37-year-old Ray Robinson on a split decision at New York's Yankee Stadium on September 23, 1957, but surrendered it again to Sugar Ray in Chicago Stadium on March 26, 1958. In their New York contest the dogged body-puncher from Canastota, New York, lost referee Al Berl's vote, but received the verdict from judges Artie Aidala and Bill Recht.

It was a gruelling battle all the way. Both men were stunned and bewildered at different stages of the fight,

Basilio, a good little man, traded punches, skill, and determination with Sugar Ray, a good big man, and at the end of 15 rounds, Carmen was the new middleweight champion. In the sequence above, Basilio traps Ray on the ropes and lands with a left hook.

but neither gave an inch. Blood streaked Carmen's left cheek as Ray tried desperately near the wind-up to put across a killer. But the final round saw Basilio still battering away. All three officials agreed that he had won that frame and many of the thousands of spectators guessed that Basilio's final-round performance had won him the decision.

It was Basilio's fifty-second victory and his greatest triumph in 71 professional fights. He had won the welter title twice, and now with the middleweight crown in his possession, he was forced to vacate the 147-pound class throne.

The fight grossed $556,467, and the paid attendance was 38,072.

Their return engagement was fought with the same viciousness. Ray made ring history by regaining the crown for the fourth time and winning it for the fifth. Less than two months short of his thirty-eighth birthday the great ring warrior conquered an almost overwhelming weariness and stuck it out to the finish, even though at times

The story of the return match in which Carmen Basilio was dethroned by Robinson is graphically told (above) in Carmen's tightly-closed left eye. From the sixth round on, Basilio was at a disadvantage. Only his courage made the bout close.

241

Ray Robinson *(above, right)* came from behind after the fifth round to roll up a margin too great for Basilio to overcome. After 15 rounds of battle, Sugar Ray's hands were raised in victory, by announcer Ben Bentley *(right)* and co-manager Harold Johnson. Robinson showed why he is called a ring marvel by succeeding in doing what never before had been accomplished—winning the middleweight crown five times. His record performance is not ever likely to be repeated.

it appeared that his aging body could stand the punishment no longer. The turning point of the battle came in the fifth round, when a left hook to the head by Ray puffed up Carmen's eye, starting the downfall of the champ. Again there was a split decision, the two judges giving it to Robinson by big margins and referee Frank Sikora seeing it as a victory for the battered Basilio.

Neither man had much fight left as the bout neared its finish, so heavy was the bombardment and so fast the pace. There were no knockdowns, although each was staggered often. 17,976 spectators paid $351,955 to see the battle, which was as thrilling a contest as anyone had seen in years. No opponent ever whipped Robinson twice.

Never has there been a boxer in any division to boast of a record like Ray's. He's a standout not only in the middleweight class but in all boxing as one of the ring's stellar performers of all time. He was born in Detroit, May 3, 1920, and made his start in the amateur field.

The N.B.A. again moved in to vacate a title for inactivity, this time Sugar Ray Robinson's. Fullmer and Basilio met at San Francisco on August 28, 1959, for the N.B.A.'s middleweight crown. Fullmer kayoed a dazed and weary Basilio in the fourteenth round, when referee Jack Downey stepped between the two battlers.

New York, Massachusetts, Europe, and the Oriental Federation recognized Robinson as champion until a twenty-nine-year-old ex-fireman from Brookline, Massachusetts, Paul Pender, won a fifteen-round split decision over the almost legendary ring marvel on January 22, 1960. It was a fast and grueling battle in which Pender let the forty-year-old Robinson take the offensive and wear himself out, while the challenger fought a defensive battle, blocking punches, then moving away.

Having knocked out Terry Downes of England in seven rounds and won a decision over Basilio, Pender fought a rematch with Downes in London on July 11, 1961. This time Pender quit at the end of the ninth round,

After the N.B.A. vacated Robinson's crown for inactivity, Fullmer met Basilio at San Francisco on August 28, 1959 and KOd him in the 14th to receive N.B.A. recognition.

Meanwhile, Robinson (left) recognized by New York, Massachusetts, Europe and Oriental Federation, lost a 15-round split decision to Paul Pender in early 1960 at Boston.

On January 14, 1961, at Boston, Pender scored a knockout in the seventh round over British challenger Terry Downes. This photo shows the bloody-faced Downes ducking under a long left thrown by Pender in the fifth round.

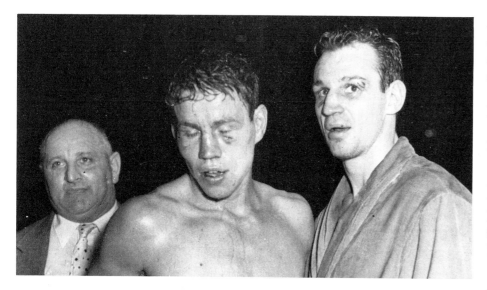

In return match in London on July 11, 1961, Pender (*right*) quits at the end of the ninth round, Downes thus winning a portion of the world middleweight championship.

Meanwhile, Dick Tiger of Nigeria was recognized as the titleholder by the World Boxing Association after defeating Fullmer in 15 rounds. (*Above*) Fullmer slips. (*Below*) Tiger and pilot Jersey Jones after Tiger clinched title via KO of Fullmer in Nigeria.

after savage warfare, and gave the champion of British Isles that portion of the world title which Pender had captured from Robinson.

Downes's reign was short-lived; Pender recaptured the title on April 7, 1962, in a fifteen-round decision in Boston.

In the meantime, the World Boxing Association title was awarded to thirty-three-year-old Dick Tiger when he won a unanimous decision over thirty-one-year-old Fullmer, on October 23, 1962, in San Francisco.

Tiger's boxing skill had overcome Fullmer's aggressive style in 1962, but it brought only a draw when the two met again on February 23 of the next year.

Tiger was finally recognized as world middleweight champion when Pender retired on May 7, 1963, but he clinched the title when he kayoed Fullmer in the seventh round on August 10, 1963, on Tiger's home soil.

Four months later, Joey Giardello's style of moving, jabbing, and sharp-shooting befuddled Tiger, and the

Joey Giardello and beaming wife are shown after Giardello captured title on 15-round decision over Tiger in 1963.

challenger won the fifteen-round decision in Atlantic City, N.J., on December 7, 1963. Both men scaled 159¾ pounds.

In a return bout Tiger landed heavier blows and sapped Giardello's strength, and he regained his title by a unanimous decision in fifteen rounds on October 21, 1965.

Flashy, happy-go-lucky Emile Griffith, born on February 3, 1938, in the Virgin Islands, became the world's next champion on April 25, 1966, when he won a fifteen-round decision over Tiger in New York. He was the

In a return bout on October 21, 1965, Tiger regained the 160-lb. title from Giardello on a unanimous 15-round decision. (*Above*) Tiger lands a right to the jaw. (*Below*) Joey connects with a left.

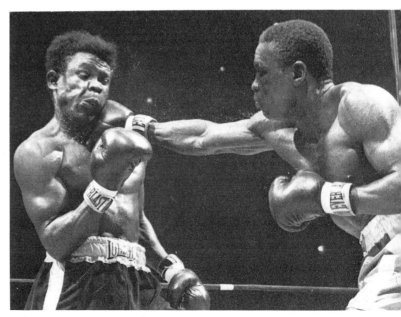

On April 25, 1966, Emile Griffith, the welterweight champion, captured the title by decisioning Tiger in 15 rounds. (*Above*) Tiger is sent to the canvas in the ninth. (*Right*) Griffith takes a hard right from Tiger which contorts his features.

On April 17, 1967, Griffith defended his crown against Italy's Nino Benvenuti, who promptly outpointed Emile over the 15-round distance at Madison Square Garden. Benvenuti, left, downed in the fourth round, and Griffith, right, hits the canvas in the second.

Benvenuti, who fought Griffith twice more, losing the title, then regaining it, met his master in Carlos Monzon, who knocked out Nino in 1970, then repeated the feat (*left*) in 1971. (*Below*) Carlos hailed.

Marvin Hagler jolts Minter with a right in taking the middleweight title at Wembley in September 1980.

Alan Minter celebrating after stopping Vito Antuofermo at Wembley in June 1980 to retain his title.

third man in the history of boxing to win the middleweight title after holding the welterweight crown, the others being Robinson and Basilio.

Just one year later Griffith was defeated by Italy's Nino Benvenuti, a romantic and handsome figure. The fifteen-round match on April 17, 1967, in New York, was a fast-paced affair in which Benvenuti used his 3½-inch height and 5¼-pound weight advantages to keep Griffith at bay while weakening his opponent with jabs.

In the 1960 Olympics, the same Olympics in which Muhammad Ali participated, Benvenuti had been named the most proficient boxer in the games over his more colorful and extroverted fellow pugilist.

Benvenuti and Griffith fought two more duels. In the first, on September 29, 1967, Griffith defeated the Italian in fifteen rounds, and the second bout, on March 4, 1968, saw Benvenuti beat Griffith by a unanimous decision.

Benvenuti's love of "the sweet life"

was his undoing, on November 7, 1970. Evenly matched at 159¾ pounds, Benvenuti and Carlos Monzon, of Argentina, met in Italy. The strong, aggressive Monzon knocked out the Italian in a stunning upset in the twelfth round with a crushing right flush on the chin.

The powerful Argentinian went on to score nine successive kayos over Emile Griffith, Frasier Scott, Jean-Claude Bouttier, Benvenuti, Denny Moyers, Tom Bogs, and Roy Dale and to win three bouts by decisions.

On February 9, 1974, he knocked out welterweight champ José Napoles in seven rounds at Paris. The 159-pound champ overpowered his game 153-pound opponent who was making a bid for the middleweight crown.

In April, 1974, however, Monzon was deprived of his title by the World Boxing Council for failing to defend same against its official challenger, Rodrigo Valdes, of Colombia, who they recognised as champion on May 25 when he knocked out Bennie Briscoe in seven rounds at Monte

Carlo. Monzon ignored this ruling and defended his title against Tony Mundine (Australia) at Buenos Aires on October 5, winning by a knockout in seven rounds. In 1975 he made two more successful defences, stopping Tony Licata in ten rounds in New York on June 30 and Gratien Tonna, of France, by a fifth round kayo in Paris on December 13.

On June 26, 1976, Monzon once again made himself undisputed world middleweight champion by outpointing the pretender to the throne, Rodrigo Valdes at Monte Carlo. This performance was repeated on July 30, 1977, again at Monte Carlo, after which Monzon announced his retirement from the ring after a reign of nearly seven years, undefeated in fourteen title defences.

Back to Valdes, who had made four successful W.B.C. title defences; against Gratien Tonna by a kayo in eleven rounds at Paris on November 30, 1974; Ramon Mendez, who was stopped in eight rounds at Cali, Colombia, on May 31, 1975; Rudy Robles, outpointed at Cartagena on August 16, and Max Cohen, who retired in the fourth round at Paris on

March 28, 1976. Immediately after Monzon's retirement, Valdes came back into the world title picture by outpointing Bennie Briscoe at Campione D'Italia on November 5, 1977, and was then recognised as undisputed champion by both the W.B.C. and W.B.A. He lost this distinction on April 22, 1978, being outpointed by Hugo Corro, from the Argentine, at San Remo. On August 5 Corro outpointed Ronnie Harris (USA) at Buenos Aires, and on November 11 he again won the decision over Valdes in the same city to remain champion.

On June 30, 1979, Corro was outpointed over 15 rounds by Vito Antuofermo (New York) and lost his title. The new champion kept his crown against Marvin Hagler (Brockton), but was held to a draw. Alan Minter gave up his British title to concentrate on winning the world crown and he did this handsomely at Las Vegas on March 16, 1980, when he outpointed the champion after a thrilling 15 rounds contest.

On June 28 at Wembley Arena, London, Minter enhanced his position as undisputed world middleweight champion by stopping Antuofermo, who retired after eight rounds, but on September 27 in the same ring, he lost his title to Marvin Hagler, the bout being stopped in round three because the Englishman had sustained a badly gashed right eyebrow. There were ugly scenes at the conclusion of the contest when some of the disappointed spectators stormed the ring and tried to assault the winner and the referee. It was a bad night for British boxing in every respect.

LIGHT MIDDLEWEIGHT CHAMPIONS (formerly known as JUNIOR MIDDLEWEIGHTS)

(Weight Limit, 154 Pounds)

DENNY MOYER, 1962; RALPH DUPAS, 1963; SANDRO MAZZINGHI, 1963; NINO BENVENUTI, 1965; KI SOO KIM, 1966; SANDRO MAZZINGHI, 1968; FREDDIE LITTLE, 1969; CARMELIO BOSSI, 1970; KOICHI WAJIMA, 1971; OSCAR ALVARADO, 1974, KOICHI WAJIMA, 1975;

In 1975 the W.B.C. withdrew its recognition of Koichi Wajima for failing to defend against Miguel De Oliveira, whom they acclaimed champion after he had beaten Jose Duran over fifteen rounds at Monte Carlo on May 7. Or November 13, however, Elisha Obed forced De Oliveira to retire in ten rounds at Paris and he was followed by Eckhard Dagge 1976-77, Rocky Mattioli (Australia and Italy) 1977-79, and Maurice Hope (Great Britain) 1979.

Meanwhile, the W.B.A. instituted its own Light-Middleweight champion in Jae Do Yuh (Korea) who knocked out former champion Koichi Wajima in seven rounds on June 7, 1975. Wajima regained the title in 1976 and he was followed by Jose Duran 1976, Miguel Angel Castellini 1976, Eddie Gazo 1977-78, and Masashi Kudo 1978-79.

ON OCTOBER 24, 1979 THE JAPANESE CHAMPION WAS OUTPOINTED BY AYUB KALULE (UGANDA) WHO LIVED IN DENMARK. HE BEAT STEVE GREGORY (U.S.A.) OVER 15 ROUNDS AT COPENHAGEN ON DECEMBER 6 AND IN 1980 MADE TWO MORE TITLE DEFENCES, OUTPOINTING MARIJAN BENES (YUGOSLAVIA) AT RANDERS ON JUNE 12 AND OUTPOINTING BUSHY BESTER (SOUTH AFRICA) AT AARHUS.

MOST INTERNATIONAL INTEREST IN THIS PERIOD, HOWEVER, WAS CONFINED TO THE W.B.C. VERSION OF THE TITLE. AFTER STOPPING MIKE BAKER (U.S.A.) IN SEVEN ROUNDS IN LONDON, ON SEPTEMBER 25, 1979, MAURICE HOPE GAVE MATTIOLI A CHANCE TO WIN BACK HIS CROWN, BUT SCORED A MORE CONVINCING VICTORY OVER THE AUSTRALIAN/ITALIAN BY STOPPING HIM IN ELEVEN ROUNDS AT WEMBLEY ARENA ON JULY 12, 1980. IN THE EARLY HOURS OF NOVEMBER 26, AFTER THE HARDEST FIGHT OF HIS CAREER, HOPE KEPT HIS TITLE, COMING OUT OF NEAR DEFEAT IN THE 11TH ROUND, TO WIN BY A CLOSE BUT UNANIMOUS POINTS VERDICT OVER CARLOS HERRERA OF THE ARGENTINE OVER 15 ROUNDS.

Maurice Hope (right) mixing it with Carlos Herrera (Argentina) while retaining his light middleweight title at Wembley, November 1980.

THE WELTERWEIGHTS

Paddington Jones weighed 145 pounds and defeated all who faced him in 1792, heavier men included. He met 185-pound heavyweight champion Jem Belcher in 1799 and lost in 33 minutes.

Jack Cooper, a gypsy, was a ring veteran and a powerfully built welterweight. After serving six months in jail for the death of Dan O'Leary in a desperate battle, he was matchd to test the ability of Young Dutch Sam, a rising star. Sam closed Cooper's eyes and cut his face to ribbons in 33 minutes.

Famous for his caricatures of society in Georgian England, Thomas Rowlandson rendered this prize ring scene (below) in 1825. It probably represents the contest between Young Dutch Sam, on left, and Harry Jones. The battle was held in Bedfordshire on October 18, 1825, with Young Sam the winner in 18 rounds.

WELTERWEIGHT DIVISION

It was not until about the middle of the nineteenth century that the gap between the lightweight and heavyweight classes (10 stone or 140 pounds and up) was somewhat closed by the adoption of both the welterweight and middleweight groups. A medium of 142 pounds was set for the former and Paddy Duffy emerged the victor and first champion. That was in 1878.

But the class soon became dormant and it was not until December 14, 1892, that we find it again active with Danny Needham and Mysterious Billy Smith fighting for the crown, which was won by the latter. Prior to that, Nonpareil Jack Dempsey and George Fulljames, each scaling well within the welterweight limit, engaged in a championship fight, but Dempsey, who carried off the honors in twenty-two rounds of heavy milling, preferred to call himself the middleweight champion and went on to defend that crown until he was shorn of it by Bob Fitzsimmons.

When Mysterious Billy Smith whipped Needham in fourteen rounds in San Francisco, he was acknowledged king of the division. There were

Harry Jones *(above)*, known as "the Sailor Boy," was an aggressive welterweight with a bruising style. With the possible exception of Paddington Jones, he fought more battles than any fighter of his time. The recorded number of bouts is 36, but he is known to have fought many more.

Young Dutch Sam *(left)* was the greatest welterweight ever produced in England. He was the son of Dutch Sam, probably the hardest hitter in pugilistic history. Young Sam was born on January 30, 1808. At 15, in his first battle, he knocked out Bill Dean. His weight was never more than 145 pounds, and he stood a little over 5' 9". He was an extraordinary phenomenon, graceful of foot, and most accurate with his blows, which were brutal. He could whip any man with only his left hand, as demonstrated in his bout with Gypsy Cooper, whom he cut to pieces with a left jab. His backer, Mr. Hughes Ball, a young man of wealth prominent in society, never lost a wager on Sam, who won all of the 16 fights he engaged in from 1823 to 1834. Young Sam died at 35.

SMITH GETS INSIDE WITH A HARD LEFT

Mysterious Billy Smith *(below)*, born in Eastport, Maine, knocked out Danny Needham for the title in 1892. He ended the bout with a left to the jaw, as illustrated above in the *New York Journal*. Smith lost to Tommy Ryan, who lost to Kid McCoy. When McCoy and Ryan vacated the class, Smith reclaimed the crown.

Tommy Ryan *(below)*, who won the crown from Smith, boxed 109 bouts from 1887 to 1907, winning 85, with 45 knockouts.

many good ringmen at his weight in the East, the best of whom was clever, speedy, sharp-shooting Tommy Ryan of Redwood, New York. After stopping Mike Shaugnessey of Detroit in twenty-three rounds, Danny Needham in seventy-six, and engaging in a draw of six with Smith, all while scaling less than 150 pounds, he challenged Billy for the championship. In a thrilling encounter that went twenty rounds, Ryan gained the crown in Minneapolis on July 26, 1894.

Ryan was one of the cleverest men in the division. Smith protested the verdict, but public sentiment favored Ryan and he was generally accepted as the titleholder. It was a bout loaded with action. The police interceded, with Ryan leading at the time.

The class, like the one above it, has been brightened with the names of boxers who will never be forgotten. Many made their mark in more than one division, while others, after losing the title, regained it.

Boxing enthusiasts were thrilled by the stirring performances of such stars as Mickey Walker, Henry Armstrong, Barney Ross, Sugar Ray Robinson, Tommy Ryan, Kid McCoy, Joe Walcott, Jimmy McLarnin, Mike Gibbons, Packey McFarland, Kid Gavilan, Ted Kid Lewis and Jack Britton among many others who made the division famous.

In Armstrong it boasted of the only boxer in ring history who held three titles simultaneously—feather, welter, and lightweight.

In Walker it had a fighter who won both welter and middleweight crowns, a two-fisted champion who was as good as a light heavyweight and heavyweight as he was in the lower sectors.

In Ray Robinson it boasts of the only titleholder to win the crown five times in the middleweight class after he had retired from the lower group.

In Ted Kid Lewis of England we find one of the few ringmen who fought with success in all divisions from bantam through heavyweight.

Sam Langford was one of the world's greatest, not only in the welter class but in each of the next higher

252

Rube Ferns, born in Pittsburgh, Kansas, in 1874, was known as "the Kansas Rube." After winning the crown from Smith in January, 1900, he won seven bouts, five by knockouts, and lost the title to Matty Matthews in October. He knocked out Matthews the following year in 10 rounds, and regained the welterweight title.

Matty Matthews (left) held the title six months. He was born in Brooklyn on July 13, 1873, and began boxing in 1891, scoring a knockout, but did not fight again until 1894, when he engaged in only one bout. He fought twice in 1895 and became active from 1896 to 1904, engaging in 79 bouts. Matthews, a good boxer, met and defeated, or held to a draw, most of the top men.

Joe Walcott, who started boxing in 1890, lost two title chances in 1898 to Mysterious Billy Smith and finally won the crown in 1901, when he stopped Rube Ferns in Canada.

groups. His bout with Jack Johnson at Chelsea, Massachusetts, in which he was outpointed, gained for Sambo recognition as one of the greats in the top division.

Kid McCoy, a pupil of Ryan, relieved Tommy of the championship at Maspeth, Long Island, March 2, 1896, in fifteen rounds, after which both retired from the division to enter the middleweight class. Mysterious

Billy Smith then reclaimed the crown. In a battle with Rube Ferns in Buffalo on January 15, 1900, Smith lost the championship to Rube on a foul in the twenty-first round. On October 16 of that year, Ferns was outpointed by Matty Matthews in fifteen rounds at Detroit, but regained the crown on May 24 of the following year when he knocked out Matty at Toronto, Canada, in the tenth round.

Then came the rise of Joe Walcott, the Barbados Demon. A short, thick-necked, furious fighting man, he knocked out Ferns at Fort Erie, Canada, in the fifth round to be acclaimed champion. When Dixie Kid won on a foul from Walcott in the twentieth round of a hectic battle in San Francisco, the decision was disputed. The winner left shortly after for England and announced his retirement from

Billy (Honey) Mellody beat Walcott for the crown and a month later won again over Joe. Mellody scored 33 knockouts since 1901, when he started, but was stopped three times. His career ended in 1913.

Mike (Twin) Sullivan won the title from Mellody on April 23, 1907, then grew out of the class. Mike and his twin brother Jack hailed from Cambridge, Massachusetts. In 67 bouts, from 1901 to 1913, Mike lost one decision, was stopped once by Stanley Ketchell and twice by Joe Gans.

Mike Glover, of Lawrence, Mississippi, was one of many who claimed the vacated title. Glover boxed from 1908 to 1916. In his last bout he lost to Ted Lewis.

Jimmy Gardner also claimed the title. Born in County Clare, Ireland, in 1885, he started in Boston in 1902 and retired in 1913 after 100 bouts, with only six losses.

the division due to weight difficulties, and Walcott reclaimed the crown.

Honey Mellody outpointed Joe in Chelsea, Massachusetts, on October 16, 1906, and he in turn was outpointed by Mike Twin Sullivan on April 23, 1907, in Los Angeles in twenty rounds, after which he gave up the crown to enter the higher division.

Now the championship was variously claimed by a group consisting of Jimmy Clabby, Ray Bronson, Jimmy Gardner, Clarence Kid Ferns, Mike Gibbons, Kid Graves, Mike Glover, Ted Kid Lewis, and Jack Britton; for several years there was no universally recognized titleholder. It was not until Lewis, a Britisher, outpointed Britton on August 31, 1915, in Boston in twelve rounds, the first of twenty bouts between the pair, that a semblance of order came out of the chaotic state.

For four years they kept fighting with varying results until on March 17, 1919, Britton knocked out Ted in Canton, Ohio, in the ninth round. Then the public conceded top laurels to Britton.

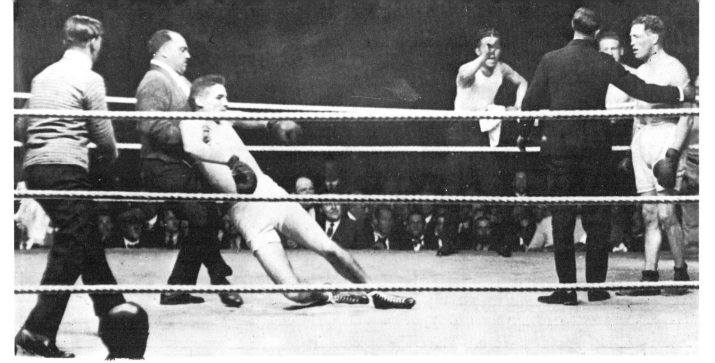

Ted Kid Lewis, who often fought Jack Britton, had a career that extended from 1910 to 1929. In 1925 Lewis lost on a foul (above) to Marcel Thuru of France, who is seen being dragged to his corner.

World War One was now on. Many of our stars of the fistic world enlisted or were drafted. The cream of the U. S. pugilists, among them Mike Gibbons and Packey McFarland, donned uniforms as boxing and physical training directors. These two were master technicians. They and Sam Langford never held a title, though Mike claimed one, but they came no better than this trio in boxing history. Though McFarland masqueraded as a lightweight, he found it difficult to make the class limit and fought mostly in the welter division with great success. The fighting qualities of the three were unexcelled.

When after the war many of the top boxers returned to normal life, Packey and Mike among them, the welter class again became the most active. The most conspicuous boxers in the class following World War One were Mickey Walker, Britton, and Lewis. Walker and Britton were matched for a Madison Square Garden bout on November 1, 1922, and Mickey, the "Toy Bulldog" from Elizabeth, New Jersey, walked off with the championship via a decision. It was

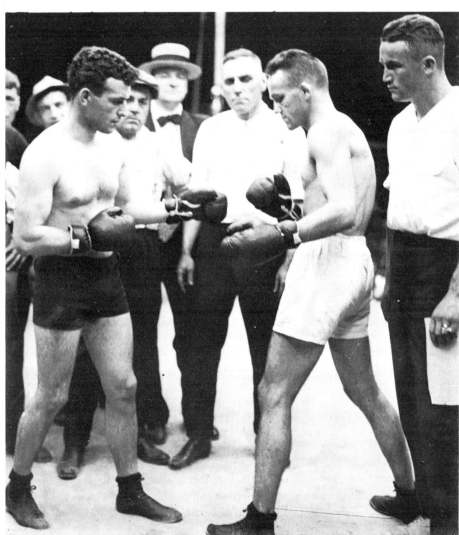

The two best ringmen in the welterweight class were Packy McFarland (left) of Chicago and Mike Gibbons, of St. Paul, who met in a no-decision battle in 1915. On the right is young heavyweight Tom Gibbons, standing behind brother Mike.

Mickey Walker (left) in his fourth year of boxing, beat Jack Britton for the crown on November 1, 1922. Britton's amazing career totaled 300 bouts from 1905 to 1930. He was knocked out once, in 1905.

The new welterweight champ visited Washington in 1922 and met Congressman Fred A. Britten (left) of Illinois, a former amateur lightweight champion of the world.

Pete Latzo, born in Coloraine, Pennsylvania, had been boxing since 1919 when he met and defeated Walker in 1926. Pete defended his crown twice, then lost it to Joe Dundee in 1927. He retired in 1934 after a knockout by Teddy Yarosz.

an excellent match in which the fans were treated to fifteen rounds of fine boxing and heavy hitting.

The Elizabeth battler held on to the title about four years before he was dethroned by Pete Latzo on May 20, 1926, in ten rounds at Scranton, Pennsylvania.

Latzo wasn't as fortunate as Walker. He held on to the crown only a little more than a year, losing it to Joe Dundee of Baltimore on June 3, 1927, in fifteen rounds at the Polo Grounds. Joe, a brother of Vince, who later was a middleweight champion, dropped the title to Jackie Fields of Chicago on July 25, 1929, at Detroit, when the referee awarded the decision to Fields on a foul in the second round.

The welter class went into a tailspin after Dundee had gained the crown, and for a time it passed back and forth among a group consisting of Fields, Young Jack Thompson, Tom-

Pete Latzo (above, right), pride of the Scranton, Pennsylvania, coal miners, lands a left on Mickey Walker's jaw. By keeping on top of Mickey through the 10 rounds, he became champion.

Joe Dundee (above, right), born in Italy in 1902, won the welterweight crown from Latzo in a 15-round bout. Dundee, whose real name was Sam Lazzaro, boxed from 1921 to 1930.

Manager Max Waxman (left) and Dundee appeared in a Los Angeles court in 1927 on a false advertisement charge. Dundee failed to go through with a title bout with Ace Hudkins.

Jackie Fields (right) won the championship from Dundee on a foul in two rounds in 1929, then lost it to Young Jack Thompson (left) on a decision in 15 rounds the following year.

Tommy Freeman (above) won a 15-round decision and the crown from Jack Thompson on September 5, 1930. Freeman defended the title successfully five times in 1931, then lost the crown to Thompson again at Cleveland on April 14, when he could not come out for the 13th round.

On October 23, 1931, Lou Brouillard outpointed Young Jack Thompson for the title, then lost it to Jackie Fields on January 28, 1932. Young Corbett III (real name, Ralph Giordana), shown at left missing a left hook to Jackie Fields' head, won six of 10 rounds from Fields at San Francisco in 1933 and was crowned welterweight champion.

Jimmy McLarnin, a perfect ringman and a lethal puncher who moved up from the lightweight class, met Young Corbett III for the welterweight championship in 1933 and knocked him out (above) in one round. This was McLarnin's only bout that year.

my Freeman, Lou Brouillard, and Young Corbett III.

The change for the better came with the rise of Jimmy McLarnin, who on May 29, 1933, knocked out Young Corbett in the opening round in Los Angeles to gain the top rung of the ladder. With his appearance in the field, the division received a lift. It began to thrive again, with huge gates and large attendances once more making the class an outstanding one in popularity.

McLarnin was one of the brightest stars of the era. He was a clever, sharp-shooting youngster who had come out of the amateurs in the Northwest. He was managed by shrewd Pop Foster, who brought him up from the ranks to become a star first in the flyweight class, in which he put an end to the career of the great little Filipino, Pancho Villa, whose death followed the loss of a ten rounder to

Jimmy "Baby Face" McLarnin and manager Pop Foster (above) were inseparable. Born in Belfast, Ireland, December 17, 1905 and raised in Vancouver, Jimmy started in 1923, as a fly-weight. Under shrewd handling by Foster, McLarnin became one of the great stars of boxing. In 77 contests, he scored 20 knockouts in 63 victories, drew three times, lost 10, and was stopped once, by Ray Miller. As a lightweight in 1927, Jimmy concentrated on more solid punching and scored 14 knockouts in 33 bouts, the last over Corbett. He defeated 13 champions during his career, which ended in 1936.

A welterweight title match between light-weight champion Bar-ney Ross and McLarnin was steamed up by fans and, on May 28, 1934, they met. Ross won a 15-round verdict and the crown. In the ninth round Ross floored Jim-my (above) with a short right and referee Eddie Forbes moved in to start a count. The bout was a sizzler, and they were re-matched for September 17.

McLarnin lost a decision to Tony Canzoneri on May 8, 1936. On Sep-tember 3 Tony lost the lightweight title to Lou Ambers and signed to meet McLarnin on Octo-ber 5. Early in the bout, Canzoneri suffered a cut eye (left) but for 10 rounds both men fought like demons. McLarnin won the decision.

The new welterweight champ, Barney Ross, vacated the lightweight throne and gave McLarnin a return crack at the title. In a hard-fought 15-round bout on September 17, 1934, McLarnin regained the crown. Ross won three bouts after losing the title and on May 28, 1935, met McLarnin for the third time. The contest was a remarkable boxing exhibition, loaded with action. At the end of 15 rounds Ross (above, right) and McLarnin embraced. Ross was declared the winner and re-won the crown.

Barney Ross at the height of his career (above). He was born on the East Side of New York on December 23, 1909, and raised in Chicago. After an amateur career, he turned pro in 1929 and retired in 1938, after losing the title to Henry Armstrong. He lost four decisions out of a total of 82 bouts. He won 74, 24 by knockouts, drew three times. One contest was a no-decision affair.

Jimmy at Oakland, California on July 4, 1925. McLarnin went on to fame and fortune as a lightweight and welterweight.

McLarnin lost the welterweight crown to Barney Ross on May 28, 1934, in the Madison Square Garden Bowl of Long Island City, in fifteen rounds, but rewon his laurels a few months later, September 17, in the same bowl in fifteen frames. They engaged in a third bout, again a thrilling exhibition of ring cleverness combined with sharp hits, on May 28, 1935, at the Polo Grounds. Ross once more came out on top at the end of fifteen sessions.

McLarnin, a boy of wealth, engaged in only three more contests before hanging up his gloves. He lost to Tony Canzoneri, beat him and Lou Ambers in ten rounds, then quit never again to box in professional competition.

The best of all training camps were Barney Ross's at Grossinger's, a summer resort in New York's Catskill Mountains. Besides the serious training routine, there was always time for fun, as above. Officials and friends from Chicago attended all of Ross's camp sessions, and later cheered him on at ringside.

After enlisting in the United States Marines in 1942, Barney received a sharpshooter's medal (above) at the Marine Corps Base in San Diego, California. Later that year Ross was awarded the Congressional Medal of Honor, for saving 10 Marine buddies by wiping out 20 Japs from a Guadalcanal foxhole.

After McLarnin's defeat by Ross, who previously had won the lightweight championship, Barney kept the welterweight class in the spotlight with his scintillating performances. He was a very popular champion who possessed all the assets of greatness in ring warfare. He ruled three years, during which he defended his title successfully against Ceferino Garcia and Izzy Jannazzo, before losing the decision to Henry Armstrong on May 31, 1938. In addition to defeating Garcia in a championship match, he twice whipped him in ten rounders.

In 1942, Ross, who was born in New York, December 23, 1909, enlisted with the U. S. Marines. He served with distinction. For extreme bravery at the battle of Guadalcanal, he was awarded the Congressional Medal of Honor.

In Armstrong, boxing had equally

Henry "Hurricane Hank" Armstrong, battled 175 opponents from 1931 to 1945. He won 144, scoring 97 knockouts, and lost 19. He lost one on a foul, one was no-decision. He drew in eight and was knocked out twice. Hank held three titles simultaneously.

General John Phelan (left) New York boxing commissioner and Dr. William Walker (center) officiated at the weighing-in of welterweight champ Barney Ross and challenger Henry Armstrong, who held the featherweight title. Hank won the welterweight crown and later annexed his third title when he defeated Lou Ambers for the lightweight crown. There was no rule, as there is now, requiring a champion to give up a title if he wins one in a heavier class. It was put into the books because of Armstrong.

The night of May 31, 1938, saw the end of a great champion and the rise of another, when Ross (below, left) took a terrific beating for 15 rounds from Armstrong, the new champion.

Editor Nat Fleischer (left) presents The Ring Magazine feather- and welterweight championship belts to Armstrong and a medal to Joe Louis, for being the outstanding fighter of 1938.

Armstrong defended the title 19 times, scoring 16 knockouts. He lost the crown to Fritzie Zivic on October 4, 1940, and was stopped by Zivic on January 17, 1941. Referee Arthur Donovan stepped in (above) and halted the contest in the 12th round.

The fighting Zivics, left to right, were: Joe, middleweight, 1918-1922; Fritzie, welterweight, 1931-1949; Eddie, lightweight, 1932-1940; Jack, lightweight, 1919-1929; Pete, bantamweight, 1919-1929. Fritz was the only title-holder.

Fritzie Zivic (below) of Pittsburgh boxed from 1931 to 1949, during which he fought in 230 battles. He won 155, including 80 knockouts, lost 61, drew in 10 and was kayoed four times. Fritzie, the youngest of the five Zivic brothers, held the welterweight title for six months before losing it to Freddie "Red" Cochrane, on July 29, 1941, in 15 rounds.

as great a titleholder as in Ross. He was born December 12, 1912, in St. Louis, Missouri, and started his professional career in 1931, following a crack at the amateur game.

He first won the featherweight championship from Petey Sarron in Madison Square Garden in October, 1936, then the welterweight championship on May 31, 1938, and in his next contest on August 22 he defeated Lou Ambers to win the lightweight crown. He wound up the year 1938 successfully defending the welterweight title against Ceferino Garcia in fifteen rounds via a decision and halting Al Manfredo in three, after which he vacated the featherweight throne.

In 1939, besides his lightweight championship contest which he lost to Ambers, he engaged in eleven defenses of his welterweight crown. In one, he took Ernie Roderick, British Empire champion, into camp, gaining the verdict in London in fifteen rounds.

In his final contest, in 1940, he was shorn of his crown by Fritzie Zivic, who won the verdict on October 4

Except for two years in the Navy, Freddie Cochrane boxed from 1933 to 1946. Freddie lost the crown to Marty Servo on February 1, and retired. Referee Eddie Josephs helps Cochrane to his feet *(above)* after the knockout in the fourth round.

Marty Servo was forced to give up the crown in 1946, because of a nose that was badly injured when he was knocked out by Rocky Graziano. Servo *(below, right)* is explaining his decision to sport writers Lewis Burton and Bill Heinz in the boxing commission office. Promoter Mike Jacobs, wearing hat, waits for the official ruling.

in New York in fifteen rounds after Henry had engaged in six title matches besides one with Garcia in which the latter's New York version of the middleweight title was at stake. They fought a draw in Los Angeles.

Zivic held the welter championship until July 29, 1941. The Pittsburgher, born on May 8, 1913, lost it in Newark to Freddie (Red) Cochrane of Elizabeth, New Jersey. Freddie marched off to the Navy with his new crown and when World War Two was over and he was discharged, he fought Marty Servo of Schenectady, New York in Madison Square Garden on February 1, 1946, and was knocked out in the fourth round. Cochrane, born May 6, 1915, prior to losing to Servo, had been knocked out by Rocky Graziano twice in the tenth round in non-title contests after Freddie led all the way.

Servo, because of a nose ailment, was forced to retire and the New York commission named Ray Robinson as his successor following attempts to get some of the leading welters to face Sugar Ray in an elimination. The only one who would agree to such a contest was Tommy Bell, who was an easy victim on December 20, 1946, in Madison Square Garden, losing in fifteen rounds in which he was outclassed. With that victory, Ray gained the support of all other commissions as world champion.

Then Robinson vacated the throne after winning the middleweight title five years later. In a National Boxing Association elimination, Johnny Bratton of Little Rock, Arkansas, born September 9, 1927, decisioned Charlie Fusari of New Jersey on March 14, 1951, in Chicago, and this victory led to a fight with Kid Gavilan of Cuba in New York City on May 18, 1951, in which Gavilan whipped Bratton and gained the support of the N.B.A. and New York, but not that of Europe as Robinson's successor.

In Europe, Charley Humez was the top man, and it was not until after he announced his retirement from the welter class to fight as a middleweight, and after Gavilan's defeat of Billy Graham of New York, that the Cuban

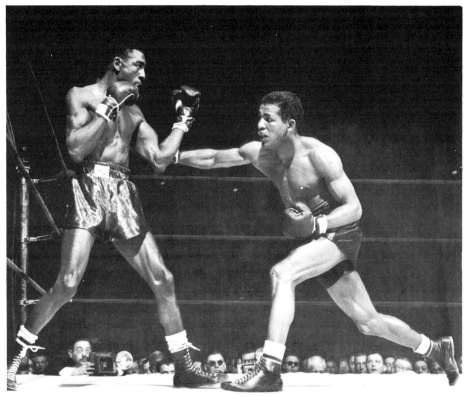

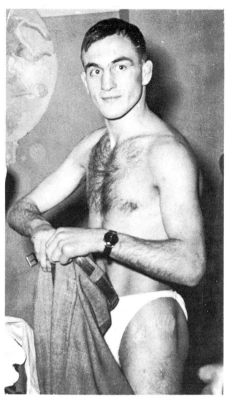

Ray Robinson was named successor to the welterweight throne and the only boxer who would meet Ray was Tommy Bell (above, left) of Youngstown, Ohio, who lost in 15 rounds. Ray defended the title eight times before winning the middleweight crown.

Charles Humez, welterweight champion of Europe, had European backing and held the key to the world championship.

Kid Gavilan (below, right), spectacular fighting machine from Camagüey, Cuba, outfought Johnny Bratton (left) on May 18, 1951, for the welterweight throne vacated by Robinson. Europe recognized the bout only as for the American title.

Kid Gavilan was given a hotly-disputed decision over Billy Graham in New York on August 29, 1951. With Humez out of the welterweight class, Gavilan was recognized as world champ. Graham *(above, right)* met Gavilan for the world title in Havana, Cuba, on October 5, 1952 and was again defeated in 15 rounds. Gavilan is shown in the seventh round, about to deliver the flashy "bolo punch" which he made famous.

Johnny Saxton is met with an uppercut to the jaw by Gavilan *(left)* during their title bout in Philadelphia on October 20, 1954. Saxton lifted the welterweight crown from the Kid in a dull 15-round bout. Gavilan, born Gerardo Gonzalez on January 6, 1926, had his first bout in 1943. Up to 1958, he had engaged in 140 fights, won 105, drew in 6, had one no-contest, and lost 28. He was never knocked out. Johnny Saxton, born in Newark, New Jersey, on July 4, 1930, won 54 out of 63 bouts from 1949 to 1957. He drew twice, lost three times, and was knocked out four times, twice by Carmen Basilio.

received world recognition as new champion. The Gavilan triumph was hotly disputed, the majority of the reporters and the public favoring Graham.

Another disputed decision, that in which Johnny Saxton of Brooklyn defeated Gavilan in Philadelphia, October 20, 1954, brought about a change in the ownership of the welter crown. Gavilan, a colorful fighter, an excellent drawing card, contested the loss, but to no avail. That same year, on April 2, he tried to win the world middleweight title in Chicago, but

was turned back by the titleholder, Bobo Olson, in fifteen rounds.

Johnny Saxton was knocked out by Tony DeMarco on April 1, 1955, in Boston in the fourteenth round to lose his crown. The loser tried for a return bout, but Carmen Basilio of Canastota, New York, beat him to it, and on June 10, 1955, Basilio stopped DeMarco in the twelfth round to gain top honors.

Saxton had been promised an engagement with Carmen if he would relinquish his rights to a contract he held for a return bout with DeMarco, but consented to let Basilio fulfill the

agreement with Tony. This fight was staged in Boston and Basilio again knocked out DeMarco in the twelfth round. Then he gave Saxton his chance.

They met in the Chicago Stadium on March 14, 1956, and in a contest in which it was almost unanimously agreed that Basilio had easily defeated his rival, the decision was against the champion.

Saxton was induced to lay his crown on the line against Carmen in a return bout at Syracuse on September 12, 1956, for which he received a

266

Tony DeMarco (above, right) became the new welterweight champion when he knocked out Saxton on April 1, 1955. Referee Mal Manning stepped in to save the glassy-eyed Saxton from further punishment. DeMarco, whose real name is Leonardo Liotta, was born in Boston on January 14, 1932. In 64 bouts, from 1948 to 1957, Tony won 54 with 31 knockouts, lost 5, drew once, and was kayoed 4 times. Less than three months after winning the crown, DeMarco was dethroned by Carmen Basilio (below, right) in 12 rounds. Carmen repeated the kayo in November. He lost the crown to Saxton in 1956 on a disputed decision, but regained it the same year, when he knocked him out. Carmen relinquished the crown in September, after winning the middleweight title.

handsome fee, and this time, Basilio made certain that no decision would be given against him by halting Johnny in the ninth round. It was a battle in which Basilio went all out from the tap of the opening gong and continued until the championship was in his hands again.

Then in a third engagement, February 22, 1957, in Cleveland, Ohio, Saxton was completely outclassed. Basilio knocked him out in the second round. Following that triumph, Carmen decided to go after Ray Robinson's middleweight crown, a bout which from the standpoint of interest was the outstanding of the year.

On September 6, 1957, Saxton was stopped by Joe Miceli of New York in the third round of a ten round contest in Washington, District of Columbia, and announced his retirement.

Vince Martinez and Virgil Akins, weigh in *(above)* under the supervision of Charles Pian *(right)* of the Missouri commission for the title bout, which ended in four rounds.

Unheralded Don Jordan *(left)* of Los Angeles scored a stunning upset on December 5, 1958, when he gave Virgil Akins a sound beating in 15 rounds and became the new welterweight champion. Jordan, 24, a 3-1 underdog, won a unanimous decision over the 30-year-old Akins, who was defending his crown for the first time. The nationally-televised contest was held in Los Angeles' Olympic Auditorium.

When Basilio defeated Robinson to become the middleweight champion, his welterweight crown became vacant, so the New York Commission and the National Boxing Association, assisted by the World Championship Committee, decided to find a successor through an elimination. Named by the group were: George Barnes of Australia, Tony DeMarco of Boston, Isaac Logart of Cuba, Vince Martinez of Paterson, New Jersey, Gaspar Ortega of Mexico, and Gil Turner of Philadelphia.

However, on the day this was announced Virgil Akins of St. Louis kayoed DeMarco in a Boston contest, and took over his place.

Logart outpointed Ortega in Cleveland, and Martinez decisioned Turner in Philadelphia. Barnes refused to come to America to compete, so the final group consisted of Logart, Turner, and Akins.

A drawing from a hat was held in the offices of *The Ring* Magazine under the direction of the author and Commissioner Helfand. Martinez drew the bye. Akins then kayoed Logart in six rounds in New York and was matched with Martinez in St. Louis on June 6, 1958.

In a one-sided contest in which Vince was floored nine times Akins became the new champion.

On December 5, 1958, Virgil Akins lost his crown to Don Jordan, who held the title for a year and a half before he succumbed to a terrific body beating dealt out by Benny (Kid) Paret. The twenty-three-year-old Paret, an ex sugar-cane cutter from Cuba, won a unanimous decision over the twenty-five-year-old

champion on May 27, 1960, in Las Vegas.

Paret and Griffith fought the first of a three-bout series that would ultimately result in the Cuban's death on April 1, 1961, in Miami. Control of the match swayed back and forth, until unexpectedly, at 1:11 of the thirteenth round, Griffith landed a left

hook to the chin, followed by a solid right that put the champion away and transferred the crown to his own head.

Paret regained the title when he won a split decision over Griffith in a return bout on September 30, 1961. The New York audience, jeering at the officials' decision, indicated that the match had been very close and controversial enough to merit a return bout.

The tragically final third bout, on March 24, 1963, left a comatose Paret on the canvas in the twelfth round,

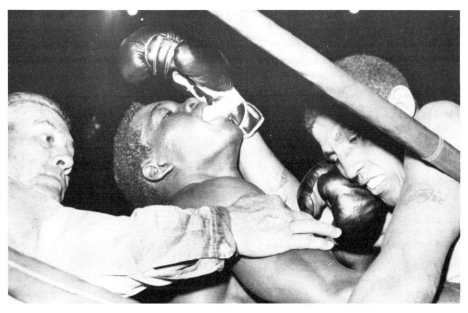

Benny (Kid) Paret, pulled away by referee Charlie Randolph, won the welterweight title from Don Jordan at Las Vegas, Nevada, May 27, 1960. Paret won a 15-round verdict.

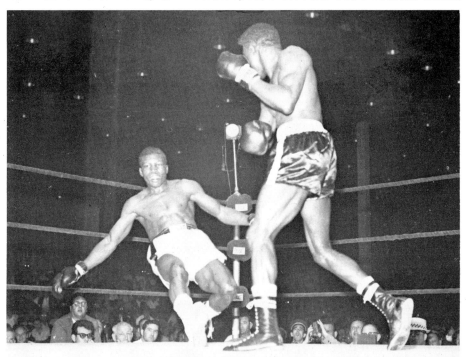

(Left) Emile Griffith administers the *coup de grace* to Paret in the 13th round of their Miami Beach bout on April 1, 1961, Emile thus capturing the 147-pound crown. Griffith (above) does a headstand while Paret still lies on the ring floor, dazed and beaten.

This sequence, from ABC-TV, shows the last few seconds of the tragic Griffith–Paret bout at Madison Square Garden on March 26, 1962, in which Paret was hammered into unconsciousness in the 12th round and died on April 3. Referee was Ruby Goldstein.

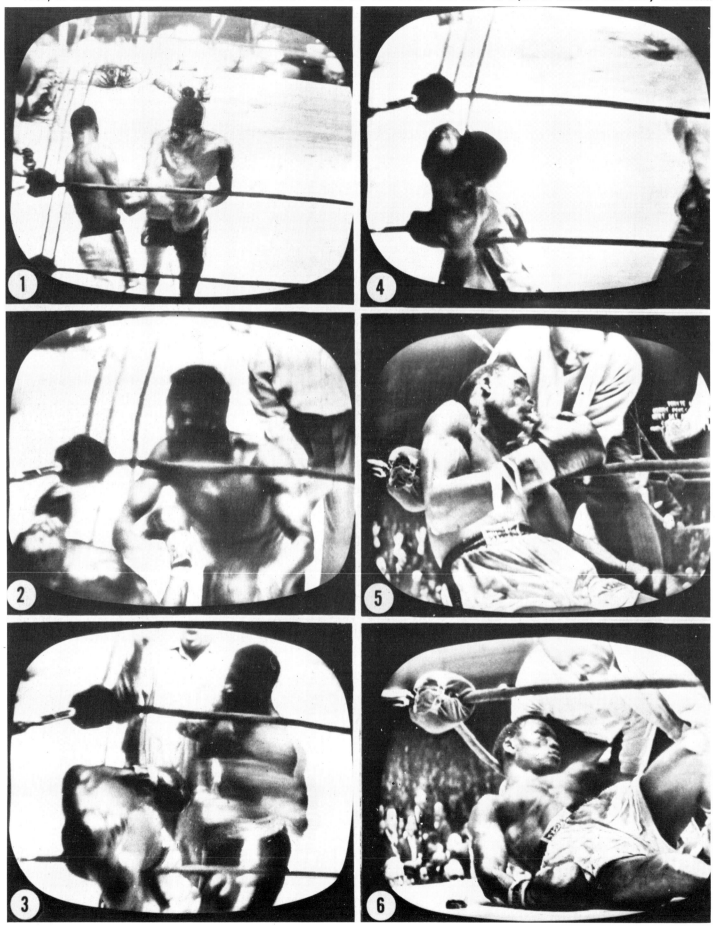

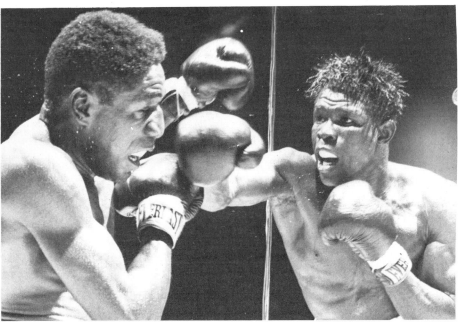

A joyous Luis Rodriguez (*left*) is held aloft by his happy handlers after a close decision over Griffith in a 15-rounder at Los Angeles on March 21, 1963. However, Emile took his crown back via a split verdict in 15 rounds at New York on June 8, 1963, (*above*) to become the first boxer in ring annals to capture the welterweight crown three times.

after an infuriated Griffith, insulted by Paret's calling him a homosexual, meted out a vicious and merciless beating while the Cuban hung on the ropes, partly out of the ring. The official count had Griffith delivering twenty-one blows before referee Ruby Goldstein halted the fight. Before the defending champion's collapse, there had been no evidence of severe injury, and Griffith had been substantially ahead on all score cards. Paret remained unconscious until he died on April 3.

Another Cuban refugee, Luis Rodriguez, briefly held the title for nearly three months after winning a close but unanimous fifteen-round decision over Griffith on March 21, 1963. He lost it again in a rematch on June 8. Awarded a close split-decision over fifteen rounds, Griffith became the first man to gain the world welterweight crown three times.

The strong, hard-hitting champion went on to win another fifteen-round split decision over Rodriguez on June 12, 1964, then three unanimous decisions over José Stable of Cuba, Brian Curvis of England, and Manuel Gonzales of the U.S., before relin-

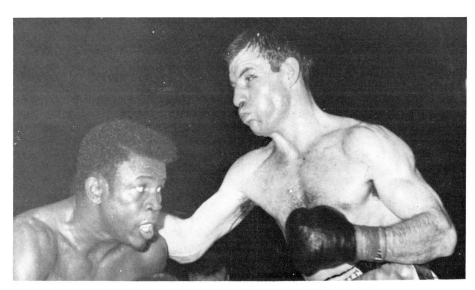

After defending his title against Rodriguez again, at Las Vegas, Griffith went to London, where he pounded out a 15-round decision over Britain's Brian Curvis on September 22, 1964.

Griffith made what was to be the final defense of his welterweight title against Manuel Gonzalez (*right*), gaining a 15-round decision at Madison Square Garden on December 10, 1965.

271

quishing his title on May 18, 1966, and stepping up to the middleweight ranks, to win that crown.

In what was accepted as a bout to decide the successor to Griffith, Curtis Cokes, with an advantage of twelve inches in reach, defeated Jean Josselin of France in Dallas on November 28, 1966, by jarring his game opponent with stinging left jabs over fifteen rounds.

This match was the result of an elimination in which Cokes had gained the W.B.A. title by defeating Gonzales and Rodriguez.

Other American contenders, Ernie Lopez of Las Vegas, Nev., and Ted Whitfield of Amherst, Mass., were defeated in bouts previous to the elimination.

José Napoles, of Mexico, hammered Cokes into submission after thirteen rounds and captured the welterweight title on April 18, 1969. Napoles, at 143 pounds, scored his forty-first knockout in sixty-one professional fights when he kayoed Cokes in ten rounds in a return bout on June 29 in Mexico City.

Billy Backus of Syracuse, who had quit boxing in 1965 because he couldn't win, returned in 1967 and in four years scored twenty-one wins out of twenty-five bouts. On December 3, 1970, he scored a stunning upset over Napoles when the bout was halted in the fourth round, the result of a gash above Napoles' left eye.

Backus, a southpaw with a plodding style, was no match for the smooth, sharpshooting Napoles when the two met in a rematch in Los Angeles on June 4, 1971. The bout was halted in the eighth round after the ring physician examined Backus's badly battered face.

On February 9, 1974 Napoles, one of the better world champions, attempted to add the middleweight title to his welterweight crown, but found conceding 6 pounds to Carlos Monzon, himself one of the best champions, too much and was knocked out in the seventh round.

Napoles was not up to form in his successful defense against the American challenger, Hedgemon Lewis, on

After Griffith vacated the crown upon becoming middleweight boss, Curtis Cokes took over the title by defeating Jean Josselin in 1966. *Above,* the action; *below,* adulation.

August 3, 1974. However, the champion outboxed and outpunched Lewis to win a knockout over his challenger when referee Ramon Berumen halted the contest in the seventh round. Even though he won, he was not the Napoles of times past. He was not as sharp or as speedy. Lewis had a bad night, and that proved the difference.

On December 14, 1974 Napoles kept on the winning trail by knocking out challenger Horacio Saldanho, of Argentina, in the third round, and

made two successful defenses in 1975 against Armando Muniz of the United States, stopping him in the twelfth round in the first encounter and gaining a decision in the second. On December 6, 1975 Napoles was challenged by John H. Stracey the British and European champion. The fight took place at Mexico City, but not before Stracey had threatened to pull out when he learned that all the officials were to be Mexican. The main doubts among Stracey's supporters concerned the unaccustomed high altitude at which their champion was fighting and his notorious slow start, a doubt which seemed justified when Napoles put Stracey down in the first round. Stracey weathered the storm and in the succeeding rounds seemed to get stronger as Napoles wilted. After putting Napoles down and battering him till his left eye was badly swollen and his right cut, Stracey's continuous pressure finally told in the sixth round, when Napoles was punched to a standstill and the referee was forced to stop the fight. Stracey's first defense, fifteen weeks later, on March 20, 1976, at Wembley, against Hedgemon Lewis, took a similar

course. Lewis began very fast, and the fight was even for five or six rounds, but Stracey's skill, strength and aggression told, and Lewis was battered and helpless when stopped in the tenth.

Stracey's wins, however, made him world champion only in the eyes of the W.B.C. as in 1975 the W.B.A. set up its own titleholder by recognising a match between Angel Espada (Puerto Rico) and Clyde Gray (Canada) as being for the vacant title. Stracey was beaten on June 22, 1976, at Wembley Arena by Carlos Palomino (Mexico), the bout being stopped in the twelfth round and the new champion made four successful title defences the following year, beating Armando Muniz, stopped fifteenth

round at Los Angeles on January 22; Dave Green (Great Britain) who was knocked out in eleven rounds, also at Wembley Arena, on June 14; Everaldo Costa, who was outpointed at Los Angeles on September 13 and Jose Palacios, who was knocked out in thirteen rounds, on December 10, also at Los Angeles. In 1978 Palomino disposed of three more challengers, beating Ryu Sormachi at Las Vegas on February 11 by the knockout route in round seven; Mimoun Mohatar, stopped in nine rounds at Las Vegas on March 18, and Armando Muniz, outpointed over fifteen rounds at Las Vegas on July 27. On January 14, 1979, however, he lost his W.B.C. title to Wilfredo Benitez (Puerto

In a stunning upset in Syracuse, N.Y., on December 3, 1970, Napoles lost his crown to Billy Backus, the bout stopped in the fourth due to a cut.

On June 4, 1971, however, Napoles regained the title, halting Backus in the eighth round at Los Angeles. (Above) They mix it in the early going.

John H. Stracey, the British and European champion, after being knocked down in the first, gets a left to Napoles' battered face and adds the world title to his collection in Mexico City on December 6, 1975.

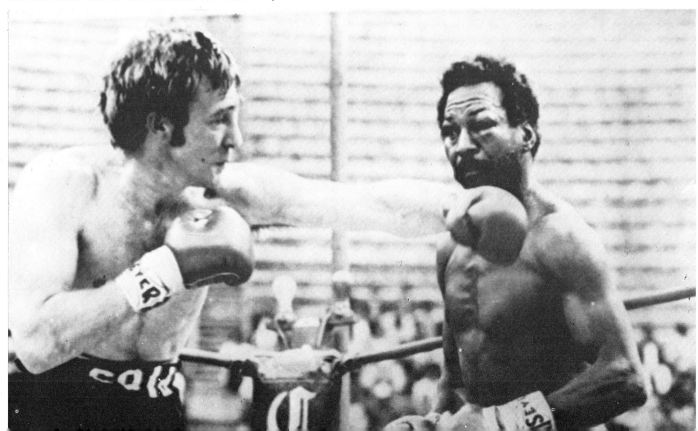

Rico) on a points decision at San Juan.

W.B.A. welter king, Angel Espada, kept his crown against Johnny Gant (USA) with a fifteen rounds points verdict at Ponce on October 11, 1975, but lost the title to Jose "Pipino" Cuevas (Mexico) in two rounds at Mexicali on July 18, 1976. The new champion successfully defended against Shoji Tsujimoto in six rounds at Kanazawa on October 27 and in 1977 overcame challenges from: Miguel Angel Campanino, ref stopped fight, second, at Mexico City, March 12; Clyde Gray, knocked out in the second at Los Angeles August 6, and Angel Espada, ref stopped fight, eleventh, at San Juan on November 19. In 1978 Cuevas remained W.B.A. champion, defeating Harold Weston (USA), the ref stopping the fight in the ninth at Los Angeles on March 4; Billy Backus, stopped in the first at Los Angeles May 20, and Pete Ranzany, stopped in the second at Sacramento on September 9. On January 30, 1979, when beating Scott Clark in two rounds at Los Angeles, Cuevas was making the eighth defence of his W.B.A. title.

A new star emerged in the W.B.C. version of the welterweight title when, after twice successfully defending the championship by outpointing Carlos Palomino (Mexico) and Harold Weston (U.S.A.), Benitez was knocked out in the 15th round by Sugar Ray Leonard, from Maryland, a gold medallist in the 1976 Olympic Games. He possessed a flamboyant style and punching power reminiscent of the young Cassius Clay, and on March 31, 1980 made an impressive first defence of his crown by knocking out Dave Green (Great Britain) in four rounds at Landover. On June 20 he suffered a shock defeat at the hands of Roberto Duran, former

Boxing found a new star attraction to replace the fading Ali when Sugar Ray Leonard won the welterweight crown, and although losing it to Duran, regained it in November 1980.

brilliant lightweight champion, being narrowly outpointed at Montreal. In a return fight at New Orleans on November 26, Leonard won back his title by forcing Duran to quit of his own accord in the eighth round.

The W.B.A. champion, Pipino Cuevas, continued to defeat his challengers, beating three in 1979 and Harold Volbrecht, the South African champion, in five rounds at Houston on April 6, 1980. At his 13th defence, on August 2 at Detroit, he was sensationally stopped in two rounds by unbeaten 21-year-old Thomas Hearns, known as The Motor City Cobra, because of his phenomenal height and reach. At Detroit on December 6 Hearns retained his title by knocking out Luis Primera (Venezuela) in six rounds.

LIGHT WELTERWEIGHT CHAMPIONS (formerly known as JUNIOR WELTERWEIGHTS)

(Weight Limit, 140 Pounds)

PINKEY MITCHELL, 1922; MUSHY CALLAHAN, 1926; JACKIE "KID" BERG, 1930; TONY CANZONERI, 1931; JOHNNY JADICK, 1931; BATTLING SHAW, 1933; TONY CANZONERI, 1933; BARNEY ROSS, 1933; TIPPY LARKIN, 1946; CARLOS ORTIZ, 1959; DUILIO LOI, 1960; EDDIE PERKINS, 1962; DUILIO LOI, 1962; EDDIE PERKINS, 1963; CARLOS HERNANDEZ, 1965; SANDRO LOPOPOLO, 1966; PAUL FUJII, 1967
IN 1967 THE W.B.A. TOOK AWAY RECOGNITION FROM FUJII FOR FAILING TO MEET PEDRE ADIGUE AND DUAL CHAMPIONS HAVE REIGNED EVER SINCE AS FOLLOWS: 1968—NICOLINO LOCHE (WBA), PEDRO ADIGUE (VACANT WBC TITLE); 1970—BRUNO ARCARI (WBC); 1972—ALFONSO FRAZER (WBA), ANTONIO CERVANTES (WBA); 1974—PERICO FERNANDEZ (VACANT WBC TITLE); 1975—SAENSAK MUSANGSURIN (WBC); 1976—WILFREDO BENITEZ (WBA), MIGUEL VELASQUEZ (WBC), SAENSAK MUSANGSURIN (WBC); 1977—ANTONIO CERVANTES (VACANT WBA TITLE); 1978—KIM SANG HYUN (WBC); 1980—SAOUL MAMBY (WBC); AARON PRYOR (WBA).

THE LIGHTWEIGHTS

Johnny Broome *(above, left)* and Johnny Hannon, fought a savage battle on January 26, 1841, for the lightweight championship. The celebrated encounter, held on a farm halfway between Birmingham and London, England, ended after one hour and 19 minutes of violent milling. Broome's superior strength was evident after the first hour of battle. He landed the heavier blows more often and Hannon was obviously weakening. When Hannon tried to rise from his second's knee to go out for the 47th round, he suddenly pitched forward and fell on the turf unconscious. Broome was awarded the $5,000 purse and championship. The scene of battle was well organized. Ordinary spectators were herded behind a roped-off arena 20 yards from the ring, while the privileged nobility settled in a circle between. Broom developed his brother Harry from a top middleweight to the heavyweight champion of England. Hannon never fought again, but furthered his reputation when he became a great teacher of boxing.

Johnny Walker *(left)*, whose real name was John Badman, was born January 1, 1819. He was given his ring name by Peter Crawley, the old English champion, in whose boxing rooms Walker was a constant visitor. Walker was powerfully built and possessed natural skill and courage. In his first bareknuckle fight, Walker battled the experienced Johnny Hannon for over three hours on November 1, 1838, before he was beaten. It took Hannon almost four hours to win their second meeting in 1839, the fight ending when Walker's shoulder was dislocated after he was thrown heavily. After beating down three challengers in 1842, Walker was recognized as lightweight champion and was never beaten thereafter.

BRILLIANT LIGHTWEIGHTS

Excepting, perhaps, the heavyweight class, no division in boxing has produced more colorful, exciting, and dramatic history than the lightweight. From the Victorian eighties when Jack McAuliffe ruled the roost, the light ranks have fairly teemed with outstanding ringmen, brilliant boxers, rugged sluggers, robust punchers, and quaint characters who, despite their strange antics in the ring and out, could really fight.

A list of the greats, champions and non-champions, those who contributed their bits to the glory of the division, shows such historic ring figures as Dick Burge, Jim Carney, Billy Myer, Young Griffo, Jack McAuliffe, Harry Gilmore, Frank Erne, George Elbows McFadden, Kid McPartland, Patsy Haley, Freddie Welsh, Joe Gans, Ad Wolgast, Benny Leonard, Joe Rivers, Battling Nelson, Matt Wells, Johnny Dundee, Willie Jackson, Matty Bald-

win, Lew Tendler, Al Singer, Sammy Mandell, Billy Petrolle, Tony Canzoneri, Lou Ambers, Jackie Kid Berg, Harry Mason, Barney Ross, Beau Jack, Henry Armstrong, Bob Montgomery, Ike Williams, Rocky Kansas, Charley White, Phil Bloom, Richie Mitchell, Pal Moran, Joe Benjamin, Joe Azevedo, Frankie Callahan, George Kid Lavigne, Joe Mandot, among many others.

It was the first episode in the classic

Dutch Sam *(above)*, inventor of the uppercut, was feared as the deadliest puncher of the London Prize Ring. He was born in Whitechapel, London, on April 4, 1775, of Jewish parents. He attracted wide attention in 1801, after he had knocked out some good lightweights and repeatedly knocked out heavier men. Sam was 5' 6½" tall and weighed only 133 pounds, but he was deep-chested and muscular. He died in 1816. His son, Young Dutch Sam, became welterweight champion in 1825.

Dick Curtis *(right)*, lightweight champion from 1820 to 1828 and popular with fast noblemen, was called "the Pet of the Fancy." After beating Barney Aaron in a fierce 55-minute battle on February 27, 1827, he remained in the ring and seconded his pal, Young Dutch Sam, who was to fight Gypsy Cooper a half hour later.

Goldfield, Nevada, gained world-wide attention when Tex Rickard, a daring young gambler, promoted the Battling Nelson-Joe Gans title fight there. The top photo is a scene of Main Street in 1905. The bottom photo is the same Main Street, one year later. Rickard put up an astoundingly large purse of $34,000. The gate receipts of $69,715 were also astounding for that era.

Battling Nelson-Joe Gans series that introduced to boxing a young gambler destined to become the world's top promoter—George Lewis 'Tex' Rickard. Goldfield, Nevada, was at the height of its boom in 1906 and a committee of local citizens, with Rickard as chairman, was appointed to promote an event that would attract outside attention to the town. Someone suggested a prize fight.

It met with favor in the eyes of Rickard, who put up $30,000 for Nelson and Gans to split, with the Battler guaranteed $20,000 and $2,000 for signing and $500 for expenses. The purse, $34,000 all told, was the biggest ever offered for a lightweight title bout up to that time, yet in the days of Jimmy McLarnin, Barney Ross,

Beau Jack, Benny Leonard, Lou Ambers, Ike Williams, Tony Canzoneri, Sammy Mandell, Al Singer, among others of their era, it was not unusual for lightweight contests to register $200,000 gates, with the fighters reaping $50,000 or more as their share. The Nelson-Gans fight ushered in the era of big gates and super-promotion in the division.

The lightweights were always in the public eye because of the speed and decisive action usually on view. Three fighters especially hold the spotlight in this class since Jack McAuliffe, born in Cork, Ireland, March 24, 1866, retired undefeated after holding the crown during the bare-knuckle days and part of the gloves era. They are Gans, Nelson, and

Benny Leonard. These are considered the greatest of all lightweights, the supermen of the group.

Whether Gans was Leonard's master or vice-versa has been a topic for discussion since Benny gained world prominence. There can be no doubt that Gans was the master of the boxers in his class when he was in his prime, and that Benny was tops among the later day lightweights.

In the earlier days, Jack McAuliffe, who defended his crown for the last time in New Orleans during the Carnival of Champions, September 5, 1892, reigned supreme from 1885 to 1896. His last defense was against Billy Myer whom he knocked out in the fifteenth round.

The title bouts in the lightweight

Arthur Chambers, born in Salford, England, started boxing at 17. He weighed 125 pounds for the Edwards fight and was taking a shellacking, until he tricked the referee into awarding him the title on a foul. Chambers lived in Philadelphia after retirement and died May 5, 1923. He was 75.

Edwards and Chambers met for the title on September 4, 1872, at Squirrel Island, Canada. Chambers rushed out for the 26th round, clinched, and screamed that he was bitten. Referee Bill Tracy, noting the teeth marks, declared Chambers the winner on a foul. Actually, Chambers' second, Tom Allen, did the biting between rounds.

Billy Edwards, born in Birmingham, England, stood 5' 5'' and weighed 126 pounds. He came to America in 1865 and beat the best lightweights around. Sneak tactics by Chambers' second cost him the title. After retirement Edwards wrote a treatise on how to box.

class in America were tussles confined mostly to foreigners until McAuliffe retired and gave an opportunity to George Kid Lavigne, a native American, to claim and successfully defend the championship for three years.

The first recorded king of the division had been Abe Hicken, whose reign extended from 1867 to 1872, when he retired. Elimination matches among Johnny Clark, Billy Edwards, and Arthur Chambers resulted in the last named taking the crown. Chambers retired in 1879 and Nonpareil Jack Dempsey forged to the front, but never claimed the laurels since he quickly outgrew the class. His pal McAuliffe asserted himself as head of the group, his claim based on the refusal of Jimmy Mitchen, top ranking lightweight to meet him in a fight for the American title.

279

Yours Truly
Jack McAuliffe
Lightweight
Champion of
the World

Jack Dempsey, the Nonpareil (above), claimed the lightweight crown, but by 1885 he outgrew the class, and Jack McAuliffe ascended the throne, reigning until 1896, when he retired. Dempsey was McAuliffe's chief second in the Carney battle.

Jem Carney, shown wearing his British championship belt, was a first class fighting man. He stood 5' 4" and his best fighting weight was 133 pounds. His battle to a draw with McAuliffe prevented Jack from winning the world crown.

Around a twenty-four-foot ring in a Revere, Massachusetts, stable on the night of November 5, 1887, sat a gathering of guests especially invited to watch a match for the world lightweight championship. Jack McAuliffe of the United States and Jem Carney, British title-holder, were the opponents. After seventy-four bloody rounds, the spectators broke into the ring, and the referee called off the proceedings.

For four hours before the affair the invited guests, because of fear of police interference, arrived in pairs at a designated hotel, and after each had passed muster, he was permitted to remain until the march to the stable under the guidance of the hotel proprietor, who led the way with a lantern.

At the barn the spectators found a Salvation Army group practicing hymns, and their presence helped throw the police off the trail.

Carney tipped the scales at 129 and McAuliffe at 126. Throughout the early rounds the men hooked and jabbed, landing few blows of any consequence. McAuliffe was dropped in the seventh round, but came back strong.

When the sixtieth round arrived, McAuliffe showed signs of fatigue. His backers, fearing the loss of their wagers, became unruly. The break came in the seventieth frame, when Carney scored a clean knockdown that looked like a finisher. Only interference by McAuliffe's friends saved him. Order was restored, and the bout went on until the seventy-fourth round,

To avoid police interference, the international lightweight battle between Jack Mc-Auliffe and Jem Carney took place inside the barn *(above)* at Revere, Massachusetts. Each fighter was allowed to select 14 persons to witness the private bout, which started at 1 A.M. and went over three hours. In the 74th round, the ring was broken into and referee Frank Stevenson called the fight a draw. A scene of the bout, a photo of McAuliffe at 65 recalling it, and the gloves he wore, are shown below.

Jimmy Carroll *(below)* a strong British lightweight, met McAuliffe on March 21, 1890, and took a terrific beating for 47 rounds, before Jack decided to score a knockout. McAuliffe, a loyal friend of Jack Dempsey, the Nonpareil, got even with Carroll, for his part in the slaughter of Dempsey by George LaBlanche in 1889. Carroll had taught George how to use the illegal "pivot blow" (striking with elbow, on backward swing). When LaBlanche tried it on Dempsey, the Nonpareil was knocked flat on his face, out cold, and it took him a long time to revive.

Carney and McAuliffe re-enacted their historic skin-tight glove battle 27 years later in London. The affair, in 1914, was refereed by Charley Mitchell, the former British heavyweight champion, who is shown walking to the center of the ring (above, left) while McAuliffe waits in the right corner and Carney in the left. The battlers got in their pet blows wearing big gloves. Carney, shown facing the camera (above, right) watches McAuliffe wind up a roundhouse right.

Young Griffo (right) born in Sydney, Australia, in 1871, started there with bare-knuckle fights and came to America in 1894. Never a title-holder, Griffo was considered one of the most skillful boxers that the ring ever produced.

when Carney again put McAuliffe down and it seemed the American could not continue. The spectators rushed the ring again. Tom McKay, the hotel proprietor, appealed to referee Stevenson to call a halt before the police arrived on the scene. Stevenson agreed and declared the contest a draw, although Carney was in the lead.

One of the most incredible figures the ring has ever known was Young Griffo, an Australian, who though actually a featherweight fought and whipped the top lightweights of his era. Griffo never was one to take his professional career seriously. Training was a nuisance to him, and he preferred hanging around barrooms and guzzling his liquor. Seldom, indeed, was Griffo sober for a fight, yet so amazingly clever was he that regardless of the state of his physical and mental condition at the moment, he invariably held his own or could and did whip his opponent.

The longest fight on record was a lightweight meeting between Andy Bowen and Jack Burke in New Or-

Jack Burke *(above)* and Andy Bowen *(right)* on April 6, 1893, fought the longest battle on record: seven hours, 19 minutes. They started at 9:15 P.M. and ended at 4:19 A.M. When the 110th round ended, they were exhausted, their eyes puffed, their arms swollen from stopping each other's blows, and their faces looking like raw beef. Referee Duffy, who refused to let the fight go to a finish as originally agreed upon, stopped it and called it a draw. The battlers split the $2,500 purse.

After George Kid Lavigne *(left)* claimed the crown, his manager, Sam Fitzpatrick *(right)*, took him to England, where Lavigne kayoed Dick Burge for the world title.

leans, April 6, 1893, a contest that waded through 110 rounds, spread across seven hours and nineteen minutes, when, exhausted, they couldn't continue and the referee halted the affair and called it a draw.

On June 1, 1896, George Kid Lavigne, born in Bay City, Michigan, December 6, 1869, succeeded to the throne left vacant by McAuliffe's retirement. Lavigne knocked out Dick Burge, British champion, in London in seventeen rounds to gain universal recognition. Burge was a scientific boxer; Lavigne, an aggressive, savage fighter. In that battle, Lavigne's mouth and nose were cut and badly bleeding while the body of his British opponent was full of blotches from the terrific pounding it had received. In the final round, heavy barrages weakened Burge. Then followed a left and right to the stomach that brought down Burge's guard and the finisher, a right to the jaw followed, giving the world crown to America.

Lavigne on July 3, 1899, at Buffalo, lost the championship to Frank Erne,

"KID" McPARTLAND

Kid McPartland, a title threat, lost a 25-round disputed decision to Lavigne on February 8, 1897. He later became a referee in New York.

George Kid Lavigne (*right*) a durable punishing fighter, was called "the Saginaw Kid." He started in 1895 and was unbeaten until 1899, when he lost a bout to Billy Smith and the title to Frank Erne. Among the top men Lavigne met were Young Griffo, whom he held to a draw, and Andy Bowen, who died from injuries following a knockout blow.

Dick Burge, England's lightweight champion (*left*), gave Kid Lavigne a stiff battle for 17 rounds on June 1, 1896, but Dick's ambition to become world champion was halted by Lavigne's cruel body punishment.

The contemporary sketches below depict the slashing battle between Lavigne and Joe Walcott, at Maspeth, Long Island, December 2, 1895. Walcott lost the decision, as had been agreed, when he failed to knock out the lightweight champion.

Almost a Finishing Touch.

T BATTLE WITH KID LAVIGNE AT BUFFALO LAST N

RANK ERNE THE WORLD'S C

AFTER TWENTY HARD ROUNDS, WITH BOTH READY

ERNE LANDING A HARD LEFT ON HIS FOE.

ship were read from Joe Gans, Kid Mc- and rushed. Uppercuts straightened him blocked. Frank puts hard right on head, Partland, George McFadden, Jim Popp and up and he remarked as a left-hander caught Toward the last the Kid landed on face Tim Kearns. him flush on the stomach. "That was a and body, while Erne jabbed him in the

Frank Erne *(left)* born in Zurich, Switzerland, on January 8, 1875, was raised in Buffalo, New York, and started boxing in 1894. His first two losses were to Martin Flaherty and George Dixon in 1897. He won over Dixon the year before in 20 rounds. Erne lifted the crown from Kid Lavigne on September 28, 1898, in a cleverly-fought 20-round bout, as illustrated in the *New York Journal* the following day.

The great Joe Gans quit to Erne in 1900. In 1902, Gans stopped Erne in one round and won the lightweight championship.

Jimmy Britt *(below)* tried to claim the title from Gans, but when they met in 1904, Britt fouled Joe in the fifth round.

Battling Nelson (*above*), "the Durable Dane," was born in Copenhagen, Denmark, on June 5, 1882. In 132 battles, from 1896 to 1923, he won 37 of 57 by knockouts, won one, lost two on fouls, had 15 no-decisions, drew in 19, lost 15 and was kayoed twice. Nelson knocked out Gans twice in title bouts.

Joe Gans (*right*), the "Old Master," was born November 25, 1874, in Philadelphia. He had 156 fights from 1891 to 1909 and won 54 of 114 by knockouts. He won five on fouls, drew 10, 18 were no-decision, lost three, and was kayoed five times. Gans was one of the all-time great ringmen.

who outpointed him in twenty rounds. The following March, Gans was stopped by Erne in the twelfth round, the Baltimore Negro quitting. But in their second engagement, at Fort Erie, May 12, 1902, an upset that aroused considerable talk enabled Gans to win the title by a knockout in the opening round. The first punch did the trick, the first time in history that a champion was disposed of with the only blow delivered.

Jimmy Britt of California set up a plea that Gans had declined to make the weight and therefore had forfeited his title. Gans proved how baseless this claim was when on October 31, 1904, he handed Britt a terrific beating, Britt striking low when nearly out in the twentieth round. By way of good measure, Gans knocked out

Nelson and Gans touch gloves *(above)* before their battle in Goldfield, Nevada, in which Tex Rickard made a successful debut as a boxing promoter. Gans displayed too much skill for Nelson during the bout. In the 42nd round Gans crumbled to the canvas from a low blow and Nelson was disqualified. The bout was profitable to Rickard despite what was then considered a fantastic purse of $34,000. When they met in 1908, Nelson's boring-in style was too much for Gans who was down five times. Nelson knocked out Joe in the 17th round *(below)* and became champion.

Britt in the sixth round on September 9, 1907.

The Goldfield battle on September 3, 1906, in which Gans won from Battling Nelson in the forty-second round on a foul, and their second bout on July 4, 1908, in San Francisco, in which the Baltimore Negro lost the championship by a knockout in the seventeenth round, were among the most spectacular battles in the lightweight class. Gans also was stopped in their next bout in Colma, California, September 9, 1908, in the twenty-first round.

The following year Gans died from pneumonia in Baltimore.

Melodramatic also was the encounter in which Nelson met defeat at the hands of Ad Wolgast, the Michigan Wildcat. Bloody, battered, desperate, game to the last, the Dane struggled on only to hear Referee Eddie Smith proclaim Wolgast, born in Cadillac, Michigan, February 8, 1888, the winner in the fortieth round of a truly Homeric engagement. That affair took place February 22, 1910, at Point Richmond, California.

One of the most extraordinary windups that ever terminated a lightweight championship contest occurred when

Bat Nelson met Ad Wolgast in a 45-round title grudge-affair in 1910. Foul rules were out except if, in the opinion of the referee, a fighter was completely incapacitated. Nelson, on the left in both photos above, and Wolgast posed before the bout, which turned out to be bloody and brutal. Nelson was in a helpless state in the 40th round and referee Ed Smith stopped the slaughter.

Packey McFarland was a rising star in 1908 when he kayoed Jimmy Britt (below) in six rounds. Britt's seconds are shown vainly coaxing Jimmy to get up. In 48 bouts Packey scored 33 knockouts and was never given a chance at the title.

Ad Wolgast had 14 bouts after winning the crown from Nelson. On July 4, 1912, Ad met Mexican Joe Rivers in a title match that had a weird ending, referred to as the double knockout. In the 13th round, Ad drove a low blow to River's body. At the same time, Rivers landed a left hook on Wolgast's jaw. Both fighters dropped *(left)*, with the champion on top. Then referee Jack Welch did an extraordinary thing. With his left hand he helped Wolgast to his feet *(below)* and with his right went through the motions of counting Rivers out. Ad staggered to his corner while Joe managed to get to his feet unaided. Welch was still counting when the bell ended the round, and spectators said he had only reached the count of eight, at most. While both fighters were in their corners being handled, Welch pointed to Wolgast as the winner, and a small riot ensued. Welch escaped harm and the decision still stands.

Wolgast and Joe Rivers fought at Vernon, California, July 4, 1912. In the thirteenth round Wolgast hooked a left to the stomach that dropped Rivers. Wolgast, unable to check his momentum, crashed on top of the Mexican. Joe got to one knee as the referee, Jack Welsh, started the count. Both fighters were helpless at the time, but Welsh, contrary to the rules, extended a helping hand to Wolgast, raised him to his feet while counting out Rivers to the amazement of the fans.

Willie Ritchie of San Francisco,

On July 4, 1911, Wolgast belted Owen Moran with a right to the stomach that had Owen gasping for breath as he was counted out in the 13th round by referee Jack Welch. Moran, a tough British lightweight, had kayoed Bat Nelson in 1910.

Willie Ritchie, covered with blankets *(right)*, had to wait for Wolgast to appear for their title bout in 1912. Ritchie held his own until the 16th round, when he was awarded the title on a foul.

born February 13, 1891, took the championship from Wolgast on a foul at Daly City, California in the six-teenth round, November 28, 1912, and lost it in turn in London to Freddie Welsh of England in twenty rounds, July 7, 1914. Ritchie, when he won the crown, had raised the limit for the class from 133 to 135 pounds. In his title defenses, he knocked out Joe Rivers in the eleventh round and fought a stirring battle of twenty rounds with Harlem Tommy Murphy and won the verdict.

In Ritchie's first title defense he knocked out Mexican Joe Rivers *(left)* on July 4, 1913. The following year, on July 7, he lost the crown to Freddie Welsh in 20 rounds in London.

Two of England's greatest, Freddie Welsh and Jem Driscoll, met *(below)* in Cardiff, Wales for the British lightweight crown. Driscoll, on his knee from a slip, lost to Welsh on a foul in the 10th round.

Freddie Welsh *(below)* boxed from 1905 to 1922. He engaged in 166 bouts, lost only three, and was kayoed once, by Benny Leonard. Winning the title from Willie Ritchie cost Welsh $500 of his own money to meet the $26,500 guaranteed to Ritchie.

Welsh reigned nearly three years before he was dethroned by Benny Leonard in a surprise knockout in the ninth round of a no-decision bout in New York at the Manhattan Casino, May 28, 1917. There was never anything sensational about Welsh's performances, other than that he was a very clever boxer. He was a light puncher, but one of the finest defensive boxers in this division's history. He was born in Pontypridd, Wales, March 5, 1886. It required a combination boxer and hitter like Leonard to penetrate his seemingly impenetrable guard and acquire the crown.

During his eight years as a champion, Leonard outclassed a field of the greatest lightweights that ever

While Benny Leonard was lightweight champion, he met Jack Britton (above, right) for the welter crown on June 26, 1922. In the 13th round, Jack dropped to one knee from a body blow and protested to referee Patsy Haley that the punch had been low. When Haley continued to count over Britton, Benny struck Jack while he was down, and was disqualified. It was said Benny had no desire to win the crown and was only trying for a draw decision.

Leonard met Johnny Dundee eight times in no-decision bouts from 1914 through 1920. Dundee (below, right) was a nine-year ring veteran when he posed with Benny before their eight-rounder on June 16, 1919, in Philadelphia.

Benny Leonard, born Benjamin Leiner in New York on April 17, 1896, boxed from 1911 to 1924 and made a comeback in 1931. He was knocked out in his first and last bout. He had a total of 209 fights, won 88, with 68 kayoes, won once and lost once on a foul, was kayoed four times, and had 115 no-decisions. He retired undefeated in 1925.

Charley White, a deadly puncher, had flattened 41 opponents with his dangerous left hook before he met Benny Leonard for the title in 1920. White connected with his famous left hook on Benny's jaw in the fifth round *(above)* and sent the champion sprawling through the ropes and out of the ring. Leonard crawled back and cautiously boxed his way out of trouble until his head cleared. In the eighth round, he cornered White and knocked him out.

The "Milwaukee Marvel," Richie Mitchell *(below, left)* gave Leonard a scare in 1921. Arising from a knockdown, Richie floored the champ, who got up dazed and dared Richie to come in and mix it. Richie became wary and was kayoed in round six.

appeared at one time in the division. Leonard could punch with sluggers and outbox the best scientific pugilists. Three times in his scintillating career as champion, one of the best the division boasted, he was on the verge of a knockout.

Charley White almost turned the trick on July 5, 1920, in Benton Harbor, Michigan; Richie Mitchell came close in Madison Square Garden, January 14, 1921, on the card for Ann Morgan's Fund for Devastated France; and Lew Tendler was talked out of a possible kayo in Jersey City, in a twelve round no-decision contest on July 27, 1922.

In the fight with White, Benny was sent over the ropes and out of the ring with a deadly left hook. White was the best left hook artist in the game. Leonard was dazed when he climbed back, but his wily generalship staved off the impending disaster. He stalled off White as he did Mitchell, until his brain cleared, then went on to give Charley a lacing and halt him.

When he fought Mitchell, Benny

Ever Hammer cut Leonard's eye early in their bout on October 18, 1916. Ben, a master of every trick in boxing, tied him up continuously (above) preventing any further damage to the eye until the 12th round, when he knocked Hammer out.

Rocky Kansas lost a 15-round decision to Leonard in a title bout in New York on February 10, 1922. Kansas met the champion again on July 4 in Michigan City, Michigan, and was stopped (right) in eight rounds.

In the eighth round on July 23, 1922, Lew Tendler (below, left) drove a vicious left to Leonard's stomach, paralyzing his legs. Leonard told Lew to "keep them up." Lew stopped to argue about the blow, long enough for life to return to Ben's legs.

Lew Tendler, a Philadelphia southpaw, posed (below) with his two-year-old son Phil in 1922. Lew was talked out of a possible kayo victory by Leonard in 1922. In the second bout on July 23, 1923, Lew lost to the champ in 15 rounds.

was dropped in the opening round, was dazed and very unsteady, yet talked his way into scaring Richie, then came back like a fighting wildcat to stop the Westerner after putting Richie on the canvas three times.

Johnny Dundee was another great fighter in both this class and the feather. He gave Leonard a lot of trouble both before and after Benny mounted the lightweight throne.

From 1914 through 1920, they fought nine times in no-decision contests.

Dundee was a fast, clever, aggressive fighter and a miracle of endurance. His trickery with the ropes baffled his opponents. He was a master at fighting off the strands. Only once did he go down for the full count when Willie Jackson, a terrific puncher, knocked him out in the first round in Philadelphia.

When Leonard retired in 1925, after a reign of seven and a half years, he claimed he did so to please his mother.

Nathan Straus, a noted New York merchant and philanthropist, was an enthusiastic follower of Leonard's ring career.

In 1931 Leonard made a comeback as a welterweight and knocked out Pal Silvers (left) in two rounds on October 6. Except for one draw, he won 18 bouts through 1932 and met Jimmy McLarnin in New York, on October 7. Paunchy and 36 years old, Leonard was an easy mark for the youthful fists of McLarnin and was counted out by referee Arthur Donovan (below, left) in the sixth round. Thus ended the extended boxing career of one of the finest ring mechanics of all time. In 1943 Benny became a popular licensed referee (below) on the staff of the New York State commission. While refereeing a bout at the St. Nicholas Arena in New York on April 17, 1947, he suddenly collapsed and died.

Jimmy McLarnin became the idol of New York with his knockouts over top lightweights, among them Ruby Goldstein, whom he kayoed *(above)* in two rounds on December 13, 1929. In spite of the great Depression, he drew sell-out crowds.

Coming down to later times, one vividly recalls the thrills that Jimmy McLarnin gave to New Yorkers when he was campaigning as a lightweight and scoring one and two round knock-outs with such persistency over likely lads of the calibre of Sid Terris and Ruby Goldstein, New York's ace performers; Phil McGraw, Stanislaus Loayza, Joe Glick, and Sgt. Sammy Baker, among other top fighters. But his most thrilling bout took place when he faced Billy Petrolle, the Fargo Express, and took a licking that might have spelled finis to the career of a less courageous, stout-hearted battler.

No one who saw that mill in the Garden in 1930 can ever forget it. Dropped in the opening round with a jaw-smash that hit him with the force of a club, Jimmy got to his feet and from then to the finish absorbed terrific punishment, yet refused to quit even when asked to do so by Referee Patsy Haley. Twice afterwards they fought and McLarnin won each in ten rounds.

Petrolle, though never a title holder,

Billy Petrolle and manager Jack Hurley *(below)* from Fargo, North Dakota, were a perfect team. Hurley arranged exciting matches and Billy executed them. From 1910 to 1934 Petrolle had 157 fights and won 85, scoring 63 knockouts.

Billy Petrolle floored Jimmy McLarnin twice with smashing rights to the jaw, in their first meeting, on November 21, 1930. The "Fargo Express" unleashed his vicious blows in the first round, but Jimmy weathered the storm and put up a sensational battle for 10 rounds. Billy was awarded the decision, but lost the verdict both times when they met on May 27 and August 20, 1931.

Jimmy Goodrich (left) and Stanislaus Loayza (above) of Iquique, Chile, met in the final match of a tournament to determine the successor for the vacant throne. Goodrich stopped Loayza in two rounds and was generally recognized as the lightweight king by boxing writers all over the country. In 110 bouts from 1923 to 1930, Jimmy won 44 and lost 33, drew 15 times, and had 18 no-decisions.

was one of the outstanding fighters of the division. His battle with Justo Suarez of Chile was another long-to-be-remembered contest which Billy won.

When Leonard retired undefeated in 1925, the New York Commission set up an elimination to decide his successor.

Jimmy Goodrich, born July 30, 1900, in Scranton, emerged the winner when he knocked out Stanislaus Loayza on July 13, 1925, at Long Island City in the second round. But he didn't retain the title long, for on December 7 of the same year, Rocky Kansas of Buffalo gained the verdict over Goodrich in fifteen rounds to relieve him of his laurels.

Then half a year later came Sammy Mandell, born February 5, 1904, in Rockford, Illinois, who on July 3, 1926, outpointed Kansas in Chicago in ten rounds and became the sceptre bearer. But on July 17, 1930, at the Yankee

Sammy Mandell is shown in his corner, ready to go out for the final round against Rocky Kansas on July 3, 1926. Mandell won easily in 10 rounds and became lightweight champion. Sammy was an extremely able ringman who boxed cleverly and possessed a sound punch. He was a pupil of Jack Blackburn, the trainer of Joe Louis, who perfected Joe's championship style. Mandell's career started in 1920. He held the title more than four years and retired in 1934. In 168 bouts, he won 82 with 28 kayoes, lost 12, drew in nine, was knocked out five times and had 60 no-decision bouts.

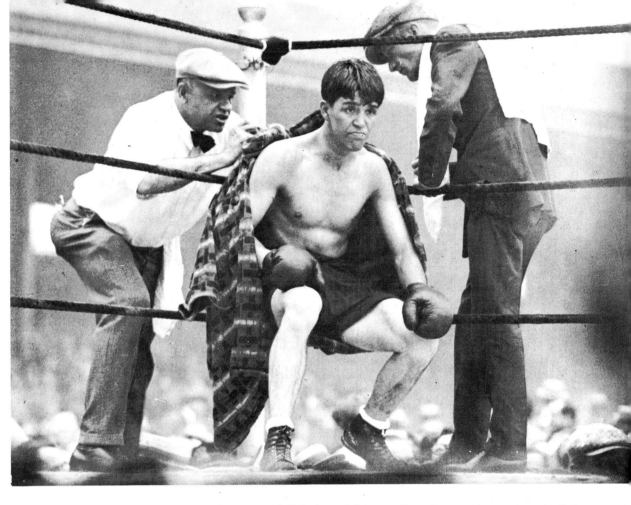

Rocky Kansas, born in 1895, was a 15-year ring veteran when he beat Goodrich for the crown on December 7, 1925. Rocky was only 5' 2'' tall, but powerful. He won 64 of 164 battles from 1911 to 1926 and had 80 no-decision bouts.

Mandell (below, right) gave Tony Canzoneri a crack at the light-weight crown on August 2, 1929, a year after Tony had lost the featherweight title. Sammy was sharp that night and outpointed Canzoneri in 10 rounds of a bout loaded with action.

Defending the light-weight crown on May 21, 1928, Sammy Mandell uncovered one of the finest exhibitions ever seen in New York, and completely out-classed Jimmy McLarnin in 15 rounds. Veteran announcer, Joe Humphries raises Mandell's arm in token of victory *(left)*, as McLarnin acknowledges defeat.

Al Singer *(below)* created a sensation on July 17, 1930, when he won the title by knocking Mandell out cold in 1.46 of the first round. Singer, a protégé of Benny Leonard, boxed from 1927 to 1935. In 70 bouts, he scored 24 kayoes while winning 60, drew twice and lost 8, four of them by knockout.

Stadium, the fans were treated to one of the biggest surprises in the division in years, when Al Singer of New York flattened clever Sammy in one round to win the championship.

Singer, born September 6, 1907, like several of his predecessors, went out in a jiffy. He lasted only a few months, for on November 14, 1930, Tony Canzoneri, born November 6, 1908, at Slidell, Louisiana, a lad with an enviable record, put Singer away in a round in Madison Square Garden.

Less than four months after winning the crown, Singer was overpowered by Tony Canzoneri on November 14, 1930, and knocked out in 1.06 of the first round. Tony forced Singer into his corner and in a flurry of blows, sent him through the ropes onto the ring apron (right), where he was counted out by referee McAvoy. Still dazed and limp, Singer was helped to his feet by Tony's manager, Sam Goldman, as Canzoneri was declared winner (below) in the fourth fastest knockout in championship history. The others were: Jackie Paterson over Peter Kane, 1943, 1.01; Emil Pladner over Frankie Genaro, 1929, 0.58; and Al McCoy over George Chip, 1914, 0.45.

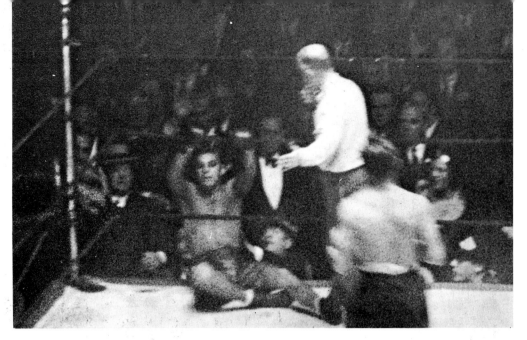

Singer is the only champion in boxing annals to have won and lost the crown by one round knockouts.

Canzoneri was a real fighting champion, a colorful pugilist and a good crowd-pleaser. He had come up from the flyweight class as an amateur and held eight titles during his career as a simon pure. He beat Benny Bass for the pro feather crown following an elimination after Dundee retired, then went on to greater heights.

He could box well and could hit.

He lost the lightweight title to Barney Ross in Chicago, June 23, 1933, and failed to regain it from Barney a short time later, Ross winning it by a very slight margin. Both affairs furnished fistic fireworks.

When Barney outgrew the division to enter the welter class, the New York Commission decided on an elimination in which Canzoneri and Lou Ambers were named to fight it out for the vacated crown. Tony won May 10, 1935, and again wore the

purple robe. He gained the verdict in fifteen rounds at the Yankee Stadium.

When he lost the championship to Ambers, September 4, 1936, in Madison Square Garden by a fifteen round decision, he gave his usual excellent performance. Tony successfully defended the title against Al Roth in fifteen rounds and on May 7, 1937, he tried to wrest the laurels from Ambers in their third match but again failed, the bout going the distance with Lou the victor. This contest was

Canzoneri risked his crown against Barney Ross, a fast coming lightweight from Chicago, who had lost only one of 48 bouts. After 10 sizzling rounds on June 23, 1933, Barney (on right) walked off with the title. In a return match on September 12, Ross repeated the victory in 15 rounds, but increasing weight later forced Barney to vacate the title. Tony was a great and busy ringman. From 1925 to 1939 he had 178 battles, winning 140 with 44 knockouts. He drew 11, had three no-decisions, was kayoed once.

Lou Ambers and Canzoneri, the top contenders for the vacated title, met on May 10, 1935. After 15 rounds Tony was again the champion. In a re-match on September 3, 1936, Lou outpointed Canzoneri in 15 rounds and became the new champion. The smiling winner (right) is flanked by his manager, Al Weill, left, and trainer Whitey Bimstein. In the "Carnival of Champions," September 23, 1937, Ambers successfully and brilliantly defended the crown against Pedro Montanez (below, left).

also fought in the Madison Square Garden arena.

On the Tournament of Champions card staged by Mike Jacobs in New York's Polo Grounds, Lou defeated Pedro Montanez of Puerto Rico in a stirring contest of fifteen rounds to retain his throne.

Then came his bout with Henry Armstrong, one of the best fought in the division in years. Before a gathering of 18,340 fans in Madison Square Garden, Homicide Hank added his

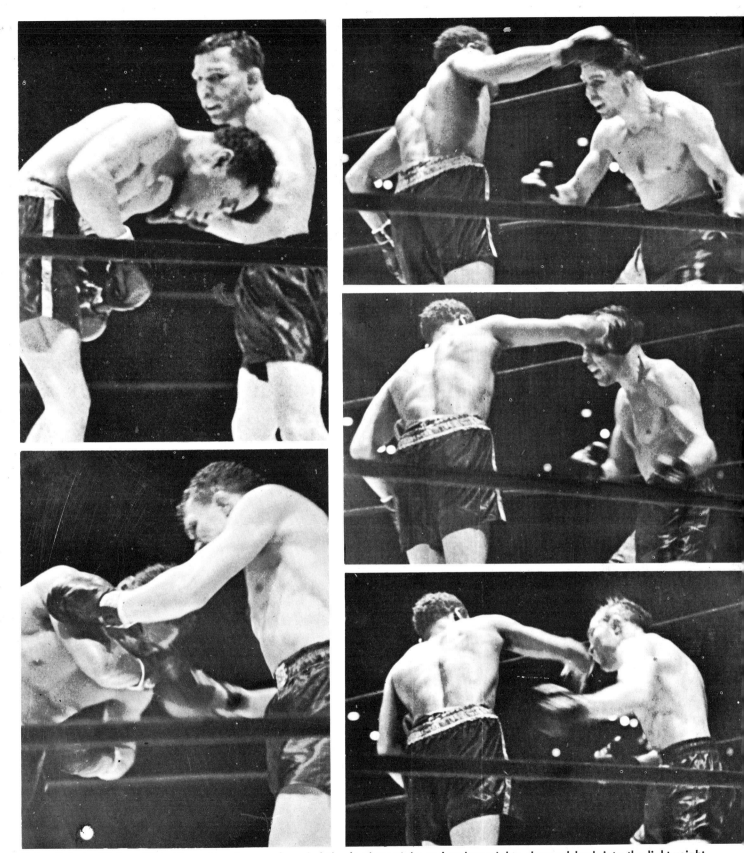

Not satisfied with two titles, Henry Armstrong, who ruled the featherweight and welterweights, dropped back into the lightweight division on August 17, 1938, and in a blood-spattered battle with Lou Ambers, won his third title. "Hammerin' Hank" was busy every second of the bout, swinging from all angles and taking advantage of split-second openings *(three photos at right)* to put over a crushing blow. The last few rounds were furious. When it seemed like Ambers was weakening, Lou would lash back with solid smashes that rocked Henry *(two photos at left)*. There wasn't a second's rest for either man throughout the battle and, at the end of 15 rounds, Armstrong, stubbornly holding his early lead in the final rounds, was the decisive winner of the lightweight crown.

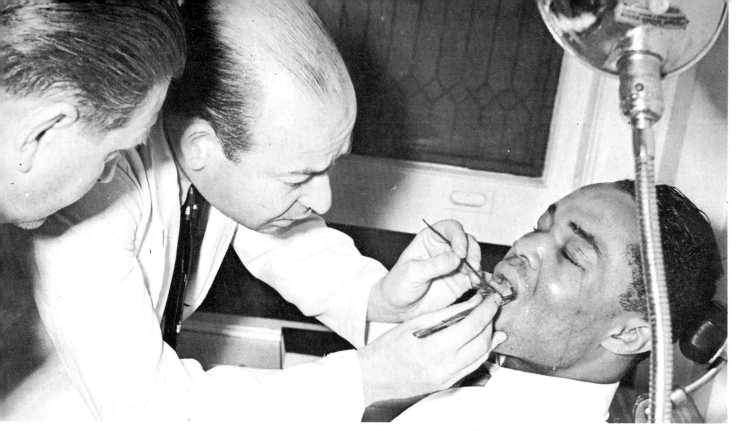

A tear trickles down the cheek of Henry Armstrong, whose mouth was badly cut while annexing Ambers' crown. Boxing Commission physician Dr. Alexander Schiff probes inside Henry's mouth the following morning, as manager Eddie Mead *(left)* looks on.

Ambers regained the crown from Armstrong in 1939. Immediately after hearing the official verdict, Lou's manager, Al Weill, leaped into the air *(left)* with joy. Low blows cost Armstrong five rounds.

third championship to his list by outpointing Ambers in fifteen rounds after having dropped the defending titleholder twice. The Herkimer boy didn't give up easily. He came back strong in the finishing rounds to have his conqueror wobbly and gory at the close of a vicious encounter.

Great was the confusion and loud the squawks when in their return engagement at the Yankee Stadium on August 22, 1939, Ambers regained the championship from Armstrong. The Herkimer Hustler, a gallant, shrewd little fighter, had Henry's right eye almost closed and his left damaged before the final bell clanged. Referee Arthur Donovan had taken five rounds away from Armstrong for what he termed low hitting, an unusual procedure in any contest, especially a title bout, and that's what brought about the howl of discontent from Henry's supporters.

Nine months later, May 10, 1940, Lou, born in Herkimer, New York, November 8, 1913, again lost the crown when he was knocked out by Lew Jenkins, born December 4, 1916, in Milburn, Texas. Jenkins turned the trick in the third round in Madison Square Garden.

Striking with deadly accuracy and the precision of a rattlesnake, the boy from the desert trails hammered the defending champ to the canvas four times and had him reeling helplessly when Referee Billy Cavanagh halted the affair. They fought again in a non-title bout on February 28, 1941, and this time Ambers was stopped in the seventh round in the same arena. It was Ambers' farewell bout. He was lying on his face when Referee Donovan intervened to save him from more punishment.

Jenkins was a colorful, hard socking ringman, whose career was highlighted by thrilling bouts in the ring and high jinx outside the ring. He first turned to boxing while in the Army, and when World War Two got under

Lew Jenkins knocked the crown from Lou Ambers' head in 1940, with whip-like jolts that almost put an end to Lou's career. Jenkins sent Lou spinning to the canvas (above) for the first of four knockdowns that rendered Ambers helpless within three rounds. When Ambers retired in 1941, he had battled 102 opponents since 1932. He won 59, with 25 knockouts. He lost six, drew in six, and was kayoed twice, by Jenkins.

When Mike Belloise was stopped by Lew Jenkins on November 21, 1939, he was the fourth victim of eight consecutive knockouts that led Lew to the title. Jenkins and manager Hymie Kaplan visit Belloise' corner after the seventh-round knockout.

Sammy Angott's clutching tactics provoked Lew Jenkins into trying to toss him over his head during their title bout in 1941. Angott went on to win a unanimous decision and the lightweight crown. Lew Jenkins had 97 bouts from 1934 to 1950. He scored 38 kayoes while winning 55. He was stopped 13 times.

Beau Jack was recognized as champion only in New York in 1942. He was sponsored by a Georgia syndicate and drew huge gates during the flush war years.

way, Lew enlisted in the Coast Guard. He served with honor and was among the crew of the first LST to hit the beach at Normandy.

After hanging up his gloves in 1948, Lew rejoined the Army and was honored for his heroic actions during the fighting in Korea. He has made a career of serving his country.

When Sammy Angott dethroned Jenkins in Madison Square Garden on December 19, 1941, the first unpopular king of the class was crowned.

Angott, born January 17, 1915 in Washington, Pennsylvania, was a clever boxer but persisted in clutching after almost every blow he delivered. It was his style, while effective, that failed to impress the fans. Sammy was the first to hang a defeat on the record of Willie Pep.

In his only defense of the crown against Allie Stolz in Madison Square Garden on May 15, 1942, he won a disputed split decision after being floored. Referee Frank Fullum, who

voted for Stolz, took two rounds away from the challenger for low hitting, and that saved Angott's crown.

He retired soon afterwards, November 13, 1942, then the following January announced a comeback as challenger for the crown he had vacated, which by now the New York Commission had awarded to Beau Jack, born in Augusta, Georgia, April 1, 1921.

The "Georgia Shoe Shine Boy," as he was dubbed, was one of the most

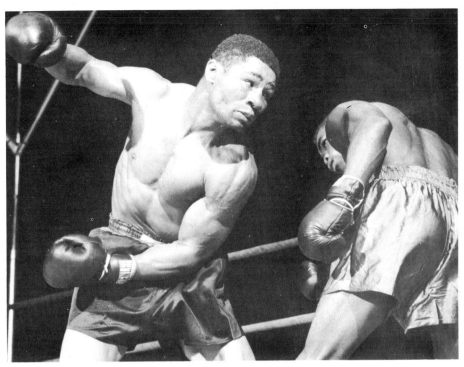

When Ike Williams *(above, right)* became undisputed lightweight champ, he gave Beau Jack a chance to regain the title on July 12, 1948. Jack was a wide-open target and was knocked out in six rounds. In a 112-bout career Jack won 83, in which he scored 40 knockouts. He lost 20, drew in five and was stopped four times.

Juan Zurita of Guadalajara, Mexico, won Angott's NBA title in 1944, scored five successive kayoes, lost the crown to Ike Williams in 1945, and retired.

Almost one year after vacating the world title, undefeated, Sammy Angott won over Slugger White and became the NBA lightweight champion. The title changed hands again on March 8, 1944, when Juan Zurita, a southpaw *(blow, left)*, outpointed Angott.

colorful lads the division had in many years. Win or lose, he drew in the throngs to Madison Square Garden. Beau Jack's popularity is attested to by the fact that in bouts in which he participated in the Garden, the total receipts were $1,578,069.

It was on May 21, 1943, that the New York Commission had Beau Jack and Bob Montgomery, the world's leading contenders, fight it out in Madison Square Garden, and Montgomery emerged the winner in fifteen rounds. But he wasn't generally accepted as the new champion, no more than was Beau Jack before him. On November 19 of that year, another match was arranged for Madison Square Garden, and Beau Jack regained the New York version of the championship.

They met for a third engagement on March 3, 1944, all bouts fought in the House that Tex Built, and Bob beat the champ in fifteen rounds, the title again changing hands. Immediately following that contest, Beau Jack joined the U. S. Army and five months later, his conqueror, born in Sumter,

South Carolina, February 10, 1919, also became a member of the armed forces.

In all their contests, both had only the support of New York as world champions. The National Boxing Association refused to go along and

sanctioned a bout between Sammy Angott and Luther Slugger White for its version of the world championship; Angott won in fifteen rounds. Then Juan Zurita, a Mexican southpaw, defeated Angott in Hollywood and he was recognized by the N.B.A.

Ike Williams became the undisputed lightweight champion of the world when he knocked out Bob Montgomery (left) on August 4, 1947, in six rounds. Ike had 42 battles from 1947 to 1951, and defended the title successfully five times. In his sixth defense of the crown, against Jimmy Carter on May 25, 1951, Ike was sent hurtling through the ropes (below) by a left hook in the 10th round, for the third knockdown of the bout. When Williams appeared hopelessly beaten in the 14th round, referee Pete Scalzo stopped the slaughter and Carter was hailed as the new lightweight champion. Ike Williams crowded 154 bouts into his career from 1940 to 1955, winning 125.

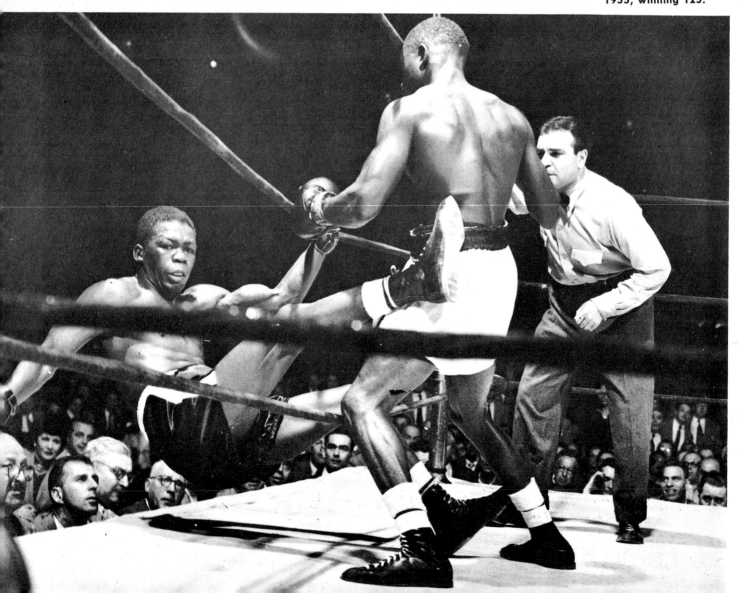

Jimmy Carter beat Lauro Salas in a title clash on April 1, 1952. In a return title bout on May 14th, Salas (right) won the crown in 15 rounds. Carter came back on October 1 and regained the title from Salas. From 1947 to 1958, Salas won 72 of 125 fights, half of them by knockout. He had nine draws, lost 42, and was knocked out four times. Carter lost the title to Paddy DeMarco (below, right) on March 5, 1954, and on November 17 he knocked Paddy out in 15 rounds and regained the crown. Carter lost the title to Wallace Bud Smith on June 29, 1955, and lost again, on October 19.

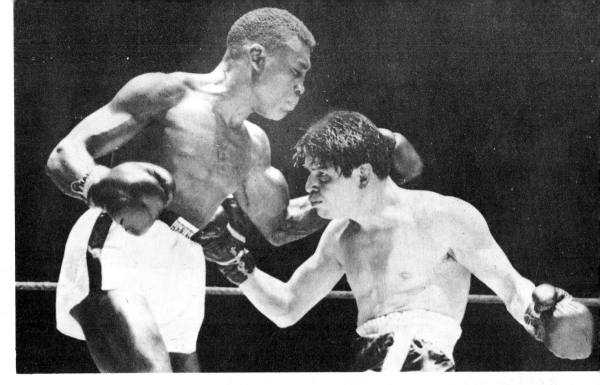

Paddy DeMarco (right) had 93 bouts from 1945 to 1957, winning 73, seven by kayo. He drew three, lost 17, and was stopped four times. Carter boxed from 1946 to 1957. He won 75 of 108 bouts, 28 by kayo, drew nine, lost 22, kayoed twice.

Ike Williams, born August 2, 1923, in Brunswick, Georgia, was pitted against Zurita in Mexico, April 18, 1945, and knocked out Juan in the second round. He then went to Europe to fight British Empire champion, Ronnie James, in Cardiff, and by stopping him in the ninth round, September 4, 1946, Williams strengthened his claim on the crown. But it was not until he knocked out Montgomery in Philadelphia on August 4, 1947, that the confusion was ended, with Williams receiving international support as world champion.

James Carter, born in Aiken, South Carolina, December 15, 1923, but a resident of New York City, was next to ascend the throne. He ended Ike's reign when he put Williams away in the fourteenth round to win the title.

A year later, in Los Angeles, Lauro Salas, a Mexican born boy from Monterey, who first saw the light of day in 1927, deposed Carter by a decision in fifteen rounds. From that point on, as was the case in the mid-dleweight division some years ago after Mickey Walker's retirement, the title kept changing hands among a group consisting of Carter, Paddy De-Marco, Wallace Bud Smith, and Joe Brown.

Carter rewon the title by decision-ing Salas in Chicago, October 15, 1952, then lost it to Paddy DeMarco of Brooklyn, born February 10, 1928, in fifteen rounds in Madison Square Garden on March 5, 1954. In the fall of that year, November 17, they engaged in a return bout in San Francisco and DeMarco, badly whipped, was stopped in the fifteenth round, Carter gaining the crown for the third time.

Then came a surprise loss, Carter

Lightweight champion Joe Brown successfully defended his crown 10 times. Joe had 130 fights between 1946 and 1970, when he retired. He won 104, 48 by knockout. He lost 12 times, nine by knockout, one by Sandy Saddler, fought 12 draws and engaged in two no-contest.

Kenny Lane, a southpaw contender from Muskegon, Michigan, started boxing in 1953. He gave Brown his toughest fight and came close to dethroning the champ.

Wallace Bud Smith (*above, left*) lost the lightweight crown to Joe Brown on August 24, 1956, at Municipal Stadium in New Orleans. Smith boxed from 1948 to 1958. He had 59 bouts, won 32 of them, drew in six, lost 21, and was knocked out eight times.

dropping the championship to Wallace Bud Smith in Boston in fifteen rounds on June 29, 1955. But Smith held it for only a year. After turning back Carter again in Cincinnati on October 19 of the same year, he was defeated by Joe Brown, a veteran, born in Baton Rouge, Louisiana, May 18, 1926, who on several occasions had retired and then made comebacks. Brown won in fifteen rounds by a decision at New Orleans on August 24, 1956, in a close bout.

They fought a return bout in Miami Beach on February 13, 1957, and this time Brown left no doubt of his superiority as he disposed of Smith in the eleventh round to retain the throne. On June 19 he again successfully put his title on the line by knocking out Orlando Zulueta of Cuba in the fifteenth round in Denver.

In 1958 Brown defended his crown

successfully twice and had three non-title fights, one as part of the inauguration program of the spacious and beautiful new Sports Stadium in Havana. The champion of Cuba, Orlando Echevarria, opposed him. Echevarria lasted less than a round in this contest on February 26. Brown had previously kayoed Ernie Williams in five rounds in Washington.

His title bouts were against Ralph Dupas in Houston on May 7, in which he stopped the New Orleans battler in the eighth round, and against Kenny Lane, whom he defeated by a slight margin in the same city on July 23. Brown had a close call in this bout, but a rally in the last rounds enabled him to pull the chestnuts out of the fire.

On November 5, in a bout in which his crown was not at stake, he lost in ten rounds to Johnny Busso in the new auditorium at Miami Beach.

When thirty-five-year-old Joe Brown lost his title to the twenty-five-year-old world junior welterweight champion, Carlos Ortiz, on April 21, 1962, in Las Vegas, "Old Bones" had established a record of eleven successful lightweight title defenses in succession, a record no one has come close to matching.

In this fight, Brown just couldn't maneuver the volatile, outspoken, Puerto Rican–born New Yorker into position to throw his well-known combination, while Ortiz kept flashing left jabs. All three officials awarded Ortiz seventy-four of a possible seventy-five points.

Ortiz underestimated Panamanian Ismael Laguna and failed to train rigorously enough for their April 10, 1965 bout in Panama City. As a result, the defending champion lost the fifteen-round decision. Laguna, rel-

Carlos Ortiz (*left*) won the lightweight title from Joe Brown by taking a 15-round verdict on April 21, 1962, at Las Vegas, Nevada. Brown had made 11 successful defenses.

Ismael Laguna of Panama pokes a left to Ortiz' face on his way to winning the crown on a 15-round decision in Panama on April 10, 1965. Ortiz had failed to train seriously.

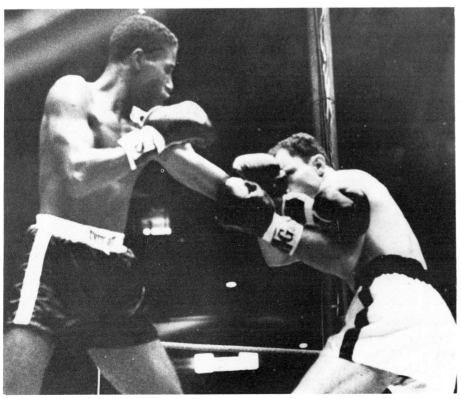

Ortiz regained his title on November 13, 1965, outpointing Laguna in 15 rounds in San Juan, Puerto Rico, and Ortiz, above, is shown successfully defending the crown against Laguna in 15 rounds at New York's Shea Stadium on August 16, 1967.

atively unknown internationally and fighting for the first time in the lightweight class, was reputed to be the fastest boxer ever seen in Panama—he had the ability to land a variety of punches with bewildering rapidity.

The ex-champion had learned his lesson. On November 13, 1965, a strong, well-conditioned Ortiz, at 135½ pounds, stepped into the ring, in Puerto Rico, for his rematch with the 133-pound Laguna.

The defending champion tried to keep up a steady jab, but he couldn't maintain the pace against the forceful attack of a stronger Ortiz, who gained a unanimous decision in fifteen rounds.

Teo Cruz, of the Dominican Republic, won a split decision over Ortiz in a grueling, consistently hard-fought bout on June 29, 1968. The decisive factor may well have been the decking of Ortiz in the first round from a

On June 29, 1968, Ortiz traveled to Santo Domingo, only to lose his precious crown to Carlos (Teo) Cruz on a split 15-round decision. Referee Zack Clayton voted for Ortiz, the two judges for Cruz. (*Top*) Cruz knocks Ortiz into the ropes. (*Left*) The foes approach each other very warily during the early going. (*Right*) Cruz being carried off by admirers after triumph.

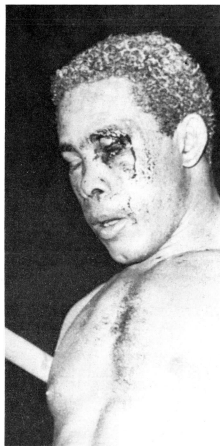

Cruz met 20-year-old Mando Ramos at Los Angeles on February 19, 1969, and was shorn of the lightweight title when the bout was halted in the 11th round because of a deep cut over Cruz' left eye, (right). Left: Cruz cuffs Ramos with both hands in first.

right cross to the jaw.

Cruz's reign was short-lived. On February 19, 1969, Mando Ramos, of California, opened a savage gash over Cruz's left eye with a looping right in the eighth round and went on to win by a knockout in the eleventh when the ring physician examined Cruz's eye for the third time and advised referee John Thomas to halt the bout.

Twenty-year-old Ramos, the youngest man to win the lightweight crown, had been befuddled in the early rounds by the Dominican's flatfooted, crouching tactics, but gaining confidence he used his $3\frac{1}{2}$-inch advantage in reach to score effectively.

Laguna recaptured the crown on March 3, 1970, in Los Angeles, when Ramos's manager decided that his fighter, with both eyes bleeding profusely, had absorbed enough punish-

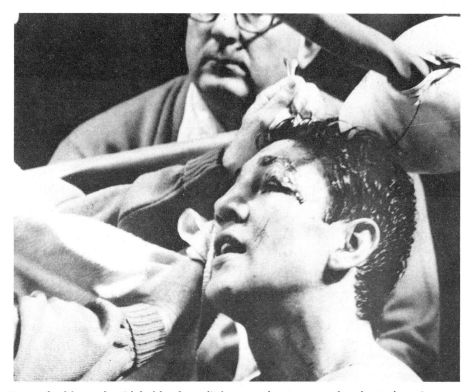

Ramos had been the titleholder for a little more than a year when he took on Laguna, who became champion again when Ramos was unable to continue after nine rounds.

313

Laguna lost the crown to Scotland's Ken Buchanan in 15 rounds in 1970 and in a return match a year later, Buchanan won easily in 15. Buchanan misses with a right.

ment after the ninth round. Laguna and Ramos scaled 135 and 134½ pounds, respectively.

Gentleman boxer Ken Buchanan became Scotland's first lightweight champion when he won a split decision over the 5-to-2-favored Laguna on September 26, 1970, in Puerto Rico.

The fight was filled with action as Laguna, at 134½ pounds, bobbed and weaved, scoring with chopping right leads and short blows on the inside, while the 134-pound Buchanan moved in behind to deliver vigorous left jabs.

In a rematch a year later, on September 13, Buchanan retained his title in a unanimous fifteen-round de-

cision.

When Buchanan met Roberto Duran, it was a battle between a clever, graceful "boxer" and a powerful "fighter." Duran, with a telling right cross, a left hook, and a jab as his assets, scored a knockout in the thirteenth round on June 26, 1972, in New York.

Upon meeting Esteban DeJesus of Puerto Rico on March 16, 1974, at Panama, Duran was out to avenge the only defeat in his record, a ten-round loss on November 17, 1972.

To even the score now, Duran knocked DeJesus out in the eleventh with a left hook to the head, a left hook to the jaw, and a right to the head. More exhausted than hurt, De-Jesus sat on his haunches as he was

counted out by referee Isaac Herrera.

On December 21, 1974, Duran KO'd Japan's contender, Masataka Takayama, in one round in Costa Rica.

He knocked out Ray Lampkin of the United States in the fourteenth at Panama in 1975 to record his thirty-fifth knockout in forty-four bouts, and the same year knocked out Leoncio Ortiz in the final round at San Juan on December 20. 1976 saw two title defences in which he beat Lou Bizzaro by a knockout in fourteen rounds at Erie on May 23 and five months later disposed of Alvaro Rojas in a single round at Hollywood on October 15. The following year Vilomar Fernandez was knocked out in thirteen rounds at Miami Beach on January 29 and Edwin Viruet was outpointed in Philadelphia over fifteen rounds on September 17. On January 21, 1978, Duran beat off a challenge from Estaban De Jesus who was knocked out in twelve rounds at Las Vegas. At the end of the year, however, at the age of only 27, Duran announced that he was giving up the lightweight title to compete as a welterweight. He had successfully defended the crown twelve times.

Duran was disciplined by the W.B.C. for failing to meet Ken Buchanan in a return title contest. Mando Ramos then outpointed Pedro Carrasco of Spain to win the vacant W.B.C. title on June 28, 1972. Chango Carmona then stopped Ramos in eight rounds at Los Angeles on September 15 and two months later Rodolfo Gonzalez took over by forcing Carmona to retire in twelve rounds at Los Angeles. On April 11, 1974, Guts Ishimatsu defeated Gonzalez by a kayo in eight rounds at Tokyo and the Japanese fighter enhanced his claim by outpointing Ken Buchanan in Tokyo on February 21, 1975. Estaban De Jesus came back into the title picture by outpointing Ishimatsu at Bayamon on May 8, 1976, and on September 11 knocked out Hector Medina in seven rounds at Bayamon. In 1977 De Jesus disposed of Buzzsaw Yamabe in six rounds on February 12 and on June 25 he knocked out Vicente Saldivar in eleven rounds, both these defences taking place at Bayamon. Then came his decisive defeat by Roberto Duran which made his W.B.C. title worthless.

314

Hard-punching Roberto Duran of Panama became king of the 135-pounders when he halted Buchanan in the 13th round at Madison Square Garden on June 26, 1972. Duran's blows, above, send the Scotsman through the ropes. (*Below, left*) Referee Johnny LoBianco pulls Duran away as Buchanan falls to the canvas at the end of the 13th round, and Buchanan, in pain, clutches his groin on the way down. Ken claimed he was fouled by the Panamanian at close quarters, but the referee ruled otherwise.

When Duran relinquished the title in 1979, both the World Boxing Council and the World Boxing Association set up their own champions. On April 17, 1979, Jim Watt of Scotland, knocked out Alfredo Pitalua (Colombia) in twelve rounds at Glasgow to win the W.B.C. crown, the second Scotsman to become world lightweight champion. He made a successful first defence by knocking out Robert Vasquez (U.S.A.) in nine rounds on November 3, then on March 14, 1980, he beat Irishman Charlie Nash, who was stopped in four rounds, again in Glasgow. On June 7, at Ibrox Park, Glasgow, he outpointed Howard Davis (U.S.A.) and defeated his third American challenger on November 1 at Glasgow, his opponent, Sean O'Grady, being stopped in the 12th round because of a badly gashed forehead.

On June 16, 1979, Ernesto Espana (Venezuela) won the vacant W.B.A. title by knocking out Claude Noel

Roberto Duran avoided a flurry of wild blows by Esteban DeJesus in eleventh round, then knocked out DeJesus who is shown taking count in Panama City title bout.

Jim Watt successfully defended his middleweight title three times in 1980, but suffered bad cuts around the eyes and mouth against Sean O'Grady (U.S.A.) *below* and was down in the first against Irishman Charlie Nash, who receives a right to the chin (*below right*).

(Trinidad) in 13 rounds at San Juan. He successfully defended against Johnny Lira (U.S.A.) by a knockout in ten rounds at Chicago on August 4. On March 2, 1980 he was stopped in nine rounds by Hilmer Kenty (U.S.A.) at Detroit. The new W.B.A. champion made three defences in 1980, stopping Yong Oh Ho (Korea) in nine rounds at Detroit on August 2; beating former champion, Ernesto Espana in four rounds at San Juan, on September 20 and outpointing Vilomar Fernandez at Detroit on November 8.

JUNIOR LIGHTWEIGHT CHAMPIONS

(Weight Limit, 130 Pounds)

JOHNNY DUNDEE, 1921; JACK BERNSTEIN, 1923; JOHNNY DUNDEE, 1923; STEVE "KID" SULLIVAN, 1924; MIKE BALLARINO, 1925; TOD MORGAN, 1925; BENNY BASS, 1929; KID CHOCOLATE, 1931; FRANKIE KLICK, 1933; HAROLD GOMES, 1959; FLASH ELORDE, 1960; YOSHIAKI NUMATA, 1967; HIROSHI KOBOYASHI, 1967;
FOR FAILING TO DEFEND HIS TITLE AGAINST THEIR CHOSEN CHALLENGER, THE W.B.C. DEPRIVED KOBOYASHI OF HIS CHAMPIONSHIP AND AFTER THAT THE TWO OPPOSING CONTROLLING BODIES RECOGNISED CHAMPIONS AS FOLLOWS: 1969—RENE BARRINGTON (WBC); 1970—YOSHIAKI NUMATA (WBC); 1971—ALFREDO MARCANO (WBA); 1972—BEN VILLAFLOR (WBA); 1973—KUNIAKI SHIBATA (WBA), BEN VILLAFLOR (WBA); 1974—KUNIAKI SHIBATA (WBC); 1975-7—ALFREDO ESCALERA (WBC); 1976-8—SAM SERRANO (WBA); 1978—ALEXIS ARGUELLO (WBC).
1980—ARGUELLO RELINQUISHED WBC TITLE, AND ON DECEMBER 11 RAFAEL LIMON (MEXICO) BEAT IDELFONSO BETHELMI (VENEZUELA), THE REFEREE STOPPING THE FIGHT IN THE FIFTEENTH, TO WIN THE VACANT TITLE AT LOS ANGELES. 1980—YASATSUNE UEHARA (JAPAN) (WBA).

THE FEATHERWEIGHTS

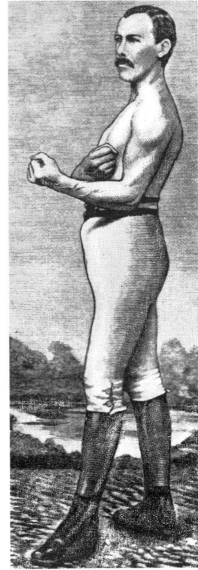

Dick Hollywood (*above*) of New York, was a pioneer bare-knuckles champion, who claimed the featherweight crown in 1867 after defeating Johnny Keating of Cincinnati.

Owen Swift (*left*) was probably England's greatest little man, but his courage was not enough to handle the powerfully heavier Hammer Lane, who terminated their battle (*above*) with crushing body slams to the turf. Swift carried the bruising battle on May 5, 1836, to 100 rounds, lasting over two hours. Born in 1814, Owen made his ring debut at the age of 15 and won 11 major battles before he was 20. He never weighed more than 128 pounds and lost only two battles in a 10-year career, the first as a youngster, the other when he met Lane. Swift gained two tragic ring victories. The results of his blows killed Anthony Noon (*right*) in 1834, for which he served six months in prison, and Brighton Bill, in 1838. He was acquitted of Bill's death and quit fighting.

318

MIGHTY MITES OF THE ROPED SQUARE

The activity in the three lower divisions—featherweight, bantam and flyweight—has dwindled considerably in the past few years owing to the scarcity of talent. Most of the boxers in the three bottom classes are from the Pacific Coast or from Mexico and other foreign countries, particularly bantams and flyweights. Good little battlers were plentiful in boxing's early days when the ring's greatest stars performed. Abe Attell, Terry McGovern, Casper Leon, George Dixon, Dave Sullivan, Jimmy Barry, Jimmy Wilde, Joe Lynch, Johnny Buff, Frankie Burns, Johnny Coulon, Kid Williams, Al Brown, Benny Lynch, Pancho Villa, Pete Herman among the old timers, and the marvelous Willie Pep among the more recent, have standout records.

In Australia the fans thought the world of Australian Billy Murphy in the feather class. In America in the early days of boxing, shortly after the gloves era got under way, George Dixon was considered tops. So evenly matched were many of the best men in the feather class that it is difficult to pick one as the greatest. Young Griffo of Australia was never defeated as a featherweight. He, like Attell and Pep, was a ring marvel. Abe Attell was so good, he had great difficulty in obtaining matches with men his weight. He had to face lightweights and often even went beyond that scale. Johnny Kilbane as a feather also often had to go out of his class to keep in action.

Two ounce gloves were just beginning to replace bare-knuckle fighting when during the late eighties Dal Hawkins and Freddy Bogan fought seventy-five rounds in San Francisco for the American featherweight crown. The fight, held indoors in 1889, was halted at five A.M. and was resumed the following day when Hawkins won by a knockout in the fifteenth round to assume the top spot in the division.

Hawkins outgrew the class, the weight of which at the time was 118 to 122 pounds, and Harry Gilmore claimed the crown. But Gilmore never went into a title defense. He offered to make 122 pounds for Ike Weir, the clever "Belfast Spider," who refused to accept the terms. Gilmore then entered the next higher division, leaving it to Weir and Frank Murphy of England to fight it out for the vacant throne. They fought a draw of eighty rounds at Kouts, Indiana, on March 31, 1889.

Murphy met Australian Billy Mur-

Dal Hawkins (left) was born in San Francisco, in 1871. He won the featherweight crown after battling Fred Bogan a total of 90 rounds. Ike Weir (right) born near Belfast, Ireland, in 1867, claimed the title when Hawkins outgrew the class.

Frank Murphy (above, left) and Ike Weir battled for the featherweight title in 1889. They fought to an 80-round draw with skin-tight gloves for a purse of $1,500. The contest was broken up by the police.

"Torpedo" Billy Murphy of Australia knocked out Weir in 14 rounds. The Americans insisted that the bout was for the British crown and not the world title.

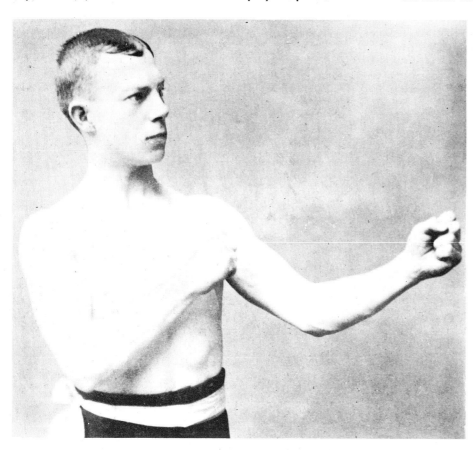

Cal McCarthy (left) of Troy, New York, held George Dixon to a 70-round draw in 1890, but was kayoed by Dixon in 1891.

the British Empire title and since Cal McCarthy and George Dixon, born July 29, 1870, were America's leading feathers who had graduated from the bantam division, they were matched for the American championship. "Little Chocolate" stopped McCarthy in the twenty-second round in Troy, New York, and was proclaimed title-holder. Through his manager, the weight was set at 115 pounds limit.

Australian Billy Murphy in the meantime had gone back to Australia and Johnny Griffin claimed his crown. After Weir and Griffin had fought a draw of four rounds, a bout stopped by the police, Tom O'Rourke, manager of Dixon, decided on a ruse. He took George to San Francisco to box Abe Willis, the British champion, and when on July 28, 1891, Dixon halted his opponent in five rounds, Dixon became the acknowledged world champion and for the first time a universal titleholder headed the division.

Because of his light weight, Dixon, really a bantam—a 115 pound boxer— took the best in the field into camp.

phy at San Francisco two months later and they fought twenty-seven rounds to a draw. On January 13, 1890, Weir and Billy Murphy met in San Francisco and Murphy was acclaimed champion when he knocked out Ike in the fourteenth round.

The American sports scribes refused to accept this as a championship bout, declaring that the battle settled only

Johnny Griffin, born in 1869, in Braintree, Massachusetts, knocked out undefeated Jimmy Lynch of New York in five rounds *(above)* on September 26, 1892, for the American title. The referee was Al Smith. Lynch is being carried to his corner *(circle)* by his second, Joe Choyinski, the heavyweight title contender. Griffin had claimed the title when Murphy left for Australia.

George Dixon leaps over the ropes and into the arms of his manager, Tom O'Rourke *(below)* after stopping Abe Willis, the British Empire champion, in the fifth round. The bout, billed as for the featherweight championship of the world, was held at the California Athletic Club in San Francisco, with Harry Cook as referee. The purse was $4,250 to the winner and $750 to the loser.

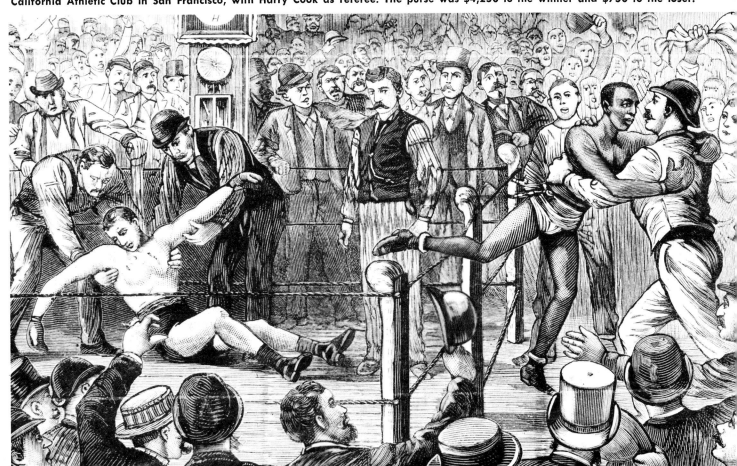

Solly Smith, a clever 19-year-old boxer from Los Angeles, gained the featherweight championship when he clearly outpointed the veteran George Dixon (left) in 1897, before an overflow crowd in San Francisco. Smith had been knocked out by Dixon in 1893 in his eighth pro bout, when he was only 15 years old. Dixon felt the 20-round loss of his title deeply and broke down in his dressing room (above) with only his manager, Tom O'Rourke, to console him.

Dave Sullivan (below, right) made sport-page headlines when he won the title from Solly Smith (below, left). Sullivan was born in Cork, Ireland, in May, 1887.

SOLLY SMITH'S ARM WAS BROKEN.

Even Then He Went Through a Whole Round Before Giving Up.

The Bout Unsatisfactory, but Dave Sullivan Got the Purse.

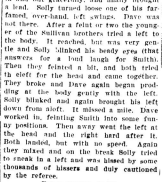

Before Dave Sullivan and Solly Smith met at the Greater New York Athletic Club last night there was a chance to put a damper on argument as to which was the better featherweight by saying, "Well, I'll bet you." Now the chance to argue the point still remains with no chance of

It was announced that the men were to break clear at the word, and they backed to corners. Then every one took a long breath and the bell clanged.

For full thirty seconds they feinted. Dave acted very nicely, he smiled, moved in and out gracefully, and finally brought a lead. Solly turned loose one of his far-famed, over-hand, left swings. Dave was not there. After a feint or two the younger of the Sullivan brothers tried a left to the body. It reached, but was very gentle and Solly blinked his beady eyes (that answers for a loud laugh for Smith). Then they feinted a bit, and both tried th eleft for the head and came together. They broke and Dave again began prodding at the body gently with the left. Solly blinked and again brought his left down from aloft. It missed a mile. Dave worked in, feinting Smith into some funny positions. Then away went the left at the head and the right hard after it. Both landed, but with no speed. Again they mixed and on the break Solly tried to sneak in a left and was hissed by some thousands of hissers and duly cautioned by the referee.

Dave Grows Bold.

In the second Dave grew bolder and jabbed his left into the body fairly good before Solly understood. Then Mr. Smith retaliated with his overhand left. Dave was inside of it. Again Dave jabbed his left fair to the works and still again. Then he smiled what is known as the Johnny Wise smile and tried at the head. Smith blocked and again tried the left like a south-paw cricket bowler. Dave was away and then in with his jab to the body. Then "bang" went the right to the

half round. Dave pushed him off, jabbed at the body and again came the swing. Again it missed and Dave got to the head with left and the body with right. Dave had done no damage so far, but he looked to have Smith guessing hard.

In the third Dave began his body jab-

He was on the three days carnival card that was featured by the Sullivan-Corbett battle and on September 6, 1892, he knocked out Jack Skelly, a very good boxer from New York with a fine amateur record, at the Olympic Club of New Orleans, in the eighth round. That was Jack's initial bout as a professional.

Quite a complication existed in the early days of the class because of the many title claimants. After the Skelly fight, O'Rourke again raised the weight, this time to 126 pounds, when he found Dixon's foes were making it tough for him. At that weight he matched "Little Chocolate" with Solly Smith at San Francisco, October 4, 1897, Smith getting the verdict at the end of twenty rounds. Smith then made a match with Dave Sullivan for Coney Island, September 26, 1898. Handicapped by a broken arm, Smith quit in the fifth round.

Dixon then challenged Sullivan and at the Lenox A. C. of New York, on November 11, 1898, "Little Chocolate" stopped his opponent in the tenth

AROUND THE RINGSIDE

DIXON RUSHING SULLIVAN TO THE ROPES

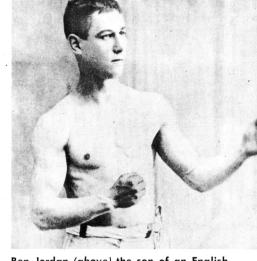

Ben Jordan (above) the son of an English minister, beat Dixon in 25 rounds in 1898 and claimed the title. He was knocked out by Eddie Santry in 1899, as the sport cartoon (below) humorously shows.

JORDAN GIVES HIMSELF UP TO ASTRONOMY IN THE 16TH ROUND

round. Each scaled 118 pounds.

Meanwhile Ben Jordan of England, who laid claim to the championship after he had outpointed Dixon in twenty-five rounds in New York on July 1, 1898, had in turn been knocked out by Eddie Santry of Chicago on October 10, 1899, in sixteen rounds. Hence Santry, though he previously had lost to Dixon, asserted himself king of the division. Dixon then cleared the path for international recognition by whipping Santry in six rounds, then boxing a draw of twenty with him.

By now Dixon was on the down-grade and Terry McGovern, "The Brooklyn Terror," had come to the fore. He had beaten all comers, many by knockouts, and on January 9, 1900, at the Broadway A. C., "Little Chocolate" lost his crown to him. Dixon was knocked out in the eighth round.

McGovern, born in Jamestown, Pennsylvania, March 9, 1880, and Dixon were two of the top ringmen in the division. Dixon battled fearlessly against great odds until, in the eighth

George Dixon regained the crown when Dave Sullivan was disqualified after his seconds entered the ring in the 10th round, to prevent a knockout. The newspaper cartoon (above) depicts the action and some of the characters at ringside.

Eddie Santry claimed the title after his knockout of Jordan. On July 14, 1899, Dixon won a six-round decision over Santry, and one month later they fought a 20-round draw, as illustrated (below) in the New York Journal.

DIXON'S AND SANTRY'S CONTRASTING STYLES

DIXON-SANTRY BATTLE

Betting Santry

"Terrible Terry" McGovern (above, right) started in 1897 and ended in 1908. In 77 bouts, he won 59, 34 by knockout, lost two, boxed four draws and 10 no-decision bouts, and was kayoed twice. His brother Hugh (left) boxed from 1902 to 1905.

When McGovern knocked out Dixon, he was absolutely invincible. He had scored eight consecutive knockouts and went on to make it 12. On July 16, 1900, he met Frank Erne, the lightweight champion, who agreed to come in at 128 pounds and knock out Terry in 10 rounds, or take the loser's end of the purse. Although no championship was involved under those terms, Terry disposed of Erne in just three rounds at Madison Square Garden. The illustration (above) which appeared in the New York Herald, shows Erne down for the second time and his second (left) is about to throw in the towel, to save him from further punishment.

Terry is shown on the left, displaying his favorite blow, a right hand to the stomach, after slipping under his opponent's right-hand lead. Terry's vicious body blows, in rapid succession, set his victims up for the knockout.

The sporting world was content to agree that Terry McGovern would rule the feather-weight roost for years to come. But a stunning upset occurred on Thanksgiving Day in 1901, when Young Corbett (above, right) knocked Terry out in two rounds. In a return bout at San Francisco Corbett again kayoed McGovern, this time in 11 rounds.

Young Corbett (William H. Rothwell) was born in Denver, Colorado, in 1880. He fought only in the West, where he scored 22 knockouts from 1897 to 1901, before he invaded the East to fight McGovern.

Abe Attell (below, right) posed with his brother, Monte, claimed the throne when Corbett could no longer make weight.

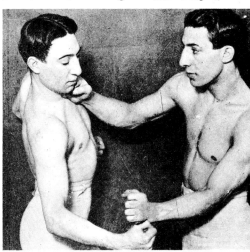

round, Referee Johnny White stepped in and halted the affair to save "Little Chocolate."

The following year, on Thanksgiving Day, November 28, a confident Mc-Govern faced Young Corbett, born in Denver, Colorado, October 4, 1880, in a battle for the feather crown. Mc-Govern set the weight limit at 126 pounds though he had won the title at 122. The contest at Hartford, Con-necticut, lasted less than two rounds. It was a terrific battle despite its short-ness, with "Terrible Terry" dropping the title.

Terry, who was discovered and de-veloped by Sam H. Harris, the the-atrical producer, got his start at the Greenwood Sporting Club of South Brooklyn, New York. He was a much harder hitter than was Dixon. He was a cruel puncher, fast and accurate.

Before his defeat by Corbett, he went all out putting his rivals out of the way. Among others he whipped were Jack Ward, Eddie Santry, Oscar Gardner, Tommy White, Pedlar Pal-mer, Frank Erne, and Joe Bernstein. He halted Joe Gans in Chicago in the

second round, a bout that was termed a "fake" and resulted in the killing of boxing in the Windy City.

One of his best performances was against Palmer, the British champion, on September 12, 1899, at Tuckahoe, New York. In that contest Terry won the world bantam crown by knocking the Britisher out in less than one round. Terry vacated the bantam class at the end of the year when he became overweight.

Corbett, McGovern's successor as feather king, put Terry down in the first round with an uppercut to the chin and put him away for keeps with several body punches followed by a hook to the jaw. Corbett defeated Kid Broad and Joe Bernstein, besides fighting no decision contests with Ed-die Lenny, Young Erne and Crockey Boyle, then vacated the throne.

When Young Corbett found that he was putting on weight, he decided to retire from the class and enter the lightweight division. Then with the championship vacant, Abe Attell, a rising young clever featherweight from San Francisco, California, where

Abe Attell (above, right) and "Harlem" Tommy Murphy engaged in one of the bloodiest fights ever seen. They met on March 9, 1912, in Daly City, California, two weeks after Attell had lost his title to Johnny Kilbane. Both fighters were covered with blood during the entire 20 rounds of fighting. Murphy won the referee's decision.

"Brooklyn" Tommy Sullivan, a seven-year veteran, knocked out Attell in 1904, but was deprived of the title for being over the featherweight limit for the fight.

he was born on Washington's birthday, 1884, laid claim to the throne. On October 20, 1901, Dixon, in an attempt to regain the championship, drew with Attell in twenty rounds, then faced him again a week later, October 28, and lost to Attell in fifteen rounds. Now Abe declared himself the successor to Corbett and announced his willingness to defend against all comers.

The "Little Hebrew," as he was called, engaged in many fifteen and twenty rounds contests with success but there were others, like Tommy Sullivan, who disputed Attell's right to top honors. After Abe had stopped Harry Forbes in five rounds in what was advertised as a championship match, he tackled Sullivan in St. Louis, October 13, 1904, in defense of his laurels and was knocked out in the fifth round. Attell insisted that Sullivan had not made the class weight and continued to assert his rights to

the crown. He was backed by the press in his claim and on April 30, 1908, Abe cleared up the confusion by knocking Sullivan out in the fourth round.

Now Attell received universal recognition, though for many months before this he kept successfully defending his claim against the cream of the division. During that period his greatest bouts were with Owen Moran of England, with whom he drew in twenty-five rounds and again in twenty-three.

Attell held the title for almost eleven years, including the disputed period, before he was dethroned by Johnny Kilbane, born in Cleveland, Ohio, April 18, 1889. During that long reign he faced the world's best in three divisions with considerable success. Among the many stars whom he met were Frankie Neil, Kid Herman, Jimmy Walsh, Brooklyn Tommy Sullivan, Battling Nelson, Matty Baldwin,

Jem Driscoll *(above)*, the British feather-weight champion, met Attell on February 19, 1909, in a 10-round no-decision contest. Driscoll completely outboxed and out-fought Attell, but could not gain the crown unless he scored a knockout.

Big Mackay, Harry Forbes, Harlem Tommy Murphy, Pal Moore, Matt Wells, Patsy Kline, K.O. Brown, and Jem Driscoll, the British champion. His bouts with Tommy Murphy, like that with Driscoll, hold a special place in the history of the class as outstanding thrillers.

The fight with Driscoll was a masterpiece of ring cleverness in which the Britisher got the better of his opponent. Driscoll was so clever on that occasion that Attell often found his punches, usually most effective, hitting the ozone. Driscoll came to America heralded as a wizard and he lived up to his reputation. The throng that witnessed the bout at the National A. C. of New York saw wily Attell miss more often than ever before. It was a battle of ring cleverness.

Kilbane stunned the boxing world when he outclassed Attell in twenty rounds on February 22, 1912, in Vernon, California, to relieve Abe of

Johnny Kilbane raises his arms in joy *(above)* after receiving a popular 20-round decision in 1912 that ended Abe Attell's almost 11-year reign on the featherweight throne. Kilbane had been credited with a four-round knockout over Attell at Cleveland in 1911, when Attell quit, claiming his shoulder was broken.

Kilbane *(right)* started boxing in 1907 and retired in 1923. He engaged in 141 contests, of which he lost only four.

Eugene Criqui (below), a French war hero, whose shattered jaw was made over by plastic surgery, ended Kilbane's 11-year reign in 1923 in six rounds (above). Criqui had scored 28 kayoes in 55 bouts after returning from the war in 1917.

Criqui won the title on June 2 and lost it to Johnny Dundee on July 26. He wore the crown only 54 days. The gallant Frenchman was knocked down early in the fight (below), but managed to go the distance, losing the decision in 15 rounds.

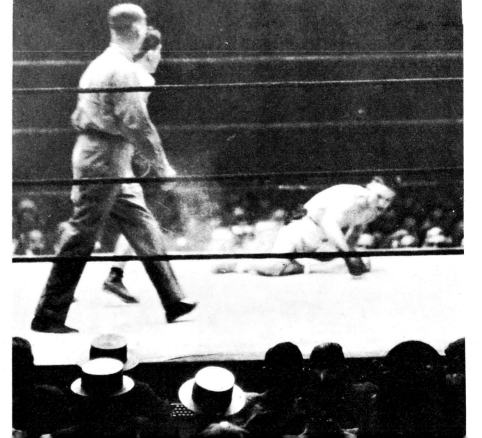

Johnny Dundee *(left)* was a 21-year ring veteran. He started in 1910 and hung up his gloves in 1932. In that time, he battled 320 opponents, losing to 31. After winning the featherweight crown, he went to Rome with manager Jimmy Johnston, where during a visit to the Vatican, they posed *(above)* before a bust of Pope Leo X.

Louis ''Kid'' Kaplan, born in Russia in 1902, succeeded Dundee to the throne when he knocked out Danny Kramer in an elimination tournament in 1925. In training for the January bout, Kaplan posed with his sisters *(below)* outside his work-gym.

his laurels. Kilbane, though not as clever as Abe, was a scientific boxer with a fairly good punch. Most of his ring battles were no-decision affairs.

Eugene Criqui of France was the next title holder. He knocked out Kilbane in six rounds at the Polo Grounds on June 2, 1923, but held on to his championship for only one month and twenty-four days when he was dethroned by Johnny Dundee in the same arena in fifteen rounds.

In 1925 Dundee outgrew the featherweight class. Following an elimination, Louis Kid Kaplan of Meriden, Connecticut, replaced Dundee. The latter, called the "Scotch Wop," born in Shaikai, Italy, November 22, 1893, was one of the ring marvels of his era. Equally good as a lightweight and as a feather, he fought the best in each class. On April 29, 1913, Dundee fought a draw with Kilbane. The bout went twenty rounds and Kilbane was lucky to retain his featherweight crown.

Kaplan, one of the best pugilists ever developed in Connecticut, surrendered his title in 1927, because like

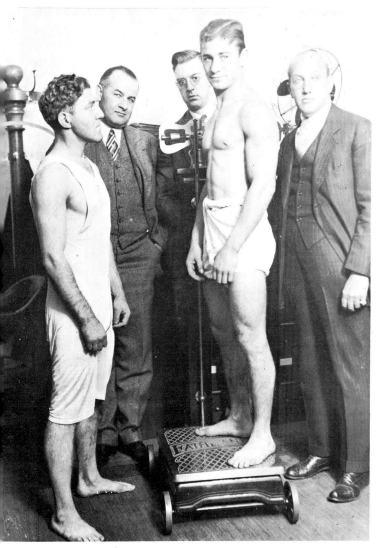

When Kaplan vacated the title, the logical contenders, Red Chapman *(left)* and Benny Bass, on the scales, met in a 10-round contest. Bass was an easy winner. Earlier in 1927, Bass won from Chapman when he was fouled in the first round.

Young Tony Canzoneri, who had been boxing three years, met Bass in February of 1928. Tony *(above, left)* walked off with the decision and the featherweight crown, only to lose it eight months later to André Routis, in 15 rounds.

André Routis, born in Bordeaux, France, in 1900, gained the title from Canzoneri in a fast 15-round bout. Routis, who started in 1919, won the bantamweight title of France in 1924 and had a fair record before coming to America in 1926. After campaigning here for two years, Routis won the title, then lost it one year later.

many other champions he no longer could make 126 pounds. Benny Bass and Red Chapman of Boston, the leading contenders, fought for the right to succeed him. Bass, born December 4, 1902, in Kiev, Russia, outpointed his rival and was crowned king, September 12, 1927. He was beaten on a decision in fifteen rounds February 10, 1928, by Tony Canzoneri who hailed from New York, though born in Louisiana.

Another Frenchman soon took over when Andre Routis outpointed Canzoneri in the Garden on September 28, 1928, in fifteen rounds. A few days short of a year later, the Frenchman lost the championship to Battling Battalino in the latter's native city, Hartford, Connecticut, via a decision at

Routis found Bat Battalino too strong and tough. At the end of 15 rounds on September 23, 1929, Battalino's hand was raised as the new featherweight champion, in Hartford, Connecticut.

Bat Battalino was a rugged ringman who started boxing in 1927 and after 22 bouts won the featherweight title. He defended the crown successfully five times and met the best men in the class. Vacated the title in 1932, and retired in 1940.

Kid Chocolate, the Cuban bonbon, was a truly finished ringman. He was an excellent boxer, with an abundance of ring skill and a good puncher. In 161 bouts from 1928 to 1938, he won 145, 64 by knockouts. When he knocked out Lew Feldman *(below)* on October 13, 1932, he won New York recognition as featherweight champion.

the end of fifteen rounds. Routis, born July 16, 1900 in Bordeaux, found Battalino, born February 10, 1908, far too strong and sturdy for him. The latter's rushing tactics and inside work bewildered the foreigner.

When Battalino outgrew the class, an elimination was staged both by New York and the National Boxing Association, with Tommy Paul gaining N.B.A. support through his victory over Johnny Pena in Detroit, May 26, 1932, and Kid Chocolate of Havana, Cuba, receiving New York's blessing when he knocked out Lew Feldman in the twelfth round. But when Freddie Miller on January 13, 1933, outpointed Paul to win the N.B.A. crown, Chocolate relinquished his claim to enter the junior lightweight class.

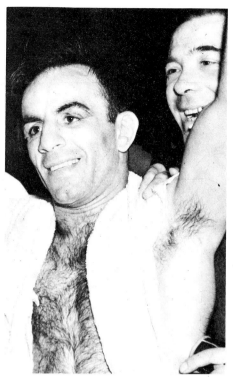

Petey Sarron, who won the title from Miller, boxed from 1928 to 1939. In 97 bouts he won 71, with only 17 knockouts.

Freddie Miller, born on April 3, 1911, in Cincinnati, Ohio, was one of the ring's busiest boxers. From 1928 to 1940 he engaged in 237 fights, winning 199. After losing a title bout to Bat Battalino in 1931, he gained the crown by defeating Tommy Paul in 1933. Freddie is shown above reading a cable from America in his Liverpool, England, hotel room, following his victory over Nel Tarleton in 1934.

Henry Armstrong (below, right) knocked out Petey Sarron for the first of three titles. Armstrong, kayoed in his first pro bout in 1931, had an indifferent record until 1937 when he scored 26 knockouts in 27 bouts, including that with Sarron and won one decision. He then went after the light and welterweight titles.

Freddie went abroad and proceeded to clean up the cream of foreign contenders in travels about Europe. There he lost only two out of thirty battles and received universal recognition as champion. His campaign was very similar to that of Tommy Burns in the heavyweight division many years before him.

On May 11, 1936, in Washington, D. C., Miller was defeated by Petey Sarron, born in Birmingham, Alabama, and Petey became the wearer of the crown. Sarron, like Miller, was a world traveller. He was a very active boxer who took part in more than 100 contests in many parts of America, England, and South Africa.

It was in Johannesburg, after he had won a twelve rounds decision from Miller in what was designated a world championship bout, that "The Ring Editor," following the rise of Henry Armstrong to fistic heights, arranged with Mike Jacobs to bring Sarron back to the States and pit Armstrong against him in a title bout. Sarron received a guarantee of $37,500.

The bout was fought in Madison

Mike Belloise, New York's featherweight champion, fought from 1932 to 1947.

Harry Jeffra, former bantam champ, lost the featherweight crown to Archibald.

Joey Archibald defeated Belloise for the title in 1938, lost it to Jeffra in 1940, and regained it in 1941. Joey entered the ring in 1932 and quit in 1943.

Chalky Wright became champion when he knocked out Archibald. Wright's career extended from 1928 to 1948. He had 124 battles, won 36, and stopped 52 men.

Square Garden, October 29, 1937, with Armstrong winning by a knockout in the sixth round. It was Mike Jacobs' first affair as promoter in Madison Square Garden.

Armstrong didn't defend his crown. He decided to go for higher laurels. He had his eyes on the welterweight and lightweight titles. These he won, as already stated, and after gaining the lightweight championship he gave up the title he had won from Sarron.

Following Armstrong's abdication of the throne, the New York State Commission put its stamp of approval on a contest between Mike Belloise, New York featherweight champion, and Joey Archibald, born December 5, 1915, of Providence, Rhode Island. This was to decide Henry's successor. Archibald, recognized by the N.B.A. as its outstanding challenger, defeated Belloise in fifteen rounds in the St. Nicholas Club of New York and gained international recognition.

Then came a bout between him and Harry Jeffra of Baltimore. Jeffra, born November 30, 1914, won in fifteen rounds on May 20, 1940. He lost the title back to Archibald in Washington, via a decision on May 12, 1941, after which, on September 11 of that year, Chalky Wright knocked out Archibald in the eleventh round in the Capitol City to gain top honors. Wright, who saw the light of day on February 10, 1912, at Durango, Mexico, had his crown vacated by the N.B.A. when he refused to meet Petey Scalzo of New York, born August 1, 1917, and the National Boxing Association declared him the title holder. But in the eyes of the fight enthusiasts, there was no doubt Archibald was the rightful owner when he regained it from Jeffra and that the crown then passed on to Wright.

As a result of this dispute, when Scalzo was knocked out in five rounds by Richie Lemos, a Los Angeles boy, born February 6, 1920, the N.B.A. recognized him as new champion. That bout took place on July 1, 1941. The following November, Lemos lost his title to Jackie Wilson, born in 1909 in Arkansas. Wilson was heralded as king of the division by his backers, but Wright still was generally recog-

333

The NBA featherweight champs, who defeated one another in succession, are (above, left to right) Pete Scalzo, of New York; Richie Lemos, of California; Jackie Wilson, of Pittsburgh. (Below) Jackie Callura of Canada and Phil Terranova of New York. They all claimed the crown, but Chalky Wright was the rightful champion.

Sal Bartolo (above) was the last of the NBA champs, after whipping Terranova. Sal was beaten by Willie Pep in 1943.

Willie Pep (below, right) defeated Chalky Wright for the crown on November 20, 1942, and again in 1944. Pep, who started his pro career in 1940, is still active in the ring and is rated among the world's greatest featherweights of all time.

nized as champion and when on November 20, 1942, Willie Pep defeated Chalky in Madison Square Garden, one of the greatest feathers of all time was acknowledged head of the division by the New York Commission and soon received popular approval.

On January 18, 1943, Jackie Wilson lost his N.B.A. crown to Jackie Callura of Canada and from him the N.B.A. title passed on to Phil Terranova of New York by a knockout in eight rounds. Then followed Sal Bartolo, of Boston, Massachusetts, who on March 10, 1944, whipped Phil in fifteen rounds. These bouts were all for N.B.A. laurels only.

Through all this confusion, the one who received the greatest world support was Pep. Willie, born in Middletown, Connecticut, September 19, 1922, takes his place among the greatest feathers of all time.

Clever, sharp, a beautiful boxer, a good hitter, exceedingly expert in countering, side-stepping, blocking and feinting, Pep for many years remained unexcelled. He started his career as an amateur, winning several titles, then turned pro and won sixty-two fights in a row before losing his first fight to lightweight Sammy Angott. After that loss he won all his

Willie Pep lost the first bout of his career to Sammy Angott on March 19, 1943, after running up a string of 62 consecutive victories. Angott, who had given up the lightweight title the year before, clutched and scrambled Willie all over the ring for 10 rounds and gave him very little chance to do any fighting. The photo on the left shows Pep about to fall out of the ring, when Angott's leaning body became too much for him to hold up. Throughout the bout, Pep's arms were tied up by Angott (above) every time the latter went into a clinch, which was often. After the bout, a weary Willie Pep was given an ice-bag treatment in his dressing room.

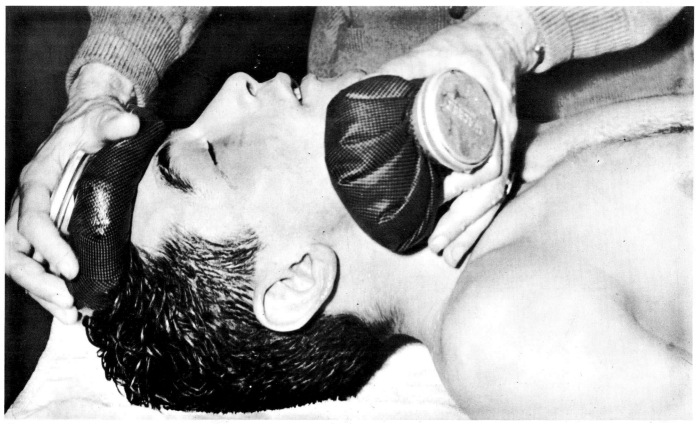

The fourth Sandy Saddler-Willie Pep featherweight title match on September 26, 1951, turned into a wild boxing-wrestling contest. Both were guilty of thumbing and fouling. In the sixth and eighth rounds *(above)* they wrestled to the mat, with Pep winning both falls. Sandy opened a deep cut over Pep's right eye in the second round and floored Willie with a left. Pep squatted in the corner *(below)* as referee Ray Miller tolled off a count of eight.

bouts except a draw with Jimmy Mc-Allister, until he was stopped by Sandy Saddler in 1948, a total of 134 victories out of 136 bouts. With the second knockout by Saddler, Pep had engaged in a total of 156 fights, of which he lost one, drew in one, and was stopped twice.

To clinch his claim to world honors, Pep whipped the N.B.A. champion, Sal Bartolo; beat Wright in a return match; and took the measure of Terranova, Jock Leslie, and Humberto Sierra, each of whom questioned his right to top honors.

Pep gave many scintillating performances as champion. His record stands out among the members of his division. To add to his unique career, he served in the U. S. Army and then in the Navy during the Second World War. Though he was badly injured in an airplane accident and was refused a renewal of his license by the New York Commission, as late as 1957

Saddler retained his title, when Pep (left) failed to come out for the 10th round. As confusion reigned in Pep's corner as to whether he could continue or not, one of the judges, Arthur Aidala (above), listens to boisterous accusations by Saddler's manager, Charley Johnston, of being influenced in judging by Dr. Vincent Nardiello, the boxing commission physician. At the left of Aidala is George Bannon, the official timekeeper, who has served in that capacity for more than 50 years.

he was still engaged in boxing in N.B.A. states.

Saddler, born in Boston, Massachusetts, June 25, 1926, started his career as a flyweight. He won twenty-eight out of thirty-eight of his first fights as a pro by knockouts. He defeated the champions of seven countries before winning the world crown by a knockout in the fourth round. He was not a clever boxer, but a strong, sturdy, two-fisted, rough battler who was accused by his opponents and the public of engaging in unfair tactics to win his bouts. Like Saron and Miller, he fought in many parts of the world.

In a return contest with Pep on February 11, 1949, in Madison Square Garden, he lost his crown by a decision in fifteen rounds, but regained it in a third bout on September 26, 1951, at the Yankee Stadium, stopping Willie in the eighth round of a rough affair in which Pep, with a shoulder injury, couldn't continue.

After Willie Pep's eye was cut open in the second round, he staggered Sandy with a right to the jaw (above) and then landed 13 straight blows without a return.

Hogan (Kid) Bassey, born in 1932 in Nigeria, is the new featherweight champion. He started his boxing career in 1949.

Cherif Hamia, the European featherweight champion, was driven into the ropes (above) and knocked out by Kid Bassey, who then became the undisputed featherweight champion. Bassey's most important win in America was over Willie Pep.

Miguel Berrios, who was defeated by Kid Bassey for the crown, has since retired from the ring because of an eye injury.

Carmelo Costa, lost to Berrios in the elimination tournament in 1957. Costa, born in 1934, started boxing in 1952.

When Sandy was inducted in the Army in 1952, Percy Bassett of Philadelphia was named the "Interim Champion" by the N.B.A. But the action of the N.B.A. was not taken seriously by other supervising organizations since Bassett's record was ordinary.

Saddler was badly injured in an automobile accident in the latter part of 1956 and after consultations with members of the Medical Advisory Board of the Boxing Commission, he abdicated his throne. Named for an elimination were Miguel Berrios of Puerto Rico; Hogan Kid Bassey of Calabar, Nigeria, British Empire Champion; Carmelo Costa of Brooklyn; and Cherif Hamia of France, champion of Europe. Berrios beat Costa, and Bassey defeated Berrios. Then Hamia, who had drawn a bye, faced Bassey in Paris, France, on June 24, 1957, and was knocked out in the tenth round. With that victory, Bassey, born June 3, 1932, became Saddler's successor.

After a three-round kayo of Ricardo Moreno on April 1, 1958, Bassey had two important non-title bouts in the United States—against Willie Pep in Boston on September 20 and Carmelo Costa in New York on October 31. Out-maneuvered by Willie Pep in the early going, Bassey's heavy fists took their toll on Pep's aging body, and Willie was knocked out in the ninth round. Costa was floored twice in the third round, but was saved by the bell. From then on it was a pursuit, and Bassey chased his man the rest of the way to win a unanimous decision.

The United States regained the featherweight title when Davy Moore kayoed Hogan K. Bassey in thirteen rounds on March 18, 1959, in an unusually vicious and bloody battle. The Nigerian was outclassed by the more aggressive, sharper-hitting challenger, who had never before fought more than ten rounds and seemed able to absorb all of Bassey's punches.

Moore lost his title and, two days later, his life, when he met Cuban-born Mexican Sugar Ramos on March 21, 1963, for the sixth defense of his title.

The bout was close through nine rounds. In the tenth, Moore landed a left hook that sent Ramos into the

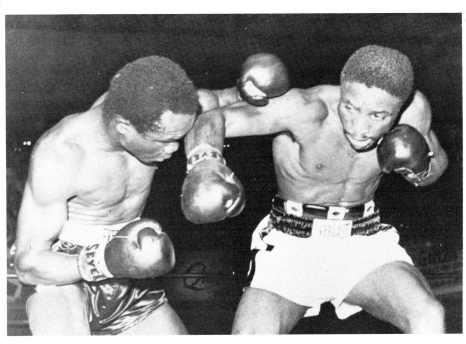

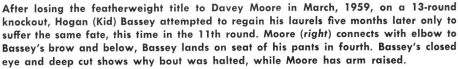

After losing the featherweight title to Davey Moore in March, 1959, on a 13-round knockout, Hogan (Kid) Bassey attempted to regain his laurels five months later only to suffer the same fate, this time in the 11th round. Moore (*right*) connects with elbow to Bassey's brow and below, Bassey lands on seat of his pants in fourth. Bassey's closed eye and deep cut shows why bout was halted, while Moore has arm raised.

Moore had been champion for four years when he took on Ultiminio (Sugar) Ramos, in a bout which would end in tragedy. Above is a scene from the video tape showing Moore's head striking the lower rope after he was knocked down by Ramos in the 10th. Below we see Moore slumped over the middle strand as referee George Latka stops the bout. Moore, who went into a coma, never regained consciousness, died two days later.

ropes. The Cuban came back with a rush, and after dropping Moore twice, Ramos let loose a furious two-fisted attack that sent the dazed and hurt Moore through the ropes as the bell rang. At this point referee George Latte halted the fight. An hour after the fight was over, Moore collapsed into a coma. He never regained consciousness.

After three successful defenses, Ramos was worn down and beaten to a pulp in the tenth and eleventh rounds of a bout on September 26, 1964, against fellow Mexican Vicente Saldivar. When the 124-pound Ramos was unable to answer the twelfth-round bell, twenty-one-year-old Saldivar, at 125 pounds, became the featherweight champion of the world.

Saldivar, a southpaw who had been

called a pocket-version Rocky Marciano, successfully defended his title six times over the ensuing three years before retiring from the ring in 1967.

In 1964 he kayoed Fino Rosales of Mexico in eleven rounds. The following year he kayoed Raul Rojas in fifteen rounds at Los Angeles and won a fifteen-round decision over Howard Winstone of Wales. During 1966 he defended the title twice, knocking out Floyd Robertson in two rounds and beating Mitsunori Seki of Japan in fifteen.

Johnny Famechon, a twenty-three-

Ramos more than met his match in the person of Vincente Saldivar, a southpaw, who administered a terrible beating to the Cuban.

(*Right*) Saldivar is on the attack against Japan's Mitsunori Seki, whom he defeated twice, once by knockout, in championship bouts.

Floyd Robertson of Ghana was another Saldivar victim, along with Fino Rosales, Raul Rojas and Howard Winstone, beaten thrice.

year-old Australian, was awarded a disputed decision over Spain's José Legra in a fifteen-round bout in London on January 21, 1969, for the vacant world title. He lost it again four months later, when the stronger and more aggressive Saldivar returned to the ring and regained the crown on May 9 by a unanimous decision. The following day, Famechon announced his retirement.

In a stunning upset, the 125-pound Saldivar was knocked out by Japan's 126-pound Kuniaki Shibata on December 11, 1970, when the bloodied defending champion failed to come out for the fourteenth round.

Mexico's Clemente Sanchez, in one of the best showings of his career and his only fight in a year, battered Shibata out of action at 2:26 of the third round on May 19, 1972, in

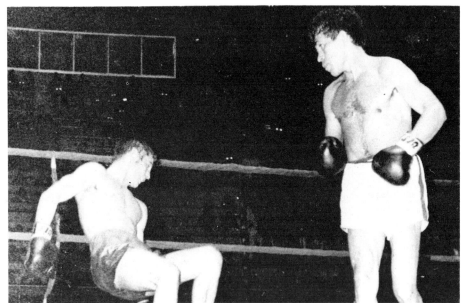

After his third victory over Winstone, Saldivar retired. Johnny Famechon (*above*) won vacant title, beating José Legra.

Saldivar launched a comeback in 1969, which culminated in his regaining his old title on a 15-round win over Famechon.

The Mexican's second reign was shortlived, however, for in his very first defense, Saldivar (*below*) was halted in 13 rounds by Kuniaki Shibata of Japan (*below, left*) at Tijuana, Mexico. Saldiver, quit in 1973.

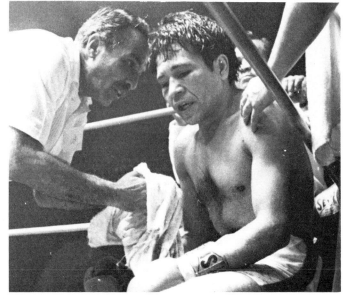

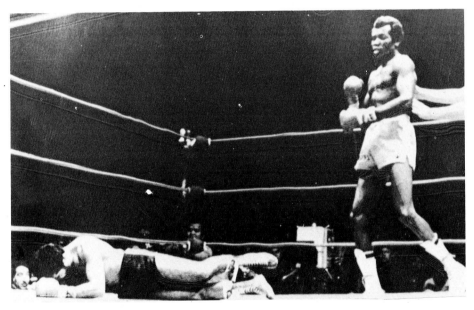

The 126-pound title again changed hands, once more via the knockout route, when Clemente Sanchez KO'd Shibata in three.

Confusion reigned when José Legra halted Sanchez in 10 (*left*). The latter was overweight, however, so no title was at stake.

Tokyo. Both men scaled 126.

On the day of the Sanchez-Legra match at Monterey, December 16, 1972, Sanchez appeared at the weigh-in to announce that he could not make the weight and was vacating the title. It was decided that the bout would go on, but as a nontitle fight.

When Legra kayoed Sanchez in the tenth round, the World Boxing Council recognized him as champion, while the W.B.A. awarded its portion of the world title to Ernesto Marcel, of Panama, who had defeated Antonio Gomez on August 19, 1972, for the W.B.A. title.

Marcel retired in June 1974, having defended his title four times. At this point the W.B.A. named Ruben Olivares, former bantamweight champion, and Zensuke Utagawa, of Japan, to meet for the title. On July 9, 1974, Olivares kayoed Utagawa in the seventh round at Los Angeles.

Olivares lost his title to Alexis Arguello, of Nicaragua, who knocked him out in the thirteenth round in 1975, and Arguello successfully defended three times in 1975, getting a decision against Leonel Hernandez of Venezuela, stopping Roberto Riasco of Panama in the second, and knocking out Royal Kobayashi of Japan in the fifth in Tokyo. At the end of 1976, however, Arguello gave up his W.B.A. title to compete in the Junior-Lightweight class.

Meanwhile, Eder Jofre, of Brazil, another former bantam champ, had won a fifteen-round split decision over Legra on May 5, 1973, in Brasilia, to win the W.B.C. version of the crown.

Jofre went on to defend his W.B.C. title with a four-round kayo over Saldivar on October 20, 1973, in Sao Paulo, Brazil.

When Jofre refused to fight Venezuela's Alfredo Marcano, the W.B.C. took away Jofre's title in June 1974 and named Marcano and U.S. champion Bobby Chacon as the contenders.

Three months later, on September 7, Chacon knocked out Marcano in nine torrid rounds at Caracas and

Hard-hitting Ruben Olivares *(right)*, ex-bantam champion, stopped Zensuke Utagawa *(above)* for the vacant W.B.A. crown after Ernesto Marcel who had defended four times, retired.

became the W.B.C. featherweight champion.

After defeating Jesus Estrada of Mexico with a second-round knockout in 1975, Chacon lost his title to the former W.B.A. champion, Ruben Olivares who stopped him in the second. Olivares' reign as W.B.C. champion lasted only three months, and in September 1975 he lost a decision to British Commonwealth champion David Kotei of Ghana.

Kotei kept his W.B.C. title until November 6, 1976, when he was outpointed by Danny Lopez (USA) before his own people in Accra. Lopez successfully defended his crown by stopping Jose Torres in seven rounds at Los Angeles on September 13, 1977, and on February 15, 1978, again beat Kotei, this time stopping him in six rounds at Las Vegas. On April 23 he disposed of Brazilian challenger, Jose De Paula in six rounds at Los Angeles. On September 15, at New Orleans, he kept his crown by knocking out Juam Malvarez in two rounds and on October 21 he won over Fel Clemente, who was disqualified in round four at Pessaro.

Meanwhile, the W.B.A. filled its vacant featherweight throne when Rafael Ortega outpointed Francisco Coronado at Panama City on January 15, 1977, but on December 12 he lost the title to Cecilio Lastra on a points verdict at Torrelavega. On April 16, 1978, Eusebio Pedroza became champion by stopping Lastra in thirteen rounds at Panama and he kept the title throughout the year by first stopping Ernesto Herrera in twelve rounds at Panama on July 2 and outpointing Enrique Solis, of Puerto Rico, at San Juan on November 27. Pedro made his third successful W.B.A. title defence on January 9, 1979, when he forced Royal Kobayashi (Japan) to retire in the thirteenth round at Tokyo.

He made three further defences in 1979, knocking out Hector Carrasquilla (Panama) in the eleventh; Ruben Olivares (Mexico) in the twelfth; and Johnny Aba (Papua) in the eleventh. In 1980 he continued his demolition of W.B.A. challengers by defeating Shig Nemoto (Japan) on points in 15 rounds; Kim Sa Wang (S. Korea), knocked out in the ninth; and Rocky Lockridge (U.S.A.) on points over 15 rounds.

Danny Lopez kept his W.B.C. title throughout 1979, knocking out Roberto Castanon (U.S.A.) in the second; Mike Ayala (U.S.A.) in the fifteenth; and Jose Caba (Dominica) in the third. On February 2, 1980 he was beaten by 21-year-old Salvador Sanchez (Mexico) who stopped him in 13 rounds at Phoenix, Arizona. Then, after outpointing Ruben Castillo (U.S.A.) over 15 rounds, at Tucson, Arizona on April 12, Sanchez gave Lopez a chance to recover the W.B.C. crown, but stopped him in 14 rounds at Las Vegas on June 21. On September 13 he made his third defence by outpointing Patrick Ford (Guyana) over 15 rounds at San Antonio. On December 13 at El Paso, Sanchez kept his crown by outpointing Juan Laporte (Brooklyn).

LIGHT-FEATHER or SUPER-BANTAMWEIGHTS

(Weight Limit, 122 Pounds)

THIS NEW WEIGHT CLASS WAS INTRODUCED BY THE WORLD BOXING COUNCIL ON APRIL 3, 1976, WHEN RIGOBERTO RIASCO (PANAMA) CAUSED WARUINGE NAKAYAMA TO RETIRE IN EIGHT ROUNDS AT PANAMA CITY. SUBSEQUENT WBC CHAMPIONS HAVE BEEN: 1976—ROYAL KOBAYASHI, DON KYUN YUN; 1976—80—WILFREDO GOMEZ (PUERTO RICO), 13 DEFENCES. ON NOVEMBER 26, 1977, THE WORLD BOXING ASSOCIATION MOVED INTO THE ACTION WHEN SOON HWAN HONG (KOREA) KNOCKED OUT HECTOR CARRASQUILLA AT PANAMA CITY FOR THEIR VACANT TITLE. SUBSEQUENT CHAMPIONS: 1978—80—RICARDO CARDONA (COLOMBIA); 1980—LEO RANDOLPH (U.S.A.); SERGIO PALMA (ARGENTINA).

THE BANTAMWEIGHTS
AND FLYWEIGHTS

THEY WRESTLED.

DOWN WENT THE VICTIM

fight between Andy Kelly and Charley Lynch, which had been talked of for some time previously. Both were tough little specimens of the lightweight order. Kelly's height was about 5 feet 5 inches, and his usual weight was not more than 115 pounds, but at the fight was not over 108. Lynch was about two inches less in stature, but nearly ten pounds heavier. Their seconds and backers were on the boat, and "mirth and jollity ruled the hour" until arriving near the ground selected by the commissary, which was about a mile and a quarter from Huyler's Landing, and was as convenient as could be desired. By about 5.30 on Thursday morning the ring was ready in orthodox style, and the lads shied their castors into the arena of contest. The toss for choice of corners was won by Kelly and he, of course, took the southeast for a bright and warm September sun was soon to arrive. The seconds readily made their toilets according to the most approved fashions of the P. R. Kelly's colors were pink and white stripes, Lynch's were black. Their belts, of course, agreed with the handkerchiefs on the middle stake post.

When the men peeled, the betting, which had been in Lynch's favor, was not at all decreased on observing the almost effeminate but decidedly feeble condition of Kelly, who had caught a cold on the night of Young Wallace's exhibition (Aug. 29), and had never fully rallied from its depressing effects. Lynch was not only more stocky in his growth, but in fine development of muscle; his back and chest looked like a sack of almighty hard potatoes. Kelly, however, had a longer reach as well as height, and he carried himself with a very jaunty and winning air.

Having previously seen both men spar beautifully it was natural we should form some opinion of the probabilities. Knowing that Lynch had a fashion of half turning his fists just before and just after delivering a blow, and knowing that Kelly could strike like lightning, we thought that Kelly might win, provided the battle did not last too long for his lack of bodily strength. Such a sad ter-

Two of the best bantams in the United States were Charley Lynch and Andy Kelly. On September 18, 1856, they battered each other for nearly two hours, going 86 rounds. In the final round, Kelly walked to the center of the ring and fell in a sitting position, unconscious. He was carried to his corner and died soon afterward.

One month after the fatal bout with Kelly, Lynch went to England, where he fought the British champ, Simon Finighty, to a draw after two hours of mauling. Two years later, he returned to England for another bout with Finighty. They met on August 2, 1859. The fight was fairly even, going into the 20th round, when Finighty's second, George Brown, annoyingly followed his man around the ring. Brown tried to step between the fighters to hinder Lynch's attack and Lynch hauled off a right-hander (above), sending him sprawling across the turf. Lynch won in the 43rd round, when Finighty, weakened by body blows, shuffled to the scratch, offered his hand, and acknowledged defeat.

346

Times have changed in the rugged sock market.

Bantamweights and flyweights, once so popular and prosperous in the American boxing scene, today are a dime a dozen, if that many can be found in America. While throughout the rest of the world, particularly Mexico, the Philippines, Japan among other places in the Orient, and in Great Britain, France and Italy, they constitute the greatest portion of those who make professional boxing their vocation, in the United States they have become practically extinct.

Many of boxing's most illustrious performers were our little men, those who scaled from 100 to 115 pounds. Such ring immortals as George Dixon, Jimmy Barry, Casper Leon, and Tommy Kelly ("The Harlem Spider") reached headline status when they scaled 110 pounds, the bantam limit at the time. Then there were such master mechanics as Harry Harris, "The Bean Stalk champion"; Clarence and Harry Forbes, Johnny Coulon, Frankie Burns, Johnny Buff, Eddie Campi, and Kid Williams. Among others who quickly graduated into the higher divisions but started as bantams were Johnny Dundee, Jimmy McLarnin, Willie Jackson, Lew Tendler, Tony Canzoneri, and the hardest hitter, in the divisions from bantam through lightweight, George K.O. Chaney of Baltimore.

The bantam and flyweight classes hit their peaks of popularity during the lush, flamboyant, post-World War One era of the early twenties, when Tex Rickard, then holding forth in Madison Square Garden, was the kingpin of world promoters and the sport was flourishing all over the land. That was the era when such mighty mites as Joe Lynch, Pete Herman, Memphis Pal Moore, Little Jack Sharkey, Joe Burman, Midget Smith, Earl Puryea, Carl Tremaine, Frankie Jerome, Abe Goldstein, Young Montreal, Bud Taylor, Frankie Genaro, Pancho Villa, Cannonball Eddie Martin, Charley Phil Rosenberg and Fidel LaBarba, to list only a few of the many, packed the arenas. There was hardly a city, town, or hamlet in the nation in that era that didn't boast of at least one good little fighter.

Gradually the tiny tikes began to fade in both quality and quantity. During the thirties, following the depression, the flyweight class practically disappeared in America though the bantams held out for another decade. Then the decline took place at a rapid rate. When Manuel Ortiz of El Centro, California, born in 1917, went to Johannesburg and on May 31, 1950, lost his world title to Vic Toweel in fifteen rounds, that just about finished the 118 pounders as major factors in the American boxing curriculum.

It is unfortunate indeed that boxing finds the little fellows extinct as major attractions in the United States, since there were few more active divisions in the general international scene than the bantams and flyweights. Three of the greatest fighting men in the classes generally referred to as the gamecock groups were Jimmy Wilde, the "Mighty Atom" from Wales; George Dixon, "Little Chocolate," from Halifax, Nova Scotia; and Pancho Villa, the little "Yellow Man." Born at Iloilo, Philippines, August 1, 1901, Villa was brought from Manila to America by Frank Churchill. Villa put an end to the long and meritorious career of Wilde, then on the down grade. Jimmy was stopped in a hair-raising fight at the Polo Grounds. The Wilde-Villa-Dixon trio furnished the fans with many thrillers that made ring history.

There is no authentic record of the bantamweight division during the London Prize Ring days, but it is generally conceded that Charley Lynch was the American titleholder in 1856 when he went to England and laid

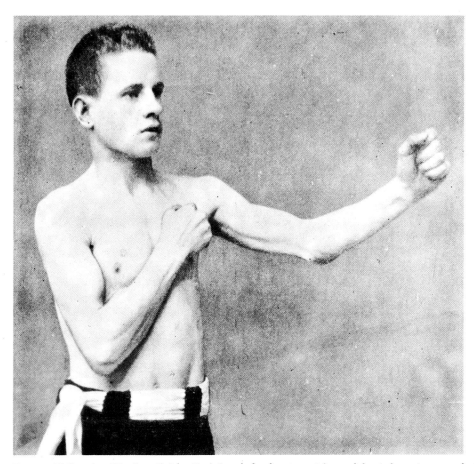

Tommy Kelly, the "Harlem Spider," claimed the bantam title and boxed a nine-round draw with George Dixon, in 1888.

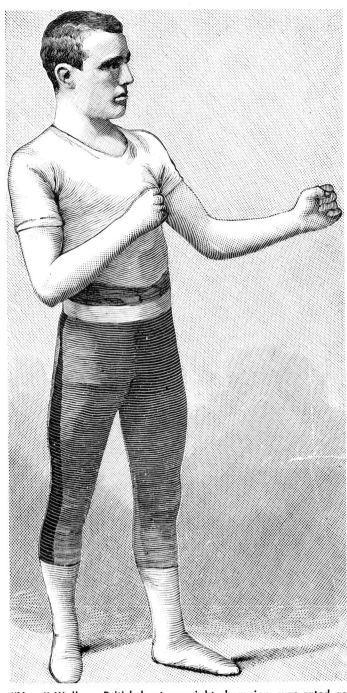

George Dixon, called "Little Chocolate," declared he would meet any challenger for the bantamweight crown, at 112 pounds.

"Nunc" Wallace, British bantamweight champion, was rated as unbeatable. Dixon knocked him out on June 27, 1890, in London.

claim to the world title when he defeated Simon Finighty in forty-three rounds. He then returned to America and retired. The New Yorker weighed 112 pounds.

We next hear of a title bout in the division when Tommy "Harlem Spider" Kelly, a New Yorker, drew with George Dixon in Boston in nine rounds with the weight limit set at 105 pounds. Manager O'Rourke, han-

dling Dixon, claimed the championship for his boy and issued a defi to all comers who contested Dixon's right to the honors to face him at 112 pound limit. The increase in weight was brought on by the inability of Dixon to fight at his best at the lower figures.

In 1890, Dixon engaged Cal McCarthy of New York in a draw of seventy rounds, fighting with two

ounce gloves. Then, with Tom O'Rourke, he sailed for England four months later to box Nunc Wallace, British bantam champion. Dixon in that bout won universal support as bantam king when he halted Wallace in the eighteenth round. He then added Jimmy Murphy to his list of victims, stopping him in the fortieth round in Providence, Rhode Island. With that triumph he vacated the

Jimmy Barry (left) born in Chicago, on March 7, 1870, was an outstanding ringman. In 68 contests, from 1891 to 1899, when he retired, he was never defeated. His meeting in 1897 with the British champion, Walter Croot, in London, ended tragically. Barry's right dropped Croot, whose skull struck the ring floor with such force he died from a brain injury. Barry was exonerated, fought a few more battles, and retired.

Casper Leon (above) was knocked out by Barry for the American title. He was born December 8, 1872, in Palermo, Sicily.

They called him "Terrible Terry" McGovern and the character cartoon (right), by the famous "Tad," most certainly makes him appear so. Terry was compactly built, fast, and packed a middleweight punch. He was born in Johnstown, Pennsylvania, of Irish stock and raised in Brooklyn. As a bantam, from 1897 to 1899, McGovern had 45 battles, winning 22 by knockout. He won the featherweight crown in his first bout in 1900.

bantam throne and set sail for the feather crown.

With Dixon's retirement, Jimmy Barry of Chicago claimed the crown. He and Casper Leon of New York, the best boy in the East, fought at Lamont, Illinois, September 15, 1894, and Barry won by a knockout in the twenty-eighth round and was accepted as new champion in the 112 pound class, then listed as the bantam division.

With the ownership of the title in dispute so far as the British were concerned, Barry accepted a challenge from Walter Croot, British titleholder, fought him in London, December 6,

1897, and knocked him out in the sixteenth round to win the international crown. Croot died the following day from a brain injury.

Barry, upset by the mishap, fought several more times, including a bout with Leon on December 29, 1898, a draw of twenty rounds, and a draw of six with Harry Harris of Chicago the following September, then retired undefeated.

Terry McGovern now claimed the crown based on his fine record, studded with knockouts and decision victories. To gain universal recognition, he agreed to fight Pedlar Palmer of Great Britain and at Tuckahoe,

Manager Sam Harris and boxer Terry McGovern were typical fashion plates of their day. After piloting McGovern to two world titles, Harris became a noted producer in the theatrical field.

A great fighter, Terry McGovern was almost as adept at baseball and turned down several offers to play professionally. He often practiced with major league New York and Brooklyn teams.

One of the briefest title bouts in ring history was the international meeting of Pedlar Palmer (left), the British champion, and McGovern, the American representative. With the disputed world bantamweight laurels at stake, Palmer and McGovern met at Tuckahoe, New York, September 12, 1899. The clever Palmer was given no opportunity to display his vaunted skill. Overwhelmed by the rushing, hardhitting McGovern, he was kayoed in one minute, 15 seconds.

350

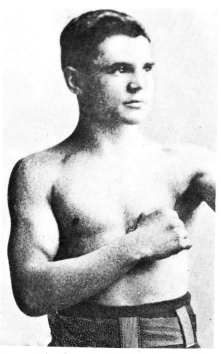

How a contemporary artist portrayed the McGovern-Palmer finish. They had started boxing when the timekeeper accidentally hit the bell and referee Siler sent the boxers to their corners for a new start, which ended disastrously for Palmer.

New York, as already told, he knocked out Palmer in the first round. For that fight McGovern raised the weight from 112 to 116 pounds, but since the bout was postponed a day because of rain, they did not weigh in again. McGovern had set a new poundage for the bantam class.

In 1900 McGovern vacated the class to go into the higher sector, and Harry Harris, born in Chicago, Illinois, November 18, 1880, asserted his rights to top honors. Of course his claim was disputed, and to clinch international support he went abroad, won a decision in fifteen rounds from Pedlar Palmer, who was still British champion, and became the recognized king of the class. Like most of his predecessors, he soon became overweight and quit to fight as a feather.

Then Harry Forbes, born in Rockford, Illinois, May 13, 1879, came into

Harry Harris, born in Chicago in 1800, started boxing at 16. He beat Palmer in 1901 and claimed the open bantam title.

Harry Forbes nominated himself champion when Harris entered the featherweight ranks. Forbes boxed from 1897 to 1912.

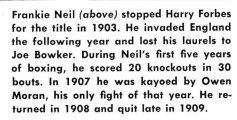

Jimmy Walsh (left) a scrappy little bantamweight champion, was 5' 2" in height. He was 15 years old for his first bout in 1901 and met all of the top bantams until 1913, when he retired. He was recognized as world champion in 1905, when he defeated the British champ, Digger Stanley.

Frankie Neil (above) stopped Harry Forbes for the title in 1903. He invaded England the following year and lost his laurels to Joe Bowker. During Neil's first five years of boxing, he scored 20 knockouts in 30 bouts. In 1907 he was kayoed by Owen Moran, his only fight of that year. He returned in 1908 and quit late in 1909.

the picture. He declared himself the champion and carried on for almost three years when Frankie Neil, of San Francisco, born July 25, 1883, stopped him in the second round in California, August 13, 1903, and became champion.

Neil defended his crown successfully against Billy DeCoursey, whom he halted in fifteen rounds, fought a draw of twenty with Johnny Reagan, knocked out Forbes in three rounds, and headed for London to fight Joe Bowker, then British king. Joe beat him in twenty rounds at 118 pounds, the British weight limit, on October 17, 1904, to become the crown wearer.

With Bowker's retirement, both Digger Stanley of London and Jimmy Walsh of Newton, Massachusetts, claimed the vacated throne. Walsh, born in 1886, fought Stanley in Chelsea, Massachusetts, October 20, 1905,

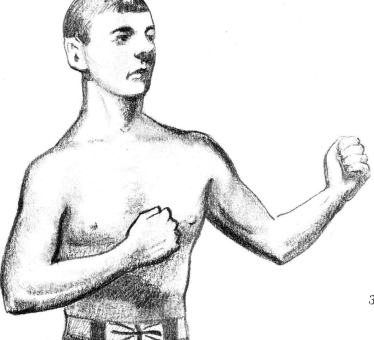

Joe Bowker (left) clearly outpointed Frankie Neil for the world bantamweight crown, before a capacity crowd at the National Sporting Club, in London. Unable to maintain the weight, he relinquished the title shortly after. An extremely clever boxer, Bowker enjoyed a long career—from 1901 to 1919.

Johnny Coulon (above, left) Canadian-born Chicagoan, rightfully claimed the crown when he twice whipped Kid Murphy in 1908 and twice defeated the British champ, Jim Kendrick, in 1910. Coulon boxed from 1905 to 1917 and 1921.

Kid Williams (above, right) was born in Denmark and reared in Baltimore, Maryland. An aggressive puncher, he met all challengers after knocking out Coulon. Williams' career started in 1910, when he was 27 years old, and ended in 1925.

Johnny "Kewpie" Ertle (right) claimed the title when he won from Williams on a foul in 1915. Most of the boxing authorities ignored his claim and continued to recognize Williams as the champion.

and settled the matter of supremacy by winning in fifteen rounds. By 1907 both had outgrown the class.

In 1908 Kid Murphy of New Jersey claimed the crown as U. S. Champion. He was defeated twice that year in U. S. title bouts at Peoria, Illinois, by Johnny Coulon of Chicago, who was born February 12, 1889 in Toronto, Canada. In 1910 Coulon clinched international support when he defeated British champion Jim Kendrick at New Orleans twice: on February 19 in ten rounds, then on March 6 in the nineteenth round.

Kid Williams, a stocky lad from Baltimore, born December 5, 1893, in Denmark, succeeded Coulon, whom he knocked out in the third round on June 9, 1914, at Vernon, California. He fought a draw of twenty rounds with Frankie Burns of Jersey City in New Orleans in a title bout; drew in twenty with Pete Herman, February

7 of the following year in the same city; then lost the crown to Herman in twenty rounds in New Orleans, January 9, 1917, on a decision by Billy

Rocap, the referee. Williams had lost on a foul to Johnny Ertle of St. Paul on September 10, 1915, but the consensus among the scribes failed to

353

Pete Herman, a fine little ringman out of New Orleans, who fought from 1913 to 1922, gained a 20-round decision and the title from Kid Williams in 1917. Herman held the crown until 1920, dropping it to Joe Lynch in 15 rounds. Posing with Lynch before their return title match in 1921, Herman (above, left) regained the title. In photo on right, Pete waves to cheering fans.

Johnny Buff, a 33-year-old New Jersey veteran, won the American flyweight title from Frankie Mason, on February 11, 1921, and on September 23 garnered the bantamweight laurels in a surprise victory over Pete Herman. Buff lost both titles in his only bouts in 1922. He was knocked out by Joe Lynch for the bantam crown and by Pancho Villa for the flyweight title.

sustain Ertle's claim and Johnny never received the honors accorded a champion.

A New Yorker, Joe Lynch, succeeded Herman. He gained the laurels when, after a number of successful title defenses by Herman, the latter lost in fifteen rounds via decision in the old Madison Square Garden. Herman had an excellent record. One of his best bouts was a victory over Frankie Burns in New Orleans, November 5, 1917.

Following World War One, while in England, Herman stopped Jimmy Wilde in seventeen rounds and on July 25 of that year, 1921, he regained the title that he had lost to Lynch on December 22, 1920, by defeating him in Brooklyn, in fifteen rounds. He lost the championship to Johnny Buff, born June 12, 1888 in Perth Amboy, New Jersey, in the old Madison Square Garden on September 23, 1921.

Herman retired, became blind, and in later years was a night club operator and a member of the Louisiana Boxing Commission.

As in the case of Herman, Joe Lynch regained the title when he knocked out Buff at the New York Velodrome, July 10, 1922, in fourteen rounds. The following year he was matched with Joe Burman. When he refused to go through with the bout, the New York Commission declared the championship vacant and designated Burman and Abe Goldstein to fight for the vacant throne.

Goldstein won but didn't receive the support of world bodies as newly crowned king. A bout was then arranged between Goldstein and Lynch, and the former won the championship by outpointing Joe in fifteen rounds in Madison Square Garden, March 21, 1924. Nine months later, December 19, in the same arena, Cannonball Eddie Martin dethroned Goldstein in fifteen rounds. Goldstein was born in New York in 1900; Martin was born March 3, 1903, in Brooklyn.

On March 20, 1925, Charley Phil

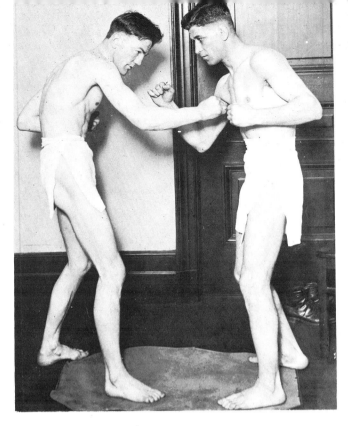

Joe Lynch *(far left)* spars with Abe Goldstein at weighing-in ceremonies for their championship fight in 1924. Goldstein *(above, right)* won the crown in a hard-fought battle. Neighborhood rivalries stimulated excitement in those days. Lynch's followers, from the Irish section of New York's West Side and Goldstein's, from the Jewish section of Harlem, filled Madison Square Garden with constant cheering during the thrilling bout.

Charley Phil Rosenberg, of New York *(below, right)* decisioned Eddie Martin, who held the crown only three months. Although Rosenberg beat Bushy Graham of Utica *(left)*, he failed to make the weight and the bantamweight title was declared vacant.

Eddie "Cannonball" Martin, a rugged Brooklynite who had been boxing three years, dethroned Goldstein in 15 rounds.

Rosenberg, another New Yorker, born August 15, 1902, relieved Martin of the crown, beating him in fifteen rounds in the Garden. Then on February 4, 1927, Rosenberg was deprived of his laurels when he was unable to make the weight for a championship bout with Bushy Graham, born in Italy, June 8, 1903.

Now came the usual confusion following an abdication or when a

Tragedy marked the rapid climb of Bud Taylor, of Terre Haute, Indiana, to the bantam-weight championship. On January 11, 1924, Taylor (left, above) punished Frankie Jerome, of the Bronx, so severely that Jerome, knocked out in the 12th round, died in a hospital. On February 9, 1928, Taylor, then claiming the disputed bantam title, was floored (below) by Joey Sangor, in a non-title match in Chicago. Bud protested that he had been fouled, but Sangor was credited with a seven-round knockout.

Panama Al Brown, was proclaimed champion in 1929, but campaigned in Europe, where he lost the crown to Baltazar Sang-chili, in Valencia, Spain, on June 1, 1935.

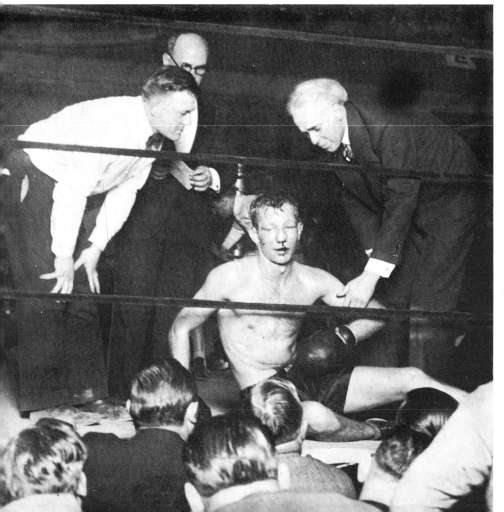

champion was shorn of his title. The N.B.A. and New York started elimina-tions. Bud Taylor, born July 5, 1903 in Terra Haute, Indiana, defeated Tony Canzoneri to win the N.B.A. recognition, and Al Brown of Panama, born July 5, 1902, after defeating Videl Gregorio, was proclaimed king in New York on June 18, 1929. Since Taylor had retired from the division on August 21, 1928, Brown had the field clear to himself. Instead of fighting in the United States, he decided to cam-paign abroad, an act that caused the New York Commission to withdraw its support. But Brown's record was so good that he was universally recog-nized as champion.

Like some of the other fighters who, when the title was in dispute, went overseas to take on all comers, Brown whipped Eugene Huat, French cham-pion, in fifteen rounds; Pete Sanstol, Scandinavian title holder, in Montreal in fifteen; Huat again in fifteen in

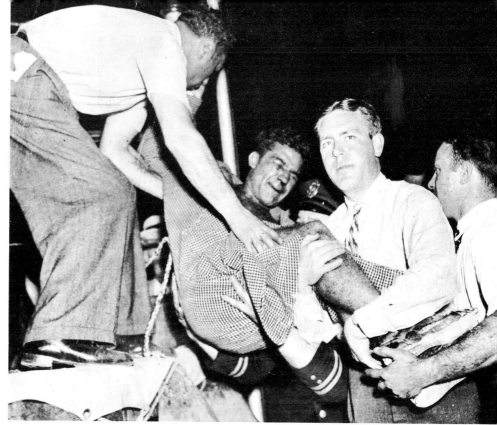

Baltazar Sangchili *(left, above)*, who had been boxing six years, mostly in Spain, when he deposed Brown as world champion, lost the crown to Tony Marino *(left, below)* of Pittsburgh. Sangchili had dropped Tony in the first round and was giving him a lacing, when in a dramatic finish in the 14th round, Marino rallied and knocked out Sangchili, who had to be carried *(above)* from the ring. On January 30, 1937, Marino battled Indian Quintana and died the next day from a brain injury.

Canada; Kid Francis in Marseilles in fifteen; stopped Emile Pladner in one round in Paris; won in twelve from Dom Bernasconi in Italy; defeated Young Perez in fifteen in Paris. Then, on June 1, 1935, he dropped the crown to Baltazar Sangchili of Spain in Valencia, in fifteen rounds.

Sangchilli, born October 15, 1911, in Valencia, came to America to press his claim when New York refused to recognize him as champion. He tackled Tony Marino, New York's title holder, on June 26, 1936, and was stopped in the fourteenth round. Marino, born in Pittsburgh in 1912, then fought Sixto Escobar, born March 23, 1913, in Barcelona, Puerto Rico, and was kayoed in the thirteenth round. Now, the field clear again, the commissions throughout the world accepted Sixto as the new world title-holder.

On September 23, 1937, on the Tournament of Champions card

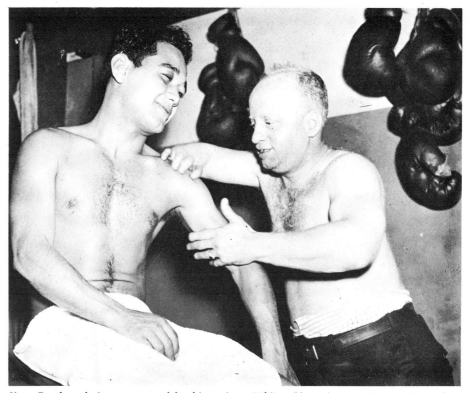

Sixto Escobar, being massaged by his trainer, Whitey Bimstein, was Puerto Rico's first world champion. After knocking out Tony Marino in 1936, Escobar lost and regained the title, but in 1939 increasing weight forced him to abandon his laurels.

357

Escobar and his main rival, Harry Jeffra, of Baltimore *(right)*, who staged a give-and-take series for the crown, pose before their final bout in Puerto Rico in 1938.

Lou Salica, who won and lost the title to Escobar, became champion again by winning an elimination tournament in 1941.

Manuel Ortiz, a popular California boxer, outpointed Salica in 1942 and became the Pacific Coast's first bantam champion.

Harold Dade was champion for a brief period in 1947. Ten weeks after beating Ortiz, he lost to Manuel in a return bout.

The bantam title went to South Africa in 1950, when Vic Toweel outpointed Ortiz. Toweel's reign ended in 1952 when he was knocked out *(below)* by Jimmy Carruthers.

staged by Mike Jacobs, Harry Jeffra of Baltimore took the crown from Escobar, winning the decision at the end of fifteen rounds. A few months later, in San Juan, Puerto Rico, Escobar regained his laurels, beating Jeffra in fifteen rounds. Escobar gave up his crown on October 4, 1939, to fight as a featherweight, and another series of eliminations took place.

George Pace, born in Cleveland, February 2, 1916, and Lou Salica, born in New York City, July 26, 1913, were the leading contenders, the former with N.B.A. support, and Salica the New York champion. They fought a fifteen round draw at Toronto, on March 4, 1940. Then, on September 24, 1940 at New York, Salica won a fifteen round decision and support of both commissions.

Salica was outpointed by Manuel Ortiz, born in El Centro, California, August 7, 1942, in twelve rounds, and thereafter Ortiz defended his title eight times in 1943, four times in 1944, joined the U. S. Army in 1945, then defended successfully three more times in 1946. On January 6, 1947, he lost the championship to Harold Dade in San Francisco, but two months later, on March 11 in Los Angeles, Ortiz regained the crown. He defended the title successfully in Honolulu, Manila, Mexico, and Honolulu again, then decided to take a trip to South Africa, and on May 31, 1950,

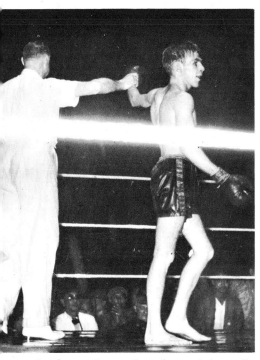

Southpaw Jimmy Carruthers of Australia is declared victor over Chamrern Songkitrat by referee Bill Henneberry in 1954's "Battle of the Typhoon." Carruthers then retired, undefeated. He had won the bantam crown in his 15th bout.

he dropped the crown to Vic Toweel, who earned the decision in fifteen rounds.

Vic held it two years, defending it three times, then lost it to Jimmy Carruthers, of Paddington, New South Wales, Australia, born July 5, 1929. Jimmy knocked out Toweel in the first round on November 15, 1952, stopped him again on March 21 the following year in ten rounds, successfully defended the crown against Henry Pappy Gault of America in fifteen rounds in Sydney, Australia, on November 13, 1953, then wound up his career by gaining a decision in a championship bout in Bangkok, Thailand in what has been called the "Battle of the Typhoon" in twelve rounds.

It was one of the most weird affairs ever staged, with a terrific downpour drenching fighters and spectators, the ring flooded, the lights shattered every few minutes, and the boys boxing barefooted to avoid slipping. A record gathering of 59,760 persons paid $227,304 to see the battle.

Tremendous excitement prevailed during the match between Carruthers and Songkitrat (above, right). Boxing was comparatively new in Thailand, and Songkitrat was the first native to fight for a world title. Barefoot to avoid slipping, they battled through a tropical rainstorm. The fight was halted twice to clear the canvas of debris, including shattered ring lightbulbs. Between rounds an umbrella was held over Chamrern (right) while his corner men worked over him. The closely-fought battle, held in Bangkok on May 2, 1954, set new bantamweight attendance records. A crowd of 59,760 jammed the National Stadium and braved a fierce storm to see their idol make a gallant but futile bid for the title.

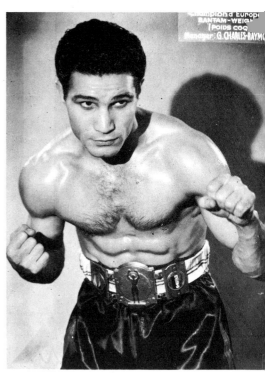

Deaf-mute Marion D'Agata (above, left) of Italy, was raised aloft by enthusiastic fans in Rome, after he knocked out Robert Cohen (right) for the title in 1956. Cohen announced his retirement. D'Agata lost the crown in 15 rounds to Alphonse Halimi in 1957

Alphonse Halimi (right) settled a dispute over the rightful owner of the bantamweight crown, by outpointing the NBA champion, Raul Raton Macias (left), a stiff puncher from Mexico. Champion Halimi, starting in 1955, has scored 12 knockouts in 23 bouts.

With Carruthers' retirement, the New York Commission, the World Championship Committee, and all supervising boxing bodies except the N.B.A. accepted a bout between Robert Cohen, European champion, and Chamrern Songkitrat, champion of the Orient and the boy who lost so gallantly to Carruthers in the above mentioned "Battle of the Typhoon" in Bangkok, to decide the new world sceptre wearer. Cohen, born in Bone, Algeria, November 15, 1930, defeated Songkitrat, but when he failed to accept a match with the N.B.A. challenger, Raul Raton Macias of Mexico, the N.B.A. named Macias its champion. He and Songkitrat, already beaten by Cohen, fought in San Francisco on March 9, 1955, and Macias stopped the Thailander in the eleventh round. Only the N.B.A. regarded this as a title match. The contract stipulated it was a non-championship bout.

When on June 29, 1956, Mario D'Agata of Arezzo, Italy, European champion, knocked out Cohen in the sixth round in Rome, Italy, he was recognized as logical successor to the crown by all except the N.B.A., and when D'Agata, the deaf-mute, was outpointed in Paris in fifteen rounds by Alphonse Halimi, born in Constantine, Algeria, February 18, 1932, Halimi reached the top rung of the ladder as world title holder.

Halimi's first defense of his crown was in Los Angeles against champion (so-called by the NBA) Raul (Raton) Macias of Mexico. Alphonse gave his challenger a bad beating over the closing rounds, to retain his title easily.

The bruising, crowding tactics of Joe Becerra, of Mexico, gave him a slight edge over defending champion Alphonse Halimi through seven brutal rounds on July 8, 1959. A crushing right to the body and a left hook to the jaw dropped the Frenchman for good in the eighth round, giving Becerra the bantamweight crown.

When Becerra was kayoed in the eighth round in a nontitle fight against Elroy Sanchez on August 30, 1960, he announced his retirement.

The N.B.A. and the European Boxing Union arranged eliminations to determine Becerra's successor. The European title was awarded to Alphonse Halimi, over the booing and stamping of the crowd, in a narrow fifteen-round decision over Freddy Gilroy, of Ireland, on October 15,

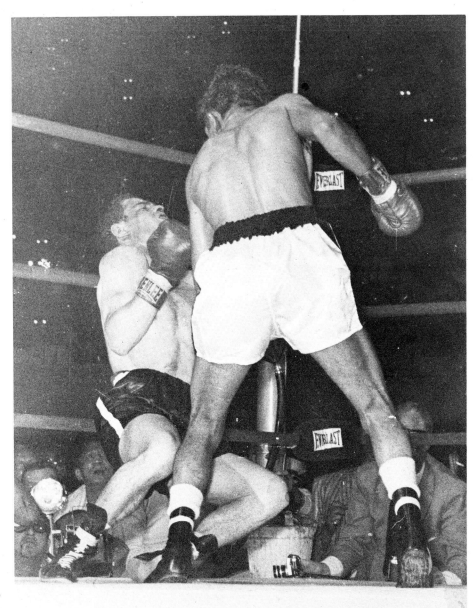

Halimi got much more than he bargained for in the person of Joe Becerra, who won the title by knocking out Alphonse in 8th.

After being halted by Eloy Sanchez in a non-title bout in 1960, Becerra (*below, center*) retired. Eder Jofre (*left*) stopped Sanchez (*right*) in sixth round for the American championship, in bout held in L.A.

In London, meanwhile, Jack Solomons (*far right, center*) promoted a Freddie Gilroy–Halimi bout, latter winning in 15 rounds.

Jofre, shown at left lifting Sanchez in the air after stopping him, met Italy's Piero Rollo four months later after Halimi refused to box him. Jofre won universal recognition after knocking out Rollo in the 10th (above). Eder was to reign four years.

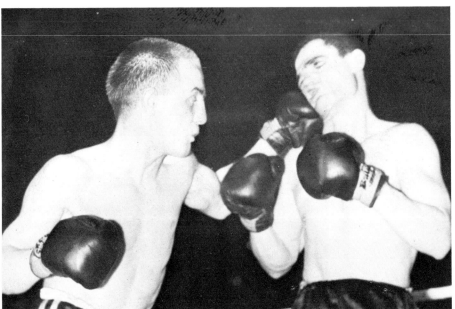

The European Boxing Union refused to go along with the other bodies, however, preferring to recognize winner of a Johnny Caldwell–Halimi bout. Caldwell (left) won in 15.

1960, in London. Shortly afterward, on November 18, in Los Angeles, Eder Jofre won the American title when he caught Eloy Sanchez flush on the jaw with a powerful right for a knockout victory in the sixth round.

Although the winners were supposed to battle for the international title, Halimi refused to accept Jofre. As a result, a match was arranged for Jofre with Italy's Piero Rollo, who was kayoed upon failing to answer the bell for the tenth round on March 21, 1961. With this victory, Jofre was recognized champion by *The Ring* magazine, the N.B.A., and the South American Boxing Federation.

Meanwhile, Johnny Caldwell beat Halimi with a blistering attack over fifteen rounds on May 30, 1961, in

London, to become the European Boxing Union champion.

An international bantamweight champion was finally crowned on January 18, 1962, when Jofre stalked and pummeled Caldwell until the helpless Irishman's manager threw in the towel in the tenth round.

Having defended his title successfully seven times since beating Sanchez in 1961, the 118-pound Jofre succumbed to the windmill style of the 117-pound Fighting Harada of Japan in a fifteen-round decision on May 17, 1965, at Tokyo.

Lionel Rose, of Australia, stepping in as a last-minute substitute for Mexican Jesus Pimental on February 26, 1968, went on to win a unanimous fifteen-round decision over Harada with faster punching and harder hitting.

In Rose's third defense he was knocked out by Ruben Olivares, of Mexico, in the fifth round on August 22, 1969. Olivares had consistently been the aggressor, displaying a furious and constantly moving left hook.

Olivares, a flashy fellow who liked high living, lost his title to Chucho Castillo in the fourteenth, when the ring physician decided cuts around Olivares' left eye were too severe for him to continue. The bout took place in Los Angeles on October 16, 1970, with both men weighing 118 pounds.

In a return bout, April 3, 1971, Olivares regained the crown from Castillo, who was badly outclassed in fifteen rounds.

Rafael Herrera, a fellow Mexican, kayoed Olivares for the title at 1:28 of the eighth round on March 19, 1973, but lost it four months later, on July 30, to Panamanian Enrique Pinder in a fifteen-round decision.

Pinder held the title slightly longer than his predecessor, losing it to Mexico's Romeo Anaya on January 20, 1973, in Panama, in a three-round kayo.

South Africa's 114-pound Arnold Taylor, survived four knockdowns, landed a right cross to the 117¾-pound Anaya's jaw and scored a fourteenth-round knockout for the title, on November 3, 1973.

On July 3, 1974, Soo Hwan Hong of Korea put Taylor down four times in gaining a decision in Durban, but after a successful defense against Fernando Cabanela of the Philippines, he lost his title to Alfonso Zamora of

Eder continued on his merry way, defeating Herman Marques, Joe Medel, Katsutoshi Aoki, Johnny Jamito and Bernardo Carabello until losing to Masahiko "Fighting" Harada in fifteen rounds. Harada, lifted in victory by handlers, KO'd Pone Kingpetch in 1962 for flyweight title, lost it to Kingpetch in 1963 and entered bantamweight class in 1965.

Mexico, who knocked him out in the fourth. Zamora retained his crown when stopping Thanoujit Sukhotai of Thailand in the fourth round on March 14, 1975, and Socrates Batoto, kayo second, at Mexico City on December 6.

In 1976 Zamaro successfully defended his W.B.A. crown three times as follows: April 3, Eusebio Pedroza, kayo second, at Mexicali; July 10, Gilberto Illueca, kayo third, at Juarez; October 16, Soo Hwan Hong, stopped twelfth, at Inchon. But in 1977 he met only one challenger and was knocked out in ten rounds by Jorge Lujan (Panama) at Los Angeles, on November 19. In 1978 Lujan retained his title by stopping Roberto Rubaldino (Mexico) in eleven rounds at San Antonio on March 18, and Alberto Davila, who was outpointed over fifteen rounds at New Orleans on September 15.

Back to the W.B.C. who stripped Enrique Pinder of his title in 1972 and on April 14, 1973, Rafael Herrera was installed as their champion when he stopped Rodolfo Martinez in twelve rounds at Monterrey. He kept his crown by outpointing Venice Borkorsor at Inglewood on October 13, 1973, and on May 25, 1974, he knocked out Romeo Anaya in six rounds at Mexico City. The following December 7, however, he dropped the title to his old rival Rodolfo Martinez, who stopped him in four rounds at Merida.

Martinez made two winning de-

Lionel Rose an Australian Aborigine, took Harada's measure and his title on a 15-round decision in Tokyo in February, 1968. Rose was so overjoyed he bowls over one of his aides.

Ruben Olivares, who had KO'd Rose, was beaten in turn by Chucho Castillo on a 14-round stoppage.

Olivares, who regained the crown from Castillo in 1971, lost the title to Rafael Herrera (below).

Panamanian Enrique Pinder became ruler of the class by defeating Herrera. Pinder, however. was stopped by Romeo Anaya (below) in three rounds. Pinder suffered the same fate in a return.

fences in 1975, stopping Nestor Jiminez in seven rounds at Bogota on May 31, and outpointing Hisami Numata over fifteen rounds at Sendai on October 8. On January 30, 1976, he again outpointed Venice Borkorsor over fifteen rounds, this time at Bangkok, but on May 8 lost his title to Carlos Zarate, who knocked him out in nine rounds at Inglewood.

The new Mexican champion soon showed he was in star class as a fighter and hard puncher. He had won forty-one consecutive contests since turning professional, forty of them inside the scheduled distance and was unbeaten. At once he set off to meet and beat all comers and on August 28, 1976, made the first defence of his W.B.C. title, stopping Paul Ferreri in twelve rounds at Inglewood. On November 13 he knocked out Philip Waruinge in four rounds at Culiacan. In 1977 he made four more successful defences as follows: February 5 Fernando Cabanela, stopped third, at Mexico City; April 23, Alfonso Zamora, kayo fourth, at Inglewood; October 29, Danito Batista, stopped sixth, at Los Angeles; December 2, Juan Rodriguez, stopped fifth, at Madrid.

Zarate began 1978 in the same devastating fashion, on February 25 stopping Alberto Davila in eight rounds at Los Angeles. On June 10 he knocked out Emilio Hernandez in four rounds at Las Vegas. At this time he had defended his title eight times, none of his challengers being able to stay the course against his dynamic punching. But on October 27, 1978, his great winning run came to an end. In attempting to become a dual champion, he took on the Super-Bantam W.B.C. titleholder, Wlfredo Gomez, but was stopped in five rounds at San Juan. This Champion versus Champion fight brought 11,000 fans into the Roberto Clemente Stadium while a further 28,000 watched the contest

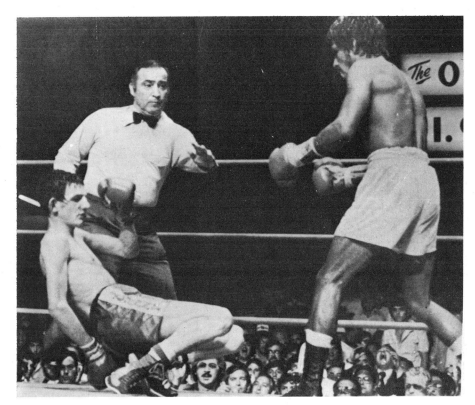

Lupe Pintor knocks out Welshman Johnny Owen in the twelfth round in Los Angeles, September, 1980. Owen later died in hospital.

on video in an adjoining open-air arena. Gomez received 175,000 dollars and Zarate 70,000 dollars. He was down for the third time when British referee Harry Gibbs called a halt. Zarate retained his W.B.C. bantamweight title.

He defended this successfully on March 10, 1979 by knocking out Mensah Kpalogo (Togo, W. Africa) in three rounds at Los Angeles, but lost his title on June 3, being outpointed over 15 rounds by Lupe Pintor (Mexico) at Las Vegas. On February 9, 1980 Pintor kept his crown by stopping Alberto Sandoval (U.S.A.) in 12 rounds at Los Angeles, but was held to a draw by Eijiro Murata (Japan) at Tokyo on June 11. On September 19 came his tragic defence against Johnny Owen of Wales at Los Angeles. Owen, holder of the British, Commonwealth and European

titles, was knocked out in round 12 and never regained consciousness, dying in a Los Angeles hospital 46 days later.

On December 19, 1980 Lupe Pintor retained his title, beating Alberto Davilla (Los Angeles) on points over 15 rounds at Las Vegas.

On April 8, 1979, Jorge Lujan kept his W.B.A. version of the championship by knocking out Cleo Garcia (Nicaragua) in the 15th round at Las Vegas, and he performed an identical feat by disposing of Roberto Rubaldino (Mexico) at McAllen on October 6. On April 2, 1980 at Tokyo, he stopped Shuichi Isogami (Japan) in nine rounds, but on August 29 he lost his title to Julian Solis (Puerto Rico) on a 15 rounds points defeat at Miami. In the same ring on November 14, Solis was stopped in 14 rounds, losing his championship to Jeff Chandler (U.S.A.).

SUPER FLYWEIGHT CHAMPIONS

(Weight Limit, 115 Pounds)

ON FEBRUARY 2, 1980, THE WORLD BOXING COUNCIL INTRODUCED A NEW SUPER FLYWEIGHT DIVISION (115 POUNDS) AND THE FIRST CHAMPION WAS RAFAEL ORONO (VENEZUELA) WHO OUTPOINTED SEUN HOON LEE (KOREA) OVER 15 ROUNDS AT CARACAS. ORONO MADE THREE SUCCESSFUL TITLE DEFENCES IN 1980, OUTPOINTING RAMON SORIA (ARGENTINA) 15 ROUNDS; DRAWING WITH WILLIE JENSEN (U.S.A.) AND STOPPING JOVITA RENGIFO (VENEZUELA) IN THREE ROUNDS.

The two mightiest mites in England were Joe Hoiles, known as "the Spider" and Jem Herbert, "the Pocket Hercules." Both weighed about 105 pounds. Hoiles, at 5' 6", was two inches taller. On January 29, 1850, they fought the most furious battle ever staged by small men in England. Hoiles' long arms cut and blinded the rushing Herbert for more than two hours. Unable to see, Jem groped around trying to grab Hoiles whenever he came in to hit. Herbert would not quit, but his seconds threw in the sponge.

One month after Pete Herman lost his bantamweight crown to Joe Lynch, he went to England and stopped Jimmy Wilde in 17 rounds of an overweight bout. Wilde, nearing the end of his career, was sent reeling out of the ring by Herman.

Young Zulu Kid represented the United States in the newly-created flyweight class, for which England set the weight at 108 pounds. In an international bout with Jimmy Wilde at London in 1916, he was knocked out in 11 rounds. Zulu Kid was born in Potenza, Italy, and was only 4' 11" tall. He started boxing in 1912 and met all of the good little men until 1924. He was a good boxer and most of his bouts were no-decision affairs.

SPEEDY AND SKILLFUL FLYWEIGHTS

The first official flyweight champion was Jimmy Wilde. The class was created in England and the poundage at the time was 108 pounds. America followed suit the same year and accepted the group as a new division in boxing. The first championship bout was one that brought together Wilde and the Zulu Kid of America and Jimmy knocked out the American in the eleventh round in London on De-

cember 18, 1916, to gain top honors.

He held the title for a long time. With World War One on, Wilde competed in exhibitions and odd bouts in England until after the armistice was signed, after which he came to America and stirred up interest in the class. During a six months' stay, the Welshman was a busy campaigner, fighting such stars as Jack Sharkey, Mike Ertle, Babe Asher, Micky Russell, Frankie

Mason, Zulu Kid, Battling Murray, Bobby Dyson, and Patsy Wallace. He then returned to his native country, where on January 13, 1921, he was stopped by Pete Herman in a non-title bout in seventeen rounds.

For two years he remained idle until Tom O'Rourke, former manager of George Dixon and Joe Walcott, brought him to the United States to defend his title at the Polo Grounds

Jimmy Wilde (left), the "Mighty Atom," was a remarkable Welshman who held the world flyweight title. One of the greatest little fighting men of all time, he scored 75 knockouts during his career from 1911 to 1923. Pete Herman (above) of New Orleans proved too strong for Wilde in their bout on January 13, 1921. Although Herman had been boxing for seven years, this was his first bout on foreign soil.

Pancho Villa *(above, left)* posing with Johnny Buff before their clash for the American flyweight title in 1921, was the best ringman ever developed in the Philippine Islands. The referee, Patsy Haley, counted Buff out in the 11th round.

One year after winning the American title, Villa watched an aging Jimmy Wilde weigh in for their world championship match in New York. Among the many ring notables present was Philadelphia Jack O'Brien, seen standing directly behind Villa.

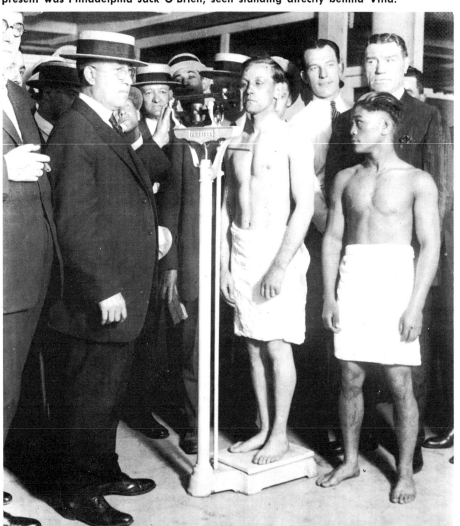

against Pancho Villa. In that affair, one of the most stirring bouts ever fought in the division, Pancho stopped "The Mighty Atom" in the seventh round. Villa was one of the classiest performers the division ever had. He was Jack Dempsey in miniature. A clever, tireless, relentless, hard-hitting flyweight, he was a colorful lad who drew the crowd at the gate. He had won the American flyweight title from Johnny Buff and lost it to Frankie Genaro and was now after the world crown.

The triumph of Villa came after 1.46 of fighting in the seventh round of a contest that will long be remembered. While it lasted, it was a battle royal. The crowd found itself rooting madly for the little Welshman could neither offset Villa's speed nor discount his volley of punches. Wild acclaim greeted the skill of the Filipino. Never since Battling Nelson was counted out on his feet in forty rounds by Ad Wolgast in 1910 in California did a champion pass more gloriously than did Wilde that night.

From the second round on, the pallid little Welshman didn't have a chance. Just as the bell sounded at the end of the second, Villa landed one flush on the jaw and down went the champion, flat. He was dragged to his corner and the rest of the fight was a test of endurance as well as one of the finest shows of the eternal fighting spirit that has ever been seen in a ring battle. Wilde's seconds called the punch that dropped him a foul, and most of the ringsiders agreed that it had been tossed after the bell rang. In England, such a blow would have brought about Pancho's disqualification.

In the third round, Wilde came out of his corner reeling and partially blinded, but he pressed into the Filipino like a panther. Villa was at him and shot rights and lefts into his face. Wilde reeled, but he would not give ground.

Wilde was rocked several times, but there was no letup in his attempt to keep going. Seldom was there such a display of endurance seen by a New York fight gathering since the time of

Nelson, the man they called the Durable Dane.

The sheer gameness of the Welsh mite convinced the spectators that he might still have a chance, frail and wobbly though he seemed. His remarkable reign as one of the greatest of world champions was about to come to a sickening end, but never did he fail to display the fighting qualities of a true title holder. His showing, and that of the mighty tyke of the Orient, placed that battle among the super-fistic contests of all time.

Wilde's finish was pathetic, for a brave little man went face down into the resin after taking a cruel beating. He had walked into the cannon's mouth, a sad, almost defiant smile on his face, made unsightly by the spiteful fists of the great little Filipino. A right hand blow put an end to the fight.

At the time, both of Wilde's eyes were swollen and closed until only a tiny slit gave him a sight of the slant-eyed terror in front of him. Age was horribly spiked and gaffed, youth was strutting from the fight unmarked, a vast crowd shrieking the praise of a

Villa's spectacular career ended tragically with this fight against Jimmy McLarnin in Oakland, California, on July 4, 1925. Pancho, suffering from infected teeth, insisted on going through with the bout. Villa *(left)* lost the decision, and the poison, spreading through his body, sent him to the hospital, where he died 10 days later.

strange little fellow from Manila who had just been crowned king.

Villa had a quick and tragic end. He fought Jimmy McLarnin on July 4, 1925, in Oakland, California, and died ten days later from blood poisoning from an infected tooth, the result of this contest.

After Fidel LaBarba had gained universal recognition as world flyweight king, he met Elky Clark, the British champion, who is seen lying flat on his face from a blow on the jaw in the first round. LaBarba received the verdict at the end of 12 rounds.

Confusion reigned in the flyweight division in 1933. Frankie Genaro (left) NBA title-holder and Midget Wolgast, New York champ, fought for the crown, but the verdict was a draw.

Fidel LaBarba started in 1924, when he won the amateur flyweight championship in the Olympics at Paris. After retiring in 1933, he completed his studies at Stanford University.

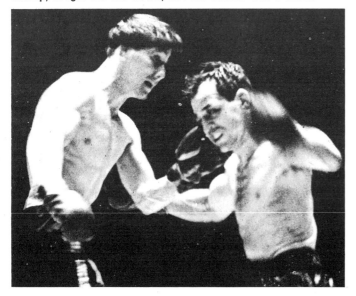

With Villa's passing, Frankie Genaro claimed the crown. He was outpointed on August 22, 1925, by Fidel LaBarba, born September 29, 1905, in New York City. LaBarba retired in 1927, and Corporal Izzy Schwartz of New York, born October 23, 1902, followed him to the throne after he whipped Newsboy Brown in New York City in fifteen rounds. Only New York accepted the Corporal as champion.

The N.B.A. refused to go along with that. Conditions in the class became greatly confused until an elimination was staged in 1929 in which Midget Wolgast outpointed Black Bill and the Midget got New York's support. Wolgast, born in Philadelphia, July 18, 1910, and Frankie Genaro then fought a draw of fifteen rounds in New York, and since Genaro was recognized by the N.B.A. as king of the class, two champions were in the field.

Genaro went to Paris, where he was knocked out in the second round on October 26, 1931, by Young Perez, born in Tunis, October 18, 1911. Perez claimed the world honors. A year later, Jackie Brown of England took over when he knocked out Perez in the thirteenth round to win European support.

The confusion continued as Small Montana, born in Negros, Philippines, February 24, 1913, outpointed Wol-

370

When La Barba retired temporarily in 1927, Corporal Izzy Schwartz whipped Newsboy Brown, and gained New York support.

Jackie Brown, a strong British flyweight, stopped Young Perez on October 31, 1932, in England, for the world crown.

Frankie Genaro, the American NBA champion, received a royal welcome in Paris upon his arrival for the flyweight contest with Young Perez. Genaro proved an easy opponent (below) for the French champion, who stopped him in two rounds. The French Federation of Boxing, as a result of this bout, declared Perez the world's flyweight champion.

One of the greatest flyweights in recent years, was a Scot, Benny Lynch, seen below with his hand raised in victory over the American champion, Small Montana. Lynch's triumph over Montana in Glasgow ended all confusion in the flyweight ranks.

gast for the U. S. crown and went abroad to seek a bout to decide world honors. In the meantime a great flyweight, Benny Lynch, born in Glasgow, Scotland, April 2, 1913, came forth to show his wares, and he took the measure of Jackie Brown at Manchester, stopping him in two rounds.

Lynch now was generally accepted as world champion, and when Montana challenged him, the Filipino was defeated in fifteen rounds, thus en-

Benny Lynch was officially shorn of his title on June 29, 1938, for failing to make weight for his bout in Paisley, Scotland, with Jackie Jurich of California. They were re-matched the same afternoon at catch-weights. Benny floored Jurich six times and knocked him out in the 12th round. Lynch died in Scotland in 1946, by then a physical wreck.

Rinty Monaghan, pride of Belfast, Ireland, who sang and danced after each bout, knocked out Paterson for the title.

Peter Kane, a sharp puncher from England, decisioned Jack Jurich in Liverpool, and claimed the vacant flyweight crown.

Jackie Paterson, Scotland's clever, hard-punching flyweight, won the title with a one-round knockout over Peter Kane.

with Best wishes to my FANS in the U.S.A.

Rinty Monaghan

abling Lynch to end all confusion in the division.

When Lynch retired, Jackie Jurich of California and Peter Kane of England, the last two men to face Lynch in title bouts, fought on September 22, 1938, at Liverpool. Kane won, thus claiming world honors.

In most boxing circles Kane was recognized as world champion. During the war he was unable to defend his crown and temporarily vacated the throne, so that in 1941 and 1942 the championship was vacant. Then on June 19, 1943, Jackie Paterson of Scotland knocked out Kane in one round to gain international recognition, and on March 23, 1948, an Irish lad, Rinty Monaghan of Belfast, stopped Paterson in seven rounds to win the crown.

Rinty Monaghan, born August 21,

"Barrow Boy" Terry Allen, the first Englishman to win the flyweight championship in 37 years, has his hand raised by referee De Young, in token of victory over Honoré Pratesi, of France. The 15-round bout was held in London, on April 25, 1950.

Yoshio Shirai gave Japan a day to remember when on May 19, 1952, he won the world flyweight crown from Dado Marino in Tokyo. Shirai (above), the first to win a world title for his country, waves to his admirers before leaving the ring.

1920, in Belfast retired on April 25, 1950, and Terry Allen, born August 11, 1925, gained top ranking by defeating Honoré Pratesi of France in fifteen rounds in the Harringay Arena of London and became champion. He in turn was outpointed in fifteen rounds on August 1, 1950 in Hawaii by Dado Marino of Hawaii, born in Honolulu, August 26, 1916.

Then, for the first time in history, a world championship was won by a Japanese when Yoshio Shirai of Tokyo, born November 23, 1923, gained the verdict over Marino, May 19, 1952, at Tokyo in fifteen rounds. They fought again on November 15 of that year in

When Terry Allen, a world-traveller, journeyed to Honolulu to defend his title, he lost it to Salvador "Dado" Marino (right) in 15 rounds. Allen used a crouching position to good advantage, befuddling Marino in the early stages, but his style was later solved. Dado's left was effective as the bout neared its end. He piled up points and won a close but well-earned victory.

Pascual Perez, a vicious puncher from Argentina, lifted the crown from Yoshio Shirai, Japan's first world champion, in Tokyo on November 26, 1954. Referee Jack Sullivan raises Perez' hand *(below)* as new champion. Between them is manager Lozaro Koci. In a return bout, Perez knocked out Shirai *(above)* in the fifth round. In a title bout on December 15, 1958, Perez retained his crown by winning a unanimous 15-round decision over Philippine flyweight champion Dommy Ursua in Manila.

Tokyo, and Shirai won in fifteen rounds, to retain his crown. Tanny Campo of Manila tried to wrest it from him but also lost, as did Terry Allen as well as Leo Espinosa of the Philippines, all in fifteen round contests.

Then came a bout with Pascual Perez, a heavy-socking lad from Buenos Aires, who, after fighting a draw of ten rounds with Shirai in Perez's country, defeated Shirai in fifteen rounds in Tokyo on November 26, 1954, to win world honors. The Argentinian, born in Tupunagte, Mendoza, Argentina, March 4, 1926, became a fighting champion. He knocked out Shirai in five rounds; defeated Leo Espinosa in fifteen; halted Oscar Suarez in eleven; Ricardo Valdez in five; Dai Dower in the first; and Luis Angel Jimenez in ten—all championship fights.

Perez defended his title seventeen times from 1955 to 1959. On April 16, 1960, the thirty-four-year-old champ could not hold his own against a young aggressive opponent, Pone Kingpetch of Tailand, and lost the crown in a fifteen-round split decision, at Bangkok. In a return bout, September 22, at Los Angeles, Perez was knocked out in eight rounds.

Fighting Harada, ranked only tenth in the flyweight division, kayoed the Thai champion in the eleventh round, October 10, 1962, at Tokyo in a vicious encounter.

Kingpetch became the first flyweight ever to regain the title. On January 12, 1963, at Bangkok, he reversed the pattern of his first fight with Harada, forcing the fight and keeping his foe on the defensive, thereby gaining a split decision.

Japan's Hiroyuki Ebihara, at twenty-three, had youth and strength to his advantage, while the twenty-

The veteran Perez, titleholder since 1954, finally met his match after 17 successful defenses, in Thailand's Pone Kingpetch, who dethroned the 34-year-old Argentinian on a split 15-round decision in Bangkok (*above*), despite suffering a deep cut over his eye. Kingpetch, his hand raised in victory (*right*), wears his new title belt.

Kingpetch, an idol in Thailand, lost the title to Japan's Fighting Harada on an 11-round knockout. However, in a return, Kingpetch regained the crown on a 15-round verdict. Late *Ring* editor Nat Fleischer (*hand to forehead*) was one of the judges.

seven-year-old champ had height and reach when they met at Tokyo, September 18, 1963. Ebihara overwhelmed Kingpetch, dropping him for a mandatory eight-count, then a volley of lefts and rights left Kingpetch prone and Ebihara the new champion in 2:07 of the first round.

Taking his training more seriously for his rematch with Ebihara, Kingpetch regained the title, for the second time, in fifteen action-packed rounds, on January 23, 1964 at Bangkok.

Salvatore Burruni of Italy, consistently beat defending champion King-

petch to the punch, hammering away with both hands to the face and body to gain a unanimous decision for the title, April 23, 1965 at Rome.

Scotsman Walter McGowan, British and Empire champion, became world champ when he decisioned Burruni at Tokyo, on June 14, 1966, by making

Kingpetch became an ex-champion for the second time when he ran into a Japanese buzzsaw named Hiroyuki Ebihara, who flattened the Thailander in the first round at Tokyo. *Above*, the second and final knockdown, and *right*, the new champion's happy handlers congratulate him while the dazed ex-titleholder receives assistance from his cornermen. It was a far different story four months later when Pone recaptured the flyweight crown for the second time by outpointing Ebihara in 15 rounds at Bangkok.

Kingpetch did not fight for more than a year. When he did, he lost his title to Italy's Salvatore Burruni in a 15-rounder.

the Italian run after him, then stepping in to deliver blows to Burruni's body.

Six months later, December 30, the title again changed hands when Chartchai Chionoi, of Thailand, kayoed McGowan at Bangkok. The attending physician, after examining a deep nose wound McGowan had received in the second round, halted the bout in round nine.

In his fifth defense in three years, Chionoi, at 110¾ pounds, lost the title to 111¾-pound Efren Torres at Mexico City, on February 23, 1969, when referee Arthur Mercante stopped the bout in the eighth round after the Thai's eye had swollen shut from Torres' constant jabbing.

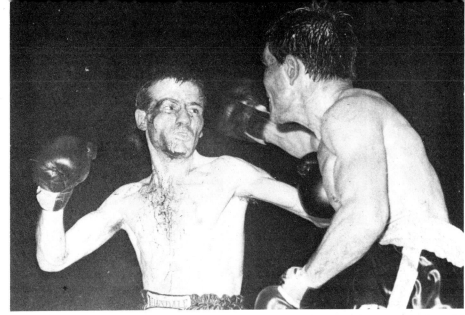

Walter McGowan became the first Briton to win the flyweight title in more than 15 years when he defeated Burruni at London in June, 1966, taking a 15-round decision.

Referee Sangvien Hiranyalekha raises hand of Chartchai Chionoi (*above, right*) after he was declared winner and new champion when McGowan (*above*) was unable to continue after 50 seconds of the ninth round due to a deep cut on his nose. (*Right*) *Ring* editor Nat Fleischer joins Chionoi in paying respects to the King of Thailand, who presents belt.

In a rematch, March 20, 1970, at Bangkok, Chionoi, using a classic left jab and lethal right hook, regained the flyweight crown, giving the Mexican champion very little room to do any damage with his powerful jabs.

Erbito Salvarria of the Philippines stopped Chionoi, on December 7, 1970, at Bangkok. The twenty-four-year-old Salvarria knocked down Chionoi, a few seconds into the second round with a staggering right hook, then decked the Thai twice more before the fight was stopped.

The explosive Salvarria found himself in the unfamiliar position of defending against the Thailand southpaw, Venice Borkorsor, who threw jabs and left hooks at the outclassed Filipino. Borkorsor won a unanimous decision.

When Borkorsor gave up the fly-weight title on July 10, 1973, to fight as a bantamweight, the World Boxing Council selected Betulio Gonzales of Venezuela as their champion, while the World Boxing Association gave its title to Chionoi.

Gonzales lost his crown to Shoji Oguma of Japan, who won a fifteen-round split decision on October 1, 1974 in Tokyo, but Oguma lost a decision in his first defense against Miguel Canto of Mexico. Canto defended successfully twice in 1975, getting a decision against Gonzales at Monterey and stopping Jiro Takada of Japan in the eleventh at Merida.

Meanwhile Chionoi, after a defense against a Swiss challenger Fritz Chervet, who lost a decision, himself lost his W.B.A. title to Susumu Hanagata of Japan, who stopped Chionoi in the sixth at Yokohama. Hanagata then lost to previous champion Erbito Salvarria, who gained a decision at Toyama. Salvarria confirmed himself as W.B.A. champion on September 16, 1975, at Yokohama, by gaining a second decision over Hanagata in the return.

On February 27, 1976, Alfonso Lopez took over the title by stopping Salavarria in the final round at Manila,

Efren Torres became the new title holder when stopping Chionoi in the eighth round. *Left:* Torres attacking in the fifth. In a rematch 13 months later, the battlers bow to each other (*below left*) and Chionoi cries for joy (*below*) after regaining his crown.

but after warding off a challenge from Shoji Oguma, who was outpointed at Tokyo on April 21, Lopez dropped his crown to Guty Espadas (Mexico) on a thirteen rounds stoppage at Los Angeles on October 2. Espadas caused Jiro Takada to retire in seven rounds at Tokyo on New Year's Day, 1977, and then stopped former champion, Alfonso Lopez in thirteen rounds in a return match at Merida on April 30. He next stopped Kimio Furesawa at Tokyo on January 2, 1978, but on August 13 at Maracay, was outpointed by Betulio Gonzalez (Venezuela). The new W.B.A. champion kept his crown against Martin Vargas, who was stopped in twelve rounds at Maracay on November 4. On January 29, 1979, however, he was held to a draw over fifteen rounds by Japanese challenger, Shoji Oguma at Hamatsu.

Miguel Canto (Mexico) maintained his hold on the W.B.C. version of the flyweight title on December 15, 1975, by outpointing Ignacio Espinal at Merida, then went through the next three years without losing his championship as follows: 1976—May 15, Susumu Hanagata w.pts.15 Merida; October 3, Betulio Gonzalez w.pts.15 Caracas; November 19, Orlando Javierto w.pts.15 Los Angeles. 1977—April 24, Reyes Arnal w.pts.15 Caracas; June 15—Kimio Furesawa w.pts.15 Tokyo; September 17, Martin Vargas w.pts.15 Merida; November 30, Martin Vargas w.pts.15 Santiago. 1978—February 4 Shoji Oguma w.pts. 15 Koriyama; April 18, Shoji Oguma w.pts.15 Tokyo; November 20, Tacomrom Viboochai w.pts.15 Houston.

On February 10, 1979, Canto outpointed challenger Antonio Avelar

Mexican challenger Miguel Canto (*right*) using his right hand effectively won the W.B.C. flyweight crown from southpaw defending champ Shoji Oguma of Japan in 15 rounds.

(Mexico) to give him a total of 14 successful defences. On March 18, however, the W.B.C. title changed hands when he lost on points to Chan Hee Park of Korea. In a return championship fight on September 9, he could only secure a draw. Chan Hee Park beat Tsutomu Igarashi (Japan) pts. 15 on May 20; Guty Espadas (Mexico) k.o. 2 on December 16; Arnel Allozal (Philippines) pts. 15 on February 9, 1980; Alberto Morales (Mexico) pts. 15 on April 12. Shoji Oguma (Japan) knocked out Chan Hee Park in nine rounds at Seoul on May 18, 1980 and kept his title by defeating Sung Jun Kim (Korea) on July 28 and Chan Hee

Park (return title fight) on October 18, both being points wins over 15 rounds.

Back to the W.B.A. title. Betulio Gonzalez knocked out Ojuma in 12 rounds of a return fight on July 6, 1979, then lost his crown to Luis Ibarra (Panama) on a points decision at Maracay on November 17. On February 16, 1980 Ibarra was knocked out in two rounds by Tae Shik Kim (Korea) at Seoul, who outpointed Arnel Arrozal (Philippines) in his first defence.

Tae Shik Kim was outpointed in turn by Peter Mathebula on December 13, 1980 at Los Angeles. Mathebula thus became the first black South African boxer to win a world title.

LIGHT-FLYWEIGHTS

(Weight Limit, 108 Pounds)

THIS, NOW THE LOWEST WEIGHT CLASS IN BOXING, WAS INTRODUCED ON APRIL 4, 1975, BY THE WORLD BOXING COUNCIL WHEN FRANCO UDELLA (ITALY) WON IN 12 ROUNDS ON THE DISQUALIFICATION OF VALENTINE MARTINEZ AT MILAN. UDELLA NEVER DEFENDED THE TITLE AND ON SEPTEMBER 13, 1975, LUIS ESTABA (VENEZUELA) KNOCKED OUT RAFAEL LOBERA IN THE FOURTH ROUND FOR THE VACANT CROWN AT CARACAS. ON AUGUST 23, 1975, JAIME RIOS (PANAMA) BEAT RIGOBERTO MARCANO ON POINTS AT PANAMA CITY FOR THE VACANT W.B.A. TITLE. SINCE THEN BOTH GOVERNING BODIES HAVE RECOGNISED THE FOLLOWING TITLE-HOLDERS AT THIS WEIGHT: W.B.C. 1976—78 LUIS ESTABA (ELEVEN SUCCESSFUL TITLE DEFENCES);

1978—FREDDIE CASTILLO, NETRNOI VORASINGH, KIM SUNG-JUN (KOREA). WBA 1976—JUAN GUZMAN, YOKO GUSHIKEN (JAPAN), WHO MADE THREE DEFENCES IN 1977, FOUR IN 1978, FOUR IN 1979 AND THREE IN 1980, MAKING A RECORD TOTAL OF 14 SUCCESSFUL CHAMPIONSHIP DEFENCES.

KIM SUNG-JUN MADE THREE DEFENCES OF HIS WBC TITLE IN 1979, BUT LOST HIS CROWN TO SHIGEO NAKAJIMA (JAPAN) ON JANUARY 3, 1980. HILARIO ZAPATA (PANAMA) OUTPOINTED NAKAJIMA ON MARCH 24 AND REMAINED CHAMPION WITH FOUR DEFENCES DURING THE YEAR.

INDEX